THE COLUMBIA ANTHOLOGY OF
AMERICAN POETRY

The Columbia Anthology of

AMERICAN
POETRY

EDITED BY

JAY PARINI

COLUMBIA UNIVERSITY PRESS

NEW YORK

Columbia University Press
New York   Chichester, West Sussex

Copyright © 1995 Columbia University Press

Library of Congress Cataloging-in-Publication Data

The Columbia anthology of American poetry   /   edited by Jay Parini.
   p.   cm.
   "A Columbia anthology."
   Includes index.
   ISBN 0-231-08122-7
   1. American poetry.   I. Parini, Jay.
PS584.C66   1995
811.008—dc20   94-32423
                                            CIP

Printed in the United States of America

c 10 9 8 7 6

CONTENTS

Ezra Pound (1885–1972)

"H.D." (Hilda Doolittle) (1886–1961)

Robinson Jeffers (1887–1962)

Elinor Wylie (1887–1928)

Marianne Moore (1887–1972)

John Crowe Ransom (1888–1974)

T. S. Eliot (1888–1965)

Conrad Aiken (1889–1973)

Claude McKay (1890–1948)

Archibald MacLeish (1892–1983)

Edna St. Vincent Millay (1892–1950)

Charles Reznikoff (1894–1976)

Jean Toomer (1894–1967)

e. e. cummings (1894–1962)

Louise Bogan (1897–1970)

Arna Bontemps (1902–1973)

Countee Cullen (1903–1946)

Louis Zukofsky (1904–1978)

Richard Eberhart (1904–   )

Stanley Kunitz (1905–   )

Robert Penn Warren (1905–1989)

Theodore Roethke (1908–1963)

Charles Olson (1910–1970)

Galway Kinnell (1927–)

James Wright (1927–1980)

Anne Sexton (1928–1974)

Peter Davison (1928–)

Philip Levine (1928–)

John Hollander (1929–)

Robert Pack (1929–)

Adrienne Rich (1929–)

Gary Snyder (1930–)

INTRODUCTION

> The United States themselves are essentially the greatest poem.
> —Walt Whitman, Preface to *Leaves of Grass*

What, besides geographical boundaries, do the varied poets in *The Columbia Anthology of American Poetry* share? What sort of poetry has this country offered to the world? While there may be no single tradition of poetry in America, any serious reader must be struck by the quasi-religious or metaphysical stance adopted by so many of our best poets. Emerson's essays have meant so much to our poets for good reason; he was the first American thinker to understand in an original way that the burden of the New World was deeply antinomian and that American poets must look not only at the wonders of its landscape but inside themselves for validation and inspiration. Consequently, American poetry acquired its peculiarly vatic if not esoteric quality rather early, and this "visionary" strain often seemed to contradict the democratic strain common to American discourse. The quintessential Emersonian note is sounded in *Nature* (1836): "Man is the dwarf of himself. Once he was permeated and dissolved by spirit." The project of consciousness, for the seer and poet, is to reconnect with the original self, from which "sprang the sun and the moon." This act of religious archaeology is, according to Emerson, the proper work of the poet. In his rather Orphic theology, the world "proceeds from the same spirit as the body of man. It is a remoter and inferior incarnation of God, a projection of God in the unconscious." Thus, the work of the human imagination involves an act of recovery, the unearthing of a mystical knowledge that restores the individual soul to its divine substance. It involves a gradual (or, in a more mystical vein, instantaneous) waking to full consciousness.

Emerson shone more brightly and truly in his prose than in his poems, which tend to be gnomic and restrained, but Whitman famously answered the Master's call with his own incomparable exuberance of vision. It was in 1842 that he wandered into a lecture hall in Manhattan and heard Emerson declaim what has become an American poetic credo:

> The poets are thus liberating gods. The ancient British bards had for the title of their order, "Those who are free throughout the world." They are free, and they make free. An imaginative book renders us much more service at first, by stimulating us through its tropes, than afterward,

when we arrive at the precise sense of the author. I think nothing is of
any value in books excepting the transcendental and extraordinary.

Whitman's first edition of *Leaves of Grass* (1855) transformed American
poetry into something vibrant, original, and fiercely egalitarian. In his preface
to that volume he declared: "The United States are themselves the greatest
poem," echoing a line from Emerson. Poets, not presidents, are the "common
referees" of the nation. They absorb the traditions of the past, including Euro-
pean traditions, and turn them into something new and distinctly native. Claim-
ing to have been influenced by Italian opera, with its superb "vocalism," he
outlined a new aesthetics of the voice: "What vocalism most needs in these
States, not only in the few choicer words and phrases, but in our whole talk, is
ease, sonorous strength, breadth and openness." He continued to argue
throughout his long life for what he called "bodily knowledge," an awareness in
which body and soul work together to intuit and reform the world in language.
Even in the saddest of his poems, "When Lilacs Last in the Dooryard Bloom'd,"
there is an underlying belief in the recovery and transformational power of this
knowledge. Whitman cries out:

Lo, body and soul—this land,
My own Manhattan with spires, and the sparkling and hurrying tides, and
    the ships,
The varied and ample land, the South and the North in the light, Ohio's
    shores and flashing Missouri,
And ever the far-spreading prairies cover'd with grass and corn.

The contradictory currents in American poetry from the Puritan Anne
Bradstreet through Whittier and Emerson found a fresh and weirdly original
manifestation in Whitman's flexible, idiosyncratic, demotic, democratic, vatic,
ebulliant, and wistful voice, which remains the central voice in our poetry.
Poets have ever since had to ignore or go around or submit to Whitman. Ezra
Pound put it memorably in "A Pact":

I make a pact with you, Walt Whitman—
I have detested you long enough.
I come to you as a grown child
Who has had a pig-headed father;
I am old enough now to make friends.
It was you that broke the new wood,
Now is a time for carving.
We have one sap and one root—
Let there be commerce between us.

That penultimate line is crucial: "We have one sap and one root." Pound implies a common source: the new wood, which is the American landscape as the embodiment of the American spirit. This land was, in a sense, our destiny: "The land was ours before we were the land's," says Robert Frost in "The Gift Outright."

> She was our land more than a hundred years
> Before we were her people. She was ours
> In Massachusetts, in Virginia,
> But we were England's, still colonials,
> Possessing what we still were unpossessed by,
> Possessed by what we now no more possessed.

Building on Whitman, Frost preaches "salvation in surrender" to this primordial landscape, to the demands of the environment, to its bloody history of possession and repossession.

The line of poets who responded directly to Whitman, often embracing his manner as much as the spirit of his work, is a long one. One hears the characteristic Whitmanian note boldly sounded in different ways by Carl Sandburg, the most self-consciously "democratic" of our poets, by William Carlos Williams, whose *Collected Poems* might be seen as a catalog of American imagery, by Robinson Jeffers, Theodore Roethke, Louis Zukofsky, Charles Olson, Muriel Rukeyser, Allen Ginsberg, James Dickey, Denise Levertov, James Wright, John Ashbery, Adrienne Rich, and so many others. Each poet recreates Whitman in his or her own image, taking one aspect of the great ancestor as the dominant strain in an act of (often unconscious) misreading. Whitman was, for modern American poets, what Milton was to the Romantics: a source of authority that had to be deconstructed, then reconstructed according to the emerging dialectics of the moment.

Whitman turns up in unexpected places, too—in the lyrics of the Imagists Amy Lowell and "H. D." (Hilda Doolittle), in the wistful catalogs of T. S. Eliot in *The Waste Land* or *Four Quartets*, in the chants of N. Scott Momaday and Simon J. Ortiz. But the question of influence is not so much the point here; rather, Whitman's demonstration of originality, his blatant dissociation from the dominant strains of English and European poetry, was itself an inspiration to the group he himself called "the poets-to-come." He understood that democracy itself, especially in its Jacksonian incarnation, demanded a new response to the world in terms of what it considered "poetic."

Alexis de Tocqueville, with his peculiar gift of foresight, predicted the nature of the poetry that a democracy might produce:

> It may be foreseen . . . that poets living in democratic times will
> prefer the delineation of passions and ideas to that of persons and

achievements. The language, the dress, and the daily actions of men in democracies are repugnant to conceptions of the ideal. . . . This forces the poet constantly to search below the external surface which is palpable to the senses, in order to read the inner soul; and nothing lends itself more to the delineation of the ideal than the scrutiny of the hidden depths in the immaterial nature of man.

This passage may guide the reader of this collection, who will find our poets almost obsessively fixed on what Tocqueville calls "man alone." Separated from the citadels and hushed corridors of Europe, with their massive libraries and thickly structured, hierarchical modes of thought and communication, the American Adam and Eve found themselves naked, gazing upon the vast richness of a bewildering absence. American reality had to be created, and it was built on the Dissenting tradition, where the inner light mattered a good deal more than anything that could be offered by the mediation of external authority or tradition. Humankind stood alone before God and Nature, having to invent itself, its voice and vision.

Our first poets, of course, were transplanted English poets, and one finds little in Bradstreet, Wigglesworth, or Edward Taylor, all born in England, that seems especially American. These were English Metaphysicals abroad, and their work is probably best read beside Donne, Herbert, Crashaw, or Vaughan. The stylistic similarities are obvious enough: a rough muscularity of expression, an obsession with extended metaphors or "conceits," and the use of commonplace, even domestic, imagery in the contemplation of otherwordly subjects. The Puritan aspect of their verse is reflected in a tendency to dwell on humanity's sinfulness, life's brevity, and the consequent need for salvation. The theme of paradise lost and regained lies at the heart of this tradition, as in Michael Wigglesworth's "The Day of Doom" (1662), which was immensely popular in its day.

Poetry, for Taylor especially, was quite literally a form of religious practice, with links to traditions of prayer and meditation. In this, he had much in common with Donne and Herbert, who often thought of poetry in terms of specific traditions of contemplation. Taylor mirrored his English counterparts by culling everyday life for metaphors that sometimes shock with their absurdity. As he watched a spider snagging a fly or contemplated a chilled wasp as it came to life in bright sunshine, his mind began to race after allegories. In "Let by Rain," one of the best of the Puritan lyrics, a Christian besieged by doubt is compared to a man ducking the rain by racing between buildings:

> Ye Flippering Soule,
>   Why dost between the Nippers dwell?
> Not stay, nor goe. Not yea, nor yet Controle,
>   Doth this doe well?

> Rise journy'ng when the skies fall weeping showers
> Not o'er nor under th'Clouds and Cloudy Powers.

This vein of "conceited" poetry fell out of favor in the mid-eighteenth century, but it resurfaced in the twentieth in a powerfully generative way. Among the numerous poets who looked back to the Puritans for inspiration were Eliot, John Crowe Ransom, Allen Tate, Robert Lowell, and Amy Clampitt.

The major poets of the early to mid-nineteenth century, such as Edgar Allan Poe and Henry Wadsworth Longfellow, also adhered to English verse forms and techniques, although their material became increasingly American. Longfellow and the so-called Schoolhouse Poets (Whittier, James Russell Lowell, Oliver Wendell Holmes) attracted wide audiences both at home and abroad, although much of their work now seems mannered and self-consciously "poetic." One of the main drives of the modernist movement had to do with sweeping away the archaic and "poetic" in poetry, thus bringing the poet's line closer to the language actually spoken by men and women. But it is important to recall how influential this early work was in its day. Longfellow's first book, *Evangeline* (1847), portrays the effects of displacement on people driven from their home by colonizing powers, and it captured the imagination of the young republic. *The Song of Hiawatha* (1855) became something of a national folk epic and a popular subject for artists, composers, and writers of libretti across Europe. Only slightly less popular were "Paul Revere's Ride," "Azrael," and other narrative poems, the best of which were gathered in *Tales of a Wayside Inn* (1863–1873). While the narrative poems are less read today than they once were, Longfellow's lyrics, such as "Mezzo Cammin," "The Jewish Cemetery at Newport," and "The Cross of Snow," remain popular. The sonority, deft phrasing, and mythic energy of this work have much in common with the Victorian poet Tennyson, who became the most widely read English poet of his century.

Longfellow's contemporary Edgar Allan Poe was another writer who caught the eye of Europe with his poems as well as his macabre stories. *The Raven and Other Poems* (1845) dazzled readers, and it remains a central volume in any account of nineteenth-century American poetry. An admirer of Coleridge, Poe believed with his English counterpart that a poem "is opposed to a work of science by having, for its *immediate* object, pleasure, not truth." He also admired Tennyson, whom he called "the greatest Poet in England, at present," and he is a more Tennysonian poet than any of his contemporaries, imitating the elder poet's sad lyricism, his note of perpetual lamentation, and his reverence for beauty in its darker aspects. No poet has ever written more sonorously, with a more heavily mournful tone, than Poe. "The Raven" is a marvelous piece of narrative, but Poe was also an extraordinary lyricist, as in the haunting "To Helen."

The original accent of American poetry, per se, was not really sounded until William Cullen Bryant, in 1830, addressed a friend leaving these shores for a visit to the Old World in "To Cole, the Painter, Departing for Europe." He understands completely what separates the American from the European experience of the world:

> Fair scenes shall greet thee where thou goest—fair,
>   But different—everywhere the trace of men,
>   Paths, homes, graves, ruins, from the lowest glen
> To where life shrinks from the fierce Alpine air,
>   Gaze on them, till the tears shall dim thy sight,
>   But keep that earlier, wilder image bright.

That "earlier, wilder image" was the American visionary gleam, heard again in the beautiful opening lines of "The Prairies," published by Bryant only three years later:

> These are the Gardens of the Desert, these
> The unshorn fields, boundless and beautiful,
> For which the speech of England has no name—
> The Prairies. I behold them for the first,
> And my heart swells, while the dilated sight
> Takes in the encircling vastness.

Bryant's "dilated sight" goes to the heart of the visionary strain, the dominant strain in our poetry. Whereas the English poet might be obsessed by place-names, the American poet-seer does not really care whether it is Nebraska or South Dakota that stimulates his vision. As Tocqueville says, "democracy diverts the imagination from all that is external to man and fixes it on man alone." Bryant's dilation of the eye is crucial, paralleling what is perhaps the most famous passage in all American literature, where Emerson, in *Nature* (1836), crossed a "bare common" in Massachusetts at twilight under a cloudy sky and discovered that dilation of sight that Whittier had already marked: "Standing on the bare ground,—my head bathed by the blithe air and uplifted into infinite space,—all mean egotism vanishes. I become a transparent eyeball; I am nothing; I see all; the currents of the Universal Being circulate through me; I am part and parcel of God."

Passages like this one stimulated the Transcendental movement, which is uniquely American in texture. Emerson was himself the primary poet of this movement, and his fellow Transcendentalists, such as Henry David Thoreau, Christopher Pearse Cranch, William Ellery Channing (the younger), Jones Very, and Margaret Fuller, among others, preferred a kind of gnomic verse in which compressed statement was much prized. Typical of these poems was "Gnosis," by Cranch, which opens:

> Thought is deeper than all speech,
>   Feeling deeper than all thought:
> Souls to souls can never teach
>   What unto themselves was taught.
>
> We are spirits clad in veils;
>   Man by man was never seen;
> All our deep communing fails
>   To remove the shadowy screen.

Cranch celebrates the effort to move beyond language into a deeper kind of knowledge than that available to the eye, to become a "transparent eyeball" seeing everything in a heightened moment of perception. The compulsive, arresting (and "non-visual") gaze that penetrates the bright surface of the world to reveal the spirit beneath it all arises everywhere in these poets. Jones Very, a little younger than Emerson, addresses a flower in "The Columbine" in typical fashion: "Still, still my eye will gaze long fixed on thee, / Till I forget that I am called a man, / And at thy side fast-rooted seem to be."

One thing the Transcendentalists hoped to transcend was individuality itself, and they avoided the cultivation of an autobiographical persona, preferring the anonymous lyric voice. This disbelief in subjectivity, marked by an awareness of the failure of an integrated self to command the world, is the theme of "Days," Emerson's most successful single poem and a prime expression of the Transcendental movement:

> Daughters of Time, the hypocritic Days,
> Muffled and dumb like barefoot dervishes,
> And marching single in an endless file,
> Bring diadems and fagots in their hands.
> To each they offer gifts after his will,
> Bread, kingdoms, stars, and sky that holds them all.
> I, in my pleached garden, watched the pomp,
> Forgot my morning wishes, hastily
> Took a few herbs and apples, and the Day
> Turned and departed silent. I, too late,
> Under her solemn fillet saw the scorn.

Emerson opens with no sense of an individual speaker; not until the painful seventh line does the poet step forward, unequal to the task of proper contemplation, too frail of spirit to contain the multitudinous day that has confronted him. The poem begins in awe and ends in frustration as the poet slips from impersonal authority to fragile subjectivity.

It would take a poet of Whitman's imaginative force to step up to reality, bright-eyed and benign, unfazed by existence, in order to confront the harsh, brilliant, loud, and multifaceted things of this world. He strode the planet wide-eyed "As Adam early in the morning, / Walking forth from the bower refresh'd with sleep." It is this mode of refreshed revisionary cognizance that leads, ultimately, to Wallace Stevens's "The Idea of Order at Key West" or Hart Crane's "Cape Hatteras" section of "The Bridge," to A. R. Ammons's "Corsons Inlet," or to Robert Penn Warren's sublime "Heart of Autumn."

In an oblique but important way, the Transcendental movement inspired the astonishing body of work produced by Emily Dickinson. When she was fourteen, in 1844, she first read Emerson's essay "The Poet," in which the poet was defined as "a man of the people." Emerson argued eloquently that the odds and ends of everyday life were the proper stuff of poetry, that metaphors must be culled from daily existence. His evocations of "the poet" were, however, masculine in the extreme:

> The poet is representative. He stands among partial men for the complete man, and apprises us not of his wealth, but of our commonwealth. The young man reveres men of genius, because, to speak truly, they are more himself than he is. . . . [The poet] unlocks our chains, and admits us to a new scene. . . . Every verse or sentence, possessing this virtue, will take care of its own immortality. The religions of the world are the ejaculations of a few imaginative men.

The genius of Dickinson was to appropriate the notion of representation, to make herself—a reclusive spinster living in a small town in New England—a representative person; she gathered in her poems the details of domestic life, and she did so with such concentration, anger, oddity, and fire that her poems practically burn a hole through the page, as in "He fumbles at your spirit":

> He fumbles at your spirit
>   As players at the keys
> Before they drop full music on;
>   He stuns you by degrees,
>
> Prepares your brittle substance
>   For the ethereal blow,
> By fainter hammers, further heard,
>   Then nearer, then so slow
>
> Your breath has time to straighten,
>   Your brain to bubble cool,—

> Deals one imperial thunderbolt
> That scalps your naked soul.

Thus, God—or some large, dark force—becomes a quasi-malevolent fumbler who prepares his victim for the ultimate deathblow. The imagery begins in a rather sweet manner, with "keys" and "music" invoked casually as the unnamed player at the piano warms up. This deft conceit (a technique inherited from the Puritans) continues in the second stanza with the notion of "hammers" striking and with notes eerily "further heard, / Then nearer." The disruptive last stanza, with its weird importation of cooking imagery (the brain bubbling cool!), gives way to the scalping of the naked soul. The reader is left, breathless and surprised, startled into a fresh awareness of life's entropic movement, which culminates in sudden, violent cessation.

Dickinson's preoccupation with death lends her work a peculiar ferocity; her poems are nearly all crisis-oriented, involving ultimate questions. The capaciousness of Whitman is banished from her taut lyrics, which somehow make a virtue out of rhythmical sameness, employing the well-known Common Measure found in church hymnals. Indeed, the conventional form of her lyrics only adds to their strangeness, as if Dickinson should not be saying such things as "I felt a funeral in my brain" or "I died for beauty, but was scarce / Adjusted in the tomb" in such a holy form. Her work has often been called "cryptic," and it is. It is full of dazzling puzzles, patterns to be traced, doors to be unlocked; there are many levels of ambiguity in almost every stanza as the poet strives to "Tell all the truth but tell it slant."

In a sense, Whitman and Dickinson represent the opposite poles of American verse, although they have a common source in Emerson. Both were highly original poets whose work has an air of challenge about it. Whitman wanted to stake his claim, to include all of America in his verse. There is a vastness to *Leaves of Grass* that was part of his reach for universality, his bid to become Representative Man; Dickinson, in her fierce exclusion of everything that did not matter dearly to her, staked her claim on the individual soul, which she took to be representative as well. Defiantly and uniquely, each succeeded, opening up paths for American poetry.

It has often been noted that Dickinson was especially important for women poets who came after her. The traditional canon of English verse was a bastion of male exclusivity, and what must immediately strike the casual reader of this anthology is the number of women poets that America has produced, beginning with Anne Bradstreet. Some of these poets from the nineteenth century were extremely popular in their day—Phillis Wheatley, Lydia Huntley Sigourney, Lydia Maria Child, Sarah Helen Whitman, Elizabeth Oakes-Smith, Frances Sargent Osgood, Alice Cary, Frances E. W. Harper, Emma Lazarus, Louise Imogen Guiney. While much of their verse would have to be called "conventional," the same must be said of most poets of the nineteenth century: only

Whitman and Dickinson wrote with an originality of vision and style equal to, say, Wordsworth or Keats.

The modernist movement in poetry was largely American in its origins. T. S. Eliot, Ezra Pound, Robert Frost, Wallace Stevens, Amy Lowell, Marianne Moore, and H.D., each in his or her own way, contributed to the founding of this international movement, which cut across the arts. In poetry, modernism is a loosely fitting tag for early-twentieth-century poets who wanted to "break the back of the goddamn iamb," as Ezra Pound said. These poets wanted to shake poetry loose from the rhetoric that one sees in the worst late-nineteenth-century poets on both sides of the Atlantic. They sought to bring the speaking voice back into poetry and believed in the primacy of the image. Imagism, a movement founded by Amy Lowell and H.D. and joined by Ezra Pound, promoted the idea of concreteness in verse. In some ways, the modernist movement was so successful that not until recently has narrative or discursive verse been again prized by poets and critics.

Robert Frost certainly brought his own poetry close to the speaking voice of ordinary New England farmers, especially in such dramatic poems as "Home Burial." It is a mistake, however, to think of him as merely a farmer-poet. He was an extremely sophisticated writer whose training in Latin and Greek verse is brilliantly hidden but nevertheless informs his work throughout. Frost is a pastoral poet in the line of Virgil, an urban poet who writes about country people for an educated audience. But his vision and originality were such that few serious readers of American poetry can resist his alluring cadences, the broken but subtly musical patterns of human speech at its most succinct, as heard in the opening lines of his incomparable " 'Out, Out—' ":

> The buzz-saw snarled and rattled in the yard
> And made dust and dropped stove-length sticks of wood,
> Sweet-scented stuff when the breeze drew across it.
> And from there those that lifted eyes could count
> Five mountain ranges one behind the other
> Under the sunset far into Vermont.

While writing in the most traditional kind of Wordsworthian blank verse, Frost adapted the line to represent a recognizably American voice. The laconic phrasing, the concreteness of the diction ("snarled and rattled"), the colloquial ease and overall compactness of the movement from line to line—this is the work of a master craftsman. Frost summoned a dark, ruined landscape populated by down-at-the-heels farmers, itinerant workers, and lonely country wives; his poems speak of human isolation, of broken communities, of quiet yearnings for another, better world. He was a dour Emersonian, a poet who (like Emerson) read nature as a symbol of the spirit, who cast his eye upon objects and studied them for their metaphorical power. But the reality that emerges in his work has nothing of Emerson's optimism. "I have been one acquainted with the night," he says in one poem. Indeed, he frequently writes about winter, with "Snow falling and night falling fast, oh, fast." He examines the seemingly amoral aspects of the universe in "Design," his most challenging sonnet, and found it "appalling" (playing on the root sense of that word, "to make white").

Frost's gaudy counterpart was Wallace Stevens, who next to Whitman has proven to be the most generative of poets, yielding a crop of mighty contemporaries as different as James Merrill and John Ashbery. Stevens's one subject was poetry itself, which he took to be the primary mode of human inquiry. Although he most often worked in blank verse, the sound of his poetry is deeply personal, at times idiosyncratic in the way of any truly original stylist. In "Of Modern Poetry," he put forward a modernist credo, saying that poetry must now become "The poem of the mind in the act of finding / What will suffice."

> It has not always had
> To find: the scene was set; it repeated what
> Was in the script.

But now these repetitions of the past will not do. Now:

> It has to be living, to learn the speech of the place.
> It has to face the men of the time and to meet
> The women of the time. It has to think about war
> And it has to find what will suffice. It has
> To construct a new stage.

It should be noted that Stevens, like Eliot and Pound, had strong European affinities. He had almost no interest in writing poetry that was especially American but looked to the Continent for inspiration. It could well be argued that English poets of the day were cut off from Europe in a way that American poets were not; the Americans were thus able to comprehend what Eliot called "the mind of Europe." Stevens himself reaches back to Latin poets like Virgil and Lucretius, to Dante, and to French symbolism (Baudelaire, Valéry, and Laforgue were seminal poets for him, as were the Cubist painters). Stevens also appropriates the English blank verse line, incorporating into it a peculiarly Latinate diction. "French and English constitute a single language," he proclaims, rather oddly but instructively, in a collection of *pensées* called "Adagia." Nevertheless, there is something unmistakably American about him in the end. As Helen Vendler says, "Stevens interrogates the adequacy of America to poetry and of poetry to America more often than any of his contemporaries except Williams, and spent more time walking the American countryside and recording it than the other Modernists."

Indeed, Stevens celebrates our natural world with a freshness that is breath-taking, as in "Sunday Morning":

> Deer walk upon our mountains, and the quail
> Whistle about us their spontaneous cries;
> Sweet berries ripen in the wilderness.

His work studies the seasons with exactness and love, finding metaphors everywhere. He was a poet of weather, and he favored the "poetry of earth" over the "poetry of heaven"; his refusal of the Divine is a major theme in his poetry. In some ways he anticipated the existentialists, insisting on his own brand of humanism, with humanity as the measure of all things. He was always questing for what he called Central Man, a version of Emerson's Representative Man.

Stevens was able to teach future poets that poetry is always, in the end, metaphysical, a language that mediates between "the mind and sky." It is always a search for "what will suffice," and in the end, "it must give pleasure." He pioneered in the development of the long poem as a sequence of symbolic lyrics, and he understood the mysterious relation of syntax to argument better than most. While retaining more than a modicum of British prosody in his manner, he brought an American idiom to bear in his verse line that was at once unique and generative.

T. S. Eliot and Ezra Pound were also central participants in the modernist movement and, in different ways, as influential. Eliot, in particular, remains a difficult poet to write about in terms of American poetry, although he was probably the central poet for the generation of Southern writers that included John Crowe Ransom, Allen Tate, and Robert Penn Warren. Certainly, as a critic, Eliot's critical dicta were taken seriously, and he had a massive influence on American literary scholarship, leaving behind him a trail of critical terms: "objective correlative," "dissociation of sensibility," "tradition," "classicism." "The Love Song of J. Alfred Prufrock," "Gerontion," and—most important—*The Waste Land*, are central texts of literary modernism, although a danger exists that they will be read as "examples" of something instead of as endlessly complex and rewarding poems in their own right. As a stylist, Eliot walked the narrow line between free verse and formal verse more delicately than any poet before or after, and, like Stevens, he perfected the art of the lyric sequence. In his longer poems, he developed a kind of symbolic architecture that was crucial for later poets—for Hart Crane, for example, whose romancing of modernism in "The Bridge" owes a great deal to *The Waste Land*. In an essay called "Fifty Years of American Poetry," Randall Jarrell took brilliant stock of Eliot's achievement:

Won't the future say to us in helpless astonishment: "But did you actually believe that all these things about objective correlatives, classicism, the tradition, applied to his poetry? Surely you must have seen that he was one of the most subjective and daemonic poets who ever lived, the victim and helpless beneficiary of his own inexorable compulsions, obsessions? . . . But for you, of course, after the first few years, his poetry existed undersea, thousands of feet below that deluge of exegesis, explication, source listing, scholarship, and criticism that overwhelmed it. And yet how bravely and personally it survived, its eye neither coral nor mother-of-pearl but plainly human, full of human anguish!

Pound, like his friend William Carlos Williams, fathered a long line of poets, many of whom (like Charles Olson and Charles Wright) would seem to have little in common. Whole "schools" were founded on Pound's Imagist aesthetics (objectivists, Beats, Black Mountain poets, Language poets—an astonishing assembly!). It should be noted that Whitman "grandfathered" many of the same poets: Pound made his "Pact" with Whitman early. In "What I Feel about Walt Whitman" (1909), he said with typical hyperbole and self-parading:

[Whitman] is America. His crudity is an exceeding great stench, but it is America. He is the hollow place in the rock that echoes with his time. He does "chant the crucial stage" and he is the "voice triumphant." He is disgusting. He is an exceedingly nauseating pill, but he accomplishes his mission.

Whitman, this "nauseating pill," stayed with Pound to the end, right through his decades of writing *The Cantos*—which became his version of *Leaves of Grass*—an expansive poem-to-end-all-poems that takes all of human history for its theme. While *The Cantos*, taken as a whole, has failed to convince anyone but a few isolated critics of its greatness, Pound remains a brilliant lyricist in the shorter poems and, even here and there, in *The Cantos*. His ear, as Eliot noted, was perfect, and the sound of his poetry is grainy, angular, odd, and fresh.

Imagism was a movement that approached poetic design in the elliptical manner of dream-sequences; traditional narrative (or even logical) connections were dropped in favor of juxtaposition and suggestion. Pound's 1913 list of Imagist "tenets" became a centerpiece of the movement:

I. Direct treatment of the "thing," whether subjective or objective.
II. To use absolutely no word that does not contribute to the presentation.
III. As regarding rhythm: to compose in sequence of the musical phrase, not in sequence of the metronome.

In Pound's "In a Station of the Metro," for example, "apparition" stands beside "petals on a wet, black bough," making a physical and emotional connection that becomes, at last, a poetic "idea." The purpose of the Imagist poem, said Pound, was "to recreate the precise instant when a thing outward and objective transforms itself, or darts into a thing inward and subjective." Not for nothing was Pound attracted to Chinese poetry, and his "translations" or "imitations" of ancient Chinese poets (gathered in *Cathay*, 1915) are alluring.

William Carlos Williams, in a sense, was the most severe Imagist of them all, and a poem like "The Red Wheelbarrow" comes directly out of this extraordinarily influential movement, as do the best poems of Amy Lowell, H.D., Carl Sandburg, and others. Of these, Williams has proven an extremely durable and especially American poet. A friend of Pound, he rejected the flight to Europe, and he eschewed European materials. The Imagist demand for concrete objects was right up Williams's alley: a doctor in Paterson, New Jersey, he had a vast array of native imagery at his doorstep, and he used it. His work is full of portraits of local people, his friends and neighbors, as in "Woman Walking," where he cries:

> —what a blessing it is
> to see you in the street again,
> powerful woman,
> coming with swinging haunches,
> breasts straight forward,
> supple shoulders, full arms
> and strong, soft hands (I've felt them)
> carrying the heavy basket.

In his use of what he called the "variable foot," in his attendance to local materials, and in the offhandedness that conceals a deep, almost mythic, sense of design, Williams inspired poets like Marianne Moore, his contemporary, as well as such later poets as Denise Levertov, Robert Creeley, Robert Duncan, Robert Lowell, and Allen Ginsberg, all of whom have explicitly paid homage to Williams. Charles Olson, in his Maximus poems, looked specifically to *Paterson*, Williams's highly original epic, for a way of sidestepping the problem of egotism that he believed had ruined Pound's *Cantos*. Williams was able to celebrate the local detail in a way that Pound could never manage, and this has been a continuing inspiration to poets.

As a quick perusal of this book ought to suggest, the twentieth century has witnessed the strong emergence in this country of women poets. Marianne Moore and Elizabeth Bishop are among its major poets, and it seems increasingly clear that Laura Riding Jackson must be counted with them. All three of these looked to H.D. as an example. Moore, in reviewing H.D.'s "Hymen"

(1923), praised the "magic and compressed energy of the author's imagination." Her "faithfulness to fact" was noted with approval. Most pointedly, she remarked on her awareness of gender:

> Talk of weapons and the tendency to match one's intellectual and emotional vigor with the violence of nature, gives a martial, an apparently masculine tone to such writing as H.D.'s, the more so that women are regarded as belonging necessarily to either of two classes— that of the intellectual freelance or that of the eternally sleeping beauty. . . . There is, however, a connection between weapons and beauty. Cowardice and beauty are at swords' points, and in H.D.'s work, suggested by the absence of subterfuge, cowardice and the ambition to dominate by brute force, we have heroics which do not confuse transcendence with domination and which in their indestructibleness, are the core of tranquility and of intellectual equilibrium.

Moore herself, and Bishop later, did not confuse "transcendence with domination," and their poetry is remarkable for the way it allows the world to emerge almost untainted by "personality." The Imagist commandment to present the "thing itself" undergirds their aesthetics. Even in her longer poems, in "Marriage," for example, there is a vividness produced by Moore's concreteness that becomes a form of objectivity:

> Below the incandescent stars
> below the incandescent fruit,
> the strange experience of beauty;
> its existence is too much;
> it tears one to pieces
> and each fresh wave of consciousness
> is poison.

"Marriage" is so far beyond the sentimentality one associates with poems on this subject that the reader is left somewhat breathless.

Moore, like H.D. and Gertrude Stein, continued to experiment with poetic form and expression throughout her long career, and while her achievement now seems idiosyncratic, her example was vital for later women poets. Her reticence, her scrupulous attention to the "thing itself," the modesty of her lyric "I," which is used sparingly in her work, her brave meandering (a refusal to batten herself to "male" narrowness of logic?), her astringent refusal of all forms of sentimentality: these have all mattered to later women poets, many of whom she rallied behind in their early careers. (Moore personally "sponsored" Elizabeth Bishop, for example, in a 1935 anthology called *Trial Balances*.)

Among the other important women poets who wrote earlier in this century are Sara Teasdale, Elinor Wylie, Edna St. Vincent Millay, and Léonie Adams. Millay, in particular, was a rich and complex poet whose work has only begun to be rediscovered. These poets were not much affected by modernism, although the bright images in their poems suggest that they had been reading Amy Lowell, H.D., Pound, Moore, and Williams. I have tried to represent this group, but I regret that much more of their work could not have been included. These poets were all more or less traditional, adhering to late Victorian norms, but the best of their work—Millay's "The Buck in the Snow" or "Ragged Island," for example—deserves our close attention and respect.

In mid- to late-twentieth-century poetry, the heirs of H.D., Millay, and Moore include Gwendolyn Brooks, Amy Clampitt, Elizabeth Bishop, Muriel Rukeyser, Mona Van Duyn, Anne Sexton, Adrienne Rich, Denise Levertov, Sylvia Plath, Anne Stevenson (a much neglected poet), Mary Oliver, Nancy Willard, Erica Jong, Louise Glück, and so many others. The fact that the canon of American poetry can no longer be seen as a male enclosure is terribly important, and the consequences of this will take a generation to process.

Among the achievements of poets writing early in this century were those of the poets who belonged to the so-called Harlem Renaissance. A huge outpouring of poetry by writers of African descent occurred in the second and third decades of this century, and several famous anthologies appeared in the early twenties, bringing the existence of these poets to light. Foremost were James Weldon Johnson's *Book of American Negro Poetry* (1922) and *Negro Poets and Their Poems* (1923), edited by Robert Kerlin. Soon Langston Hughes, Countee Cullen, Jean Toomer, Arna Bontemps, and Gwendolyn Bennett acquired a following. In the introduction to his anthology, Johnson traced the history of African American poetry from the eighteenth century to the present. Pointing to poets from Phillis Wheatley to Paul Laurence Dunbar, Johnson reflected:

> What the colored poet in the United States needs to do is something like what Synge did for the Irish; he needs to find a form that will express the racial spirit by symbols from within rather than by symbols from without, such as the mere mutilation of English spelling and pronunciation. He needs a form that is freer and larger than dialect, but which will still hold the racial flavor; a form expressing the imagery, the idioms, the peculiar turns of thought, and the distinctive humor and pathos, too, of the Negro, but which will also be capable of voicing the deepest and highest emotions and aspirations, and allow of the widest range of subjects and the widest scope of treatment.

As Arnold Rampersad has noted: "For James Weldon Johnson (as he made clear in his 1933 autobiography *Along This Way*) and Langston Hughes—

certainly two highly influential figures—Walt Whitman's *Leaves of Grass* was the volume that inspired their own flight from the old kind of dialect verse, and set in motion their search—in ways, to be sure, often contrary to Whitman's—for an aesthetic that reflected the realities of African American language, culture, and history." Whitman again emerges as the powerful precursor, although one must not suggest that poets like McKay and Hughes did not possess a radical sense of their own originality.

McKay's aggressive stance made him extremely attractive to a generation of new African-American poets. Hughes, however, became the central poet of this movement when he published *The Weary Blues* in 1926. The title poem in that collection was the first to make use of the basic blues form, and its inventiveness astounded readers, who had never before seen lines like these: "Droning a drowsy syncopated tune, / Rocking back and forth to a mellow croon, / I heard a Negro play." Countee Cullen also came into prominence in the twenties and thirties, and he was in some ways the opposite of Hughes, consciously imitating English poets like Keats, Shelley, and A. E. Housman. His best-known poem, "Heritage," wonders what Africa means to the African American of his day, whether it be

> Copper sun or scarlet sea,
> Jungle star or jungle track,
> Strong bronzed men, or regal black
> Women from whose loins I sprang
> When the birds of Eden sang?

"What is Africa to me?" Cullen asks. His answer is complex, suggesting that he is pleased by the triumph of Christian values over paganism ("I belong to Jesus Christ, / Preacher of humility; / Heathen gods are naught to me") yet secretly thrilled that certain African impulses remain unchecked within him ("Not yet has my heart or head / In the least way realized / They are I are civilized").

Melvin B. Tolson and Anne Spencer were extremely gifted poets, and Tolson's *Harlem Gallery* (not published until 1965 but written much earlier) is among the few examples of modernist influence within the Harlem Renaissance group. Arna Bontemps, who never published a full-length book of his own, was also a fine lyric poet in the traditional sense; his poetic line was sharp and clear, and one hears in his lines a strange combination of Negro spiritual and English Romantic verse, as in the stately opening stanza of "A Black Man Talks of Reaping":

> I have sown beside all waters in my day
> I planted deep within my heart the fear
> That wind or fowl would take the grain away.
> I planted safe against this stark, lean year.

The Harlem Renaissance writers showed African-American poets a way to bring the imagery and sound of their experience into poetry, and a clear line can be drawn from them, and from Hughes in particular, to later African-American poets Gwendolyn Brooks, Robert Hayden, Imamu Amiri Baraka, Jay Wright, Don Lee (Haki R. Madhubuti), Sonia Sanchez, Nikki Giovanni, and Rita Dove. Each of these poets, and dozens more, have found original ways to deal with racial difference, often making use of original African materials.

Recent American poetry remains tremendously varied, but I made a firm decision not to include poets born after the Second World War, a move founded on the observation that most anthologies of this sort become extremely arbitrary in the last few pages. Nevertheless, a considerable range of contemporary poetry is represented, including Adrienne Rich, James Merrill, Philip Levine, Charles Wright, and Louise Glück, each of whom has produced a major and influential body of work that repays close reading.

It is also in the nature of anthologies to have gaps: I have merely skimmed the cream, as I see it, of American poetry, putting between covers those few hundred pages of verse that would be for me essential reading on some future desert island. I have omitted the usually obligatory sections that contain anonymous poems—folk poetry, as it were. These poems—"The Yankee Man o' War," "Go Down, Moses," "The Big Rock Candy Mountain," "Frankie and Johnny," "John Henry," "The Old Chisholm Trail," and so forth—are really song lyrics, and they strike this editor as ill suited to an anthology of poems that are better read than sung.

Poetry lies at the heart of any national culture, and American culture is no different from any other. Poetry is the highest expression in language of our deepest longings, and it represents our most concentrated efforts to find a language adequate to our experience. The fact that American experience has been so varied is reflected in the different traditions of expression represented here. The terse New England measures of Emily Dickinson seem a continent away from Ginsberg's ramble in "A Supermarket in California," just as Sara Teasdale's gentle lyrics seem remote from Robert Lowell's thunderous tones in "A Quaker Graveyard in Nantucket." The wit of W. D. Snodgrass's "April Inventory" could hardly look stranger beside Sylvia Plath's frightening "Daddy." It is a tribute to the American spirit that such a range of poetry is so readily generated and absorbed.

THE COLUMBIA ANTHOLOGY OF
AMERICAN POETRY

Anne Bradstreet

(1 6 1 2 – 1 6 7 2)

CONTEMPLATIONS

Some time now past in the autumnal tide,
    When Phoebus wanted but one hour to bed,
The trees all richly clad, yet void of pride,
    Were gilded o'er by his rich golden head;
Their leaves and fruits seemed painted, but were true
Of green, of red, of yellow, mixéd hue.
Rapt were my senses at this delectable view.

I wist not what to wish, yet sure, thought I,
    If so much excellence abide below
How excellent is He that dwells on high,
    Whose power and beauty by his works we know!
Sure He is goodness, wisdom, glory, light,
That hath this under world so richly dight.
More heaven than earth was here, no winter and no night.

Then on a stately oak I cast mine eye,
    Whose ruffling top the clouds seemed to aspire.
How long since thou wast in thine infancy?
    Thy strength and stature more thy years admire.
Hath hundred winters passed since thou wast born,
Or thousand since thou break'st thy shell of horn?
If so, all these as naught eternity doth scorn.

Then higher on the glistering sun I gazed,
    Whose beams were shaded by the leafy tree;
The more I looked the more I grew amazed,
    And softly said, What glory's like to thee?
Soul of this world, this universe's eye,
No wonder some made thee a deity.
Had I not better known, alas, the same had I.

Thou as a bridegroom from thy chamber rushes,
    And as a strong man joys to run a race;

The morn doth usher thee with smiles and blushes,
    The earth reflects her glances in thy face.
Birds, insects, animals, with vegetive,
Thy heart from death and dulness doth revive,
And in the darksome womb of fruitful nature dive.

Thy swift annual and diurnal course,
    Thy daily straight and yearly oblique path,
Thy pleasing fervor, and thy scorching force
    All mortals here the feeling knowledge hath.
Thy presence makes it day, thy absence night.
Quaternal seasons causéd by thy might.
Hail, creature full of sweetness, beauty, and delight!

Art thou so full of glory that no eye
    Hath strength thy shining rays once to behold?
And is thy splendid throne erect so high
    As to approach it can no earthly mould?
How full of glory then must thy Creator be
Who gave this bright light luster unto thee?
Admired, adored, forever be that Majesty.

Silent, alone, where none or saw or heard,
    In pathless paths I led my wandering feet;
My humble eyes to lofty skies I reared,
    To sing some song my amazéd muse thought meet.
My great Creator I would magnify
That nature had thus decked liberally.
But ah, and ah again, my imbecility!

I heard the merry grasshopper then sing,
    The black-clad cricket bear a second part;
They kept one tune and played on the same string,
    Seeming to glory in their little art.
Shall creatures abject thus their voices raise,
And in their kind resound their maker's praise,
Whilst I as mute can warble forth no higher lays?

When present times look back to ages past,
    And men in being fancy those are dead,
It makes things gone perpetually to last,
    And calls back months and years that long since fled;

It makes a man more aged in conceit
Than was Methuselah or his grandsire great
While of their persons and their acts his mind doth treat.

Sometimes in Eden fair he seems to be,
    Sees glorious Adam there made lord of all,
Fancies the apple dangle on the tree
    That turned his sovereign to a naked thrall,
Who like a miscreant was driven from that place
To get his bread with pain and sweat of face—
A penalty imposed on his backsliding race.

Here sits our grandam in retired place,
    And in her lap her bloody Cain new born;
The weeping imp oft looks her in the face,
    Bewails his unknown hap and fate forlorn.
His mother sighs to think of paradise,
And how she lost her bliss to be more wise,
Believing him that was and is father of lies.

Here Cain and Abel come to sacrifice;
    Fruits of the earth and fatlings each doth bring.
On Abel's gift the fire descends from skies,
    But no such sign on false Cain's offering.
With sullen hateful looks he goes his ways,
Hath thousand thoughts to end his brother's days,
Upon whose blood his future good he hopes to raise.

There Abel keeps his sheep, no ill he thinks;
    His brother comes, then acts his fratricide;
The virgin earth of blood her first draught drinks,
    But since that time she often hath been cloyed.
The wretch with ghastly face and dreadful mind
Thinks each he sees will serve him in his kind,
Though none on earth but kindred near then could he find.

Who fancies not his looks now at the bar,
    His face like death, his heart with horror fraught,
Nor malefactor ever felt like war
    When deep despair with wish of life hath sought.
Branded with guilt, and crushed with treble woes,

A vagabond to land of Nod he goes,
A city builds, that walls might him secure from foes.

Who thinks not oft upon the fathers' ages,
    Their long descent, how nephews' sons they saw,
The starry observations of those sages,
    And how their precepts to their sons were law;
How Adam sighed to see his progeny
Clothed all in his black sinful livery,
Who neither guilt nor yet the punishment could fly?

Our life compare we with their length of days,
    Who to the tenth of theirs doth now arrive?
And though thus short, we shorten many ways,
    Living so little while we are alive—
In eating, drinking, sleeping, vain delight;
So unawares comes on perpetual night,
And puts all pleasures vain unto eternal flight.

When I behold the heavens as in their prime,
    And then the earth, though old, still clad in green,
The stones and trees insensible of time,
    Nor age nor wrinkle on their front are seen;
If winter come, and greenness then doth fade,
A spring returns, and they're more youthful made.
But man grows old, lies down, remains where once he's laid.

By birth more noble than those creatures all,
    Yet seems by nature and by custom cursed—
No sooner born but grief and care make fall
    That state obliterate he had at first;
Nor youth, nor strength, nor wisdom spring again,
Nor habitations long their names retain,
But in oblivion to the final day remain.

Shall I then praise the heavens, the trees, the earth,
    Because their beauty and their strength last longer?
Shall I wish there or never to had birth,
    Because they're bigger and their bodies stronger?
Nay, they shall darken, perish, fade, and die,
And when unmade so ever shall they lie;
But man was made for endless immortality.

Under the cooling shadow of a stately elm
   Close sat I by a goodly river's side
Where gliding streams the rocks did overwhelm;
   A lonely place, with pleasures dignified.
I once that loved the shady woods so well
Now thought the rivers did the trees excel,
And if the sun would ever shine there would I dwell.

While on the stealing stream I fixed mine eye
   Which to the longed-for ocean held its course,
I marked nor crooks nor rubs that there did lie
   Could hinder aught, but still augment its force.
O happy flood, quoth I, that holds thy race
Till thou arrive at thy beloved place,
Nor is it rocks or shoals that can obstruct thy pace.

Nor is it enough that thou alone mayst slide,
   But hundred brooks in thy clear waves do meet;
So hand in hand along with thee they glide
   To Thetis' house, where all embrace and greet.
Thou emblem true of what I count the best,
Oh, could I lead my rivulets to rest!
So may we press to that vast mansion ever blest!

Ye fish which in this liquid region abide,
   That for each season have your habitation,
Now salt, now fresh, where you think best to glide,
   To unknown coasts to give a visitation,
In lakes and ponds you leave your numerous fry;
So nature taught, and yet you know not why,
You watery folk that know not your felicity.

Look how the wantons frisk to taste the air,
   Then to the colder bottom straight they dive;
Eftsoon to Neptune's glassy hall repair
   To see what trade the great ones there do drive;
Who forage o'er the spacious sea-green field,
And take the trembling prey before it yield;
Whose armor is their scales, their spreading fins their shield.

While musing thus with contemplation fed,
   And thousand fancies buzzing in my brain,

The sweet-tongued philomel perched o'er my head,
  And chanted forth a most melodious strain,
Which rapt me so with wonder and delight
I judged my hearing better than my sight,
And wished me wings with her a while to take my flight.

O merry bird, said I, that fears no snares,
  That neither toils nor hoards up in thy barn,
Feels no sad thoughts, nor cruciating cares
  To gain more good or shun what might thee harm,
Thy clothes ne'er wear, thy meat is everywhere,
Thy bed a bough, thy drink the water clear,
Reminds not what is past, nor what's to come dost fear!

The dawning morn with songs thou dost prevent,
  Settest hundred notes unto thy feathered crew;
So each one tunes his pretty instrument,
  And, warbling out the old, begins anew.
And thus they pass their youth in summer season,
Then follow thee into a better region
Where winter's never felt by that sweet airy legion.

Man, at the best a creature frail and vain,
  In knowledge ignorant, in strength but weak,
Subject to sorrows, losses, sickness, pain,
  Each storm his state, his mind, his body break,
From some of these he never finds cessation,
But day or night, within, without, vexation,
Troubles from foes, from friends, from dearest, nearest relation.

And yet this sinful creature, frail and vain,
  This lump of wretchedness, of sin and sorrow,
This weather-beaten vessel racked with pain,
  Joys not in hope of an eternal morrow;
Nor all his losses, crosses, and vexation,
In weight, in frequency, and long duration,
Can make him deeply groan for that divine translation.

The mariner that on smooth waves doth glide
  Sings merrily, and steers his bark with ease,
As if he had command of wind and tide,
  And now become great master of the seas;
But suddenly a storm spoils all the sport,

And makes him long for a more quiet port,
Which 'gainst all adverse winds may serve for fort.

So he that faileth in this world of pleasure,
    Feeding on sweets, that never bit of the sour,
That's full of friends, of honor, and of treasure,
    Fond fool, he takes this earth e'en for heaven's bower.
But sad affliction comes, and makes him see
Here's neither honor, wealth, nor safety;
Only above is found all with security.

O time, the fatal wreck of mortal things,
That draws oblivion's curtains over kings!
Their sumptuous monuments men know them not,
Their names without a record are forgot,
Their parts, their ports, their pomps, all laid in the dust,
Nor wit, nor gold, nor buildings 'scape time's rust.
But he whose name is graved in the white stone
Shall last and shine when all of these are gone.

BEFORE THE BIRTH
OF ONE OF HER CHILDREN

All things within this fading world hath end,
Adversity doth still our joys attend;
No ties so strong, no friends so dear and sweet,
But with death's parting blow is sure to meet.
The sentence past is most irrevocable,
A common thing, yet oh, inevitable.
How soon, my Dear, death may my steps attend,
How soon't may be thy lot to lose thy friend,
We both are ignorant, yet love bids me
These farewell lines to recommend to thee,
That when that knot's untied that made us one,
I may seem thine, who in effect am none.
And if I see not half my days that's due,
What nature would, God grant to yours and you;
The many faults that well you know I have
Let be interred in my oblivious grave;

If any worth or virtue were in me,
Let that live freshly in thy memory
And when thou feel'st no grief, as I no harms,
Yet love thy dead, who long lay in thine arms.
And when thy loss shall be repaid with gains
Look to my little babes, my dear remains.
And if thou love thyself, or loved'st me,
These O protect from step-dame's injury.
And if chance to thine eyes shall bring this verse,
With some sad sighs honour my absent hearse;
And kiss this paper for thy love's dear sake,
Who with salt tears this last farewell did take.

TO MY DEAR AND LOVING HUSBAND

If ever two were one, then surely we.
If ever man were loved by wife, then thee;
If ever wife was happy in a man,
Compare with me, ye women, if you can.
I prize thy love more than whole mines of gold
Or all the riches that the East doth hold.
My love is such that rivers cannot quench,
Nor ought but love from thee, give recompense.
Thy love is such I can no way repay,
The heavens reward thee manifold, I pray.
Then while we live, in love let's so persevere
That when we live no more, we may live ever.

THE AUTHOR TO HER BOOK

Thou ill-formed offspring of my feeble brain,
Who after birth didst by my side remain,
Till snatched from thence by friends, less wise than true,
Who thee abroad, exposed to public view,
Made thee in rags, halting to th' press to trudge,
Where errors were not lessened (all may judge).

At thy return my blushing was not small,
My rambling brat (in print) should mother call,
I cast thee by as one unfit for light,
Thy visage was so irksome in my sight;
Yet being mine own, at length affection would
Thy blemishes amend, if so I could:
I washed thy face, but more defects I saw,
And rubbing off a spot still made a flaw.
I stretched thy joints to make thee even feet,
Yet still thou run'st more hobbling than is meet;
In better dress to trim thee was my mind,
But nought save homespun cloth i' th' house I find.
In this array 'mongst vulgars may'st thou roam.
In critic's hands beware thou dost not come,
And take thy way where yet thou art not known;
If for thy father asked, say thou hadst none;
And for thy mother, she alas is poor,
Which caused her thus to send thee out of door.

IN MEMORY OF MY DEAR GRANDCHILD ELIZABETH BRADSTREET, WHO DECEASED AUGUST, 1665, BEING A YEAR AND HALF OLD

1

Farewell dear babe, my heart's too much content,
Farewell sweet babe, the pleasure of mine eye,
Farewell fair flower that for a space was lent,
Then ta'en away unto eternity.
Blest babe, why should I once bewail thy fate,
Or sigh thy days so soon were terminate,
Sith thou art settled in an everlasting state.

2

By nature trees do rot when they are grown,
And plums and apples thoroughly ripe do fall,
And corn and grass are in their season mown,
And time brings down what is both strong and tall.

But plants new set to be eradicate,
And buds new blown to have so short a date,
Is by His hand alone that guides nature and fate.

ON MY DEAR GRANDCHILD
SIMON BRADSTREET
WHO DIED ON 16 NOVEMBER, 1669,
BEING BUT A MONTH, AND ONE DAY OLD

No sooner came, but gone, and fall'n asleep,
Acquaintance short, yet parting caused us weep;
Three flowers, two scarcely blown, the last i' th' bud,
Cropt by th' Almighty's hand; yet is He good.
With dreadful awe before Him let's be mute,
Such was His will, but why, let's not dispute,
With humble hearts and mouths put in the dust,
Let's say He's merciful as well as just.
He will return and make up all our losses,
And smile again after our bitter crosses
Go pretty babe, go rest with sisters twain;
Among the blest in endless joys remain.

HERE FOLLOWS SOME VERSES UPON THE
BURNING OF OUR HOUSE JULY 10TH, 1666.
COPIED OUT OF A LOOSE PAPER

In silent night when rest I took
For sorrow near I did not look
I wakened was with thund'ring noise
And piteous shrieks of dreadful voice.
That fearful sound of "Fire!" and "Fire!"
Let no man know is my desire.
I, starting up, the light did spy,

And to my God my heart did cry
To strengthen me in my distress
And not to leave me succorless.
Then, coming out, beheld a space
The flame consume my dwelling place.
And when I could no longer look,
I blest His name that gave and took,
That laid my goods now in the dust.
Yea, so it was, and so 'twas just.
It was His own, it was not mine,
Far be it that I should repine;
He might of all justly bereft
But yet sufficient for us left.
When by the ruins oft I past
My sorrowing eyes aside did cast,
And here and there the places spy
Where oft I sat and long did lie:
Here stood that trunk, and there that chest,
There lay that store I counted best.
My pleasant things in ashes lie,
And them behold no more shall I.
Under thy roof no guest shall sit,
Nor at thy table eat a bit.
No pleasant tale shall e'er be told,
Nor things recounted done of old.
No candle e'er shall shine in thee,
Nor bridegroom's voice e'er heard shall be.
In silence ever shall thou lie,
Adieu, Adieu, all's vanity.
Then straight I 'gin my heart to chide,
And did thy wealth on earth abide?
Didst fix thy hope on mold'ring dust?
The arm of flesh didst make thy trust?
Raise up thy thoughts above the sky
That dunghill mists away may fly.
Thou hast an house on high erect,
Framed by that mighty Architect,
With glory richly furnished,
Stands permanent though this be fled.
It's purchased and paid for too
By Him who hath enough to do.
A price so vast as is unknown

Yet by His gift is made thine own;
There's wealth enough, I need no more,
Farewell, my pelf, farewell my store.
The world no longer let me love,
My hope and treasure lies above.

AS WEARY PILGRIM

As weary pilgrim, now at rest,
    Hugs with delight his silent nest,
His wasted limbs now lie full soft
    That mirey steps have trodden oft,
Blesses himself to think upon
    His dangers past, and travails done.
The burning sun no more shall heat,
    Nor stormy rains on him shall beat.
The briars and thorns no more shall scratch,
    Nor hungry wolves at him shall catch.
He erring paths no more shall tread,
    Nor wild fruits eat instead of bread.
For waters cold he doth not long
    For thirst no more shall parch his tongue.
No rugged stones his feet shall gall,
    Nor stumps nor rocks cause him to fall.
All cares and fears he bids farewell
    And means in safety now to dwell.
A pilgrim I, on earth perplexed
    With sins, with cares and sorrows vext,
By age and pains brought to decay,
    And my clay house mold'ring away.
Oh, how I long to be at rest
    And soar on high among the blest.
This body shall in silence sleep,
    Mine eyes no more shall ever weep,
No fainting fits shall me assail,
    Nor grinding pains my body frail,
With cares and fears ne'er cumb'red be
    Nor losses know, nor sorrows see.
What though my flesh shall there consume,
    It is the bed Christ did perfume,

And when a few years shall be gone,
    This mortal shall be clothed upon.
A corrupt carcass down it lays,
    A glorious body it shall rise.
In weakness and dishonour sown,
    In power 'tis raised by Christ alone.
Then soul and body shall unite
    And of their Maker have the sight.
Such lasting joys shall there behold
    As ear ne'er heard nor tongue e'er told.
Lord make me ready for that day,
    Then come, dear Bridegroom, come away.

Michael Wigglesworth

(1 6 3 1 – 1 7 0 5)

From THE DAY OF DOOM

1

The security of the
world before
Christ's coming to
judgment.
Luke 12:19

Still was the night, serene and bright,
    when all men sleeping lay;
Calm was the season, and carnal reason
    thought so 'twould last for ay.
Soul, take thine ease, let sorrow cease,
    much good thou hast in store:
This was their song, their cups among,
    the evening before.

2

Matt. 25:5

Wallowing in all kind of sin,
    vile wretches lay secure:
The best of men had scarcely then
    their lamps kept in good ure.
Virgins unwise, who through disguise
    amongst the best were number'd,
Had clos'd their eyes; yea, and the wise
    through sloth and frailty slumber'd.

3

Matt. 24:37, 38

Like as of old, when men grow bold
    God's threat'nings to contemn,
Who stopt their ear, and would not hear,
    when mercy warned them:
But took their course, without remorse,
    till God began to power
Destruction the world upon
    in a tempestuous shower.

4

They put away the evil day,
    And drown'd their care and fears,
Till drown'd were they, and swept away
    by vengeance unawares:

1 Thess. 5:3

So at the last, whilst men sleep fast
    in their security,
Supris'd they are in such a snare
    as cometh suddenly.

5

The suddenness,
majesty, &
terror of Christ's
appearing.
Matt. 25:6
2 Pet. 3:10

For at midnight broke forth a light,
    which turn'd the night to day,
And speedily an hideous cry
    did all the world dismay.
Sinners awake, their hearts do ache,
    trembling their loins surpriseth;
Amaz'd with fear, by what they hear,
    each one of them ariseth.

6

They rush from beds with giddy heads,
    and to their windows run,
Viewing this light, which shines more bright
    then doth the noon-day Sun.

Matt. 24:29, 30

Straightway appears (they see't with tears)
    the Son of God most dread;
Who with his train comes on amain
    To judge both quick and dead.

7

2 Pet. 3:10

Before his face the heavn's gave place,
    and skies are rent asunder,
With mighty voice, and hideous noise,
    more terrible than thunder.
His brightness damps Heav'n's glorious lamps
    and makes them hide their heads,
As if afraid and quite dismay'd,
    they quit their wonted steads.

8

Ye sons of men that durst contemn
　　the threat'nings of God's word,
How cheer you now? your hearts, I trow,
　　are thrill'd as with a sword.
Now atheist blind, whose brutish mind
　　a God could never see,
Dost thou perceive, dost now believe,
　　that Christ thy Judge shall be?

9

Stout courages, (whose hardiness
　　could death and Hell out-face)
Are you as bold now you behold
　　your Judge draw near apace?
They cry, no, no: Alas! and woe!
　　our courage all is gone:
Our hardiness (fool hardiness)
　　hath us undone, undone.

10

No heart so bold, but now grows cold
　　and almost dead with fear:
Rev. 6:16   No eye so dry, but now can cry,
　　and pour out many a tear.
Earth's potentates and pow'rful states,
　　Captains and men of might
Are quite abasht, their courage dasht
　　at this most dreadful sight.

11

Mean men lament, great men do rent
　　their robes, and tear their hair:
Matt. 24:30   They do not spare their flesh to tear
　　through horrible despair.
All kindreds wail: all hearts do fail:
　　horror the world doth fill
With weeping eyes, and loud out-cries,
　　yet knows not how to kill.

12

Rev. 6:15, 16   Some hide themselves in caves and delves,
                      in places under ground:
                  Some rashly leap into the deep,
                      to scape by being drown'd:
                  Some to the rocks (O senseless blocks!)
                      and woody mountains run,
                  That there they might this fearful sight,
                      and dreaded presence shun.

13

                  In vain do they to mountains say,
                      "Fall on us, and us hide
                  From Judge's ire, more hot than fire,
                      for who may it abide?"
                  No hiding place can from his face,
                      sinners at all conceal,
                  Whose flaming eyes hid things doth 'spy,
                      and darkest things reveal.

14

                  The Judge draws nigh, exalted high
Matt. 25:31   upon a lofty throne,
                  Amidst the throng of angels strong,
                      lo, Israel's Holy One!
                  The excellence of whose presence
                      and awful majesty,
                  Amazeth Nature, and every creature,
                      doth more than terrify.

15

Rev. 6:14   The mountains smoke, the hills are shook,
                      the earth is rent and torn,
                  As if she should be clean dissolv'd
                      or from the center born.
                  The sea doth roar, forsakes the shore,
                      and shrinks away for fear;
                  The wild beasts flee into the sea,
                      so soon as he draws near.

16

Whose glory bright, whose wondrous might,
    whose power imperial,
So far surpass whatever was
    in realms terrestrial;
That tongues of men (nor angel's pen)
    cannot the same express,
And therefore I must pass it by,
    lest speaking should transgress.

17

1 Thess. 4:16   Before his throne a trump is blown,
Resurrection   Proclaiming th' Day of Doom:
of the dead.   Forthwith he cries, "*Ye Dead arise,*
John 5:28, 29   *and unto Judgment come.*"
                      No sooner said, but 'tis obey'd;
                          Sepulchers open'd are:
                      Dead bodies all rise at his call,
                          and's mighty power declare.

18

Both sea and land, at his command,
    their dead at once surrender:
The fire and air constrained are
    also their dead to tender.
The mighty word of this great Lord
    links body and soul together
Both of the just, and the unjust,
    to part no more for ever.

19

The living   The same translates, from Mortal states
changed.   to immortality,
                      All that survive, and be alive,
                          i' th' twinkling of an eye:
Luke 20:36   That so they may abide for ay
1 Cor. 15:52   to endless weal or woe;
                      Both the renate and reprobate
                          are made to dy no more.

20

All brought
to Judgment.
Matt. 24:31

His winged hosts flie through all coasts,
   together gathering
Both good and bad, both quick and dead,
   and all to Judgment bring.
Out of their holes those creeping moles,
   that hid themselves for fear,
By force they take, and quickly make
   before the Judge appear.

21

2 Cor. 5:10
The sheep
separated from
the goats.
Matt. 25

Thus every one before the throne
   of Christ the Judge is brought,
Both righteous and impious
   that good or ill had wrought.
A separation, and diff'ring station
   by Christ appointed is
(To sinners sad) 'twixt good and bad,
   'twixt heirs of woe and bliss.

22

Who are
Christ's sheep.
Matt. 5:10, 11

At Christ's right hand the sheep do stand,
   his holy martyrs, who
For his dear name suffering shame,
   calamity and woe,
Like champions stood, and with their blood
   their testimony sealed;
Whose innocence without offense,
   to Christ their Judge appealed.

23

Heb. 12:5, 6, 7

Next unto whom there find a room
   all Christ's afflicted ones,
Who being chastised, neither despised
   nor sank amidst their groans:
Who by the rod were turn'd to God,
   and loved him the more,
Not murmuring nor quarrelling
   when they were chast'ned sore.

24

Luke 7:41, 47
Moreover, such as loved much,
    that had not such a trial,
As might constrain to so great pain,
    and such deep self-denial:
Yet ready were the cross to bear,
    when Christ them call'd thereto,
And did rejoice to hear his voice,
    they're counted sheep also.

25

John 21:15
Matt. 19:14
John 3:3
Christ's flock of lambs there also stands,
    whose faith was weak, yet true;
All sound believers (Gospel receivers)
    whose grace was small, but grew:
And them among an infant throng
    of babes, for whom Christ dy'd;
Whom for his own, by ways unknown
    to men, he sanctify'd.

26

Rev. 6:11
Phil. 3:21
All stand before their Saviour
    in long white robes yclad,
Their countenance full of pleasance,
    appearing wondrous glad.
O glorious sight! Behold how bright
    dust heaps are made to shine,
Conformed so their Lord unto,
    whose glory is divine.

27

*The goats
described or the
several sorts of
reprobates on
the left hand.*
Matt. 24:51
At Christ's left hand the goats do stand,
    all whining hypocrites,
Who for self-ends did seem Christ's friends,
    but foster'd guileful sprites;
Who sheep resembled, but they dissembled
    (their hearts were not sincere);

Who once did throng Christ's lambs among,
but now must not come near.

28

Luke 11:24, 26

Heb. 6:4, 5, 6

Heb. 10:29

Apostates and run-aways,
such as have Christ forsaken,
Of whom the Devil, with seven more evil,
hath fresh possession taken:
Sinners in grain reserv'd to pain
and torments most severe:
Because 'gainst light they sinn'd with spite,
are also placed there.

29

Luke 12:47

Prov. 1:24, 26

John 3:19

There also stand a num'rous band,
that no profession made
Of godliness, nor to redress
their ways at all essay'd:
Who better knew, but (sinful crew)
Gospel and law despised;
Who all Christ's knocks withstood like blocks
and would not be advised.

30

Gal. 3:10

1 Cor. 6:9

Rev. 21:8

Moreover, there with them appear
a number, numberless
Of great and small, vile wretches all,
that did God's law transgress:
Idolators, false worshippers,
Prophaners of God's name,
Who not at all thereon did call,
or took in vain the same.

31

Exod. 20:7, 8

Blasphemers lewd, and swearers shrewd,
Scoffers at purity,
They hated God, contemn'd his rod,
and lov'd security;

Sabbath-polluters, saints persecuters,
    Presumptuous men and proud,
2 Thes. 1:6, 8, 9   Who never lov'd those that reprov'd;
    all stand amongst this crowd.

32

Heb. 13:4   Adulterers and whoremongers
1 Cor. 6:10   were there, with all unchaste:
There covetous, and ravenous,
    that riches got too fast:
Who us'd vile ways themselves to raise
    t'estates and worldly wealth,
Oppression by, or knavery,
    by force, or fraud, or stealth.

33

Zech. 5:3, 4   Moreover, there together were
Gal. 5:19, 20, 21   Children flagitious,
And parents who did them undo
    by nurture vicious.
False-witness-bearers, and self-forswearers,
    Murd'rers, and men of blood,
Witches, inchanters, and ale-house-haunters,
    beyond account there stood.

        *   *   *

219

The saints rejoice   The saints behold with courage bold,
to see Judgment   and thankful wonderment,
executed upon the   To see all those that were their foes
wicked world.   thus sent to punishment:
Ps. 58:10   Then do they sing unto their King
Rev. 19:1, 2, 3   a song of endless praise:
They praise his name, and do proclaim
    that just are all his ways.

220

They ascend with
Christ into Heaven
triumphing.
Matt. 25:46
1 John 3:2
I Cor. 13:12

Thus with great joy and melody
   to Heav'n they all ascend,
Him there to praise with sweetest lays,
   and hymns that never end,
Where with long rest they shall be blest,
   and nought shall them annoy:
Where they shall see as seen they be,
   and whom they love enjoy.

221

Their eternal
happiness and
incomparable
glory there.

O glorious place! where face to face
   Jehovah may be seen,
By such as were sinners whilere
   and no dark veil between.
Where the sun shine, and light divine,
   of God's bright countenance,
Doth rest upon them every one,
   with sweetest influence.

222

O blessed state of the renate!
   O wondrous happiness,
To which they're brought, beyond what thought
   can reach, or words express!
Rev. 21:4
Griefs water-course, and sorrows source,
   are turn'd to joyful streams.
Their old distress and heaviness
   are vanished like dreams.

223

For God above in arms of love
   doth dearly them embrace.
Ps. 16:11
And fills their sprites with such delights,
   and pleasures in his grace;
As shall not fail, nor yet grow stale
   through frequency of use:

Nor do they fear God's favor there,
    to forfeit by abuse:

224

Heb. 12:23   For there the saints are perfect saints,
    and holy ones indeed,
From all the sin that dwelt within
    their mortal bodies freed:
Made kings and priests to God through Christ's
Rev. 1:6, 22:5   dear loves transcendency,
There to remain, and there to reign
    with him eternally.

Edward Taylor

(1 6 4 2 ? – 1 7 2 9)

LET BY RAIN

Ye Flippering Soule,
  Why dost between the Nippers dwell?
Not stay, nor goe. Not yea, nor yet Controle.
  Doth this doe well?
      Rise journy'ng when the skies fall weeping Showers.
      Not o're nor under th'Clouds and Cloudy Powers.

Not yea, nor noe:
  On tiptoes thus? Why sit on thorns?
Resolve the matter: Stay thyselfe or goe.
  Be n't both wayes born.
      Wager thyselfe against thy surplice, see,
      And win thy Coate: or let thy Coate Win thee.

Is this th'Effect,
  To leaven thus my Spirits all?
To make my heart a Crabtree Cask direct?
  A Verjuicte Hall?
      As Bottle Ale, whose Spirits prisond nurst
      When jog'd, the bung with Violence doth burst?

Shall I be made
  A sparkling Wildfire Shop
Where my dull Spirits at the Fireball trade
  Do frisk and hop?
      And while the Hammer doth the Anvill pay,
      The fireball matter sparkles ery way.

One sorry fret,
  An anvill Sparke, rose higher
And in thy Temple falling almost set
  The house on fire.
      Such fireballs droping in the Temple Flame
      Burns up the building: Lord forbid the same.

45

THE REFLEXION

Lord, art thou at the table head above
   Meat, med'cine, sweetness, sparkling beauties to
Enamor souls with flaming flakes of love,
   And not my trencher, nor my cup o'erflow?
   Be n't I a bidden guest? Oh! sweat mine eye.
   O'erflow with tears: Oh! draw thy fountains dry.

Shall I not smell thy sweet, oh! Sharon's rose?
   Shall not mine eye salute thy beauty? Why?
Shall thy sweet leaves their beautious sweets upclose?
   As half ashamed my sight should on them lie?
   Woe's me! for this my sighs shall be in grain
   Offer'd on sorrow's altar for the same.

Had not my soul's thy conduit, pipes stopped been
   With mud, what ravishment would'st thou convey?
Let grace's golden spade dig till the spring
   Of tears arise, and clear this filth away.
   Lord, let thy spirit raise my sighings till
   These pipes my soul do with thy sweetness fill.

Earth once was paradise of Heaven below
   Till inkfac'd sin had it with poison stocked
And chased this paradise away into
   Heav'n's upmost loft, and it in glory locked.
   But thou, sweet Lord, hast with thy golden key
   Unlocked the door, and made, a golden day.

Once at thy feast, I saw thee pearl-like stand
   'Tween Heaven, and earth where heaven's bright glory all
In streams fell on thee, as a floodgate and,
   Like sunbeams through thee on the world to fall.
   Oh! sugar sweet then! my dear sweet Lord, I see
   Saints' Heavens-lost happiness restor'd by thee.

Shall Heaven, and earth's bright glory all up lie
   Like sunbeams bundled in the sun, in thee?
Dost thou sit rose at table head, where I
   Do sit, and carv'st no morsel sweet for me?

So much before, so little now! Sprindge, Lord,
Thy rosy leaves, and me their glee afford.

Shall not thy rose my garden fresh perfume?
   Shall not thy beauty my dull heart assail?
Shall not thy golden gleams run through this gloom?
   Shall my black velvet mask thy fair face veil?
   Pass o'er my faults: shine forth, bright sun: arise
   Enthrone thy rosy-self within mine eyes.

MEDITATION 8 (FIRST SERIES)

John 6:51. *I am the living bread.*

I kenning through astronomy divine
   The world's bright battlement, wherein I spy
A golden path my pencil cannot line,
   From that bright throne unto my threshold lie.
   And while my puzzled thoughts about it pour,
   I find the bread of life in't at my door.

When that this bird of paradise put in
   This wicker cage (my corpse) to tweedle praise
Had pecked the fruit forbade: and so did fling
   Away its food; and lost its golden days;
   It fell into celestial famine sore:
   And never could attain a morsel more.

Alas! alas! Poor bird, what wilt thou do?
   The creature's field no food for souls e'er gave.
And if thou knock at angels doors they show
   An empty barrel: they no soul bread have.
   Alas! Poor bird, the world's white loaf is done.
   And cannot yield thee here the smallest crumb.

In this sad state, God's tender bowels run
   Out streams of grace: and he to end all strife
The purest wheat in Heaven, his dear-dear Son
   Grinds, and kneads up into this bread of life.

Which bread of life from Heaven down came and stands
Dished on thy table up by angel's hands.

Did God mold up this bread in Heaven, and bake,
   Which from his table came, and to thine goeth?
Doth he bespeak thee thus, this soul bread take.
   Come eat thy fill of this thy God's white loaf?
   It's food too fine for angels, yet come, take
   And eat thy fill. It's Heaven's sugar cake.

What grace is this knead in this loaf? This thing
   Souls are but petty things it to admire.
Yee angels, help: This fill would to the brim
   Heav'n's whelm'd-down crystal meal bowl, yea and higher.
   This bread of life dropped in thy mouth, doth cry.
   Eat, eat me, soul, and thou shalt never die.

MEDITATION 150 (SECOND SERIES)

Canticles 7:3. *Thy two breasts are like two young roes that are twins.*

My Blessed Lord, how doth thy beautious spouse
   In stately stature rise in comeliness?
With her two breasts like two little roes that browse
   Among the lilies in their shining dress
   Like stately milk pails ever full and flow
   With spiritual milk to make her babes to grow.

Celestial nectar wealthier far than wine
   Wrought in the spirit's brew house and up tunned
Within these vessels which are trussed up fine
   Likened to two pretty, neat twin roes that run'd
   Most pleasantly by their dam's sides like cades
   And suckle with their milk Christ's spiritual babes.

Lord put these nibbles then my mouth into
   And suckle me therewith I humbly pray,
Then with this milk thy spiritual babe I'dst grow,
   And these two milk pails shall themselves display

Like to these pretty twins in pairs round neat
And shall sing forth thy praise over this meat.

UPON A SPIDER CATCHING A FLY

Thou sorrow, venom elf.
  Is this thy play,
To spin a web out of thyself
  To catch a fly?
    For why?

I saw a pettish wasp
  Fall foul therein.
Whom yet thy whorl pins did not clasp
  Lest he should fling
    His sting.

But as afraid, remote
  Didst stand hereat
And with thy little fingers stroke
  And gently tap
    His back.

Thus gently him didst treat
  Lest he should pet,
And in a froppish, waspish heat
  Should greatly fret
    Thy net.

Whereas the silly fly,
  Caught by its leg
Thou by the throat tookst hastily
  And 'hind the head
    Bite dead.

This goes to pot, that not
  Nature doth call.
Strive not above what strength hath got
  Lest in the brawl
    Thou fall.

This fray seems thus to us.
   Hell's spider gets
His intrails spun to whip cords thus
   And wove to nets
     And sets.

To tangle Adam's race
   In's stratigems
To their destructions, spoil'd, made base
   By venom things
     Damn'd sins.

But mighty, gracious Lord
   Communicate
Thy grace to break the cord, afford
   Us glory's gate
     And state.

We'll nightingale sing like
   When pearched on high
In glory's cage, thy glory, bright,
   And thankfully,
     For joy.

HUSWIFERY

Make me, O Lord, thy spinning wheel complete.
   Thy Holy Word my distaff make for me.
Make mine affections thy swift flyers neat
   And make my soul thy holy spool to be.
   My conversation make to be thy reel
   And reel the yarn thereon spun of thy wheel.

Make me thy loom then, knit therein this twine:
   And make thy Holy Spirit, Lord, wind quills:
Then weave the web thyself. The yarn is fine.
   Thine ordinances make my fulling mills.
   Then dye the same in heavenly colors choice,
   All pinked with varnished flowers of paradise.

Then clothe therewith mine understanding, will,
   Affections, judgment, conscience, memory
My words, and actions, that their shine may fill
   My ways with glory and thee glorify.
   Then mine apparel shall display before ye
   That I am clothed in holy robes for glory.

UPON WEDLOCK,
AND DEATH OF CHILDREN

A curious knot God made in paradise,
   And drew it out enameled neatly fresh.
It was the true-love knot, more sweet than spice
   And set with all the flowers of grace's dress.
   It's wedding's knot, that ne'er can be untied.
   No Alexander's sword can it divide

The slips here planted, gay and glorious grow:
   Unless an hellish breath do singe their plumes.
Here primrose, cowslips, roses, lilies blow
   With violets and pinks that void perfumes.
   Whose beautious leaves o'erlaid with honey dew.
   And chanting birds chirp out sweet music true.

When in this knot I planted was, my stock
   Soon knotted, and a manly flower outbroke.
And after it my branch again did knot.
   Brought out another flower its sweet breathed mate.
   One knot gave one t'other the t'other's place.
   Whence chuckling smiles fought in each other's face.

But oh! a glorious hand from glory came
   Guarded with angels, soon did crop this flower
Which almost tore the root up of the same
   At that unlooked for, dolesome, darksome hour.
   In prayer to Christ perfumed it did ascend,
   And angels bright did it to Heaven tend.

But pausing on't, this sweet perfum'd my thought,
   Christ would in glory have a flower, choice, prime,

And having choice, chose this my branch forth brought.
   Lord take't. I thank thee, thou takst ought of mine,
   It is my pledge in glory, part of me
   Is now in it, Lord, glorified with thee.

But praying o'er my branch, my branch did sprout
   And bore another manly flower, and gay
And after that another, sweet broke out.
   The which the former hand soon got away.
   But oh! the tortures, vomit, screechings, groans,
   And six weeks' fever would pierce hearts like stones.

Grief o'er doth flow: and nature fault would find
   Were not thy Will, my spell, charm, joy, and gem:
That as I said, I say, take, Lord, they're thine.
   I piecemeal pass to glory bright in them.
   I joy, may I sweet flowers for glory breed,
   Whether thou getst them green, or lets them seed.

Philip Freneau

(1752 – 1832)

ON THE EMIGRATION TO AMERICA

AND PEOPLING THE WESTERN COUNTRY

To western woods, and lonely plains,
Palemon from the crowd departs,
Where Nature's wildest genius reigns,
To tame the soil, and plant the arts—
What wonders there shall freedom show,
What mighty states successive grow!

From Europe's proud, despotic shores
Hither the stranger takes his way,
And in our new found world explores
A happier soil, a milder sway,
Where no proud despot holds him down,
No slaves insult him with a crown.

What charming scenes attract the eye,
On wild Ohio's savage stream!
There Nature reigns, whose works outvie
The boldest pattern art can frame;
There ages past have rolled away,
And forests bloomed but to decay.

From these fair plains, these rural seats,
So long concealed, so lately known,
The unsocial Indian far retreats,
To make some other clime his own,
When other streams, less pleasing, flow,
And darker forests round him grow.

Great Sire of floods! whose varied wave
Through climes and countries takes its way,
To whom creating Nature gave
Ten thousand steams to swell thy sway!

No longer shall they useless prove,
Nor idly through the forests rove;

Nor longer shall your princely flood
From distant lakes be swelled in vain,
Nor longer through a darksome wood
Advance, unnoticed, to the main,
Far other ends, the heavens decree—
And commerce plans new freights for thee.

While virtue warms the generous breast,
There heaven-born freedom shall reside,
Nor shall the voice of war molest,
Nor Europe's all-aspiring pride—
There Reason shall new laws devise,
And order from confusion rise.

Forsaking kings and regal state,
With all their pomp and fancied bliss,
The traveller owns, convinced though late,
No realm so free, so blest as this—
The east is half to slaves consigned,
Where kings and priests enchain the mind.

O come the time, and haste the day,
When man shall man no longer crush,
When Reason shall enforce her sway,
Nor these fair regions raise our blush,
Where still the African complains,
And mourns his yet unbroken chains.

Far brighter scenes a future age,
The muse predicts, these States will hail,
Whose genius may the world engage,
Whose deeds may over death prevail,
And happier systems bring to view,
Than all the eastern sages knew.

THE WILD HONEY SUCKLE

Fair flower, that dost so comely grow,
Hid in this silent, dull retreat,
Untouched thy honied blossoms blow,

Unseen thy little branches greet:
   No roving foot shall crush thee here,
   No busy hand provoke a tear.

By Nature's self in white arrayed,
She bade thee shun the vulgar eye,
And planted here the guardian shade,
And sent soft waters murmuring by;
   Thus quietly thy summer goes,
   Thy days declining to repose.

Smit with those charms, that must decay,
I grieve to see your future doom;
They died—nor were those flowers more gay,
The flowers that did in Eden bloom;
   Unpitying frosts, and Autumn's power
   Shall leave no vestige of this flower.

From morning suns and evening dews
At first thy little being came:
If nothing once, you nothing lose,
For when you die you are the same;
   The space between, is but an hour,
   The frail duration of a flower.

THE INDIAN BURYING GROUND

In spite of all the learned have said,
I still my old opinion keep;
The *posture*, that *we* give the dead,
Points out the soul's eternal sleep.

Not so the ancients of these lands—
The Indian, when from life released,
Again is seated with his friends,
And shares again the joyous feast.

His imaged birds, and painted bowl,
And venison, for a journey dressed,

Bespeak the nature of the soul,
ACTIVITY, that knows no rest.

His bow, for action ready bent,
And arrows, with a head of stone,
Can only mean that life is spent,
And not the old ideas gone.

Thou, stranger, that shalt come this way,
No fraud upon the dead commit—
Observe the swelling turf, and say
They do not *lie*, but here they *sit*.

Here still a lofty rock remains,
On which the curious eye may trace
(Now wasted, half, by wearing rains)
The fancies of a ruder race.

Here still an aged elm aspires,
Beneath whose far-projecting shade
(And which the shepherd still admires)
The children of the forest played!

There oft a restless Indian queen
(Pale *Shebah*, with her braided hair)
And many a barbarous form is seen
To chide the man that lingers there.

By midnight moons, o'er moistening dews,
In habit for the chase arrayed,
The hunter still the deer pursues,
The hunter and the deer, a shade!

And long shall timorous fancy see
The painted chief, and pointed spear,
And Reason's self shall bow the knee
To shadows and delusions here.

ON MR. PAINE'S RIGHTS OF MAN

Thus briefly sketched the sacred RIGHTS OF MAN,
How inconsistent with the ROYAL PLAN!
Which for itself exclusive honour craves,
Where some are masters born, and millions slaves.
With what contempt must every eye look down
On that base, childish bauble called a *crown*,
The gilded bait, that lures the crowd, to come,
Bow down their necks, and meet a slavish doom;
The source of half the miseries men endure,
The quack that kills them, while it seems to cure.
　　Roused by the REASON of his manly page,
Once more shall PAINE a listening world engage:
From Reason's source, a bold reform he brings,
In raising up *mankind*, he pulls down *kings*,
Who, source of discord, patrons of all wrong,
On blood and murder have been fed too long:
Hid from the world, and tutored to be base,
The curse, the scourge, the ruin of our race,
Their's was the task, a dull designing few,
To shackle beings that they scarcely knew,
Who made this globe the residence of slaves,
And built their thrones on systems formed by knaves
—Advance, bright years, to work their final fall,
And haste the period that shall crush them all.
Who, that has read and scann'd the historic page
But glows, at every line, with kindling rage,
To see by them the rights of men aspersed,
Freedom restrain'd, and Nature's law reversed,
Men, ranked with beasts, by monarchs *will'd* away,
And bound young fools, or madmen to obey:
Now driven to wars, and now oppressed at home,
Compelled in crowds o'er distant seas to roam,
From India's climes the plundered prize to bring
To glad the strumpet, or to glut the king.
　　COLUMBIA, hail! immortal be thy reign:
Without a king, we till the smiling plain;
Without a king, we trace the unbounded sea,
And traffic round the globe, through each degree;
Each foreign clime our honour'd flag reveres,

Which asks no monarch, to support the STARS:
Without a *king*, the laws maintain their sway,
While honour bids each generous heart obey.
Be ours the task the ambitious to restrain,
And this great lesson teach—that kings are vain;
That warring realms to certain ruin haste,
That kings subsist by war, and wars are waste:
So shall our nation, form'd on Virtue's plan.
Remain the guardian of the Rights of Man,
A vast Republic, famed through every clime,
Without a king, to see the end of time.

TO AN AUTHOR

Your leaves bound up compact and fair,
In neat array at length prepare,
To pass their hour on learning's stage,
To meet the surly critic's rage;
The statesman's slight, the smatterer's sneer—
Were these, indeed, your only fear,
You might be tranquil and resigned:
What most should touch your fluttering mind;
Is that, few critics will be found
To sift your works, and deal the wound.

Thus, when one fleeting year is past
On some bye-shelf *your* book is cast—
Another comes, with *something new*,
And drives you fairly out of view:
With some to praise, *but more to blame*,
The mind returns to—whence it came;
And some alive, who *scarce could read*
Will publish satires on the dead.

Thrice happy Dryden, who could meet
Some rival bard in every street!
When all were bent on writing well
It was some credit to excel:—

Thrice happy Dryden, who could find
A *Milbourne* for his sport designed—

And *Pope*, who saw the harmless rage
Of *Dennis* bursting o'er his page
Might justly spurn the *critic's aim*,
Who only helped to swell his fame.

On these bleak climes by Fortune thrown,
Where rigid *Reason* reigns alone,
Where lovely *Fancy* has no sway,
Nor magic forms about us play—
Nor nature takes her summer hue
Tell me, what has the muse to do?—

An age employed in edging steel
Can no poetic raptures feel;
No solitude's attracting power,
No leisure of the noon day hour,
No shaded stream, no quiet grove
Can this fantastic century move;

The muse of love in no request—
Go—try your fortune with the rest,
One of the nine you should engage,
To meet the follies of the age:—
On *one*, we fear, your choice must fall—
The least engaging of them all—
Her visage stern—an angry style—
A clouded brow—malicious smile—
A mind on *murdered victims* placed—
She, only she, can please the taste!

ON OBSERVING A
LARGE RED-STREAK APPLE

In spite of ice, in spite of snow,
In spite of all the winds that blow,
In spite of hail and biting frost,
Suspended here I see you tossed
You still retain your wonted hold
Though days are short and nights are cold.

Amidst this system of decay
How could you have one wish to stay?
If fate or fancy kept you there
They meant you for a *Solitaire*.
Were it not better to descend,
Or in the cider mill to end
Than thus to shiver in the storm
And not a leaf to keep you warm—
A moment then, had buried all,
Nor you have doomed so late a fall.

But should the stem to which you cling
Uphold you to another spring,
Another race would round you rise
And view the *stranger* with surprize,
And, peeping from the blossoms say
Away old dotard, get away!

Alas! small pleasure can there be
To dwell, a hermit, on the tree—
Your old companions, all, are gone,
Have dropt and perished, every one;
You only stay to face the blast,
A sad memento of the past.

Phillis Wheatley

(1753 - 1784)

ON BEING BROUGHT
FROM AFRICA TO AMERICA

'Twas mercy brought me from my *Pagan* land,
Taught my benighted soul to understand
That there's a God, that there's a *Saviour* too:
Once I redemption neither sought nor knew.
Some view our sable race with scornful eye,
"Their colour is a diabolic die."
Remember, *Christians*, *Negros*, black as *Cain*,
May be refin'd, and join th' angelic train.

ON THE DEATH OF THE
REV. MR. GEORGE WHITEFIELD
1770

Hail, happy saint, on thine immortal throne,
Possest of glory, life and bliss unknown;
We hear no more the music of thy tongue,
Thy wonted auditories cease to throng.
Thy sermons in unequall'd accents flow'd,
And ev'ry bosom with devotion glow'd;
Thou didst in strains of eloquence refin'd
Inflame the heart, and captivate the mind.
Unhappy we the setting sun deplore,
So glorious once, but ah! it shines no more.

Behold the prophet in his tow'ring flight!
He leaves the earth for heav'n's unmeasur'd height,
And worlds unknown receive him from our sight.
There *Whitefield* wings with rapid course his way,

And sails to *Zion* through vast seas of day.
Thy pray'rs, great saint, and thine incessant cries
Have pierc'd the bosom of thy native skies.
Thou moon hast seen, and all the stars of light,
How he has wrestled with his God by night.

He pray'd that grace in ev'ry heart might dwell,
He long'd to see *America* excel;
He charg'd its youth that ev'ry grace divine
Should with full lustre in their conduct shine;
That Saviour, which his soul did first receive,
The greatest gift that ev'n a God can give,
He freely offer'd to the num'rous throng,
That on his lips with list'ning pleasure hung.

   "Take him, ye wretched, for your only good,
"Take him ye starving sinners, for your food;
"Ye thirsty, come to this life-giving stream,
"Ye preachers, take him for your joyful theme;
"Take him my dear *Americans*, he said,
"Be your complaints on this kind bosom laid:
"Take him, ye *Africans*, he longs for you,
"*Impartial Saviour* is his title due:
"Wash'd in the fountain of redeeming blood,
"You shall be sons, and kings, and priests to God."

   Great *Countess*, we *Americans* revere
Thy name, and mingle in thy grief sincere;
New England deeply feels, the *Orphans* mourn,
Their more than father will no more return.

   But, though arrested by the hand of death,
Whitefield no more exerts his lab'ring breath,
Yet let us view him in th' eternal skies,
Let ev'ry heart to this bright vision rise;
While the tomb safe retains its sacred trust,
Till life divine re-animates his dust.

THOUGHTS ON THE WORKS OF PROVIDENCE

Arise, my soul, on wings enraptur'd, rise
To praise the monarch of the earth and skies,
Whose goodness and beneficence appear
As round its centre moves the rolling year,
Or when the morning glows with rosy charms,
Or the sun slumbers in the ocean's arms:
Of light divine be a rich portion lent
To guide my soul, and favour my intent.
Celestial muse, my arduous flight sustain,
And raise my mind to a seraphic strain!

    Ador'd for ever be the God unseen,
Which round the sun revolves this vast machine,
Though to his eye its mass a point appears:
Ador'd the God that whirls surrounding spheres,
Which first ordain'd that mighty *Sol* should reign
The peerless monarch of th' ethereal train:
Of miles twice forty millions is his height,
And yet his radiance dazzles mortal sight
So far beneath—from him th' extended earth
Vigour derives, and ev'ry flow'ry birth:
Vast through her orb she moves with easy grace
Around her *Phœbus* in unbounded space;
True to her course th' impetuous storm derides,
Triumphant o'er the winds, and surging tides.

    Almighty, in these wond'rous works of thine,
What *Pow'r*, what *Wisdom*, and what *Goodness* shine?
And are thy wonders, Lord, by men explor'd,
And yet creating glory unador'd!

    Creation smiles in various beauty gay,
While day to night, and night succeeds to day:
That *Wisdom*, which attends *Jehovah's* ways,
Shines most conspicuous in the solar rays:
Without them, destitute of heat and light,
This world would be the reign of endless night:
In their excess how would our race complain,
Abhorring life! how hate its length'ned chain!
From air adust what num'rous ills would rise?

What dire contagion taint the burning skies?
What pestilential vapours, fraught with death,
Would rise, and overspread the lands beneath?

   Hail, smiling morn, that from the orient main
Ascending dost adorn the heav'nly plain!
So rich, so various are thy beauteous dies,
That spread through all the circuit of the skies,
That, full of thee, my soul in rapture soars,
And thy great God, the cause of all adores.

O'er beings infinite his love extends,
His *Wisdom* rules them, and his *Pow'r* defends.
When tasks diurnal tire the human frame,
The spirits faint, and dim the vital flame,
Then too that ever active bounty shines,
Which not infinity of space confines.
The sable veil, and *Night* in silence draws,
Conceals effects, but shes th' *Almighty Cause*;
Night seals in sleep the wide creation fair,
And all is peaceful but the brow of care.
Again, gay *Phœbus*, as the day before,
Wakes ev'ry eye, but what shall wake no more;
Again the face of nature is renew'd,
Which still appears harmonious, fair, and good.
May grateful strains salute the smiling morn,
Before its beams the eastern hills adorn!

   Shall day to day, and night to night conspire
To show the goodness of the Almighty Sire?
This mental voice shall man regardless hear,
And never, never raise the filial pray'r?
To-day, O hearken, nor your folly mourn
For time mispent, that never will return.
   But see the sons of vegetation rise,
And spread their leafy banners to the skies.
All-wise Almighty providence we trace
In trees, and plants, and all the flow'ry race;
As clear as in the nobler frame of man,
All lovely copies of the Maker's plan.
The pow'r the same that forms a ray of light,
That call'd creation from eternal night.

"Let there be light," he said: from his profound
Old *Chaos* heard, and trembled at the sound:
Swift as the word, inspir'd by pow'r divine,
Behold the light around its maker shine,
The first fair product of th' omnific God,
And now through all his works diffus'd abroad.

As reason's pow'rs by day our God disclose,
So we may trace him in the night's repose:
Say what is sleep? and dreams how passing strange!
When action ceases, and ideas range
Licentious and unbounded o'er the plains,
Where *Fancy's* queen in giddy triumph reigns.
Here in soft strains the dreaming lover sigh
To a kind fair, or rave in jealousy;
On pleasure now, and now on vengeance bent,
The lab'ring passions struggle for a vent.
What pow'r, Oh man! thy *reason* then restores,
So long suspended in nocturnal hours?
What secret hand returns the mental train,
And gives improv'd thine active pow'rs again?
From thee, O man, what gratitude should rise!
And, when from balmy sleep thou op'st thine eyes,
Let first thoughts be praises to the skies.
How merciful our God who thus imparts
O'erflowing tides of joy to human hearts,
When wants and woes might be our righteous lot,
Our God forgetting, by our God forgot!

Among the mental pow'rs a question rose,
"What must the image of th' Eternal shows?"
When thus to *Reason* (so let *Fancy* rove)
Her great companion spoke immortal *Love*.

"Say, mighty pow'r, how long shall strife prevail,
"And with its murmurs load the whisp'ring gale?
"Refer the cause to *Recollection's* shrine,
"Who loud proclaims my origin divine,
"The cause whence heav'n and earth began to be,
"And is not man immortaliz'd by me?
"*Reason* let this most causeless strife subside."
Thus *Love* pronounc'd, and *Reason* thus reply'd.

"Thy birth, celestial queen! 'tis mine to own,
"In thee resplendent is the Godhead shown;
"Thy words persuade, my soul enraptur'd feels
"Resistless beauty which thy smile reveals."
Ardent she spoke, and, kindling at her charms,
She clasp'd the blooming goddess in her arms.

Infinite *Love* wher'er we turn our eyes
Appears: this ev'ry creature's wants supplies;
This most is heard in *Nature's* constant voice,
This makes the morn, and this the eve rejoice;
This bids the fost'ring rains and dews descend
To nourish all, to serve one gen'ral end,
The good of man; yet man ungrateful pays
But little homage, and but little praise.
To him, whose works array'd with mercy shine,
What songs should rise, how constant, how divine!

TO S. M., A YOUNG AFRICAN PAINTER, ON SEEING HIS WORKS

To show the lab'ring bosom's deep intent,
And thought in living characters to paint,
When first thy pencil did those beauties give,
And breathing figures learnt from thee to live,
How did those prospects give my soul delight,
A new creation rushing on my sight?
Still, wond'rous youth! each noble path pursue,
On deathless glories fix thine ardent view:
Still may the painter's and the poet's fire
To aid thy pencil, and thy verse conspire!
And may the charms of each seraphic theme
Conduct thy footsteps to immortal fame!
High to the blissful wonders of the skies
Elate thy soul, and raise thy wishful eyes.
Thrice happy, when exalted to survey
That splendid city, crown'd with endless day,
Whose twice six gates on radiant hinges ring:
Celestial *Salem* blooms in endless spring.

Calm and serene thy moments glide along,
And may the muse inspire each future song!
Still, with the sweets of contemplation bless'd,
May peace with balmy winds your soul invest!
But when these shades of time are chas'd away,
And darkness ends in everlasting day,
On what seraphic pinions shall we move,
And view the landscapes in the realms above?
There shall thy tongue in heav'nly murmurs flow,
And there my muse with heav'nly transport glow:
No more to tell of *Damon's* tender sighs,
Or rising radiance of *Aurora's* eyes,
For nobler themes demand a nobler strain,
And purer language on th' ethereal plain.
Cease, gentle muse! the solemn gloom of night
Now seals the fair creation from my sight.

Joel Barlow

(1 7 5 4 – 1 8 1 2)

ADVICE TO A RAVEN IN RUSSIA

December, 1812

Black fool, why winter here? These frozen skies,
Worn by your wings and deafen'd by your cries,
Should warn you hence, where milder suns invite,
And day alternates with his mother night.
You fear perhaps your food will fail you there,
Your human carnage, that delicious fare
That lured you hither, following still your friend
The great Napoleon to the world's bleak end.
You fear, because the southern climes pour'd forth
Their clustering nations to infest the north,
Barvarians, Austrians, those who Drink the Po
And those who skirt the Tuscan seas below,
With all Germania, Neustria, Belgia, Gaul,
Doom'd here to wade thro slaughter to their fall,
You fear he left behind no wars, to feed
His feather'd canibals and nurse the breed.
Fear not, my screamer, call your greedy train,
Sweep over Europe, hurry back to Spain,
You'll find his legions there; the valliant crew
Please best their master when they toil for you.
Abundant there they spread the country o'er
And taint the breeze with every nation's gore,
Iberian, Lusian, British widely strown,
But still more wide and copious flows their own.
Go where you will; Calabria, Malta, Greece,
Egypt and Syria still his fame increase,
Domingo's fatten'd isle and India's plains
Glow deep with purple drawn from Gallic veins.
No Raven's wing can stretch the flight so far
As the torn bandrols of Napoleon's war.
Choose then your climate, fix your best abode,
He'll make you deserts and he'll bring you blood.

How could you fear a dearth? have not mankind,
Tho slain by millions, millions left behind?
Has not CONSCRIPTION still the power to weild
Her annual faulchion o'er the human field?
A faithful harvester! or if a man
Escape that gleaner, shall he scape the ban?
The triple BAN, that like the hound of hell
Gripes with three joles, to hold his victim well.

Fear nothing then, hatch fast your ravenous brood,
Teach them to cry to Bonaparte for food;
They'll be like you, of all his suppliant train,
The only class that never cries in vain.
For see what mutual benefits you lend!
(The surest way to fix the mutual friend)
While on his slaughter'd troops your tribes are fed,
You cleanse his camp and carry off his dead.
Imperial Scavenger! but now you know
Your work is vain amid these hills of snow.
His tentless troops are marbled thro with frost
And change to crystal when the breath is lost.
Mere trunks of ice, tho limb'd like human frames
And lately warm'd with life's endearing flames,
They cannot taint the air, the world impest,
Nor can you tear one fiber from their breast.
No! from their visual sockets, as they lie,
With beak and claws you cannot pluck an eye.
The frozen orb, preserving still its form,
Defies your talons as it braves the storm,
But stands and stares to God, as if to know
In what curst hands he leaves his world below.

Fly then, or starve; tho all the dreadful road
From Minsk to Moskow with their bodies strow'd
May count some Myriads, yet they can't suffice
To feed you more beneath these dreary skies.
Go back, and winter in the wilds of Spain;
Feast there awhile, and in the next campaign
Rejoin your master; for you'll find him then,
With his new million of the race of men,
Clothed in his thunders, all his flags unfurl'd,
Raging and storming o'er the prostrate world.

War after war his hungry soul requires,
State after State shall sink beneath his fires,
Yet other Spains in victim smoke shall rise

And other Moskows suffocate the skies,
Each land lie reeking with its people's slain
And not a stream run bloodless to the main.
Till men resume their souls, and dare to shed
Earth's total vengeance on the monster's head,
Hurl from his blood-built throne this king of woes,
Dash him to dust, and let the world repose.

Richard Henry Wilde

(1789 – 1847)

THE LAMENT OF THE CAPTIVE

My life is like the summer rose
   That opens to the morning sky,
And, ere the shades of evening close,
   Is scattered on the ground to die:
Yet on that rose's humble bed
The softest dews of night are shed;
As if she wept such waste to see—
But none shall drop a tear for me!

My life is like the autumn leaf
   That trembles in the moon's pale ray,
Its hold is frail—its date is brief—
   Restless, and soon to pass away:
Yet when that leaf shall fall and fade,
The parent tree will mourn its shade,
The wind bewail the leafless tree,
But none shall breathe a sigh for me!

My life is like the print, which feet
   Have left on TAMPA's desert strand,
Soon as the rising tide shall beat,
   Their track will vanish from the sand:
Yet, as if grieving to efface
All vestige of the human race,
On that lone shore loud moans the sea,
But none shall thus lament for me!

Lydia Huntley Sigourney

(1791 – 1865)

INDIAN NAMES

"How can the red men be forgotten, while so many of our states
and territories, bays, lakes and rivers, are indelibly stamped by
names of their giving?"

Ye say they all have passed away,
   That noble race and brave,
That their light canoes have vanished
   From off the crested wave;
That 'mid the forests where they roamed
   There rings no hunter shout,
But their names is on your waters,
   Ye may not wash it out.

'Tis where Ontario's billow
   Like Ocean's surge is curled,
Where strong Niagara's thunders wake
   The echo of the world.
Where red Missouri bringeth
   Rich tribute from the west,
And Rappahannock sweetly sleeps
   On green Virginia's breast.

Ye say their cone-like cabins,
   That clustered o'er the vale,
Have fled away like withered leaves
   Before the autumn gale,
But their memory liveth on your hills,
   Their baptism on your shore,
Your everlasting rivers speak
   Their dialect of yore.

Old Massachusetts wears it,
   Within her lordly crown,
And broad Ohio bears it,
   Amid his young renown;

Connecticut hath wreathed it
   Where her quiet foliage waves,
And bold Kentucky breathed it hoarse
   Through all her ancient caves.

Wachuset hides its lingering voice
   Within his rocky heart,
And Alleghany graves its tone
   Throughout his lofty chart;
Monadnock on his forehead hoar
   Doth seal the sacred trust,
Your mountains build their monument,
   Though ye destroy their dust.

Ye call these red-browed brethren
   The insects of an hour,
Crushed like the noteless worm amid
   The regions of their power;
Ye drive them from their father's lands,
   Ye break of faith the seal,
But can ye from the court of Heaven
   Exclude their last appeal?

Ye see their unresisting tribes,
   With toilsome step and slow,
On through the trackless desert pass,
   A caravan of woe;
Think ye the Eternal's ear is deaf?
   His sleepless vision dim?
Think ye the *soul's blood* may not cry
   From that far land to him?

THE STARS

Make friendship with the stars.
                 Go forth at night,
And talk with Aldebaran, where he flames
In the cold forehead of the wintry sky.
Turn to the sister Pleiades, and ask

If there be death in Heaven? A blight to fall
Upon the brightness of unfrosted hair?
A severing of fond hearts? A place of graves?
Our sympathies are with you, stricken stars,
Clustering so closely round the lost one's place.
Too well we know the hopeless toil to hide
The chasm in love's fond circle. The lone seat
Where the meek grandsire, with his silver locks,
Reclined so happily; the fireside chair
Whence the fond mother fled; the cradle turn'd
Against the wall, and empty; well we know
The untold anguish, when some dear one falls.
How oft the life-blood trickling from our hearts,
Reveals a kindred spirit torn away!
Tears are our birth-right, gentle sister train.
And more we love you, if like us ye mourn.
—Ho! bold Orion, with thy lion-shield;
What tidings from the chase? what monster slain?
Runn'st thou a tilt with Taurus? or dost rear
Thy weapon for more stately tournament?
'Twere better, sure, to be a son of peace
Among those quiet stars, than raise the rout
Of rebel tumult, and of wild affray,
Or feel ambition with its scorpion sting
Transfix thy heel, and like Napoleon fall.
Fair queen, Cassiopeia! is thy court
Well peopled with chivalric hearts, that pay
Due homage to thy beauty? Thy levee,
Is it still throng'd as in thy palmy youth?
Is there no change of dynasty? No dread
Of revolution 'mid the titled peers
That age on age have served thee? Teach us how
To make our sway perennial, in the hearts
Of those who love us, so that when our bloom
And spring-tide wither, they in phalanx firm
May gird us round, and make life's evening bright.
—But thou, O Sentinel, with sleepless eye,
Guarding the northern battlement of heaven,
For whom the seven pure spirits nightly burn
Their torches, marking out, with glittering spire,
Both hours and seasons on thy dial-plate,
How turns the storm-tost mariner to thee!
The poor lost Indian, having nothing left

In his own ancient realm, not even the bones
Of his dead fathers, lifts his brow to thee,
And glads his broken spirit with thy beam.
The weary caravan, with chiming bells,
Making strange music 'mid the desert sands,
Guides, by thy pillar'd fires, its nightly march.
Reprov'st thou not our faith so oft untrue
To its Great Pole Star, when some surging wave
Foams o'er our feet, or thorns beset our way?
—Speak out the wisdom of thy hoary years,
Arcturus! Patriarch! Mentor of the train,
That gather radiance from thy golden urn.
We are of yesterday, short-sighted sons
Of this dim orb, and all our proudest lore
Is but the alphabet of ignorance:
Yet ere we trace its little round, we die.
Give us thy counsel, ere we pass away.
—Lyra, sweet Lyra, sweeping on with song,
While glorious Summer decks the listening flowers,
Teach us thy melodies; for sinful cares
Make discord in our hearts. Hast thou the ear
Of the fair planets that encircle thee,
As children round the hearth-stone? Canst thou quell
Their woes with music? or their infant eyes
Lull to soft sleep? Do thy young daughters join
Thy evening song? Or does thine Orphean art
Touch the warm pulses of the neighbor stars
And constellations, till they higher lift
The pilgrim-staff to run their glorious way?
—Hail, mighty Sirius! monarch of the suns,
Whose golden sceptre subject worlds obey;
May we, in this poor planet speak to thee?
Thou highest dweller, 'mid the highest heaven,
Say, art thou nearer to His Throne, whose nod
Doth govern all things?
                        Hearest thou the strong wing
Of the Archangel, as it broadly sweeps
The empyrean, to the farthest orb,
Bearing Heaven's watch-word? Knowest thou what report
The red-hair'd Comet, on his car of flame,
Brings the recording seraph? Hast thou heard
One whisper through the open gate of Heaven
When the pale stars shall fall, and yon blue vault

Be as a shrivell'd scroll?
                    Thou answer'st not!
Why question we with thee, Eternal Fire?
We, frail, and blind, to whom our own dark moon,
With its few phases, is a mystery!
Back to the dust, most arrogant! Be still!
Deep silence is thy wisdom! Ask no more!
But let thy life be one long sigh of prayer,
One hymn of praise, till from the broken clay,
At its last gasp, the unquench'd spirit rise,
And, unforgotten, 'mid unnumber'd worlds,
Ascend to Him, from whom its essence came.

TO THE FIRST SLAVE SHIP

First of that train which cursed the wave,
    And from the rifled cabin bore,
Inheritor of wo,—*the slave*
    To bless his palm-tree's shade no more.

Dire engine!—o'er the troubled main
    Borne on in unresisted state,—
Know'st thou within thy dark domain
    The secrets of thy prison'd freight?—

Hear'st thou *their* moans whom hope hath fled?—
    Wild cries, in agonizing starts?—
Know'st thou thy humid sails are spread
    With ceaseless sighs from broken hearts?—

The fetter'd chieftain's burning tear,—
    The parted lover's mute despair,—
The childless mother's pang severe,—
    The orphan's misery, are there.

Ah!—could'st thou from the scroll of fate
    The annal read of future years,
Stripes,—tortures,—unrelenting hate.
    And death-gasps drown'd in slavery's tears.

Down,—down,—beneath the cleaving main
    Thou fain would'st plunge where monsters lie,
Rather than ope the gates of pain
    For time and for Eternity.—

Oh Afric!—what has been thy crime?—
    That thus like Eden's fratricide,
A mark is set upon thy clime,
    And every brother shuns thy side.—

Yet are thy wrongs, thou long-distrest!—
    Thy burdens, by the world unweigh'd,
Safe in that *Unforgetful Breast*
    Where all the sins of earth are laid.—

Poor outcast slave!—Our guilty land
    Should tremble while she drinks thy tears,
Or sees in vengeful silence stand,
    The beacon of thy shorten'd years;—

Should shrink to hear her sons proclaim
    The sacred truth that heaven is just,—
Shrink even at her Judge's name,—
    "Jehovah,—Saviour of the opprest."

The Sun upon thy forehead frown'd,
    But Man more cruel far than he,
Dark fetters on thy spirit bound:—
    Look to the mansions of the free!

Look to that realm where chains unbind,—
    Where the pale tyrant drops his rod,
And where the patient sufferers find
    A friend,—a father in their God.

William Cullen Bryant

(1 7 9 4 – 1 8 7 8)

TO COLE, THE PAINTER,
DEPARTING FOR EUROPE

Thine eyes shall see the light of distant skies;
   Yet, Cole! thy heart shall bear to Europe's strand
   A living image of our own bright land,
Such as upon thy glorious canvas lies;
Lone lakes—savannas where the bison roves—
   Rocks rich with summer garlands—solemn streams—
   Skies, where the desert eagle wheels and screams—
Spring bloom and autumn blaze of boundless groves.

Fair scenes shall greet thee where thou goest—fair,
   But different—everywhere the trace of men,
   Paths, homes, graves, ruins, from the lowest glen
To where life shrinks from the fierce Alpine air.
   Gaze on them, till the tears shall dim thy sight,
   But keep that earlier, wilder image bright.

A WINTER PIECE

   The time has been that these wild solitudes,
Yet beautiful as wild—were trod by me
Oftener than now; and when the ills of life
Had chafed my spirit—when the unsteady pulse
Beat with strange flutterings—I would wander forth
And seek the woods. The sunshine on my path
Was to me as a friend. The swelling hills,
The quiet dells retiring far between,
With gentle invitation to explore
Their windings, were a calm society
That talked with me and soothed me. Then the chant

Of birds, and chime of brooks, and soft caress
Of the fresh sylvan air, made me forget
The thoughts that broke my peace, and I began
To gather simples by the fountain's brink,
And lose myself in day-dreams. While I stood
In nature's loneliness, I was with one
With whom I early grew familiar, one
Who never had a frown for me, whose voice
Never rebuked me for the hours I stole
From cares I loved not, but of which the world
Deems highest, to converse with her. When shrieked
The bleak November winds, and smote the woods,
And the brown fields were herbless, and the shades,
That met above the merry rivulet,
Were spoiled, I sought, I loved them still,—they seemed
Like old companions in adversity.
Still there was beauty in my walks; the brook,
Bordered with sparkling frost-work, was as gay
As with its fringe of summer flowers. Afar,
The village with its spires, the path of streams,
And dim receding valleys, hid before
By interposing trees, lay visible
Through the bare grove, and my familiar haunts
Seemed new to me. Nor was I slow to come
Among them, when the clouds, from their still skirts,
Had shaken down on earth the feathery snow,
And all was white. The pure keen air abroad,
Albeit it breathed no scent of herb, nor heard
Love call of bird nor merry hum of bee,
Was not the air of death. Bright mosses crept
Over the spotted trunks, and the close buds,
That lay along the boughs, instinct with life,
Patient, and waiting the soft breath of Spring,
Feared not the piercing spirit of the North.
The snow-bird twittered on the beechen bough,
And 'neath the hemlock, whose thick branches bent
Beneath its bright cold burden, and kept dry
A circle, on the earth, of withered leaves,
The partridge found a shelter. Through the snow
The rabbit sprang away. The lighter track
Of fox, and the racoon's broad path were there,
Crossing each other. From his hollow tree,
The squirrel was abroad, gathering the nuts

Just fallen, that asked the winter cold and sway
Of winter blast, to shake them from their hold.
    But winter has yet brighter scenes,—he boasts
Splendors beyond what gorgeous summer knows;
Or autumn, with his many fruits, and woods
All flushed with many hues. Come, when the rains
Have glazed the snow, and clothed the trees with ice;
While the slant sun of February pours
Into the bowers a flood of light. Approach!
The encrusted surface shall upbear thy steps,
And the broad arching portals of the grove
Welcome thy entering. Look! the massy trunks
Are cased in the pure chrystal, each light spray,
Nodding and tinkling in the breath of heaven,
Is studded with its trembling water-drops,
That stream with rainbow radiance as they move.
But round the parent stem the long low boughs
Bend, in a glittering ring, and arbors hide
The grassy floor. Oh! you might deem the spot,
The spacious cavern of the virgin mine,
Deep in the womb of earth—where the gems grow,
And diamonds put forth radiant rods and bud
With amethyst and topaz—and the place
Lit up, most royally, with the pure beam
That dwells in them. Or haply the vast hall
Of fairy palace, that outlasts the night,
And fades not in the glory of the sun;—
Where chrystal columns send forth slender shafts
And crossing arches; and fantastic aisles
Wind from the sight in brightness, and are lost
Among the crowded pillars. Raise thine eye,—
Thou seest no cavern roof, no palace vault;
There the blue sky and the white drifting cloud
Look in. Again the wildered fancy dreams
Of spouting fountains, frozen as they rose,
And fixed, with all their branching jets, in air,
And all their sluices sealed. All, all is light;
Light without shade. But all shall pass away
With the next sun. From numberless vast trunks,
Loosened, the crashing ice shall make a sound
Like the far roar of rivers, and the eve
Shall close o'er the brown woods as it was wont.
    And it is pleasant, when the noisy streams

Are just set free, and milder suns melt off
The plashy snow, save only the firm drift
In the deep glen or the close shade of pines,—
'Tis pleasant to behold the wreaths of smoke
Roll up among the maples of the hill,
Where the shrill sound of youthful voices wakes
The shriller echo, as the clear pure lymph,
That from the wounded trees, in twinkling drops,
Falls, 'mid the golden brightness of the morn,
Is gathered in with brimming pails, and oft,
Wielded by sturdy hands, the stroke of axe
Makes the woods ring. Along the quiet air,
Come and float calmly off the soft light clouds,
Such as you see in summer, and the winds
Scarce stir the branches. Lodged in sunny cleft,
Where the cold breezes come not, blooms alone
The little wind-flower, whose just opened eye
Is blue as the spring heaven it gazes at—
Startling the loiterer in the naked groves
With unexpected beauty, for the time
Of blossoms and green leaves is yet afar.
And ere it comes, the encountering winds shall oft
Muster their wrath again, and rapid clouds
Shade heaven, and bounding on the frozen earth
Shall fall their volleyed stores, rounded like hail,
And white like snow, and the loud North again
Shall buffet the vexed forests in his rage.

THE PRAIRIES

These are the Gardens of the Desert, these
The unshorn fields, boundless and beautiful,
For which the speech of England has no name—
The Prairies. I behold them for the first,
And my heart swells, while the dilated sight
Takes in the encircling vastness. Lo! they stretch
In airy undulations, far away,
As if the ocean, in his gentlest swell,
Stood still, with all his rounded billows fixed,

And motionless for ever.—Motionless?—
No—they are all unchained again. The clouds
Sweep over with their shadows, and, beneath,
The surface rolls and fluctuates to the eye;
Dark hollows seem to glide along and chase
The sunny ridges. Breezes of the South!
Who toss the golden and the flame-like flowers,
And pass the prairie-hawk that, poised on high,
Flaps his broad wings, yet moves not—ye have played
Among the palms of Mexico and vines
Of Texas, and have crisped the limpid brooks
That from the fountains of Sonora glide
Into the calm Pacific—have ye fanned
A nobler or a lovelier scene than this?
Man hath no part in all this glorious work:
The hand that built the firmament hath heaved
And smoothed these verdant swells, and sown their slopes
With herbage, planted them with island groves,
And hedged them round with forests. Fitting floor
For this magnificent temple of the sky—
With flowers whose glory and whose multitude
Rival the constellations! The great heavens
Seem to stoop down upon the scene in love,—
A nearer vault, and of a tenderer blue,
Than that which bends above the eastern hills.
    As o'er the verdant waste I guide my steed,
Among the high rank grass that sweeps his sides,
The hollow beating of his footstep seems
A sacrilegious sound. I think of those
Upon whose rest he tramples. Are they here—
The dead of other days?—and did the dust
Of these fair solitudes once stir with life
And burn with passion? Let the mighty mounds
That overlook the rivers, or that rise
In the dim forest crowded with old oaks,
Answer. A race, that long has passed away,
Built them;—a disciplined and populous race
Heaped, with long toil, the earth, while yet the Greek
Was hewing the Pentelicus to forms
Of symmetry, and rearing on its rock
The glittering Parthenon. These ample fields
Nourished their harvests, here their herds were fed,
When haply by their stalls the bison lowed,

And bowed his maned shoulder to the yoke.
All day this desert murmured with their toils,
Till twilight blushed and lovers walked, and wooed
In a forgotten language, and old tunes,
From instruments of unremembered form,
Gave the soft winds a voice. The red man came—
The roaming hunter tribes, warlike and fierce,
And the mound-builders vanished from the earth.
The solitude of centuries untold
Has settled where they dwelt. The prairie wolf
Hunts in their meadows, and his fresh-dug den
Yawns by my path. The gopher mines the ground
Where stood their swarming cities. All is gone—
All—save the piles of earth that hold their bones—
The platforms where they worshipped unknown gods.
The barriers which they builded from the soil
To keep the foe at bay—till o'er the walls
The wild beleaguerers broke, and, one by one,
The strongholds of the plain were forced, and heaped
With corpses. The brown vultures of the wood
Flocked to those vast uncovered sepulchres,
And sat, unscared and silent, at their feast.
Haply some solitary fugitive,
Lurking in marsh and forest, till the sense
Of desolation and of fear became
Bitterer than death, yielded himself to die.
Man's better nature triumphed. Kindly words
Welcomed and soothed him; the rude conquerors
Seated the captive with their chiefs; he chose
A bride among their maidens, and at length
Seemed to forget,—yet ne'er forgot,—the wife
Of his first love, and her sweet little ones
Butchered, amid their shrieks, with all his race.
　Thus change the forms of being. Thus arise
Races of living things, glorious in strength,
And perish, as the quickening breath of God
Fills them, or is withdrawn. The red man too—
Has left the blooming wilds he ranged so long,
And, nearer to the Rocky Mountains, sought
A wider hunting-ground. The beaver builds
No longer by these streams, but far away,
On waters whose blue surface ne'er gave back
The white man's face—among Missouri's springs,

And pools whose issues swell the Oregan,
He rears his little Venice. In these plains
The bison feeds no more. Twice twenty leagues
Beyond remotest smoke of hunter's camp,
Roams the majestic brute, in herds that shake
The earth with thundering steps—yet here I meet
His ancient footprints stamped beside the pool.
   Still this great solitude is quick with life.
Myriads of insects, gaudy as the flowers
They flutter over, gentle quadrupeds,
And birds, that scarce have learned the fear of man,
Are here, and sliding reptiles of the ground,
Startlingly beautiful. The graceful deer
Bounds to the wood at my approach. The bee,
A more adventurous colonist than man,
With whom he came across the eastern deep,
Fills the savannas with his murmurings,
And hides his sweets, as in the golden age,
Within the hollow oak. I listen long
To his domestic hum, and think I hear
The sound of that advancing multitude
Which soon shall fill these deserts. From the ground
Comes up the laugh of children, the soft voice
Of maidens, and the sweet and solemn hymn
Of Sabbath worshippers. The low of herds
Blends with the rustling of the heavy grain
Over the dark-brown furrows. All at once
A fresher wind sweeps by, and breaks my dream,
And I am in the wilderness alone.

THANATOPSIS

To him who in the love of Nature holds
Communion with her visible forms, she speaks
A various language; for his gayer hours
She has a voice of gladness, and a smile
And eloquence of beauty, and she glides
Into his darker musings, with a mild
And healing sympathy, that steals away
Their sharpness, ere he is aware. When thoughts

Of the last bitter hour come like a blight
Over thy spirit, and sad images
Of the stern agony, and shroud, and pall,
And breathless darkness, and the narrow house,
Make thee to shudder, and grow sick at heart;—
Go forth, under the open sky, and list
To Nature's teachings, while from all around—
Earth and her waters, and the depths of air—
Comes a still voice.—

                Yet a few days, and thee
The all-beholding sun shall see no more
In all his course; nor yet in the cold ground,
Where thy pale form was laid, with many tears,
Nor in the embrace of ocean, shall exist
Thy image. Earth, that nourished thee, shall claim
Thy growth, to be resolved to earth again,
And, lost each human trace, surrendering up
Thine individual being, shalt thou go
To mix for ever with the elements,
To be a brother to the insensible rock
And to the sluggish clod, which the rude swain
Turns with his share, and treads upon. The oak
Shall send his roots abroad, and pierce thy mould.

   Yet not to thine eternal resting-place
Shalt thou retire alone, nor couldst thou wish
Couch more magnificent. Thou shalt lie down
With patriarchs of the infant world—with kings,
The powerful of the earth—the wise, the good,
Fair forms, and hoary seers of ages past,
All in one mighty sepulchre. The hills
Rock-ribbed and ancient as the sun,—the vales
Stretching in pensive quietness between;
The venerable woods—rivers that move
In majesty, and the complaining brooks
That make the meadows green; and, poured round all,
Old Ocean's gray and melancholy waste,—
Are but the solemn decorations all
Of the great tomb of man. The golden sun,
The planets, all the infinite host of heaven,
Are shining on the sad abodes of death,
Through the still lapse of ages. All that tread

The globe are but a handful to the tribes
That slumber in its bosom.—Take the wings
Of morning, pierce the Barcan wilderness,
Or lose thyself in the continuous woods
Where rolls the Oregon, and hears no sound,
Save his own dashings—yet the dead are there:
And millions in those solitudes, since first
The flight of years began, have laid them down
In their last sleep—the dead reign there alone.
So shalt thou rest, and what if thou withdraw
In silence from the living, and no friend
Take note of thy departure? All that breathe
Will share thy destiny. The gay will laugh
When thou art gone, the solemn brood of care
Plod on, and each one as before will chase
His favorite phantom; yet all these shall leave
Their mirth and their employments, and shall come
And make their bed with thee. As the long train
Of ages glides away, the sons of men,
The youth in life's fresh spring, and he who goes
In the full strength of years, matron and maid,
The speechless babe, and the gray-headed man—
Shall one by one be gathered to thy side,
By those, who in their turn shall follow them.
⹁ So live, that when thy summons comes to join
The innumerable caravan, which moves
To that mysterious realm, where each shall take
His chamber in the silent halls of death,
Thou go not, like the quarry-slave at night,
Scourged to his dungeon, but, sustained and soothed
By an unfaltering trust, approach thy grave,
Like one who wraps the drapery of his couch
About him, and lies down to pleasant dreams.

TO A WATERFOWL

Whither, midst falling dew,
While glow the heavens with the last steps of day,
Far, through their rosy depths, dost thou pursue
Thy solitary way?

Vainly the fowler's eye
Might mark thy distant flight to do thee wrong,
As, darkly painted on the crimson sky,
Thy figure floats along.

Seek'st thou the plashy brink
Of weedy lake, or marge of river wide,
Or where the rocking billows rise and sink
On the chafed ocean-side?

There is a Power whose care
Teaches thy way along that pathless coast—
The desert and illimitable air—
Lone wandering, but not lost.

All day thy wings have fanned,
At that far height, the cold, thin atmosphere,
Yet stoop not, weary, to the welcome land,
Though the dark night is near.

And soon that toil shall end;
Soon shalt thou find a summer home, and rest,
And scream among thy fellows; reeds shall bend,
Soon, o'er thy sheltered nest.

Thou'rt gone, the abyss of heaven
Hath swallowed up thy form; yet, on my heart
Deeply has sunk the lesson thou hast given,
And shall not soon depart.

He who, from zone to zone,
Guides through the boundless sky thy certain flight,
In the long way that I must tread alone,
Will lead my steps aright.

THE AFRICAN CHIEF

Chained in the market-place he stood,
A man of giant frame,
Amid the gathering multitude

That shrunk to hear his name—
All stern of look and strong of limb,
His dark eye on the ground:—
And silently they gazed on him,
As on a lion bound.

Vainly, but well that chief had fought,
He was a captive now,
Yet pride, that fortune humbles not,
Was written on his brow.
The scars his dark broad bosom wore
Showed warrior true and brave;
A prince among his tribe before,
He could not be a slave.

Then to his conqueror he spake:
"My brother is a king;
Undo this necklace from my neck,
And take this bracelet ring,
And send me where my brother reigns,
And I will fill thy hands
With store of ivory from the plains,
And gold-dust from the sands."

"Not for thy ivory nor thy gold
Will I unbind thy chain;
That bloody hand shall never hold
The battle-spear again.
A price that nation never gave
Shall yet be paid for thee;
For thou shalt be the Christian's slave,
In lands beyond the sea."

Then wept the warrior chief, and bade
To shred his locks away;
And one by one, each heavy braid
Before the victor lay.
Thick were the platted locks, and long,
And closely hidden there
Shone many a wedge of gold among
The dark and crisped hair.

"Look, feast thy greedy eye with gold
Long kept for sorest need;
Take it—thou askest sums untold—
And say that I am freed.
Take it—my wife, the long, long day,
Weeps by the cocoa-tree,
And my young children leave their play,
And ask in vain for me."

"I take thy gold, but, I have made
Thy fetters fast and strong,
And ween that by the cocoa-shade
Thy wife will wait thee long."
Strong was the agony that shook
The captive's frame to hear,
And the proud meaning of his look
Was changed to mortal fear.

His heart was broken—crazed his brain:
At once his eye grew wild;
He struggled fiercely with his chain,
Whispered, and wept, and smiled;
Yet wore not long those fatal bands,
And once, at shut of day,
They drew him forth upon the sands,
The foul hyena's prey.

James Gates Percival

(1795 – 1856)

THE CORAL GROVE

Deep in the wave is a coral grove,
Where the purple mullet, and gold-fish rove,
Where the sea-flower spreads its leaves of blue,
That never are wet with falling dew,
But in bright and changeful beauty shine,
Far down in the green and glassy brine.
The floor is of sand, like the mountain drift,
And the pearl shells spangle the flinty snow;
From coral rocks the sea plants lift
Their boughs, where the tides and billows flow;
The water is calm and still below,
For the winds and waves are absent there,
And the sands are bright as the stars that glow
In the motionless fields of upper air:
There with its waving blade of green,
The sea-flag streams through the silent water,
And the crimson leaf of the dulse is seen
To blush, like a banner bathed in slaughter:
There with a light and easy motion,
The fan-coral sweeps through the clear deep sea;
And the yellow and scarlet tufts of ocean,
Are bending like corn on the upland lea:
And life, in rare and beautiful forms,
Is sporting amid those bowers of stone,
And is safe, when the wrathful spirit of storms,
Has made the top of the wave his own:
And when the ship from his fury flies,
Where the myriad voices of ocean roar,
When the wind-god frowns in the murky skies,
And demons are waiting the wreck on shore;
Then far below in the peaceful sea,
The purple mullet, and gold-fish rove,
Where the waters murmur tranquilly,
Through the bending twigs of the coral grove.

Lydia Maria Child

(1802–1880)

THE NEW-ENGLAND BOY'S SONG
ABOUT THANKSGIVING DAY

Over the river, and through the wood,
  To grandfather's house we go;
    The horse knows the way,
    To carry the sleigh,
  Through the white and drifted snow.

Over the river, and through the wood,
  To grandfather's house away!
    We would not stop
    For doll or top,
  For 't is Thanksgiving day.

Over the river, and through the wood,
  Oh, how the wind does blow!
    It stings the toes,
    And bites the nose,
  As over the ground we go.

Over the river, and through the wood,
  With a clear blue winter sky,
    The dogs do bark,
    And children hark,
  As we go jingling by.

Over the river, and through the wood,
  To have a first-rate play—
    Hear the bells ring
    Ting a ling ding,
  Hurra for Thanksgiving day!

Over the river, and through the wood—
  No matter for winds that blow;

     Or if we get
     The sleigh upset,
Into a bank of snow.

Over the river, and through the wood,
  To see little John and Ann;
    We will kiss them all,
    And play snow-ball,
  And stay as long as we can.

Over the river, and through the wood,
  Trot fast, my dapple grey!
    Spring over the ground,
    Like a hunting hound,
  For 't is Thanksgiving day!

Over the river, and through the wood,
  And straight through the barn-yard gate;
    We seem to go
    Extremely slow,
  It is so hard to wait.

Over the river, and through the wood—
  Old Jowler hears our bells;
    He shakes his pow,
    With a loud bow wow,
  And thus the news he tells.

Over the river, and through the wood—
  When grandmother sees us come,
    She will say, Oh dear,
    The children are here,
  Bring a pie for every one.

Over the river, and through the wood—
  Now grandmother's cap I spy!
    Hurra for the fun!
    Is the pudding done?
  Hurra for the pumpkin pie!

Sarah Helen Whitman

(1 8 0 3 – 1 8 7 8)

THE MORNING-GLORY

When the peach ripens to a rosy bloom,
When purple grapes glow through the leafy gloom
Of trellised vines, bright wonder, thou dost come,
Cool as a star dropt from night's azure dome,
To light the early morning, that doth break
More softly beautiful for thy sweet sake.

Thy fleeting glory to my fancy seems
Like the strange flowers we gather in our dreams;
Hovering so lightly o'er the slender stem,
Wearing so meekly the proud diadem
Of penciled rays, that gave the name you bear
Unblamed amid the flowers, from year to year.
The tawny lily, flecked with jetty studs,
Pard-like, and dropping through long, pendent buds,
Her purple anthers; nor the poppy, bowed
In languid sleep, enfolding in a cloud
Of drowsy odors her too fervid heart,
Pierced by the day-god's barbed and burning dart;
Nor the swart sunflower, her dark brows enrolled
With their broad carcanets of living gold,—
A captive princess, following the car
Of her proud conqueror; nor that sweet star,
The evening primrose, pallid with strange dreams
Born of the wan moon's melancholy beams;
Nor any flower that doth its tendrils twine
Around my memory, hath a charm like thine.
Child of the morning, passionless and fair
As some ethereal creature of the air,
Waiting not for the bright lord of the hours
To weary of thy bloom in sultry bowers;
Nor like the summer rose, that one by one,
Yields her fair, fragrant petals to the sun,
Faint with the envenomed sweetness of his smile,

That doth to lingering death her race beguile;
But, as some spirit of the air doth fade
Into the light from its own essence rayed,
So, Glory of the morning, fair and cold,
Soon in thy circling halo dost thou fold
Thy virgin bloom, and from our vision hide
That form too fair, on earth, unsullied to abide.

A NOVEMBER LANDSCAPE

How like a rich and gorgeous picture hung
In memory's storied hall seems that fair scene
O'er which long years their mellowing tints have flung!
The way-side flowers had faded one by one,
Hoar were the hills, the meadows drear and dun,
When homeward wending, 'neath the dusky screen
Of the autumnal woods, at close of day,
As o'er a pine-clad height my pathway lay,
Lo! at a sudden turn, the vale below
Lay far outspread, all flushed with purple light;
Gray rocks and umbered woods gave back the glow
Of the last day-beams, fading into night;
While down a glen where dark Moshassuck flows,
With all its kindling lamps the distant city rose.

Ralph Waldo Emerson

(1803–1882)

EACH AND ALL

Little thinks, in the field, yon red-cloaked clown
Of thee from the hill-top looking down;
The heifer that lows in the upland farm,
Far-heard, lows not thine ear to charm;
The sexton, tolling his bell at noon,
Deems not that great Napoleon
Stops his horse, and lists with delight,
Whilst his files sweep round yon Alpine height;
Nor knowest thou what argument
Thy life to thy neighbor's creed has lent.
All are needed by each one;
Nothing is fair or good alone.
I thought the sparrow's note from heaven,
Singing at dawn on the alder bough;
I brought him home, in his nest, at even;
He sings the song, but it cheers not now,
For I did not bring home the river and sky;—
He sang to my ear,—they sang to my eye.
The delicate shells lay on the shore;
The bubbles of the latest wave
Fresh pearls to their enamel gave,
And the bellowing of the savage sea
Greeted their safe escape to me.
I wiped away the weeds and foam,
I fetched my sea-born treasures home;
But the poor, unsightly, noisome things
Had left their beauty on the shore
With the sun and the sand and the wild uproar.
The lover watched his graceful maid,
As 'mid the virgin train she strayed,
Nor knew her beauty's best attire
Was woven still by the snow-white choir.
At last she came to his hermitage,
Like the bird from the woodlands to the cage;—

95

The gay enchantment was undone,
A gentle wife, but fairy none.
Then I said, "I covet truth;
Beauty is unripe childhood's cheat;
I leave it behind with the games of youth:"—
As I spoke, beneath my feet
The ground-pine curled its pretty wreath,
Running over the club-moss burrs;
I inhaled the violet's breath;
Around me stood the oaks and firs;
Pine-cones and acorns lay on the ground;
Over me soared the eternal sky,
Full of light and of deity;
Again I saw, again I heard,
The rolling river, the morning bird;—
Beauty through my senses stole;
I yielded myself to the perfect whole.

SEA-SHORE

I heard or seemed to hear the chiding Sea
Say, Pilgrim, why so late and slow to come?
Am I not always here, thy summer home?
Is not my voice thy music, morn and eve?
My breath thy healthful climate in the heats,
My touch thy antidote, my bay thy bath?
Was ever building like my terraces?
Was ever couch magnificent as mine?
Lie on the warm rock-ledges, and there learn
A little hut suffices like a town.
I make your sculptured architecture vain,
Vain beside mine. I drive my wedges home,
And carve the coastwise mountain into caves.
Lo! here is Rome, and Nineveh, and Thebes,
Karnak, and Pyramid, and Giant's Stairs,
Half piled or prostrate; and my newest slab
Older than all thy race.

                              Behold the Sea,
The opaline, the plentiful and strong,

Yet beautiful as is the rose in June,
Fresh as the trickling rainbow of July;
Sea full of food, the nourisher of kinds,
Purger of earth, and medicine of men;
Creating a sweet climate by my breath,
Washing out harms and griefs from memory,
And, in my mathematic ebb and flow,
Giving a hint of that which changes not.
Rich are the sea-gods:—who gives gifts but they?
They grope the sea for pearls, but more than pearls:
They pluck Force thence, and give it to the wise.
For every wave is wealth to Dædalus,
Wealth to the cunning artist who can work
This matchless strength. Where shall he find, O waves!
A load your Atlas shoulders cannot lift?

   I with my hammer pounding evermore
The rocky coast, smite Andes into dust,
Strewing my bed, and, in another age,
Rebuild a continent of better men.
Then I unbar the doors: my paths lead out
The exodus of nations: I disperse
Men to all shores that front the hoary main.

   I too have arts and sorceries;
Illusion dwells forever with the wave.
I know what spells are laid. Leave me to deal
With credulous and imaginative man;
For, though he scoop my water in his palm,
A few rods off he deems it gems and clouds.
Planting strange fruits and sunshine on the shore,
I make some coast alluring, some lone isle,
To distant men, who must go there, or die.

ODE

Inscribed to W. H. Channing

Though loath to grieve
The evil time's sole patriot,

I cannot leave
My honied thought
For the priest's cant,
Or statesman's rant.

If I refuse
My study for their politique,
Which at the best is trick,
The angry Muse
Puts confusion in my brain.

But who is he that prates
Of the culture of mankind,
Of better arts and life?
Go, blindworm, go,
Behold the famous States
Harrying Mexico
With rifle and with knife!

Or who, with accent bolder,
Dare praise the freedom-loving mountaineer?
I found by thee, O rushing Contoocook!
And in thy valleys, Agiochook!
The jackals of the negro-holder.

The God who made New Hampshire
Taunted the lofty land
With little men;—
Small bat and wren
House in the oak:—
If earth-fire cleave
The upheaved land, and bury the folk,
The southern crocodile would grieve.
Virtue palters; Right is hence;
Freedom praised, but hid;
Funeral eloquence
Rattles the coffin-lid.

What boots thy zeal,
O glowing friend,
That would indignant rend
The northland from the south?

Wherefore? to what good end?
Boston Bay and Bunker Hill
Would serve things still;—
Things are of the snake.

The horseman serves the horse,
The neatherd serves the neat,
The merchant serves the purse,
The eater serves his meat;
'T is the day of the chattel,
Web to weave, and corn to grind;
Things are in the saddle,
And ride mankind.

There are two laws discrete,
Not reconciled,—
Law for man, and law for thing;
The last builds town and fleet,
But it runs wild,
And doth the man unking.

'T is fit the forest fall,
The steep be graded,
The mountain tunnelled,
The sand shaded,
The orchard planted,
The glebe tilled,
The prairie granted,
The steamer built.

Let man serve law for man;
Live for friendship, live for love,
For truth's and harmony's behoof;
The state may follow how it can,
As Olympus follows Jove.

Yet do not I implore
The wrinkled shopman to my sounding woods,
Nor bid the unwilling senator
Ask votes of thrushes in the solitudes.
Every one to his chosen work;—
Foolish hands may mix and mar;

Wise and sure the issues are.
Round they roll till dark is light,
Sex to sex, and even to odd;—
The over-god
Who marries Right to Might,
Who peoples, unpeoples,—
He who exterminates
Races by stronger races,
Black by white faces,—
Knows to bring honey
Out of the lion;
Grafts gentlest scion
On pirate and Turk.

The Cossack eats Poland,
Like stolen fruit;
Her last noble is ruined,
Her last poet mute:
Straight, into double band
The victors divide;
Half for freedom strike and stand;—
The astonished Muse finds thousands at her side.

GIVE ALL TO LOVE

Give all to love;
Obey thy heart;
Friends, kindred, days,
Estate, good-fame,
Plans, credit and the Muse,—
Nothing refuse.

'T is a brave master;
Let it have scope:
Follow it utterly,
Hope beyond hope:
High and more high
It dives into noon,
With wing unspent,

Untold intent:
But it is a god,
Knows its own path
And the outlets of the sky.

It was never for the mean;
It requireth courage stout.
Souls above doubt,
Valor unbending,
It will reward,—
They shall return
More than they were,
And ever ascending.

Leave all for love;
Yet, hear me, yet,
One word more thy heart behoved,
One pulse more of firm endeavor,—
Keep thee to-day,
To-morrow, forever,
Free as an Arab
Of thy beloved.

Cling with life to the maid;
But when the surprise,
First vague shadow of surmise
Flits across her bosom young,
Of a joy apart from thee,
Free be she, fancy-free;
Nor thou detain her vesture's hem,
Nor the palest rose she flung
From her summer diadem.

Though thou loved her as thyself,
As a self of purer clay,
Though her parting dims the day,
Stealing grace from all alive;
Heartily know,
When half-gods go,
The gods arrive.

THINE EYES STILL SHINED

Thine eyes still shined for me, though far
   I lonely roved the land or sea:
As I behold yon evening star,
   Which yet beholds not me.

This morn I climbed the misty hill
   And roamed the pastures through;
How danced thy form before my path
   Amidst the deep-eyed dew!

When the redbird spread his sable wing,
   And showed his side of flame;
When the rosebud ripened to the rose,
   In both I read thy name.

CONCORD HYMN

Sung at the completion of the Battle Monument, July 4, 1837

By the rude bridge that arched the flood,
   Their flag to April's breeze unfurled,
Here once the embattled farmers stood
   And fired the shot heard round the world.

The foe long since in silence slept;
   Alike the conqueror silent sleeps;
And Time the ruined bridge has swept
   Down the dark stream which seaward creeps.

On this green bank, by this soft stream,
   We set to-day a votive stone;
That memory may their deed redeem,
   When, like our sires, our sons are gone.

Spirit, that made those heroes dare
   To die, and leave their children free,
Bid Time and Nature gently spare
   The shaft we raise to them and thee.

BRAHMA

If the red slayer think he slays,
   Or if the slain think he is slain,
They know not well the subtle ways
   I keep, and pass, and turn again.

Far or forgot to me is near;
   Shadow and sunlight are the same;
The vanished gods to me appear;
   And one to me are shame and fame.

They reckon ill who leave me out;
   When me they fly, I am the wings;
I am the doubter and the doubt,
   And I the hymn the Brahmin sings.

The strong gods pine for my abode,
   And pine in vain the sacred Seven;
But thou, meek lover of the good!
   Find me, and turn thy back on heaven.

From THE RIVER

Awed I behold once more
My old familiar haunts; here the blue river
The same blue wonder that my infant eye
Admired, sage doubting whence the traveller came,—
Whence brought his sunny bubbles ere he washed
The fragrant flag roots in my father's fields,
And where thereafter in the world he went.
Look, here he is unaltered, save that now
He hath broke his banks & flooded all the vales
With his redundant waves.

Here is the rock where yet a simple child
I caught with bended pin my earliest fish,
Much triumphing,—And these the fields

Over whose flowers I chased the butterfly,
A blooming hunter of a fairy fine.
And hark! where overhead the ancient crows
Hold their sour conversation in the sky.
          These are the same, but I am not the same
But wiser than I was, & wise enough
Not to regret the changes, tho' they cost
Me many a sigh. Oh call not Nature dumb;
These trees & stones are audible to me,
These idle flowers, that tremble in the wind,
I understand their faery syllables,
And all their sad significance. This wind,
That rustles down the well-known forest road—
It hath a sound more eloquent than speech.
The stream, the trees, the grass, the sighing wind,
All of them utter sounds of admonishment
And grave parental love.

They are not of our race, they seem to say,
And yet have knowledge of our moral race,
And somewhat of majestic sympathy,
Something of pity for the puny clay,
That holds & boasts the immeasureable mind.

I feel as I were welcome to these trees
After long months of weary wandering,
Acknowledged by their hospitable boughs;
They know me as their son, for side by side,
They were coeval with my ancestors,
Adorned with them my country's primitive times,
And soon may give my dust their funeral shade.

DAYS

Daughters of Time, the hypocritic Days,
Muffled and dumb like barefoot dervishes,
And marching single in an endless file,
Bring diadems and fagots in their hands.
To each they offer gifts after his will,

Bread, kingdoms, stars, and sky that holds them all.
I, in my pleached garden, watched the pomp,
Forgot my morning wishes, hastily
Took a few herbs and apples, and the Day
Turned and departed silent. I, too late,
Under her solemn fillet saw the scorn.

Elizabeth Oakes-Smith

(1806–1893)

ODE TO SAPPHO

Bright, glowing Sappho! child of love and song.
  Adown the blueness of long-distant years
Beams forth thy glorious shape, and steal along
  Thy melting tones, beguiling us to tears.
      Thou priestess of great hearts,
        Thrilled with the secret fire
      By which a god imparts
        The anguish of desire—
    For meaner souls be mean content—
    Thine was a higher element.
Over Leucadia's rock thou leanest yet,
  With thy wild song, and all thy locks outspread;
The stars are in thine eyes, the moon hath set—
  The night dew falls upon thy radiant head;
      And thy resounding lyre—
        Ah! not so wildly sway:
      Thy soulful lips inspire
        And steal our hearts away!
    Swanlike and beautiful, thy dirge
    Still moans along the Ægean surge.
No unrequited love filled thy lone heart,
  But thine infinitude did on thee weigh,
And all the wildness of despair impart,
  Stealing the down from Hope's own wing away.
      Couldst thou not suffer on,
        Bearing the direful pang,
      While thy melodious tone
        Through wondering cities rang?
    Couldst thou not bear thy godlike grief?
    In godlike utterance find relief?
Devotion, fervor, might upon thee wait:
  But what were these to thine? all cold and chill,
And left thy burning heart but desolate;
  Thy wondrous beauty with despair might fill

The worshipper who bent
   Entranced at thy feet:
Too affluent the dower lent
   Where song and beauty meet!
Consumed by a Promethean fire
Wert thou, O daughter of the lyre!
Alone, above Leucadia's wave art thou,
   Most beautiful, most gifted, yet alone!
Ah! what to thee the crown from Pindar's brow!
   What the loud plaudit and the garlands thrown
      By the enraptured throng,
         When thou in matchless grace
      Didst move with lyre and song,
         And monarchs gave thee place?
   What hast thou left, proud one? what token?
   Alas! a lyre and heart—both broken!

John Greenleaf Whittier

(1 8 0 7 – 1 8 9 2)

TO MY OLD SCHOOLMASTER

An Epistle Not after the Manner of Horace

Old friend, kind friend! lightly down
Drop time's snow-flakes on thy crown!
Never be thy shadow less,
Never fail thy cheerfulness;
Care, that kills the cat, may plough
Wrinkles in the miser's brow,
Deepen envy's spiteful frown,
Draw the mouths of bigots down,
Plague ambition's dream, and sit
Heavy on the hypocrite,
Haunt the rich man's door, and ride
In the gilded coach of pride;—
Let the fiend pass!—what can he
Find to do with such as thee?
Seldom comes that evil guest
Where the conscience lies at rest,
And brown health and quiet wit
Smiling on the threshold sit.

I, the urchin unto whom,
In that smoked and dingy room,
Where the district gave thee rule
O'er its ragged winter school,
Thou didst teach the mysteries
Of those weary A B C's,—
Where, to fill the every pause
Of thy wise and learned saws,
Through the cracked and crazy wall
Came the cradle-rock and squall,
And the goodman's voice, at strife
With his shrill and tipsy wife,—
Luring us by stories old,

With a comic unction told,
More than by the eloquence
Of terse birchen arguments
(Doubtful gain, I fear), to look
With complacence on a book!—
Where the genial pedagogue
Half forgot his rogues to flog,
Citing tale or apologue,
Wise and merry in its drift
As was Phædrus' twofold gift,
Had the little rebels known it,
Risum et prudentiam monet!
I,—the man of middle years,
In whose sable locks appears
Many a warning fleck of gray,—
Looking back to that far day,
And thy primal lessons, feel
Grateful smiles my lips unseal,
As, remembering thee, I blend
Olden teacher, present friend,
Wise with antiquarian search,
In the scrolls of State and Church:
Named on history's title-page,
Parish-clerk and justice sage;
For the ferule's wholesome awe
Wielding now the sword of law.

Threshing Time's neglected sheaves,
Gathering up the scattered leaves
Which the wrinkled sibyl cast
Careless from her as she passed,—
Twofold citizen art thou,
Freeman of the past and now.
He who bore thy name of old
Midway in the heavens did hold
Over Gibeon moon and sun;
Thou hast bidden them backward run;
Of to-day the present ray
Flinging over yesterday!

Let the busy ones deride
What I deem of right thy pride:

Let the fools their treadmills grind,
Look not forward nor behind,
Shuffle in and wriggle out,
Veer with every breeze about,
Turning like a windmill sail,
Or a dog that seeks his tail;
Let them laugh to see thee fast
Tabernacled in the Past,
Working out with eye and lip
Riddles of old penmanship,
Patient as Belzoni there
Sorting out, with loving care,
Mummies of dead questions stripped
From their sevenfold manuscript!

Dabbling, in their noisy way,
In the puddles of to-day,
Little know they of that vast
Solemn ocean of the past,
On whose margin, wreck-bespread,
Thou art walking with the dead,
Questioning the stranded years,
Waking smiles by turns, and tears,
As thou callest up again
Shapes the dust has long o'erlain,—
Fair-haired woman, bearded man,
Cavalier and Puritan;
In an age whose eager view
Seeks but present things, and new,
Mad for party, sect and gold,
Teaching reverence for the old.

On that shore, with fowler's tact,
Coolly bagging fact on fact,
Naught amiss to thee can float,
Tale, or song, or anecdote;
Village gossip, centuries old,
Scandals by our grandams told,
What the pilgrim's table spread,
Where he lived, and whom he wed,
Long-drawn bill of wine and beer
For his ordination cheer,

Or the flip that wellnigh made
Glad his funeral cavalcade;
Weary prose, and poet's lines,
Flavored by their age, like wines,
Eulogistic of some quaint,
Doubtful, Puritanic saint;
Lays that quickened husking jigs,
Jests that shook grave periwigs,
When the parson had his jokes
And his glass, like other folks;
Sermons that, for mortal hours,
Taxed our fathers' vital powers,
As the long nineteenthlies poured
Downward from the sounding-board,
And, for fire of Pentecost,
Touched their beards December's frost.

Time is hastening on, and we
What our fathers are shall be,—
Shadow-shapes of memory!
Joined to that vast multitude
Where the great are but the good,
And the mind of strength shall prove
Weaker than the heart of love;
Pride of graybeard wisdom less
Than the infant's guilelessness,
And his song of sorrow more
Than the crown the Psalmist wore!
Who shall then, with pious zeal,
At our moss-grown thresholds kneel,
From a stained and stony page
Reading to a careless age,
With a patient eye like thine,
Prosing tale and limping line,
Names and words the hoary rime
Of the Past has made sublime?
Who shall work for us as well
The antiquarian's miracle?
Who to seeming life recall
Teacher grave and pupil small?
Who shall give to thee and me
Freeholds in futurity?

Well, whatever lot be mine,
Long and happy days be thine,
Ere thy full and honored age
Dates of time its latest page!
Squire for master, State for school,
Wisely lenient, live and rule;
Over grown-up knave and rogue
Play the watchful pedagogue;
Or, while pleasure smiles on duty,
At the call of youth and beauty,
Speak for them the spell of law
Which shall bar and bolt withdraw,
And the flaming sword remove
From the Paradise of Love.
Still, with undimmed eyesight, pore
Ancient tome and record o'er;
Still thy week-day lyrics croon,
Pitch in church the Sunday tune,
Showing something, in thy part,
Of the old Puritanic art,
Singer after Sternhold's heart!
In thy pew, for many a year,
Homilies from Oldbug hear,
Who to wit like that of South,
And the Syrian's golden mouth,
Doth the homely pathos add
Which the pilgrim preachers had;
Breaking, like a child at play,
Gilded idols of the day,
Cant of knave and pomp of fool
Tossing with his ridicule,
Yet, in earnest or in jest,
Ever keeping truth abreast.
And, when thou art called, at last,
To thy townsmen of the past,
Not as stranger shalt thou come;
Thou shalt find thyself at home
With the little and the big,
Woollen cap and periwig,
Madam in her high-laced ruff,
Goody in her home-made stuff,—
Wise and simple, rich and poor,
Thou hast known them all before!

TELLING THE BEES

Here is the place; right over the hill
   Runs the path I took;
You can see the gap in the old wall still,
   And the stepping-stones in the shallow brook.

There is the house, with the gate red-barred,
   And the poplars tall;
And the barn's brown length, and the cattle-yard,
   And the white horns tossing above the wall.

There are the beehives ranged in the sun;
   And down by the brink
Of the brook are her poor flowers, weed-o'errun,
   Pansy and daffodil, rose and pink.

A year has gone, as the tortoise goes,
   Heavy and slow;
And the same rose blows, and the same sun glows,
   And the same brook sings of a year ago.

There's the same sweet clover-smell in the breeze;
   And the June sun warm
Tangles his wings of fire in the trees,
   Setting, as then, over Fernside farm.

I mind me how with a lover's care
   From my Sunday coat
I brushed off the burrs, and smoothed my hair,
   And cooled at the brookside my brow and throat.

Since we parted, a month had passed,—
   To love, a year;
Down through the beeches I looked at last
   On the little red gate and the well-sweep near.

I can see it all now,—the slantwise rain
   Of light through the leaves,
The sundown's blaze on her window-pane,
   The bloom of her roses under the eaves.

Just the same as a month before,—
    The house and the trees,
The barn's brown gable, the vine by the door,—
    Nothing changed but the hives of bees.

Before them, under the garden wall,
    Forward and back,
Went drearily singing the chore-girl small,
    Draping each hive with a shred of black.

Trembling, I listened: the summer sun
    Had the chill of snow;
For I knew she was telling the bees of one
    Gone on the journey we all must go!

Then I said to myself, "My Mary weeps
    For the dead to-day:
Haply her blind old grandsire sleeps
    The fret and the pain of his age away."

But her dog whined low; on the doorway sill,
    With his cane to his chin,
The old man sat; and the chore-girl still
    Sang to the bees stealing out and in.

And the song she was singing ever since
    In my ear sounds on:—
"Stay at home, pretty bees, fly not hence!
    Mistress Mary is dead and gone!"

BARBARA FRIETCHIE

Up from the meadows rich with corn,
Clear in the cool September morn,

The clustered spires of Frederick stand
Green-walled by the hills of Maryland.

Round about them orchards sweep,
Apple and peach trees fruited deep,

Fair as the garden of the Lord
To the eyes of the famished rebel horde,

On that pleasant morn of the early fall
When Lee marched over the mountain-wall;

Over the mountains winding down,
Horse and foot, into Frederick town.

Forty flags with their silver stars,
Forty flags with their crimson bars,

Flapped in the morning wind: the sun
Of noon looked down, and saw not one.

Up rose old Barbara Frietchie then,
Bowed with her fourscore years and ten;

Bravest of all in Frederick town,
She took up the flag the men hauled down;

In her attic window the staff she set,
To show that one heart was loyal yet.

Up the street came the rebel tread,
Stonewall Jackson riding ahead.

Under his slouched hat left and right
He glanced; the old flag met his sight.

"Halt!"—the dust-brown ranks stood fast.
"Fire!"—out blazed the rifle-blast.

It shivered the window, pane and sash;
It rent the banner with seam and gash.

Quick, as it fell, from the broken staff
Dame Barbara snatched the silken scarf.

She leaned far out on the window-sill,
And shook it forth with a royal will.

"Shoot, if you must, this old gray head,
But spare your country's flag," she said.

A shade of sadness, a blush of shame,
Over the face of the leader came;

The nobler nature within him stirred
To life at that woman's deed and word;

"Who touches a hair of yon gray head
Dies like a dog! March on!" he said.

All day long through Frederick street
Sounded the tread of marching feet:

All day long that free flag tost
Over the heads of the rebel host.

Ever its torn folds rose and fell
On the loyal winds that loved it well;

And through the hill-gaps sunset light
Shone over it with a warm good-night.

Barbara Frietchie's work is o'er,
And the Rebel rides on his raids no more.

Honor to her! and let a tear
Fall, for her sake, on Stonewall's bier.

Over Barbara Frietchie's grave,
Flag of Freedom and Union, wave!

Peace and order and beauty draw
Round thy symbol of light and law;

And ever the stars above look down
On thy stars below in Frederick town!

SNOW-BOUND

A Winter Idyl

The sun that brief December day
Rose cheerless over hills of gray,
And, darkly circled, gave at noon
A sadder light than waning moon.
Slow tracing down the thickening sky
Its mute and ominous prophecy,
A portent seeming less than threat,
It sank from sight before it set.
A chill no coat, however stout,
Of homespun stuff could quite shut out,
A hard, dull bitterness of cold,
That checked, mid-vein, the circling race
Of life-blood in the sharpened face,
The coming of the snow-storm told.
The wind blew east; we heard the roar
Of Ocean on his wintry shore,
And felt the strong pulse throbbing there
Beat with low rhythm our inland air.

Meanwhile we did our nightly chores,—
Brought in the wood from out of doors,
Littered the stalls, and from the mows
Raked down the herd's-grass for the cows:
Heard the horse whinnying for his corn;
And, sharply clashing horn on horn,
Impatient down the stanchion rows
The cattle shake their walnut bows;
While, peering from his early perch
Upon the scaffold's pole of birch,
The cock his crested helmet bent
And down his querulous challenge sent.

Unwarmed by any sunset light
The gray day darkened into night,
A night made hoary with the swarm
And whirl-dance of the blinding storm,
As zigzag, wavering to and fro,
Crossed and recrossed the wingèd snow:

And ere the early bedtime came
The white drift piled the window-frame,
And through the glass the clothes-line posts
Looked in like tall and sheeted ghosts.
So all night long the storm roared on:
The morning broke without a sun;
In tiny spherule traced with lines
Of Nature's geometric signs,
In starry flake, and pellicle,
All day the hoary meteor fell;
And, when the second morning shone,
We looked upon a world unknown,
On nothing we could call our own.
Around the glistening wonder bent
The blue walls of the firmament,
No cloud above, no earth below,—
A universe of sky and snow!
The old familiar sights of ours
Took marvellous shapes; strange domes and towers
Rose up where sty or corn-crib stood,
Or garden-wall, or belt of wood;
A smooth white mound the brush-pile showed,
A fenceless drift what once was road;
The bridle-post an old man sat
With loose-flung coat and high cocked hat;
The well-curb had a Chinese roof;
And even the long sweep, high aloof,
In its slant splendor, seemed to tell
Of Pisa's leaning miracle.

A prompt, decisive man, no breath
Our father wasted: "Boys, a path!"
Well pleased, (for when did farmer boy
Count such a summons less than joy?)
Our buskins on our feet we drew;
With mittened hands, and caps drawn low,
To guard our necks and ears from snow,
We cut the solid whiteness through.
And, where the drift was deepest, made
A tunnel walled and overlaid
With dazzling crystal: we had read
Of rare Aladdin's wondrous cave,
And to our own his name we gave,

With many a wish the luck were ours
To test his lamp's supernal powers.
We reached the barn with merry din,
And roused the prisoned brutes within.
The old horse thrust his long head out,
And grave with wonder gazed about;
The cock his lusty greeting said,
And forth his speckled harem led;
The oxen lashed their tails, and hooked,
And mild reproach of hunger looked;
The hornèd patriarch of the sheep,
Like Egypt's Amun roused from sleep,
Shook his sage head with gesture mute,
And emphasized with stamp of foot.

All day the gusty north-wind bore
The loosening drift its breath before;
Low circling round its southern zone,
The sun through dazzling snow-mist shone.
No church-bell lent its Christian tone
To the savage air, no social smoke
Curled over woods of snow-hung oak.
A solitude made more intense
By dreary-voicèd elements,
The shrieking of the mindless wind,
The moaning tree-boughs swaying blind,
And on the glass the unmeaning beat
Of ghostly finger-tips of sleet.
Beyond the circle of our hearth
No welcome sound of toil or mirth
Unbound the spell, and testified
Of human life and thought outside.
We minded that the sharpest ear
The buried brooklet could not hear,
The music of whose liquid lip
Had been to us companionship,
And, in our lonely life, had grown
To have an almost human tone.

As night drew on, and, from the crest
Of wooded knolls that ridged the west,
The sun, a snow-blown traveller, sank
From sight beneath the smothering bank,

We piled, with care, our nightly stack
Of wood against the chimney-back,—
The oaken log, green, huge, and thick,
And on its top the stout back-stick;
The knotty forestick laid apart,
And filled between with curious art
The ragged brush; then, hovering near,
We watched the first red blaze appear,
Heard the sharp crackle, caught the gleam
On whitewashed wall and sagging beam,
Until the old, rude-furnished room
Burst, flower-like, into rosy bloom;
While radiant with a mimic flame
Outside the sparkling drift became,
And through the bare-boughed lilac-tree
Our own warm hearth seemed blazing free.
The crane and pendent trammels showed,
The Turks' heads on the andirons glowed;
While childish fancy, prompt to tell
The meaning of the miracle,
Whispered the old rhyme: "*Under the tree,
When fire outdoors burns merrily,
There the witches are making tea.*"

The moon above the eastern wood
Shone at its full; the hill-range stood
Transfigured in the silver flood,
Its blown snows flashing cold and keen,
Dead white, save where some sharp ravine
Took shadow, or the sombre green
Of hemlocks turned to pitchy black
Against the whiteness at their back.
For such a world and such a night
Most fitting that unwarming light,
Which only seemed where'er it fell
To make the coldness visible.

Shut in from all the world without,
We sat the clean-winged hearth about,
Content to let the north-wind roar
In baffled rage at pane and door,
While the red logs before us beat
The frost-line back with tropic heat;

And ever, when a louder blast
Shook beam and rafter as it passed,
The merrier up its roaring draught
The great throat of the chimney laughed;
The house-dog on his paws outspread
Laid to the fire his drowsy head,
The cat's dark silhouette on the wall
A couchant tiger's seemed to fall;
And, for the winter fireside meet,
Between the andirons' straddling feet,
The mug of cider simmered slow,
The apples sputtered in a row,
And, close at hand, the basket stood
With nuts from brown October's wood.

What matter how the night behaved?
What matter how the north-wind raved?
Blow high, blow low, not all its snow
Could quench our hearth-fire's ruddy glow.
O Time and Change!—with hair as gray
As was my sire's that winter day,
How strange it seems, with so much gone
Of life and love, to still live on!
Ah, brother! only I and thou
Are left of all that circle now,—
The dear home faces whereupon
That fitful firelight paled and shone.
Henceforward, listen as we will,
The voices of that hearth are still;
Look where we may, the wide earth o'er,
Those lighted faces smile no more.
We tread the paths their feet have worn,
   We sit beneath their orchard trees,
   We hear, like them, the hum of bees
And rustle of the bladed corn;
We turn the pages that they read,
   Their written words we linger o'er,
But in the sun they cast no shade,
No voice is heard, no sign is made,
   No step is on the conscious floor!
Yet Love will dream, and Faith will trust,
(Since He who knows our need is just,)
That somehow, somewhere, meet we must.

Alas for him who never sees
The stars shine through his cypress-trees!
Who, hopeless, lays his dead away,
Nor looks to see the breaking day
Across the mournful marbles play!
Who hath not learned, in hours of faith,
    The truth to flesh and sense unknown,
That Life is ever lord of Death,
    And Love can never lose its own!

We sped the time with stories old,
Wrought puzzles out, and riddles told,
Or stammered from our school-book lore
"The Chief of Gambia's golden shore."
How often since, when all the land
Was clay in Slavery's shaping hand,
As if a far-blown trumpet stirred
The languorous sin-sick air, I heard:
"Does not the voice of reason cry,
    Claim the first right which Nature gave,
From the red scourge of bondage fly,
    Nor deign to live a burdened slave!"
Our father rode again his ride
On Memphremagog's wooded side;
Sat down again to moose and samp
In trapper's hut and Indian camp;
Lived o'er the old idyllic ease
Beneath St. François' hemlock-trees;
Again for him the moonlight shone
On Norman cap and bodiced zone;
Again he heard the violin play
Which led the village dance away.
And mingled in its merry whirl
The grandam and the laughing girl.
Or, nearer home, our steps he led
Where Salisbury's level marshes spread
    Mile-wide as flies the laden bee;
Where merry mowers, hale and strong,
Swept, scythe on scythe, their swaths along
    The low green prairies of the sea.
We shared the fishing off Boar's Head,
    And round the rocky Isles of Shoals
    The hake-broil on the drift-wood coals;

The chowder on the sand-beach made,
Dipped by the hungry, steaming hot,
With spoons of clam-shell from the pot.
We heard the tales of witchcraft old,
And dream and sign and marvel told
To sleepy listeners as they lay
Stretched idly on the salted hay,
Adrift along the winding shores,
When favoring breezes deigned to blow
The square sail of the gundelow
And idle lay the useless oars.
Our mother, while she turned her wheel
Or run the new-knit stocking-heel,
Told how the Indian hordes came down
At midnight on Cocheco town,
And how her own great-uncle bore
His cruel scalp-mark to fourscore.
Recalling, in her fitting phrase,
      So rich and picturesque and free,
      (The common unrhymed poetry
Of simple life and country ways,)
The story of her early days,—
She made us welcome to her home;
Old hearths grew wide to give us room;
We stole with her a frightened look
At the gray wizard's conjuring-book,
The fame whereof went far and wide
Through all the simple country side;
We heard the hawks at twilight play,
The boat-horn on Piscataqua,
The loon's weird laughter far away;
We fished her little trout-brook, knew
What flowers in wood and meadow grew,
What sunny hillsides autumn-brown
She climbed to shake the ripe nuts down,
Saw where in sheltered cove and bay
The ducks' black squadron anchored lay,
And heard the wild-geese calling loud
Beneath the gray November cloud.

Then, haply, with a look more grave,
And soberer tone, some tale she gave
From painful Sewel's ancient tome,

Beloved in every Quaker home,
Of faith fire-winged by martyrdom,
Or Chalkley's Journal, old and quaint,—
Gentlest of skippers, rare sea-saint!—
Who, when the dreary calms prevailed,
And water-butt and bread-cask failed,
And cruel, hungry eyes pursued
His portly presence mad for food,
With dark hints muttered under breath
Of casting lots for life or death,
Offered, if Heaven withheld supplies,
To be himself the sacrifice.
Then, suddenly, as if to save
The good man from his living grave,
A ripple on the water grew,
A school of porpoise flashed in view.
"Take, eat," he said, "and be content;
These fishes in my stead are sent
By Him who gave the tangled ram
To spare the child of Abraham."

Our uncle, innocent of books,
Was rich in lore of fields and brooks,
The ancient teachers never dumb
Of Nature's unhoused lyceum.
In moons and tides and weather wise,
He read the clouds as prophecies,
And foul or fair could well divine,
By many an occult hint and sign,
Holding the cunning-warded keys
To all the woodcraft mysteries;
Himself to Nature's heart so near
That all her voices in his ear
Of beast or bird had meanings clear,
Like Apollonius of old,
Who knew the tales the sparrows told,
Or Hermes who interpreted
What the sage cranes of Nilus said;
A simple, guileless, childlike man,
Content to live where life began;
Strong only on his native grounds,
The little world of sights and sounds
Whose girdle was the parish bounds,

Whereof his fondly partial pride
The common features magnified,
As Surrey hills to mountains grew
In White of Selborne's loving view,—
He told how teal and loon he shot,
And how the eagle's eggs he got,
The feats on pond and river done,
The prodigies of rod and gun;
Till, warming with the tales he told,
Forgotten was the outside cold,
The bitter wind unheeded blew,
From ripening corn the pigeons flew,
The partridge drummed i' the wood, the mink
Went fishing down the river-brink.
In fields with bean or clover gay,
The woodchuck, like a hermit gray,
    Peered from the doorway of his cell:
The muskrat plied the mason's trade,
And tier by tier his mud-walls laid;
And from the shagbark overhead
    The grizzled squirrel dropped his shell.

Next, the dear aunt, whose smile of cheer
And voice in dreams I see and hear,—
The sweetest woman ever Fate
Perverse denied a household mate,
Who, lonely, homeless, not the less
Found peace in love's unselfishness,
And welcome wheresoe'er she went,
A calm and gracious element,
Whose presence seemed the sweet income
And womanly atmosphere of home,—
Called up her girlhood memories,
The huskings and the apple-bees,
The sleigh-rides and the summer sails.
Weaving through all the poor details
And homespun warp of circumstance
A golden woof-thread of romance.
For well she kept her genial mood
And simple faith of maidenhood;
Before her still a cloud-land lay,
The mirage loomed across her way;
The morning dew, that dries so soon

With others, glistened at her noon;
Through years of toil and soil and care,
From glossy tress to thin gray hair,
All unprofaned she held apart
The virgin fancies of the heart.
Be shame to him of woman born
Who hath for such but thought of scorn.

There, too, our elder sister plied
Her evening task the stand beside;
A full, rich nature, free to trust,
Truthful and almost sternly just,
Impulsive, earnest, prompt to act,
And make her generous thought a fact,
Keeping with many a light disguise
The secret of self-sacrifice.
O heart sore-tried! thou hast the best
That Heaven itself could give thee,—rest,
Rest from all bitter thoughts and things!
    How many a poor one's blessing went
    With thee beneath the low green tent
Whose curtain never outward swings!

As one who held herself a part
Of all she saw, and let her heart
    Against the household bosom lean,
Upon the motley-braided mat
Our youngest and our dearest sat,
Lifting her large, sweet, asking eyes,
    Now bathed in the unfading green
And holy peace of Paradise.
Oh, looking from some heavenly hill,
    Or from the shade of saintly palms,
    Or silver reach of river calms,
Do those large eyes behold me still?
With me one little year ago:—
The chill weight of the winter snow
    For months upon her grave has lain;
And now, when summer south-winds blow
    And brier and harebell bloom again,
I tread the pleasant paths we trod,
I see the violet-sprinkled sod
Whereon she leaned, too frail and weak

The hillside flowers she loved to seek,
Yet following me where'er I went
With dark eyes full of love's content.
The birds are glad; the brier-rose fills
The air with sweetness; all the hills
Stretch green to June's unclouded sky;
But still I wait with ear and eye
For something gone which should be nigh,
A loss in all familiar things,
In flower that blooms, and bird that sings.
And yet, dear heart! remembering thee,
    Am I not richer than of old?
Safe in thy immortality,
    What change can reach the wealth I hold?
    What chance can mar the pearl and gold
Thy love hath left in trust with me?
And while in life's late afternoon,
    Where cool and long the shadows grow,
I walk to meet the night that soon
    Shall shape and shadow overflow,
I cannot feel that thou art far,
Since near at need the angels are;
And when the sunset gates unbar,
    Shall I not see thee waiting stand,
And, white against the evening star,
    The welcome of thy beckoning hand?

Brisk wielder of the birch and rule,
The master of the district school
Held at the fire his favored place,
Its warm glow lit a laughing face
Fresh-hued and fair, where scarce appeared
The uncertain prophecy of beard.
He teased the mitten-blinded cat,
Played cross-pins on my uncle's hat,
Sang songs, and told us what befalls
In classic Dartmouth's college halls.
Born the wild Northern hills among,
From whence his yeoman father wrung
By patient toil subsistence scant,
Not competence and yet not want,
He early gained the power to pay
His cheerful, self-reliant way;

Could doff at ease his scholar's gown
To peddle wares from town to town:
Or through the long vacation's reach
In lonely lowland districts teach,
Where all the droll experience found
At stranger hearths in boarding round,
The moonlit skater's keen delight,
The sleigh-drive through the frosty night,
The rustic-party, with its rough
Accompaniment of blind-man's-buff,
And whirling-plate, and forfeits paid,
His winter task a pastime made.
Happy the snow-locked homes wherein
He tuned his merry violin,
Or played the athlete in the barn,
Or held the good dame's winding-yarn,
Or mirth-provoking versions told
Of classic legends rare and old,
Wherein the scenes of Greece and Rome
Had all the commonplace of home,
And little seemed at best the odds
'Twixt Yankee pedlers and old gods;
Where Pindus-born Arachthus took
The guise of any grist-mill brook,
And dread Olympus at his will
Became a huckleberry hill.

A careless boy that night he seemed;
    But at his desk he had the look
And air of one who wisely schemed,
    And hostage from the future took
    In trainëd thought and lore of book.
Large-brained, clear-eyed, of such as he
Shall Freedom's young apostles be,
Who, following in War's bloody trail,
Shall every lingering wrong assail;
All chains from limb and spirit strike,
Uplift the black and white alike;
Scatter before their swift advance
The darkness and the ignorance,
The pride, the lust, the squalid sloth,
Which nurtured Treason's monstrous growth,
Made murder pastime, and the hell

Of prison-torture possible;
The cruel lie of caste refute,
Old forms remould, and substitute
For Slavery's lash the freeman's will,
For blind routine, wise-handed skill;
A school-house plant on every hill,
Stretching in radiate nerve-lines thence
The quick wires of intelligence;
Till North and South together brought
Shall own the same electric thought,
In peace a common flag salute,
And, side by side in labor's free
And unresentful rivalry,
Harvest the fields wherein they fought.
Another guest that winter night
Flashed back from lustrous eyes the light.
Unmarked by time, and yet not young,
The honeyed music of her tongue
And words of meekness scarcely told
A nature passionate and bold,
Strong, self-concentred, spurning guide,
Its milder features dwarfed beside
Her unbent will's majestic pride.
She sat among us, at the best,
A not unfeared, half-welcome guest,
Rebuking with her cultured phrase
Our homeliness of words and ways.
A certain pard-like, treacherous grace
Swayed the lithe limbs and drooped the lash,
Lent the white teeth their dazzling flash;
And under low brows, black with night,
Rayed out at times a dangerous light;
The sharp heat-lightnings of her face
Presaging ill to him whom Fate
Condemned to share her love or hate.
A woman tropical, intense
In thought and act, in soul and sense,
She blended in a like degree
The vixen and the devotee,
Revealing with each freak or feint
   The temper of Petruchio's Kate,
The raptures of Siena's saint.
Her tapering hand and rounded wrist

Had facile power to form a fist;
The warm, dark languish of her eyes
Was never safe from wrath's surprise.
Brows saintly calm and lips devout
Knew every change of scowl and pout;
And the sweet voice had notes more high
And shrill for social battle-cry.

Since then what old cathedral town
Has missed her pilgrim staff and gown,
What convent-gate has held its lock
Against the challenge of her knock!
Through Smyrna's plague-hushed thoroughfares,
Up sea-set Malta's rocky stairs,
Gray olive slopes of hills that hem
Thy tombs and shrines, Jerusalem,
Or startling on her desert throne
The crazy Queen of Lebanon
With claims fantastic as her own,
Her tireless feet have held their way;
And still, unrestful, bowed, and gray,
She watches under Eastern skies,
    With hope each day renewed and fresh,
    The Lord's quick coming in the flesh,
Whereof she dreams and prophesies!

Where'er her troubled path may be,
    The Lord's sweet pity with her go!
The outward wayward life we see,
    The hidden springs we may not know.
Nor is it given us to discern
    What threads the fatal sisters spun,
    Through what ancestral years has run
The sorrow with the woman born,
What forged her cruel chain of moods,
What set her feet in solitudes,
    And held the love within her mute,
What mingled madness in the blood,
    A life-long discord and annoy,
    Water of tears with oil of joy,
And hid within the folded bud
    Perversities of flower and fruit.
It is not ours to separate

The tangled skein of will and fate,
To show what metes and bounds should stand
Upon the soul's debatable land,
And between choice and Providence
Divide the circle of events;
But He who knows our frame is just,
Merciful and compassionate,
And full of sweet assurances
And hope for all the language is,
That He remembereth we are dust!

At last the great logs, crumbling low,
Sent out a dull and duller glow,
The bull's-eye watch that hung in view,
Ticking its weary circuit through,
Pointed with mutely warning sign
Its black hand to the hour of nine.
That sign the pleasant circle broke:
My uncle ceased his pipe to smoke,
Knocked from its bowl the refuse gray,
And laid it tenderly away;
Then roused himself to safely cover
The dull red brands with ashes over.
And while, with care, our mother laid
The work aside, her steps she stayed
One moment, seeking to express
Her grateful sense of happiness
For food and shelter, warmth and health,
And love's contentment more than wealth,
With simple wishes (not the weak,
Vain prayers which no fulfilment seek,
But such as warm the generous heart,
O'er-prompt to do with Heaven its part)
That none might lack, that bitter night,
For bread and clothing, warmth and light.

Within our beds awhile we heard
The wind that round the gables roared,
With now and then a ruder shock,
Which made our very bedsteads rock.
We heard the loosened clapboards tost,
The board-nails snapping in the frost;
And on us, through the unplastered wall,

Felt the light sifted snow-flakes fall.
But sleep stole on, as sleep will do
When hearts are light and life is new;
Faint and more faint the murmurs grew,
Till in the summer-land of dreams
They softened to the sound of streams,
Low stir of leaves, and dip of oars,
And lapsing waves on quiet shores.

Next morn we wakened with the shout
Of merry voices high and clear;
And saw the teamsters drawing near
To break the drifted highways out.
Down the long hillside treading slow
We saw the half-buried oxen go,
Shaking the snow from heads uptost,
Their straining nostrils white with frost.
Before our door the straggling train
Drew up, an added team to gain.
The elders threshed their hands a-cold,
    Passed, with the cider-mug, their jokes
    From lip to lip; the younger folks
Down the loose snow-banks, wrestling, rolled,
Then toiled again the cavalcade
    O'er windy hill, through clogged ravine,
    And woodland paths that wound between
Low drooping pine-boughs winter-weighed.
From every barn a team afoot,
At every house a new recruit,
Where, drawn by Nature's subtlest law,
Haply the watchful young men saw
Sweet doorway pictures of the curls
And curious eyes of merry girls,
Lifting their hands in mock defence
Again the snow-ball's compliments,
And reading in each missive tost
The charm with Eden never lost.

We heard once more the sleigh-bells' sound;
    And, following where the teamsters led,
The wise old Doctor went his round,
Just pausing at our door to say,
In the brief autocratic way

Of one who, prompt at Duty's call,
Was free to urge her claim on all,
   That some poor neighbor sick abed
At night our mother's aid would need.
For, one in generous thought and deed,
   What mattered in the sufferer's sight
   The Quaker matron's inward light,
The Doctor's mail of Calvin's creed?
All hearts confess the saints elect
   Who, twain in faith, in love agree,
And melt not in an acid sect
   The Christian pearl of charity!

So days went on: a week had passed
Since the great world was heard from last.
The Almanac we studied o'er,
Read and reread our little store
Of books and pamphlets, scarce a score;
One harmless novel, mostly hid
From younger eyes, a book forbid,
And poetry, (or good or bad,
A single book was all we had,)
Where Ellwood's meek, drab-skirted Muse,
   A stranger to the heathen Nine,
   Sang, with a somewhat nasal whine,
The wars of David and the Jews.
At last the floundering carrier bore
The village paper to our door.
Lo! broadening outward as we read,
To warmer zones the horizon spread
In panoramic length unrolled
We saw the marvels that it told.
Before us passed the painted Creeks,
   And daft McGregor on his raids
   In Costa Rica's everglades.
And up Taygetos winding slow
Rode Ypsilanti's Mainote Greeks,
A Turk's head at each saddle-bow!
Welcome to us its week-old news,
Its corner for the rustic Muse,
   Its monthly gauge of snow and rain,
Its record, mingling in a breath
The wedding bell and dirge of death:

Jest, anecdote, and love-lorn tale,
The latest culprit sent to jail;
Its hue and cry of stolen and lost,
Its vendue sales and goods at cost,
    And traffic calling loud for gain.
We felt the stir of hall and street,
The pulse of life that round us beat;
The chill embargo of the snow
Was melted in the genial glow;
Wide swung again our ice-locked door,
And all the world was ours once more!

Clasp, Angel of the backward look
    And folded wings of ashen gray
    And voice of echoes far away,
The brazen covers of they book;
The weird palimpsest old and vast,
Wherein thou hid'st the spectral past;
Where, closely mingling, pale and glow
The characters of joy and woe;
The monographs of outlived years,
Or smile-illumed or dim with tears,
    Green hills of life that slope to death,
And haunts of home, whose vistaed trees
Shade off to mournful cypresses
    With the white amaranths underneath
Even while I look, I can but heed
    The restless sands' incessant fall,
Importunate hours that hours succeed,
Each clamorous with its own sharp need,
    And duty keeping pace with all.
Shut down and clasp the heavy lids;
I hear again the voice that bids
The dreamer leave his dream midway
For larger hopes and graver fears:
Life greatens in these later years,
The century's aloe flowers to-day!

Yet, haply, in some lull of life,
Some Truce of God which breaks its strife,
The worldling's eyes shall gather dew,
    Dreaming in throngful city ways
Of winter joys his boyhood knew;

And dear and early friends—the few
Who yet remain—shall pause to view
   These Flemish pictures of old days;
Sit with me by the homestead hearth,
And stretch the hands of memory forth
   To warm them at the wood-fire's blaze!
And thanks untraced to lips unknown
Shall greet me like the odors blown
From unseen meadows newly mown,
Or lilies floating in some pond,
Wood-fringed, the wayside gaze beyond;
The traveller owns the grateful sense
Of sweetness near, he knows not whence,
And, pausing, takes with forehead bare
The benediction of the air.

Henry Wadsworth Longfellow

(1807–1882)

From THE SONG OF HIAWATHA

INTRODUCTION

Should you ask me, whence these stories?
   Whence these legends and traditions,
With the odors of the forest,
With the dew and damp of meadows,
With the curling smoke of wigwams,
With the rushing of great rivers,
With their frequent repetitions,
And their wild reverberations,
As of thunder in the mountains?
I should answer, I should tell you,
   "From the forests and the prairies,
From the great lakes of the Northland,
From the land of the Ojibways,
From the land of the Dacotahs,
From the mountains, moors, and fen-lands
Where the heron, the Shuh-shuh-gah,
Feeds among the reeds and rushes.
I repeat them as I heard them
From the lips of Nawadaha,
The musician, the sweet singer."
   Should you ask where Nawadaha
Found these songs so wild and wayward,
Found these legends and traditions,
I should answer, I should tell you,
"In the bird's-nests of the forest,
In the lodges of the beaver,
In the hoof-prints of the bison,
In the eyry of the eagle!
   "All the wild-fowl sang them to him,
In the moorlands and the fen-lands,
In the melancholy marshes;

Chetowaik, the plover, sang them,
Mahng, the loon, the wild-goose, Wawa,
The blue heron, the Shuh-shuh-gah,
And the grouse, the Mushkodasa!"
    If still further you should ask me,
Saying, "Who was Nawadaha?
Tell us of this Nawadaha,"
I should answer your inquiries
Straightway in such words as follow.
    "In the vale of Tawasentha,
In the green and silent valley,
By the pleasant water-courses,
Dwelt the singer Nawadaha.
Round about the Indian village
Spread the meadows and the cornfields,
And beyond them stood the forest,
Stood the groves of singing pinetrees,
Green in Summer, white in Winter,
Ever sighing, ever singing.
    "And the pleasant water-courses,
You could trace them through the valley,
By the rushing in the Spring-time,
By the alders in the Summer,
By the white fog in the Autumn,
By the black line in the Winter;
And beside them dwelt the singer,
In the vale of Tawasentha,
In the green and silent valley.
    "There he sang of Hiawatha,
Sang the Song of Hiawatha,
Sang his wondrous birth and being,
How he prayed and how he fasted,
How he lived, and toiled, and suffered,
That the tribes of men might prosper,
That he might advance his people!"
    Ye who love the haunts of Nature,
Love the sunshine of the meadow,
Love the shadow of the forest,
Love the wind among the branches,
And the rain-shower and the snowstorm,
And the rushing of great rivers
Through their palisades of pinetrees,

And the thunder in the mountains,
Whose innumerable echoes
Flap like eagles in their eyries;—
Listen to these wild traditions,
To this Song of Hiawatha!
  Ye who love a nation's legends,
Love the ballads of a people,
That like voices from afar off
Call to us to pause and listen,
Speak in tones so plain and childlike,
Scarcely can the ear distinguish
Whether they are sung or spoken;—
Listen to this Indian Legend,
To this Song of Hiawatha!
  Ye whose hearts are fresh and simple,
Who have faith in God and Nature,
Who believe that in all ages
Every human heart is human,
That in even savage bosoms
There are longings, yearnings, strivings
For the good they comprehend not,
That the feeble hands and helpless,
Groping blindly in the darkness,
Touch God's right hand in that darkness
And are lifted up and strengthened;—
Listen to this simple story,
To this Song of Hiawatha!
  Ye, who sometimes, in your rambles
Through the green lanes of the country,
Where the tangled barberry-bushes
Hang their tufts of crimson berries
Over stone walls gray with mosses,
Pause by some neglected graveyard,
For a while to muse, and ponder
On a half effaced inscription,
Written with little skill of song-craft,
Homely phrases, but each letter
Full of hope and yet of heart-break,
Full of all the tender pathos
Of the Here and the Hereafter;—
Stay and read this rude inscription,
Read this Song of Hiawatha!

MEZZO CAMMIN

Written at Boppard on the Rhine, August 25, 1842, just before
leaving for home.

Half of my life is gone, and I have let
    The years slip from me and have not fulfilled
The aspiration of my youth, to build
    Some tower of song with lofty parapet.
Not indolence, nor pleasure, nor the fret
    Of restless passions that would not be stilled,
    But sorrow, and a care that almost killed,
    Kept me from what I may accomplish yet;
Though, half-way up the hill, I see the Past
    Lying beneath me with its sounds and sights,—
    A city in the twilight dim and vast,
With smoking roofs, soft bells, and gleaming lights,—
    And hear above me on the autumnal blast
    The cataract of Death far thundering from the heights.

THE JEWISH CEMETERY AT NEWPORT

How strange it seems! These Hebrews in their graves,
    Close by the street of this fair seaport town,
Silent beside the never-silent waves,
    At rest in all this moving up and down!

The trees are white with dust, that o'er their sleep
    Wave their broad curtains in the south-wind's breath,
While underneath these leafy tents they keep
    The long, mysterious Exodus of Death.

And these sepulchral stones, so old and brown,
    That pave with level flags their burial-place,
Seem like the tablets of the Law, thrown down
    And broken by Moses at the mountain's base.

The very names recorded here are strange,
    Of foreign accent, and of different climes;

Alvares and Rivera interchange
  With Abraham and Jacob of old times.

"Blessed by God, for he created Death!"
  The mourners said, "and Death is rest and peace;"
Then added, in the certainty of faith,
  "And giveth Life that nevermore shall cease."

Closed are the portals of their Synagogue.
  No Psalms of David now the silence break,
No Rabbi reads the ancient Decalogue
  In the grand dialect the Prophets spake.

Gone are the living, but the dead remain,
  And not neglected; for a hand unseen,
Scattering its bounty, like a summer rain,
  Still keeps their graves and their remembrance green.

How came they here? What burst of Christian hate,
  What persecution, merciless and blind,
Drove o'er the sea—that desert desolate—
  These Ishmaels and Hagars of mankind?

They lived in narrow streets and lanes obscure,
  Ghetto and Judenstrass, in mirk and mire;
Taught in the school of patience to endure
  The life of anguish and the death of fire.

All their lives long, with the unleavened bread
  And bitter herbs of exile and its fears,
The wasting famine of the heart they fed,
  And slaked its thirst with marah of their tears.

Anathema maranatha! was the cry
  That rang from town to town, from street to street:
At every gate the accursed Mordecai
  Was mocked and jeered, and spurned by Christian feet.

Pride and humiliation hand in hand
  Walked with them through the world where'er they went;
Trampled and beaten were they as the sand,
  And yet unshaken as the continent.

For in the background figures vague and vast
   Of patriarchs and of prophets rose sublime,
And all the great traditions of the Past
   They saw reflected in the coming time.

And thus forever with reverted look
   The mystic volume of the world they read,
Spelling it backward, like a Hebrew book,
   Till life became a Legend of the Dead.

But ah! what once has been shall be no more!
   The groaning earth in travail and in pain
Brings forth its races, but does not restore,
   And the dead nations never rise again.

THE CROSS OF SNOW

In the long, sleepless watches of the night,
   A gentle face—the face of one long dead—
   Looks at me from the wall, where round its head
   The night-lamp casts a halo of pale light.
Here in this room she died; and soul more white
   Never through martyrdom of fire was led
   To its repose; nor can in books be read
   The legend of a life more benedight.
There is a mountain in the distant West
   That, sun-defying, in its deep ravines
   Displays a cross of snow upon its side.
Such is the cross I wear upon my breast
   These eighteen years, through all the changing scenes
   And seasons, changeless since the day she died.

SEAWEED

When descends on the Atlantic
   The gigantic
Storm-wind of the equinox,

Landward in his wrath he scourges
        The toiling surges,
Laden with seaweed from the rocks:

From Bermuda's reefs; from edges
        Of sunken ledges,
In some far-off, bright Azore;
From Bahama, and the dashing,
        Silver-flashing
Surges of San Salvador;

From the tumbling surf, that buries
        The Orkneyan skerries,
Answering the hoarse Hebrides;
And from wrecks of ships, and drifting
        Spars, uplifting
On the desolate, rainy seas;—

Ever drifting, drifting, drifting
        On the shifting
Currents of the restless main;
Till in sheltered coves, and reaches
        Of sandy beaches,
All have found repose again.

So when storms of wild emotion
        Strike the ocean
Of the poet's soul, ere long
From each cave and rocky fastness,
        In its vastness,
Floats some fragment of a song:

From the far-off isles enchanted,
        Heaven has planted
With the golden fruit of Truth;
From the flashing surf whose vision
        Gleams Elysian
In the tropic clime of Youth;

From the strong Will, and the Endeavour
        That for ever
Wrestles with the tides of Fate;

From the wreck of Hopes far-scattered,
    Tempest-shattered,
Floating waste and desolate;—

Ever drifting, drifting, drifting,
    On the shifting
Currents of the restless heart;
Till at length in books recorded,
    They, like hoarded
Household words, no more depart.

AFTERNOON IN FEBRUARY

The day is ending,
The night is descending;
The marsh is frozen,
    The river dead.

Through clouds like ashes,
The red sun flashes
On village windows
    That glimmer red.

The snow recommences;
The buried fences
Mark no longer
    The road o'er the plain;

While through the meadows,
Like fearful shadows,
Slowly passes
    A funeral train.

The bell is pealing,
And every feeling
Within me responds
    To the dismal knell;

Shadows are trailing,
My heart is bewailing
And tolling within
   Like a funeral bell.

THE ARROW AND THE SONG

I shot an arrow into the air,
It fell to earth, I knew not where;
For, so swiftly it flew, the sight
Could not follow it in its flight.

I breathed a song into the air,
It fell to earth, I knew not where;
For who has sight so keen and strong,
That it can follow the flight of song?

Long, long afterward, in an oak
I found the arrow, still unbroke;
And the song, from beginning to end,
I found again in the heart of a friend.

PAUL REVERE'S RIDE

Listen, my children, and you shall hear
Of the midnight ride of Paul Revere,
On the eighteenth of April, in Seventy-five;
Hardly a man is now alive
Who remembers that famous day and year.
He said to his friend, "If the British march
By land or sea from the town tonight,
Hang a lantern aloft in the belfry arch
Of the North Church tower as a signal light,—
One, if by land, and two, if by sea;
And I on the opposite shore will be,
Ready to ride and spread the alarm

Through every Middlesex village and farm,
  For the country folk to be up and to arm."

Then he said, "Good night!" and with muffled oar
Silently rowed to the Charlestown shore,
Just as the moon rose over the bay,
Where swinging wide at her moorings lay
The Somerset, British man-of-war;
A phantom ship, with each mast and spar
Across the moon like a prison bar,
And a huge black hulk, that was magnified
By its own reflection in the tide.
Meanwhile, his friend, through alley and street,
Wanders and watches with eager ears,
Till in the silence around him he hears
The muster of men at the barrack door,
The sound of arms, and the tramp of feet,
And the measured tread of the grenadiers,
Marching down to their boats on the shore.

Then he climbed the tower of the Old North Church,
By the wooden stairs, with stealthy tread,
To the belfry-chamber overhead,
And startled the pigeons from their perch
On the sombre rafters, that round him made
Masses and moving shapes of shade,—
By the trembling ladder, steep and tall,
To the highest window in the wall,
Where he paused to listen and look down
A moment on the roofs of the town,
And the moonlight flowing over all.

Beneath, in the churchyard, lay the dead,
In their night-encampment on the hill,
Wrapped in silence so deep and still
That he could hear, like a sentinel's tread,
The watchful night-wind, as it went
Creeping along from tent to tent,
And seeming to whisper, "All is well!"
A moment only he feels the spell
Of the place and the hour, and the secret dread
Of the lonely belfry and the dead;
For suddenly all his thoughts are bent

On a shadowy something far away,
Where the river widens to meet the bay,—
A line of black that bends and floats
On the rising tide, like a bridge of boats.

Meanwhile, impatient to mount and ride,
Booted and spurred, with a heavy stride
On the opposite shore walked Paul Revere.
Now he patted his horse's side,
Now gazed at the landscape far and near,
Then, impetuous, stamped the earth,
And turned and tightened his saddle-girth;
But mostly he watched with eager search
The belfry-tower of the Old North Church,
As it rose above the graves on the hill,
Lonely and spectral and sombre and still.
And lo! as he looks, on the belfry's height
A glimmer, and then a stream of light!
He springs to the saddle, the bridle he turns,
But lingers and gazes, till full on his sight
A second lamp in the belfry burns!

A hurry of hoofs in a village street,
A shape in the moonlight, a bulk in the dark,
And beneath, from the pebbles, in passing, a spark
Struck out by a steed flying fearless and fleet:
That was all! And yet, through the gloom and the light,
The fate of a nation was riding that night;
And the spark struck out by that steed, in his flight,
Kindled the land into flame with its heat.

He has left the village and mounted the steep,
And beneath him, tranquil and broad and deep,
Is the Mystic, meeting the ocean tides;
And under the alders that skirt its edge,
Now soft on the sand, now loud on the ledge,
Is heard the tramp of his steed as he rides.

It was twelve by the village clock,
When he crossed the bridge into Medford town.
He heard the crowing of the cock,
And the barking of the farmer's dog,
And felt the damp of the river fog,
That rises after the sun goes down.

It was one by the village clock,
When he galloped into Lexington.
He saw the gilded weathercock
Swim in the moonlight as he passed,
And the meeting-house windows, blank and bare,
Gaze at him with a spectral glare,
As if they already stood aghast
At the bloody work they would look upon.

It was two by the village clock,
When he came to the bridge in Concord town.
He heard the bleating of the flock,
And the twitter of birds among the trees,
And felt the breath of the morning breeze
Blowing over the meadows brown.
And one was safe and asleep in his bed
Who at the bridge would be first to fall,
Who that day would be lying dead,
Pierced by a British musket-ball.

You know the rest. In the books you have read,
How the British Regulars fired and fled,—
How the farmers gave them ball for ball,
From behind each fence and farmyard wall,
Chasing the red-coats down the lane,
Then crossing the fields to emerge again
Under the trees at the turn of the road,
And only pausing to fire and load.

So through the night rode Paul Revere;
And so through the night went his cry of alarm
To every Middlesex village and farm,—
A cry of defiance and not of fear,
A voice in the darkness, a knock at the door,
And a word that shall echo forevermore!
For, borne on the night-wind of the Past,
Through all our history, to the last,
In the hour of darkness and peril and need,
The people will waken and listen to hear
The hurrying hoof-beats of that steed,
And the midnight message of Paul Revere.

Lucretia Davidson

(1808 – 1825)

AMERICA

And this was once the realm of Nature, where
Wild as the wind, though exquisitely fair,
She breathed the mountain breeze, or bowed to kiss
The dimpling waters with unbounded bliss.
Here in this Paradise of earth, where first
Wild mountain Liberty began to burst,
Once Nature's temple rose in simple grace,
The hill her throne, the world her dwelling-place.
And where are now her lakes, so still and lone,
Her thousand streams with bending shrubs o'ergrown?
Where her dark cat'racts tumbling from on high,
With rainbow arch aspiring to the sky?
Her tow'ring pines with fadeless wreaths entwined,
Her waving alders streaming to the wind?
Nor these alone,—her own,—her fav'rite child,
All fire, all feeling; man untaught and wild;
Where can the lost, lone son of Nature stray?
For art's high car is rolling on its way;
A wand'rer of the world, he flies to drown
The thoughts of days gone by and pleasures flown
In the deep draught, whose dregs are death and woe,
With slavery's iron chain concealed below.
Once through the tangled wood, with noiseless tread
And throbbing heart, the lurking warrior sped,
Aimed his sure weapon, won the prize, and turned,
While his high heart with wild ambition burned
With song and war-whoop to his native tree,
There on its bark to carve the victory.
His all of learning did that act comprise,
But still in *nature's* volume doubly wise.

The wayward stream which once, with idle bound,
Whirled on resistless in its foaming round,
Now curbed by art flows on, a wat'ry chain

148

Linking the snow-capped mountains to the main.
Where once the alder in luxuriance grew,
Or the tall pine its towering branches threw
Abroad to heaven, with dark and haughty brow,
There mark the realms of plenty smiling now;
There the full sheaf of Ceres richly glows,
And Plenty's fountain blesses as it flows;
And man, a brute when left to wander wild,
A reckless creature, Nature's lawless child,
What boundless streams of knowledge rolling now
From the full hand of art around him flow!
Improvement strides the surge, while from afar
Learning rolls onward in her silver car;
Freedom unfurls her banner o'er his head,
While peace sleeps sweetly on her native bed.

The Muse arises from the wild-wood glen,
And chants her sweet and hallowed song again,
As in those halcyon days, which bards have sung,
When hope was blushing, and when life was young.
Thus shall she rise, and thus her sons shall rear
Her sacred temple *here*, and only *here*,
While Percival, her loved and chosen priest,
Forever blessing, though himself unblest,
Shall fan the fire that blazes at her shrine,
And charm the ear with numbers half divine.

Oliver Wendell Holmes

(1 8 0 9 – 1 8 9 4)

THE CHAMBERED NAUTILUS

This is the ship of pearl, which, poets feign,
   Sails the unshadowed main,—
   The venturous bark that flings
On the sweet summer wind its purpled wings
In gulfs enchanted, where the Siren sings,
   And coral reefs lie bare,
Where the cold sea-maids rise to sun their streaming hair.

Its webs of living gauze no more unfurl;
   Wrecked is the ship of pearl!
   And every chambered cell,
Where its dim dreaming life was wont to dwell,
As the frail tenant shaped his growing shell,
   Before thee lies revealed,—
Its irised ceiling rent, its sunless crypt unsealed!

Year after year beheld the silent toil
   That spread his lustrous coil;
   Still, as the spiral grew,
He left the past year's dwelling for the new,
Stole with soft step its shining archway through,
   Built up its idle door,
Stretched in his last-found home, and knew the old no more.

Thanks for the heavenly message brought by thee,
   Child of the wandering sea,
   Cast from her lap, forlorn!
From thy dead lips a clearer note is born
Than ever Triton blew from wreathèd horn!
   While on mine ear it rings,
Through the deep caves of thought I hear a voice that sings:—

Build thee more stately mansions, O my soul,
   As the swift seasons roll!

Leave thy low-vaulted past!
Let each new temple, nobler than the last,
Shut thee from heaven with a dome more vast,
    Till thou at length art free,
Leaving thine outgrown shell by life's unresting sea!

Edgar Allan Poe

(1809–1849)

TO HELEN

Helen, thy beauty is to me
  Like those Nicéan barks of yore,
That gently, o'er a perfumed sea,
  The weary, way-worn wanderer bore
  To his own native shore.

On desperate seas long wont to roam,
  Thy hyacinth hair, thy classic face,
Thy Naiad airs have brought me home
  To the glory that was Greece,
And the grandeur that was Rome.

Lo! in yon brilliant window-niche
  How statue-like I see thee stand,
  The agate lamp within thy hand!
Ah, Psyche, from the regions which
  Are Holy-Land!

THE CITY IN THE SEA

Lo! Death has reared himself a throne
In a strange city lying alone
Far down within the dim West,
Where the good and the bad and the worst and the best
Have gone to their eternal rest.
There shrines and palaces and towers
(Time-eaten towers that tremble not!)
Resemble nothing that is ours.
Around, by lifting winds forgot,
Resignedly beneath the sky
The melancholy waters lie.

No rays from the holy heaven come down
On the long night-time of that town;
But light from out the lurid sea
Streams up the turrets silently—
Gleams up the pinnacles far and free
Up domes—up spires—up kingly halls—
Up fanes—up Babylon-like walls—
Up shadowy long-forgotten bowers
Of sculptured ivy and stone flowers—
Up many and many a marvellous shrine
Whose wreathéd friezes intertwine
The viol, the violet, and the vine.

Resignedly beneath the sky
The melancholy waters lie.
So blend the turrets and shadows there
That all seem pendulous in air,
While from a proud tower in the town
Death looks gigantically down.

There open fanes and gaping graves
Yawn level with the luminous waves;
But not the riches there that lie
In each idol's diamond eye—
Not the gaily-jewelled dead
Tempt the waters from their bed;
For no ripples curl, alas!
Along that wilderness of glass—
No swellings tell that winds may be
Upon some far-off happier sea—
No heavings hint that winds have been
On seas less hideously serene.

But lo, a stir is in the air!
The wave—there is a movement there!
As if the towers had thrust aside,
In slightly sinking, the dull tide—
As if their tops had feebly given
A void within the filmy Heaven.
The waves have now a redder glow—
The hours are breathing faint and low—
And when, amid no earthly moans,
Down, down that town shall settle hence,

Hell, rising from a thousand thrones,
Shall do it reverence.

SONNET—SILENCE

There are some qualities—some incorporate things,
    That have a double life, which thus is made
A type of that twin entity which springs
    From matter and light, evinced in solid and shade.
There is a two-fold *Silence*—sea and shore—
    Body and Soul. One dwells in lonely places,
    Newly with grass o'ergrown; some solemn graces,
Some human memories and tearful lore,
Render him terrorless: his name's "No more."
He is the corporate Silence: dread him not!
    No power hath he of evil in himself;
But should some urgent fate (untimely lot!)
    Bring thee to meet his shadow (nameless elf,
That haunteth the lone regions where hath trod
No foot of man,) commend thyself to God!

THE RAVEN

Once upon a midnight dreary, while I pondered, weak and weary,
Over many a quaint and curious volume of forgotten lore—
While I nodded, nearly napping, suddenly there came a tapping,
As of some one gently rapping, rapping at my chamber door—
" 'Tis some visiter," I muttered, "tapping at my chamber door—
        Only this and nothing more."

Ah, distinctly I remember it was in the bleak December;
And each separate dying ember wrought its ghost upon the floor.
Eagerly I wished the morrow;—vainly I had sought to borrow
From my books surcease of sorrow—sorrow for the lost Lenore—
For the rare and radiant maiden whom the angels name Lenore—
        Nameless *here* for evermore.

And the silken, sad, uncertain rustling of each purple curtain
Thrilled me—filled me with fantastic terrors never felt before;
So that now, to still the beating of my heart, I stood repeating,
" 'Tis some visiter entreating entrance at my chamber door—
Some late visiter entreating entrance at my chamber door;—
          This it is and nothing more."

Presently my soul grew stronger; hesitating then no longer,
"Sir," said I, "or Madam, truly your forgiveness I implore;
But the fact is I was napping, and so gently you came rapping,
And so faintly you came tapping, tapping at my chamber door,
That I scarce was sure I heard you"—here I opened wide the door;—
          Darkness there and nothing more.

Deep into that darkness peering, long I stood there wondering, fearing,
Doubting, dreaming dreams no mortal ever dared to dream before;
But the silence was unbroken, and the stillness gave no token,
And the only word there spoken was the whispered word, "Lenore?"
This I whispered, and an echo murmured back the word "Lenore!"
          Merely this and nothing more.

Back into the chamber turning, all my soul within me burning,
Soon again I heard a tapping somewhat louder than before.
"Surely," said I, "surely that is something at my window lattice;
Let me see, then, what thereat is, and this mystery explore—
Let my heart be still a moment and this mystery explore;—
          'Tis the wind and nothing more!"

Open here I flung the shutter, when, with many a flirt and flutter,
In there stepped a stately Raven of the saintly days of yore:
Not the least obeisance made he; not a minute stopped or stayed he;
But, with mien of lord or lady, perched above my chamber door—
Perched upon a bust of Pallas just above my chamber door—
          Perched, and sat, and nothing more.

Then this ebony bird beguiling my sad fancy into smiling,
By the grave and stern decorum of the countenance it wore;
"Though thy crest be shorn and shaven, thou," I said, "art sure no craven,
Ghastly grim and ancient Raven wandering from the Nightly shore—
Tell me what thy lordly name is on the Night's Plutonian shore!"
          Quoth the Raven "Nevermore."

Much I marvelled this ungainly fowl to hear discourse so plainly,
Though its answer little meaning—little relevancy bore;

For we cannot help agreeing that no living human being
Ever yet was blessed with seeing bird above his chamber door—
Bird or beast upon the sculptured bust above his chamber door,
      With such name as "Nevermore."

But the Raven, sitting lonely on the placid bust, spoke only
That one word, as if his soul in that one word he did outpour.
Nothing farther then he uttered—not a feather then he fluttered—
Till I scarcely more than muttered "Other friends have flown before—
On the morrow *he* will leave me, as my Hopes have flown before."
      Then the bird said "Nevermore."

Startled at the stillness broken by reply so aptly spoken,
"Doubtless," said I, "what it utters is its only stock and store
Caught from some unhappy master whom unmerciful Disaster
Followed fast and followed faster till his songs one burden bore—
Till the dirges of his Hope that melancholy burden bore
      Of 'Never—nevermore.' "

But the Raven still beguiling my sad fancy into smiling,
Straight I wheeled a cushioned seat in front of bird, and bust and door;
Then, upon the velvet sinking, I betook myself to linking
Fancy unto fancy, thinking what this ominous bird of yore—
What this grim, ungainly, ghastly, gaunt, and ominous bird of yore
      Meant in croaking "Nevermore."

This I sat engaged in guessing, but no syllable expressing
To the fowl whose fiery eyes now burned into my bosom's core;
This and more I sat divining, with my head at ease reclining
On the cushion's velvet lining that the lamp-light gloated o'er,
But whose velvet-violet lining with the lamp-light gloating o'er,
      She shall press, ah, nevermore!

Then, methought, the air grew denser, perfumed from an unseen censer
Swung by seraphim whose foot-falls tinkled on the tufted floor.
"Wretch," I cried, "thy God hath lent thee—by these angels he hath sent thee
Respite—respite and nepenthe from thy memories of Lenore;
Quaff, oh quaff this kind nepenthe and forget this lost Lenore!"
      Quoth the Raven "Nevermore."

"Prophet!" said I, "thing of evil!—prophet still, if bird or devil!—
Whether Tempter sent, or whether tempest tossed thee here ashore,
Desolate yet all undaunted, on this desert land enchanted—

On this home by Horror haunted—tell me truly, I implore—
Is there—*is* there balm in Gilead?—tell me—tell me, I implore!"
            Quoth the Raven "Nevermore."

"Prophet!" said I, "thing of evil!—prophet still, if bird or devil!—
By that Heaven that bends above us—by that God we both adore—
Tell this soul with sorrow laden if, within the distant Aidenn,
It shall clasp a sainted maiden whom the angels name Lenore—
Clasp a rare and radiant maiden whom the angels name Lenore."
            Quoth the Raven "Nevermore."

"Be that word our sign of parting, bird or fiend!" I shrieked, upstarting—
"Get thee back into the tempest and the Night's Plutonian shore!
Leave no black plume as a token of that lie thy soul hath spoken!
Leave my loneliness unbroken!—quit the bust above my door!
Take thy beak from out my heart, and take thy form from off my door!"
            Quoth the Raven "Nevermore."

And the Raven, never flitting, still is sitting, *still* is sitting
On the pallid bust of Pallas just above my chamber door;
And his eyes have all the seeming of a demon's that is dreaming,
And the lamp-light o'er him streaming throws his shadow on the floor;
And my soul from out that shadow that lies floating on the floor
            Shall be lifted—nevermore!

ELDORADO

        Gaily bedight,
        A gallant knight,
In sunshine and in shadow,
        Had journeyed long,
        Singing a song,
In search of Eldorado.

        But he grew old—
        This knight so bold—
And o'er his heart a shadow
        Fell, as he found
        No spot of ground
That looked like Eldorado.

And, as his strength
    Failed him at length
He met a pilgrim shadow—
    "Shadow," said he,
    "Where can it be—
This land of Eldorado?"

    "Over the Mountains
    Of the Moon,
Down the Valley of the Shadow,
    Ride, boldly ride,"
    The shade replied,—
"If you seek for Eldorado!"

FOR ANNIE

Thank Heaven! the crisis—
    The danger is past,
And the lingering illness
    Is over at last—
And the fever called "Living"
    Is conquered at last.

Sadly, I know
    I am shorn of my strength,
And no muscle I move
    As I lie at full length—
But no matter!—I feel
    I am better at length.

And I rest so composedly,
    Now, in my bed,
That any beholder
    Might fancy me dead—
Might start at beholding me,
    Thinking me dead.

The moaning and groaning,
    The sighing and sobbing,

Are quieted now,
　　With that horrible throbbing
At heart:—ah, that horrible,
　　Horrible throbbing!

The sickness—the nausea—
　　The pitiless pain—
Have ceased, with the fever
　　That maddened my brain—
With the fever called "Living"
　　That burned in my brain.

And oh! of all tortures
　　That torture the worst
Has abated—the terrible
　　Torture of thirst
For the napthaline river
　　Of Passion accurst:—
I have drank of a water
　　That quenches all thirst:—

Of a water that flows,
　　With a lullaby sound,
From a spring but a very few
　　Feet under ground—
From a cavern not very far
　　Down under ground.

And ah! let it never
　　Be foolishly said
That my room it is gloomy
　　And narrow my bed;
For man never slept
　　In a different bed—
And, to *sleep*, you must slumber
　　In just such a bed.

My tantalized spirit
　　Here blandly reposes,
Forgetting, or never
　　Regretting its roses—
Its old agitations
　　Of myrtles and roses:

For now, while so quietly
   Lying, it fancies
A holier odor
   About it, of pansies—
A rosemary odor,
   Commingled with pansies—
With rue and the beautiful
   Puritan pansies.

And so it lies happily,
   Bathing in many
A dream of the truth
   And the beauty of Annie—
Drowned in a bath
   Of the tresses of Annie.

She tenderly kissed me,
   She fondly caressed,
And then I fell gently
   To sleep on her breast—
Deeply to sleep
   From the heaven of her breast.

When the light was extinguished,
   She covered me warm,
And she prayed to the angels
   To keep me from harm—
To the queen of the angels
   To shield me from harm.

And I lie so composedly,
   Now, in my bed,
(Knowing her love)
   That you fancy me dead—
And I rest so contentedly,
   Now in my bed,
(With her love at my breast)
   That you fancy me dead—
That you shudder to look at me,
   Thinking me dead:—

But my heart it is brighter
   Than all of the many

Stars in the sky,
    For it sparkles with Annie—
It glows with the light
    Of the love of my Annie—
With the thought of the light
    Of the eyes of my Annie.

ANNABEL LEE

It was many and many a year ago,
    In a kingdom by the sea,
That a maiden there lived whom you may know
    By the name of Annabel Lee;—
And this maiden she lived with no other thought
    Than to love and be loved by me.

She was a child and *I* was a child,
    In this kingdom by the sea,
But we loved with a love that was more than love—
    I and my Annabel Lee—
With a love that the wingéd seraphs of Heaven
    Coveted her and me.

And this was the reason that, long ago,
    In this kingdom by the sea,
A wind blew out of a cloud by night
    Chilling my Annabel Lee;
So that her highborn kinsmen came
    And bore her away from me,
To shut her up in a sepulchre
    In this kingdom by the sea.

The angels, not half so happy in Heaven,
    Went envying her and me:—
Yes! that was the reason (as all men know,
    In this kingdom by the sea)
That the wind came out of the cloud, chilling
    And killing my Annabel Lee.

But our love it was stronger by far than the love
   Of those who were older than we—
   Of many far wiser than we—
And neither the angels in Heaven above
   Nor the demons down under the sea
Can ever dissever my soul from the soul
   Of the beautiful Annabel Lee:—

For the moon never beams without bringing me dreams
   Of the beautiful Annabel Lee;
And the stars never rise but I see the bright eyes
   Of the beautiful Annabel Lee;
And so, all the night-tide, I lie down by the side
Of my darling, my darling, my life and my bride
   In her sepulchre there by the sea—
   In her tomb by the side of the sea.

Frances Sargent Osgood

(1811–1850)

WOMAN
A Fragment

Within a frame, more glorious than the gem
To which Titania could her sylph condemn,
Fair woman's spirit dreams the hours away,
Content at times in that bright home to stay,
So that you let her deck her beauty still,
And waltz and warble at her own sweet will.
    Taught to restrain, in cold Decorum's school,
The step, the smile, to glance and dance by rule;
To smooth alike her words and waving tress,
And her pure *heart's* impetuous play repress;
Each airy impulse—every frolic thought
Forbidden, if by Fashion's law untaught,
The graceful houri of your heavenlier hours
Forgets, in gay saloons, her native bowers,
Forgets her glorious home—her angel-birth—
Content to share the passing joys of earth;
Save when, at intervals, a ray of love
Pleads to her spirit from the realms above,
Plays on her pinions shut, and softly sings
In low Æolian tones of heavenly things.
    Ah! *then* dim memories dawn upon the soul
Of that celestial home from which she stole;
She feels its fragrant airs around her blow;
She sees the immortal bowers of beauty glow;
And faint and far, but how divinely sweet!
She hears the music where its angels meet.
    Then wave her starry wings in hope and shame,
Their fire illumes the fair, transparent frame,
Fills the dark eyes with passionate thought the while,
Blooms in the blush and lightens in the smile:
No longer then the toy, the doll, the slave,
But frank, heroic, beautiful, and brave,

She rises, radiant in immortal youth,
And wildly pleads for Freedom and for Truth!

These captive Peris all around you smile,
And one I've met who might a god beguile.
She's stolen from Nature all her loveliest spells:
Upon her cheek morn's blushing splendour dwells,
The starry midnight kindles in her eyes,
The gold of sunset on her ringlets lies,
And to the ripple of a rill, 'tis said,
She tuned her voice and timed her airy tread!
    No rule restrains *her* thrilling laugh, or moulds
Her flowing robe to tyrant Fashion's folds;
No custom chains the grace in that fair girl,
That sways her willowy form or waves her careless curl.
I plead not that she share each sterner task;
The cold reformers know not what they ask;
I only seek for our transplanted fay,
That she may have—in all *fair ways*—*her way!*
    I would not see the aerial creature trip,
A blooming sailor, up some giant ship,
Some man-of-war—to reef the topsail high—
Ah! reef your *curls*—and let the *canvas* fly!
    Nor would I bid her quit her 'broidery frame,
A fairy blacksmith by the forge's flame:
No! be the fires *she* kindles only those
With which man's iron nature wildly glows.
"Strike while the iron's hot," with all your art,
But strike *Love's* anvil in his yielding heart!
    Nor should our sylph her tone's low music strain,
A listening senate with her wit to chain,
To rival Choate in rich and graceful lore,
Or challenge awful Webster to the floor,
Like that rash wight who raised the casket's lid,
And set a genius free the stars that hid.
    Not thus forego the poetry of life,
The sacred names of mother, sister, wife!
Rob not the household hearth of all its glory,
Lose not those tones of musical delight,
All man has left, to tell him the sweet story
Of his remember'd home—beyond the night.
    Yet men too proudly use their tyrant power;
They chill the soft bloom of the fairy flower;

They bind the wing, that would but soar above
In search of purer air and holier love;
They hush the heart, that fondly pleads its wrong
In plaintive prayer or in impassion'd song.
    Smile on, sweet flower! soar on, enchanted wing!
Since she ne'er asks but for *one trifling thing*,
Since but *one* want disturbs the graceful fay,
Why *let* the docile darling *have—her way!*

ELLEN LEARNING TO WALK

My beautiful trembler! how wildly she shrinks!
    And how wistful she looks while she lingers!
Papa is extremely uncivil, she thinks,—
    She but pleaded for one of his fingers!

What eloquent pleading! the hand reaching out,
    As if doubting so strange a refusal;
While her blue eyes say plainly, "What is he about
    That he does not assist me as usual?"

Come on, my pet Ellen! we won't let you slip,—
    Unclasp those soft arms from his knee, love;
I see a faint smile round that exquisite lip,
    A smile half reproach and half glee, love.

So! that's my brave baby! one foot falters forward,
    Half doubtful the other steals by it!
What, shrinking again! why, you shy little coward!
    'Twon't kill you to walk a bit!—try it!

There! steady, my darling! huzza! I have caught her!
    I clasp her, caress'd and caressing!
And she hides her bright face, as if what we had taught her
    Were something to blush for—the blessing!

Now back again! Bravo! that shout of delight,
    How it thrills to the hearts that adore her!
Joy, joy for her mother! and blest be the night
    When her little light feet first upbore her!

AH! WOMAN STILL

Ah! woman still
Must veil the shrine,
Where feeling feeds the fire divine,
Nor sing at will,
Untaught by art,
The music prison'd in her heart!
Still gay the note,
And light the lay,
The woodbird warbles on the spray,
Afar to float;
But homeward flown,
Within his nest, how changed the tone!

Oh! none can know,
Who have not heard
The music-soul that thrills the bird,
The carol low
As coo of dove
He warbles to his woodland-love!
The world would say
'Twas vain and wild,
The impassion'd lay of Nature's child;
And Feeling so
Should veil the shrine
Where softly glow her fires divine!

Christopher Pearse Cranch

(1813 – 1892)

GNOSIS

Thought is deeper than all speech,
   Feeling deeper than all thought:
Souls to souls can never teach
   What unto themselves was taught.

We are spirits clad in veils;
   Man by man was never seen;
All our deep communing fails
   To remove the shadowy screen.

Heart to heart was never known;
   Mind with mind did never meet;
We are columns left alone
   Of a temple once complete.

Like the stars that gem the sky,
   Far apart though seeming near,
In our light we scattered lie;
   All is thus but starlight here.

What is social company
   But a babbling summer stream?
What our wise philosophy
   But the glancing of a dream?

Only when the Sun of Love
   Melts the scattered stars of thought,
Only when we live above
   What the dim-eyed world hath taught,

Only when our souls are fed
   By the Fount which gave them birth,
And by inspiration led
   Which they never drew from earth,

We, like parted drops or rain,
   Swelling till they meet and run,
Shall be all absorbed again,
   Melting, flowing into one.

THE PINES AND THE SEA

Beyond the low marsh-meadows and the beach,
Seen through the hoary trunks of windy pines,
The long blue level of the ocean shines.
The distant surf, with hoarse, complaining speech,
Out from its sandy barrier seems to reach;
And while the sun behind the woods declines,
The moaning sea with sighing boughs combines,
And waves and pines make answer, each to each.
O melancholy soul, whom far and near,
In life, faith, hope, the same sad undertone
Pursues from thought to thought! thou needs must hear
An old refrain, too much, too long thine own:
'Tis thy mortality infects thine ear;
The mournful strain was in thyself alone.

Jones Very

(1817 – 1862)

THE COLUMBINE

Still, still my eye will gaze long fixed on thee,
Till I forget that I am called a man,
And at thy side fast-rooted seem to be,
And the breeze comes my cheek with thine to fan.
Upon this craggy hill our life shall pass,
A life of summer days and summer joys,
Nodding our honey-bells mid pliant grass
In which the bee half hid his time employs;
And here we'll drink with thirsty pores the rain,
And turn dew-sprinkled to the rising sun,
And look when in the flaming west again
His orb across the heaven its path has run;
Here left in darkness on the rocky steep,
My weary eyes shall close like folding flowers in sleep.

I WAS SICK AND IN PRISON

Thou hast not left the rough-barked tree to grow
Without a mate upon the river's bank;
Nor dost Thou on one flower the rain bestow,
But many a cup the glittering drops has drank;
The bird must sing to one who sings again,
Else would her note less welcome be to hear;
Nor hast Thou bid thy word descend in vain,
But soon some answering voice shall reach my ear;
Then shall the brotherhood of peace begin,
And the new song be raised that never dies,
That shall the soul from death and darkness win,
And burst the prison where the captive lies;
And one by one new-born shall join the strain,
Till earth restores her sons to heaven again.

THE LAMENT OF THE FLOWERS

I looked to find Spring's early flowers,
    In spots where they were wont to bloom;
But they had perished in their bowers;
    The haunts they loved had proved their tomb!

The alder, and the laurel green,
    Which sheltered them, had shared their fate;
And but the blackened ground was seen,
    Where hid their swelling buds of late.

From the bewildered, homeless bird,
    Whose half-built nest the flame destroys,
A low complaint of wrong I heard,
    Against the thoughtless, ruthless boys.

Sadly I heard its notes complain,
    And ask the young its haunts to spare;
Prophetic seemed the sorrowing strain,
    Sung o'er its home, but late so fair!

"No more with hues like ocean shell
    The delicate wind-flower here shall blow;
The spot that loved its form so well
    Shall ne'er again its beauty know.

"Or, if it bloom, like some pale ghost
    'T will haunt the black and shadeless dell,
Where once it bloomed a numerous host,
    Of its once pleasant bowers to tell.

"And coming years no more shall find
    The laurel green upon the hills;
The frequent fire leaves naught behind,
    But e'en the very roots it kills.

"No more upon the turnpike's side
    The rose shall shed its sweet perfume;
The traveler's joy, the summer's pride,
    Will share with them a common doom.

"No more shall these returning fling
   Round childhood's home a heavenly charm,
With song of bird in early spring,
   To glad the heart and save from harm."

NATURE

The bubbling brook doth leap when I come by,
Because my feet find measure with its call;
The birds know when the friend they love is nigh,
For I am known to them, both great and small;
The flower that on the lovely hill-side grows
Expects me there when spring its bloom has given;
And many a tree and bush my wanderings knows,
And e'en the clouds and silent stars of heaven;
For he who with his Maker walks aright,
Shall be their lord as Adam was before;
His ear shall catch each sound with new delight,
Each object wear the dress that then it wore;
And he, as when erect in soul he stood,
Hear from his Father's lips that all is good.

THE SUMACH LEAVES

Some autumn leaves a painter took,
   And with his colors caught their hues;
So true to nature did they look
   That none to praise them could refuse.

The yellow mingling with the red
   Shone beauteous in their bright decay,
And round a golden radiance shed,
   Like that which hangs o'er parting day.

Their sister leaves, that, fair as these,
   Thus far had shared a common lot,

All soiled and scattered by the breeze
  Are now by every one forgot.

Soon, trodden under foot of men,
  Their very forms will cease to be,
Nor they remembered be again,
  Till Autumn decks once more the tree.

But these shall still their beauty boast,
  To praise the painter's wondrous art,
When Autumn's glories all are lost
  And with the fading year depart;

And through the wintry months so pale
  The sumach's brilliant hues recall;
Where, waving over hill and vale,
  They gave its splendor to our fall.

Henry David Thoreau

(1 8 1 7 – 1 8 6 2)

INSPIRATION

Whate'er we leave to God, God does,
　　And blesses us;
The work we choose should be our own,
　　God lets alone.

If with light head erect I sing,
　　Though all the muses lend their force,
From my poor love of anything,
　　The verse is weak and shallow as its source.

But if with bended neck I grope,
　　Listening behind me for my wit,
With faith superior to hope,
　　More anxious to keep back than forward it,

Making my soul accomplice there
　　Unto the flame my heart hath lit,
Then will the verse forever wear,—
　　Time cannot bend the line which God hath writ.

Always the general show of things
　　Floats in review before my mind,
And such true love and reverence brings,
　　That sometimes I forget that I am blind.

But now there comes unsought, unseen,
　　Some clear, divine electuary,
And I who had but sensual been,
　　Grow sensible, and as God is, am wary.

I hearing get who had but ears,
　　And sight, who had but eyes before,
I moments live who lived but years,
　　And truth discern who knew but learning's lore.

I hear beyond the range of sound,
    I see beyond the range of sight,
New earths and skies and seas around,
    And in my day the sun doth pale his light.

A clear and ancient harmony
    Pierces my soul through all its din,
As through its utmost melody,—
    Farther behind than they—farther within.

More swift its bolt than lightning is,
    Its voice than thunder is more loud,
It doth expand my privacies
    To all, and leave me single in the crowd.

It speaks with such authority,
    With so serene and lofty tone,
That idle Time runs gadding by,
    And leaves me with Eternity alone.

Then chiefly is my natal hour,
    And only then my prime of life,
Of manhood's strength it is the flower,
    'Tis peace's end and war's beginning strife.

'T 'hath come in summer's broadest noon,
    By a grey wall or some chance place,
Unseasoned time, insulted June,
    And vexed the day with its presuming face.

Such fragrance round my couch it makes,
    More rich than are Arabian drugs,
That my soul scents its life and wakes
    The body up beneath its perfumed rugs.

Such is the Muse—the heavenly maid,
    The star that guides our mortal course,
Which shows where life's true kernel's laid,
    Its wheat's fine flower, and its undying force.

She with one breath attunes the spheres,
    And also my poor human heart,
With one impulse propels the years
    Around, and gives my throbbing pulse its start.

I will not doubt forever more,
   Nor falter from a steadfast faith,
For though the system be turned o'er,
   God takes not back the word which once he saith.

I will then trust the love untold
   Which not my worth nor want has bought,
Which wooed me young and woos me old,
   And to this evening hath me brought.

My memory I'll educate
   To know the one historic truth,
Remembering to the latest date
   The only true and sole immortal youth.

Be but thy inspiration given,
   No matter through what danger sought,
I'll fathom hell or climb to heaven,
   And yet esteem that cheap which love has bought.

      Fame cannot tempt the bard
        Who's famous with his God,
      Nor laurel him reward
        Who hath his Maker's nod.

I AM A PARCEL OF VAIN STRIVINGS TIED

I am a parcel of vain strivings tied
    By a chance bond together,
  Dangling this way and that, their links
    Were made so loose and wide,
      Methinks,
    For milder weather.

A bunch of violets without their roots,
    And sorrel intermixed,
  Encircled by a wisp of straw
    Once coiled about their shoots,
      The law
    By which I'm fixed.

A nosegay which Time clutched from out
    Those fair Elysian fields,
  With weeds and broken stems, in haste,
    Doth make the rabble rout
      That waste
    The day he yields.

And here I bloom for a short hour unseen,
    Drinking my juices up,
  With no root in the land
    To keep my branches green,
      But stand
    In a bare cup.

Some tender buds were left upon my stem
    In mimicry of life,
  But ah! the children will not know,
    Till time has withered them,
      The woe
    With which they're rife.

But now I see I was not plucked for naught,
    And after in life's vase
  Of glass set while I might survive,
    But by a kind hand brought
      Alive
    To a strange place.

That stock thus thinned will soon redeem its hours,
    And by another year,
  Such as God knows, with freer air,
    More fruits and fairer flowers
      Will bear,
    While I droop here.

LIGHT-WINGED SMOKE, ICARIAN BIRD

Light-winged Smoke, Icarian bird,
Melting thy pinions in thy upward flight,
Lark without song, and messenger of dawn,
Circling above the hamlets as thy nest;

Or else, departing dream, and shadowy form
Of midnight vision, gathering up thy skirts;
By night star-veiling, and by day
Darkening the light and blotting out the sun;
Go thou my incense upward from this hearth,
And ask the gods to pardon this clear flame.

WITHIN THE CIRCUIT OF THIS PLODDING LIFE

Within the circuit of this plodding life
There enter moments of an azure hue,
Untarnished fair as is the violet
Or anemone, when the spring strews them
By some meandering rivulet, which make
The best philosophy untrue that aims
But to console man for his grievances.
I have remembered when the winter came,
High in my chamber in the frosty nights,
When in the still light of the cheerful moon,
On every twig and rail and jutting spout,
The icy spears were adding to their length
Against the arrows of the coming sun,
How in the shimmering noon of summer past
Some unrecorded beam slanted across
The upland pastures where the Johnswort grew;
Or heard, amid the verdure of my mind,
The bee's long smothered hum, on the blue flag
Loitering amidst the mead; or busy rill,
Which now through all its course stands still and dumb
Its own memorial,—purling at its play
Along the slopes, and through the meadows next,
Until its youthful sound was hushed at last
In the staid current of the lowland stream;
Or seen the furrows shine but late upturned,
And where the fieldfare followed in the rear,
When all the fields around lay bound and hoar
Beneath a thick integument of snow.
So by God's cheap economy made rich
To go upon my winter's task again.

William Ellery Channing

(1818–1901)

From A POET'S HOPE

Lady, there is a hope that all men have,—
Some mercy for their faults, a grassy place
To rest in, and a flower-strown, gentle grave;
Another hope which purifies our race,
That, when that fearful bourne forever past,
They may find rest,—and rest so long to last.

I seek it not, I ask no rest for ever,
My path is onward to the farthest shores,—
Upbear me in your arms, unceasing river,
That from the soul's clear fountain swiftly pours,
Motionless not, until the end is won,
Which now I feel hath scarcely felt the sun.

To feel, to know, to soar unlimited
Mid throngs of light-winged angels sweeping far,
And pore upon the realms unvisited
That tessellate the unseen, unthought star,—
To be the thing that now I feebly dream,
Flashing within my faintest, deepest gleam.

Ah! caverns of my soul! how thick your shade,
Where flows that life by which I faintly see:—
Wave your bright torches, for I need your aid,
Golden-eyed demons of my ancestry!
Your son though blinded hath a light within,
A heavenly fire which ye from suns did win.

And, lady, in thy hope my life will rise
Like the air-voyager, till I upbear
These heavy curtains of my filmy eyes
Into a lighter, more celestial air:
A mortal's hope shall bear me safely on,
Till I the higher region shall have won.

James Russell Lowell

(1819–1891)

TO THE DANDELION

Dear common flower, that grow'st beside the way
Fringing the dusty road with harmless gold,
　First pledge of blithesome May,
Which children pluck, and, full of pride uphold,
　High-hearted buccaneers, o'erjoyed that they
An Eldorado in the grass have found,
Which not the rich earth's ample round
May match in wealth, thou art more dear to me
Than all the prouder summer-blooms may be.

Gold such as thine ne'er drew the Spanish prow
Through the primeval hush of Indian seas,
　Nor wrinkled the lean brow
Of age, to rob the lover's heart of ease;
　'Tis the Spring's largess, which she scatters now.
To rich and poor alike, with lavish hand,
Though most hearts never understand
To take it at God's value, but pass by
The offered wealth with unrewarded eye.

Thou art my tropics and mine Italy;
To look at thee unlocks a warmer clime;
　The eyes thou givest me
Are in the heart, and heed not space or time:
　Not in mid June the golden-cuirassed bee
Feels a more summer-like warm ravishment
In the white lily's breezy tent,
His fragrant Sybaris, than I, when first
From the dark green thy yellow circles burst.

Then think I of deep shadows on the grass,
Of meadows where in sun the cattle graze,
　Where, as the breezes pass,

179

The gleaming rushes lean a thousand ways,
   Of leaves that slumber in a cloudy mass,
Or whiten in the wind, of waters blue
That from the distance sparkle through
Some woodland gap, and of a sky above,
Where one white cloud like a stray lamb doth move.

   My childhood's earliest thoughts are linked with thee;
The sight of thee calls back the robin's song,
   Who, from the dark old tree
Beside the door, sang clearly all day long,
   And I, secure in childish piety,
Listened as if I heard an angel sing
With news from heaven, which he could bring
Fresh every day to my untainted ears
When birds and flowers and I were happy peers.

   How like a prodigal doth nature seem,
When thou, for all thy gold, so common art!
   Thou teachest me to deem
More sacredly of every human heart,
   Since each reflects in joy its scanty gleam
Of heaven, and could some wondrous secret show,
Did we but pay the love we owe,
And with a child's undoubting wisdom look
On all these living pages of God's book.

Walt Whitman

(1819 – 1892)

ONE'S-SELF I SING

One's-Self I sing, a simple separate person,
Yet utter the word Democratic, the word En-Masse.

Of physiology from top to toe I sing,
Not physiognomy alone nor brain alone is worthy for the Muse, I say the
   Form complete is worthier far,
The Female equally with the Male I sing.

Of Life immense in passion, pulse, and power,
Cheerful, for freest action form'd under the laws divine,
The Modern Man I sing.

From SONG OF MYSELF

    1

I celebrate myself, and sing myself,
And what I assume you shall assume,
For every atom belonging to me as good belongs to you.

I loafe and invite my soul,
I lean and loafe at my ease observing a spear of summer grass.

My tongue, every atom of my blood, form'd from this soil, this air,
Born here of parents born here from parents the same, and their parents the
    same,
I, now thirty-seven years old in perfect health begin,
Hoping to cease not till death.

Creeds and schools in abeyance,
Retiring back a while sufficed at what they are, but never forgotten,
I harbor for good or bad, I permit to speak at every hazard,
Nature without check with original energy.

2

Houses and rooms are full of perfumes, the shelves are crowded with perfumes,
I breathe the fragrance myself and know it and like it,
The distillation would intoxicate me also, but I shall not let it.

The atmosphere is not a perfume, it has no taste of the distillation, it is
    odorless,
It is for my mouth forever, I am in love with it,
I will go to the bank by the wood and become undisguised and naked,
I am mad for it to be in contact with me.
The smoke of my own breath,
Echoes, ripples, buzz'd whispers, love-root, silk-thread, crotch and vine,
My respiration and inspiration, the beating of my heart, the passing of blood
    and air through my lungs,
The sniff of green leaves and dry leaves, and of the shore and dark-color'd sea-
    rocks, and of hay in the barn,
The sound of the belch'd words of my voice loos'd to the eddies of the wind,
A few light kisses, a few embraces, a reaching around of arms,
The play of shine and shade on the trees as the supple boughs wag,
The delight alone or in the rush of the streets, or along the fields and hill-sides,
The feeling of health, the full-noon trill, the song of me rising from bed and
    meeting the sun.

Have you reckon'd a thousand acres much? have you reckon'd the earth much?
Have you practis'd so long to learn to read?
Have you felt so proud to get at the meaning of poems?

Stop this day and night with me and you shall possess the origin of all poems,
You shall possess the good of the earth and sun, (there are millions of suns
    left,)
You shall no longer take things at second or third hand, nor look through the
    eyes of the dead, nor feed on the spectres in books,
You shall not look through my eyes either, nor take things from me,
You shall listen to all sides and filter them from yourself.

3

I have heard what the talkers were talking, the talk of the beginning and the
    end,
But I do not talk of the beginning or the end.

There was never any more inception than there is now,
Nor any more youth or age than there is now,

And will never be any more perfection than there is now,
Nor any more heaven or hell than there is now.

Urge and urge and urge,
Always the procreant urge of the world.

Out of the dimness opposite equals advance, always substance and increase,
    always sex,
Always a knit of identity, always distinction, always a breed of life.

To elaborate is no avail, learn'd and unlearn'd feel that it is so.

Sure as the most certain sure, plumb in the uprights, well entretied, braced in
    the beams,
Stout as a horse, affectionate, haughty, electrical,
I and this mystery here we stand.

Clear and sweet is my soul, and clear and sweet is all that is not my soul.

Lack one lacks both, and the unseen is proved by the seen,
Till that becomes unseen and receives proof in its turn.

Showing the best and dividing it from the worst, age vexes age,
Knowing the perfect fitness and equanimity of things, while they discuss I am
    silent, and go bathe and admire myself.

Welcome is every organ and attribute of me, and of any man hearty and clean,
Not an inch nor a particle of an inch is vile, and none shall be less familiar
    than the rest.

I am satisfied—I see, dance, laugh, sing;
As the hugging and loving bed-fellow sleeps at my side through the night, and
    withdraws at the peep of the day with stealthy tread,
Leaving me baskets cover'd with white towels swelling the house with their
    plenty,
Shall I postpone my acceptation and realization and scream at my eyes,
That they turn from gazing after and down the road,
And forthwith cipher and show me to a cent,
Exactly the value of one and exactly the value of two, and which is ahead?

4

Trippers and askers surround me,
People I meet, the effect upon me of my early life or the ward and city I live in,
    or the nation,

The latest dates, discoveries, inventions, societies, authors old and new,
My dinner, dress, associates, looks, compliments, dues,
The real or fancied indifference of some man or woman I love,
The sickness of one of my folks or of myself, or ill-doing or loss or lack of
  money, or depressions or exaltations,
Battles, the horrors of fratricidal war, the fever of doubtful news, the fitful events;
These come to me days and nights and go from me again,
But they are not the Me myself.

Apart from the pulling and hauling stands what I am,
Stands amused, complacent, compassionating, idle, unitary,
Looks down, is erect, or bends an arm on an impalpable certain rest,
Looking with side-curved head curious what will come next,
Both in and out of the game and watching and wondering at it.

Backward I see in my own days where I sweated through fog with linguists and
  contenders,
I have no mockings or arguments, I witness and wait.

  5

I believe in you my soul, the other I am must not abase itself to you,
And you must not be abased to the other.

Loafe with me on the grass, loose the stop from your throat,
Not words, not music or rhyme I want, not custom or lecture, not even the
  best,
Only the lull I like, the hum of your valvèd voice.

I mind how once we lay such a transparent summer morning,
How you settled your head athwart my hips and gently turn'd over upon me.
And parted the shirt from my bosom-bone, and plunged your tongue to my
  bare-stript heart,
And reach'd till you felt my beard, and reach'd till you held my feet.

Swiftly arose and spread around me the peace and knowledge that pass all the
  argument of the earth,
And I know that the hand of God is the promise of my own,
And I know that the spirit of God is the brother of my own,
And that all the men ever born are also my brothers, and the women my sisters
  and lovers,
And that a kelson of the creation is love,
And limitless are leaves stiff or drooping in the fields,

And brown ants in the little wells beneath them,
And mossy scabs of the worm fence, heap'd stones, elder, mullein and poke-weed.

6

A child said *What is the grass?* fetching it to me with full hands;
How could I answer the child? I do not know what it is any more than he.

I guess it must be the flag of my disposition, out of hopeful green stuff woven.

Or I guess it is the handkerchief of the Lord,
A scented gift and remembrancer designedly dropt,
Bearing the owner's name someway in the corners, that we may see and
    remark, and say *Whose?*

Or I guess the grass is itself a child, the produced babe of the vegetation.

Or I guess it is a uniform hieroglyphic,
And it means, Sprouting alike in broad zones and narrow zones,
Growing among black folks as among white,
Kanuck, Tuckahoe, Congressman, Cuff, I give them the same, I receive them
    the same.

And now it seems to me the beautiful uncut hair of graves.

Tenderly will I use you curling grass,
It may be you transpire from the breasts of young men,
It may be if I had known them I would have loved them,
It may be you are from old people, or from offspring taken soon out of their
    mothers' laps,
And here you are the mothers' laps.

This grass is very dark to be from the white heads of old mothers,
Darker than the colorless beards of old men,
Dark to come from under the faint red roofs of mouths.

O I perceive after all so many uttering tongues,
And I perceive they do not come from the roofs of mouths for nothing.

I wish I could translate the hints about the dead young men and women,
And the hints about old men and mothers, and the offspring taken soon out of
    their laps.

What do you think has become of the young and old men?
And what do you think has become of the women and children?
They are alive and well somewhere,
The smallest sprout shows there is really no death,
And if ever there was it led forward life, and does not wait at the end to arrest
    it,
And ceas'd the moment life appear'd.

All goes onward and outward, nothing collapses,
And to die is different from what any one supposed, and luckier.

        7

Has any one supposed it lucky to be born?
I hasten to inform him or her it is just as lucky to die, and I know it.

I pass death with the dying and birth with the new-wash'd babe, and am not
    contain'd between my hat and boots,
And peruse manifold objects, no two alike and every one good,
The earth good and the stars good, and their adjuncts all good.

I am not an earth nor an adjunct of an earth,
I am the mate and companion of people, all just as immortal and fathomless as
    myself,
(They do not know how immortal, but I know.)

Every kind for itself and its own, for me mine male and female,
For me those that have been boys and that love women,
For me the man that is proud and feels how it stings to be slighted,
For me the sweet-heart and the old maid, for me mothers and the mothers of
    mothers,
For me lips that have smiled, eyes that have shed tears,
For me children and the begetters of children.

Undrape! you are not guilty to me, nor stale nor discarded,
I see through the broadcloth and gingham whether or no,
And am around, tenacious, acquisitive, tireless, and cannot be shaken away.

        8

The little one sleeps in its cradle,
I lift the gauze and look a long time, and silently brush away flies with my
    hand.

The youngster and the red-faced girl turn aside up the busy hill,
I peeringly view them from the top.

The suicide sprawls on the bloody floor of the bedroom,
I witness the corpse with its dabbled hair, I note where the pistol has fallen.

The blab of the pave, tires of carts, sluff of boot-soles, talk of the promenaders,
The heavy omnibus, the driver with his interrogating thumb, the clank of the
    shod horses on the granite floor,
The snow-sleighs, clinking, shouted jokes, pelts of snow-balls,
The hurrahs for popular favorites, the fury of rous'd mobs,
The flap of the curtain'd litter, a sick man inside borne to the hospital,
The meeting of enemies, the sudden oath, the blows and fall,
The excited crowd, the policeman with his star quickly working his passage to
    the centre of the crowd,
The impassive stones that receive and return so many echoes,
What groans of over-fed or half-starv'd who fall sunstruck or in fits,
What exclamations of women taken suddenly who hurry home and give birth
    to babes,
What living and buried speech is always vibrating here, what howls restrain'd
    by decorum,
Arrests of criminals, slights, adulterous offers made, acceptances, rejections
    with convex lips,
I mind them or the show or resonance of them—I come and I depart.

      9

The big doors of the country barn stand open and ready,
The dried grass of the harvest-time loads the slow-drawn wagon,
The clear light plays on the brown gray and green intertinged,
The armfuls are pack'd to the sagging mow.

I am there, I help, I came stretch'd atop of the load,
I felt its soft jolts, one leg reclined on the other,
I jump from the cross-beams and seize the clover and timothy,
And roll head over heels and tangle my hair full of wisps.

          *   *   *

      11

Twenty-eight young men bathe by the shore,
Twenty-eight young men and all so friendly;
Twenty-eight years of womanly life and all so lonesome.

She owns the fine house by the rise of the bank,
She hides handsome and richly drest aft the blinds of the window.

Which of the young men does she like the best?
Ah the homeliest of them is beautiful to her.

Where are you off to, lady? for I see you,
You splash in the water there, yet stay stock still in your room.

Dancing and laughing along the beach came the twenty-ninth bather,
The rest did not see her, but she saw them and loved them.

The beards of the young men glisten'd with wet, it ran from their long hair,
Little streams pass'd all over their bodies.

An unseen hand also pass'd over their bodies,
It descended tremblingly from their temples and ribs.

The young men float on their backs, their white bellies bulge to the sun, they
    do not ask who seizes fast to them,
They do not know who puffs and declines with pendant and bending arch,
They do not think whom they souse with spray.

     *   *   *

14

The wild gander leads his flock through the cool night,
Ya-honk he says, and sounds it down to me like an invitation,
The pert may suppose it meaningless, but I listening close,
Find its purpose and place up there toward the wintry sky.

The sharp-hoof'd moose of the north, the cat on the house-sill, the chickadee,
    the prairie dog,
The litter of the grunting sow as they tug at her teats,
The brood of the turkey-hen and she with her half-spread wings,
I see in them and myself the same old law.

The press of my foot to the earth springs a hundred affections,
They scorn the best I can do to relate them.
I am enamour'd of growing out-doors,
Of men that live among cattle or taste of the ocean or woods,

Of the builders and steerers of ships and the wielders of axes and mauls, and
    the drivers of horses,
I can eat and sleep with them week in and week out.

What is commonest, cheapest, nearest, easiest, is Me,
Me going in for my chances, spending for vast returns,
Adorning myself to bestow myself on the first that will take me,
Not asking the sky to come down to my good will,
Scattering it freely forever.

       *   *   *

20

Who goes there? hankering, gross, mystical, nude;
How is it I extract strength from the beef I eat?
What is a man anyhow? what am I? what are you?

All I mark as my own you shall offset it with your own,
Else it were time lost listening to me.

I do not snivel that snivel the world over,
That months are vacuums and the ground but wallow and filth.

Whimpering and truckling fold with powders for invalids, conformity, goes to
    the fourth-remov'd,
I wear my hat as I please indoors or out.

Why should I pray? why should I venerate and be ceremonious?

Having pried through the strata, analyzed to a hair, counsel'd with doctors and
    calculated close,
I find no sweeter fat than sticks to my own bones.

In all people I see myself, none more and not one a barley-corn less,
And the good or bad I say of myself I say of them.

I know I am solid and sound,
To me the converging objects of the universe perpetually flow,
All are written to me, and I must get what the writing means.

I know I am deathless,
I know this orbit of mine cannot be swept by a carpenter's compass,
I know I shall not pass like a child's carlacue cut with a burnt stick at night.

I know I am august,
I do not trouble my spirit to vindicate itself or be understood,
I see that the elementary laws never apologize,
(I reckon I behave no prouder than the level I plant my house by, after all.)

I exist as I am, that is enough,
If no other in the world be aware I sit content,
And if each and all be aware I sit content.

One world is aware and by far the largest to me, and that is myself,
And whether I come to my own to-day or in ten thousand or ten million years,
I can cheerfully take it now, or with equal cheerfulness I can wait.
My foothold is tenon'd and mortis'd in granite,
I laugh at what you call dissolution,
And I know the amplitude of time.

21

I am the poet of the Body and I am the poet of the Soul,
The pleasures of heaven are with me and the pains of hell are with me,
The first I graft and increase upon myself, the latter I translate into a new
        tongue.

I am the poet of the woman the same as the man,
And I say it is as great to be a woman as to be a man,
And I say there is nothing greater than the mother of men.

I chant the chant of dilation or pride,
We have had ducking and deprecating about enough,
I show that size is only development.

Have you outstript the rest? are you the President?
It is a trifle, they will more than arrive there every one, and still pass on.

I am he that walks with the tender and growing night,
I call to the earth and sea half-held by the night.

Press close bare-bosom'd night—press close magnetic nourishing night!
Night of south winds—night of the large few stars!
Still nodding night—mad naked summer night.

Smile O voluptuous cool-breath'd earth!
Earth of the slumbering and liquid trees!

Earth of departed sunset—earth of the mountains misty-topt!
Earth of the vitreous pour of the full moon just tinged with blue!
Earth of shine and dark mottling the tide of the river!
Earth of the limpid gray of clouds brighter and clearer for my sake!
Far-swooping elbow'd earth—rich apple blossom'd earth!
Smile, for your lover comes.

Prodigal, you have given me love—therefore I to you give love!
O unspeakable passionate love.

         *   *   *

24

Walt Whitman, a kosmos, of Manhattan the son,
Turbulent, fleshy, sensual, eating, drinking and breeding,
No sentimentalist, no stander above men and women or apart from them,
No more modest than immodest.

Unscrew the locks from the doors!
Unscrew the doors themselves from their jambs!

Whoever degrades another degrades me,
And whatever is done or said returns at last to me.

Through me the afflatus surging and surging, through me the current and index.

I speak the pass-word primeval, I give the sign of democracy,
By God! I will accept nothing which all cannot have their counterpart of on the
    same terms.

Through me many long dumb voices,
Voices of the interminable generations of prisoners and slaves,
Voices of the diseas'd and despairing and of thieves and dwarfs,
Voices of cycles of preparation and accretion,
And of the threads that connect the stars, and of wombs and of the father-stuff,
And of the rights of them the others are down upon,
Of the deform'd, trivial, flat, foolish, despised,
Fog in the air, beetles rolling balls of dung.

Through me forbidden voices,
Voices of sexes and lusts, voices veil'd and I remove the veil,
Voices indecent by me clarified and transfigur'd.

I do not press my fingers across my mouth,
I keep as delicate around the bowels as around the head and heart,
Copulation is no more rank to me than death is.

I believe in the flesh and the appetites,
Seeing, hearing, feeling, are miracles, and each part and tag of me is a
    miracle.

Divine am I inside and out, and I make holy whatever I touch or am touch'd
    from,
The scent of these arm-pits aroma finer than prayer,
This head more than churches, bibles, and all the creeds.

If I worship one thing more than another it shall be the spread of my own
    body, or any part of it,
Translucent mould of me it shall be you!
Shaded ledges and rests it shall be you!
Firm masculine colter it shall be you!
Whatever goes to the tilth of me it shall be you!
You my rich blood! your milky stream pale strippings of my life!
Breast that presses against other breasts it shall be you!
My brain it shall be your occult convolutions!
Root of wash'd sweet-flag! timorous pond-snipe! nest of guarded duplicate eggs!
    it shall be you!
Mix'd tussled hay of head, beard, brawn, it shall be you!
Trickling sap of maple, fibre of manly wheat, it shall be you!
Sun so generous it shall be you!
Vapors lighting and shading my face it shall be you!
You sweaty brooks and dews it shall be you!
Winds whose soft-tickling genitals rub against me it shall be you!
Broad muscular fields, branches of live oak, loving lounger in my winding
    paths, it shall be you!
Hands I have taken, face I have kiss'd, mortal I have ever touch'd, it shall be
    you.

I dote on myself, there is that lot of me and all so luscious,
Each moment and whatever happens thrills me with joy,
I cannot tell how my ankles bend, nor whence the cause of my faintest wish,
Nor the cause of the friendship I emit, nor the cause of the friendship I take
    again.

That I walk up my stoop, I pause to consider if it really be,
A morning-glory at my window satisfies me more than the metaphysics of
    books.

To behold the day-break!
The little light fades the immense and diaphanous shadows,
The air tastes good to my palate.

Hefts of the moving world at innocent gambols silently rising freshly exuding,
Scooting obliquely high and low.

Something I cannot see puts upward libidinous prongs,
Seas of bright juice suffuse heaven.

The earth by the sky staid with, the daily close of their junction,
The heav'd challenge from the east that moment over my head,
The mocking taunt, See then whether you shall be master!

    25

Dazzling and tremendous how quick the sun-rise would kill me,
If I could not now and always send sun-rise out of me.

We also ascend dazzling and tremendous as the sun,
We found our own O my soul in the calm and cool of the daybreak.

My voice goes after what my eyes cannot reach,
With the twirl of my tongue I encompass worlds and volumes of worlds.

Speech is the twin of my vision, it is unequal to measure itself,
It provokes me forever, it says sarcastically,
Walt you contain enough, why don't you let it out then?

Come now I will not be tantalized, you conceive too much of articulation,
Do you not know O speech how the buds beneath you are folded?
Waiting in gloom, protected by frost,
The dirt receding before my prophetical screams,
I underlying causes to balance them at last,
My knowledge my live parts, it keeping tally with the meaning of all things,
Happiness, (which whoever hears me let him or her set out in search of this
    day.)

My final merit I refuse you, I refuse putting from me what I really am,
Encompass worlds, but never try to encompass me,
I crowd your sleekest and best by simply looking toward you.

Writing and talk do not prove me,
I carry the plenum of proof and every thing else in my face,
With the hush of my lips I wholly confound the skeptic.

                    *   *   *

        30

All truths wait in all things,
They neither hasten their own delivery nor resist it,
They do not need the obstetric forceps of the surgeon,
The insignificant is as big to me as any,
(What is less or more than a touch?)

Logic and sermons never convince,
The damp of the night drives deeper into my soul.

(Only what proves itself to every man and woman is so,
Only what nobody denies is so.)

A minute and a drop of me settle my brain,
I believe the soggy clods shall become lovers and lamps,
And a compend of compends is the meat of a man or woman,
And a summit and flower there is the feeling they have for each other,
And they are to branch boundlessly out of that lesson until it becomes omnific,
And until one and all shall delight us, and we them.

        31

I believe a leaf of grass is no less than the journey-work of the stars,
And the pismire is equally perfect, and a grain of sand, and the egg of the
        wren,
And the tree-toad is a chef-d'œuvre for the highest,
And the running blackberry would adorn the parlors of heaven,
And the narrowest hinge in my hand puts to scorn all machinery,
And the cow crunching with depress'd head surpasses any statue,
And a mouse is miracle enough to stagger sextillions of infidels.

I find I incorporate gneiss, coal, long-threaded moss, fruits, grains, esculent roots,
And am stucco'd with quadrupeds and birds all over,

And have distanced what is behind me for good reasons,
But call any thing back again when I desire it.
In vain the speeding or shyness,
In vain the plutonic rocks send their old heat against my approach,
In vain the mastodon retreats beneath its own powder'd bones,
In vain objects stand leagues off and assume manifold shapes,
In vain the ocean settling in hollows and the great monsters lying low,
In vain the buzzard houses herself with the sky,
In vain the snake slides through the creepers and logs,
In vain the elk takes to the inner passes of the woods,
In vain the razor-bill'd auk sails far north to Labrador,
I follow quickly, I ascend to the nest in the fissure of the cliff.

*   *   *

36

Stretch'd and still lies the midnight,
Two great hulls motionless on the breast of the darkness,
Our vessel riddled and slowly sinking, preparations to pass to the one we have
    conquer'd,
The captain on the quarter-deck coldly giving his orders through a
    countenance white as a sheet,
Near by the corpse of the child that serv'd in the cabin,
The dead face of an old salt with long white hair and carefully curl'd whiskers,
The flames spite of all that can be done flickering aloft and below,
The husky voices of the two or three officers yet fit for duty,
Formless stacks of bodies and bodies by themselves, dabs of flesh upon the
    masts and spars,
Cut of cordage, dangle of rigging, slight shock of the soothe of waves,
Black and impassive guns, litter of powder-parcels, strong scent,
A few large stars overhead, silent and mournful shining,
Delicate sniffs of sea-breeze, smells of sedgy grass and fields by the shore,
    death-messages given in charge to survivors,
The hiss of the surgeon's knife, the gnawing teeth of this saw,
Wheeze, cluck, swash of falling blood, short wild scream, and long, dull,
    tapering groan,
These so, these irretrievable.

*   *   *

42

A call in the midst of the crowd,
My own voice, orotund sweeping and final.

Come my children,
Come my boys and girls, my women, household and intimates,
Now the performer launches his nerve, he has pass'd his prelude on the reeds
     within.

Easily written loose-finger'd chords—I feel the thrum of your climax and close.

My head slues round on my neck,
Music rolls, but not from the organ,
Folks are around me, but they are no household of mind.

Ever the hard unsunk ground,
Ever the eaters and drinkers, ever the upward and downward sun, ever the air
     and the ceaseless tides,
Ever myself and my neighbors, refreshing, wicked, real,
Ever the old inexplicable query, ever that thorn'd thumb, that breath of itches
     and thirsts,
Ever the vexer's *hoot! hoot!* till we find where the sly one hides and bring him
     forth,
Ever love, ever the sobbing liquid of life,
Ever the bandage under the chin, ever the trestles of death.

Here and there with dimes on the eyes walking,
To feed the greed of the belly the brains liberally spooning,
Tickets buying, taking, selling, but in to the feast never once going,
Many sweating, ploughing, thrashing, and then the chaff for payment
     receiving,
A few idly owning, and they the wheat continually claiming.

This is the city and I am one of the citizens,
Whatever interests the rest interests me, politics, wars, markets, newspapers,
     schools,
The mayor and councils, banks, tariffs, steamships, factories, stocks, stores,
     real estate and personal estate.

The little plentiful manikins skipping around in collars and tail'd coats,
I am aware who they are, (they are positively not worms or fleas,)
I acknowledge the duplicates of myself, the weakest and shallowest is deathless
     with me,
What I do and say the same waits for them,
Every thought that flounders in me the same flounders in them.

I know perfectly well my own egotism,
Know my omnivorous lines and must not write any less,
And would fetch you whoever you are flush with myself.
Not words of routine this song of mine,
But abruptly to question, to leap beyond yet nearer bring;
This printed and bound book—but the printer and the printing-office boy?
The well-taken photographs—but your wife or friend close and solid in your
    arms?
The black ship mail'd with iron, her mighty guns in her turrets—but the pluck
    of the captain and engineers?
In the houses the dishes and fare and furniture—but the host and hostess, and
    the look out of their eyes?
The sky up there—yet here or next door, or across the way?
The saints and sages in history—but you yourself?
Sermons, creeds, theology—but the fathomless human brain,
And what is reason? and what is love? and what is life?

*   *   *

46

I know I have the best of time and space, and was never measured and never
    will be measured.
I tramp a perpetual journey, (come listen all!)
My signs are a rain-proof coat, good shoes, and a staff cut from the woods,
No friend of mine takes his ease in my chair,
I have no chair, no church, no philosophy,
I lead no man to a dinner-table, library, exchange,
But each man and each woman of you I lead upon a knoll,
My left hand hooking you round the waist,
My right hand pointing to landscapes of continents and the public road.

Not I, not any one else can travel that road for you,
You must travel it for yourself.
It is not far, it is within reach,
Perhaps you have been on it since you were born and did not know,
Perhaps it is everywhere on water and on land.

Shoulder your duds dear son, and I will mine, and let us hasten forth,
Wonderful cities and free nations we shall fetch as we go.

If you tire, give me both burdens, and rest the chuff of your hand on my hip,
And in due time you shall repay the same service to me,
For after we start we never lie by again.

This day before dawn I ascended a hill and look'd at the crowded heaven,
And I said to my spirit *When we become the enfolders of those orbs, and the
     pleasure and knowledge of every thing in them, shall we be fill'd and
     satisfied then?*
And my spirit said *No, we but level that lift to pass and continue beyond.*

You are also asking me questions and I hear you,
I answer that I cannot answer, you must find out for yourself.

Sit a while dear son,
Here are biscuits to eat and here is milk to drink,
But as soon as you sleep and renew yourself in sweet clothes, I kiss you with a
     good-by kiss and open the gate for your egress hence.

Long enough have you dream'd contemptible dreams,
Now I wash the gum from your eyes,
You must habit yourself to the dazzle of the light and of every moment of your
     life.

Long have you timidly waded holding a plank by the shore,
Now I will you to be a bold swimmer,
To jump off in the midst of the sea, rise again, nod to me, shout, and
     laughingly dash with your hair.

47

I am the teacher of athletes,
He that by me spreads a wider breast than my own proves the width of my own,
He most honors my style who learns under it to destroy the teacher.

The boy I love, the same becomes a man not through derived power, but in his
     own right,
Wicked rather than virtuous out of conformity or fear,
Fond of his sweetheart, relishing well his steak,
Unrequited love or a slight cutting him worse than sharp steel cuts,
First-rate to ride, to fight, to hit the bull's eye, to sail a skiff, to sing a song or
     play on the banjo,
Preferring scars and the beard and faces pitted with small-pox over all latherers,
And those well-tann'd to those that keep out of the sun.

I teach straying from me, yet who can stray from me?
I follow you whoever you are from the present hour,
My words itch at your ears till you understand them.

I do not say these things for a dollar or to fill up the time while I wait for a
     boat,
(It is you talking just as much as myself, I act as the tongue of you,
Tied in your mouth, in mine it begins to be loosen'd.)

I swear I will never again mention love or death inside a house,
And I swear I will never translate myself at all, only to him or her who privately
     stays with me in the open air.

If you would understand me go to the heights or water-shore,
The nearest gnat is an explanation, and a drop or motion of waves a key,
The maul, the oar, the hand-saw, second my words.

No shutter'd room or school can commune with me,
But roughs and little children better than they.

The young mechanic is closest to me, he knows me well,
The woodman that takes his axe and jug with him shall take me with him all
     day,
The farm-boy ploughing in the field feels good at the sound of my voice,
In vessels that sail my words sail, I go with fishermen and seamen and love
     them.

The soldier camp'd or upon the march is mine,
On the night ere the pending battle many seek me, and I do not fail them,
On that solemn night (it may be their last) those that know me seek me.
My face rubs to the hunter's face when he lies down alone in his blanket,
The driver thinking of me does not mind the jolt of his wagon,
The young mother and old mother comprehend me,
The girl and the wife rest the needle a moment and forget where they are,
They and all would resume what I have told them.

48

I have said that the soul is not more than the body,
And I have said that the body is not more than the soul,
And nothing, not God, is greater to one than one's self is,
And whoever walks a furlong without sympathy walks to his own funeral drest
     in his shroud,
And I or you pocketless of a dime may purchase the pick of the earth,
And to glance with an eye or show a bean in its pod confounds the learning of
     all times,

And there is no trade or employment but the young man following it may
    become a hero,
And there is no object so soft but it makes a hub for the wheel'd universe,
And I say to any man or woman, Let your soul stand cool and composed before
    a million universes.

And I say to mankind, Be not curious about God,
For I who am curious about each am not curious about God,
(No array of terms can say how much I am at peace about God and about
    death.)

I hear and behold God in every object, yet understand God not in the least,
Nor do I understand who there can be more wonderful than myself.

Why should I wish to see God better than this day?
I see something of God each hour of the twenty-four, and each moment then,
In the faces of men and women I see God, and in my own face in the glass,
I find letters from God dropt in the street, and every one is sign'd by God's
    name,
And I leave them where they are, for I know that wheresoe'er I go,
Others will punctually come for ever and ever.

    49

And as to you Death, and you bitter hug of mortality, it is idle to try to alarm
    me.

To his work without flinching the accoucheur comes,
I see the elder-hand pressing receiving supporting,
I recline by the sills of the exquisite flexible doors,
And mark the outlet, and mark the relief and escape.

And as to you Corpse I think you are good manure, but that does not offend
    me,
I smell the white roses sweet-scented and growing,
I reach to the leafy lips, I reach to the polish'd breasts of melons.

And as to you Life I reckon you are the leavings of many deaths,
(No doubt I have died myself ten thousand times before.)

I hear you whispering there O stars of heaven,
O suns—O grass of graves—O perpetual transfers and promotions,
If you do not say any thing how can I say any thing?

Of the turbid pool that lies in the autumn forest,
Of the moon that descends the steeps of the soughing twilight,
Toss, sparkles of day and dusk—toss on the black stems that decay in the muck,
Toss to the moaning gibberish of the dry limbs.

I ascend from the moon, I ascend from the night,
I perceive that the ghastly glimmer is noonday sunbeams reflected,
And debouch to the steady and central from the offspring great or small.

50

There is that in me—I do not know what it is—but I know it is in me.

Wrench'd and sweaty—calm and cool then my body becomes,
I sleep—I sleep long.

I do not know it—it is without name—it is a word unsaid,
It is not in any dictionary, utterance, symbol.

Something it swings on more than the earth I swing on,
To it the creation is the friend whose embracing awakes me.

Perhaps I might tell more. Outlines! I plead for my brothers and sisters.

Do you see O my brothers and sisters?
It is not chaos or death—it is form, union, plan—it is eternal life—it is
      Happiness.

51

The past and present wilt—I have fill'd them, emptied them,
And proceed to fill my next fold of the future.
Listener up there! what have you to confide to me?
Look in my face while I snuff the sidle of evening,
(Talk honestly, no one else hears you, and I stay only a minute longer.)

Do I contradict myself?
Very well then I contradict myself,
(I am large, I contain multitudes.)

I concentrate toward them that are nigh, I wait on the door-slab.

Who has done his day's work? who will soonest be through with his supper?
Who wishes to walk with me?

Will you speak before I am gone? will you prove already too late?

52

The spotten hawk swoops by and accuses me, he complains of my gab and my
    loitering.

I too am not a bit tamed, I too am untranslatable,
I sound my barbaric yawp over the roofs of the world.

The last scud of day holds back for me,
It flings my likeness after the rest and true as any on the shadow'd wilds,
It coaxes me to the vapor and the dusk.

I depart as air, I shake my white locks at the runaway sun,
I effuse my flesh in eddies, and drift it in lacy jags.

I bequeath myself to the dirt to grow from the grass I love,
If you want me again look for me under your boot-soles.

You will hardly know who I am or what I mean,
But I shall be good health to you nevertheless,
And filter and fibre your blood.

Failing to fetch me at first keep encouraged,
Missing me one place search another,
I stop somewhere waiting for you.

I SAW IN LOUISIANA A LIVE-OAK GROWING

I saw in Louisiana a live-oak growing,
All alone stood it and the moss hung down from the branches,
Without any companion it grew there uttering joyous leaves of dark green,
And its look, rude, unbending, lusty, made me think of myself,
But I wonder'd how it could utter joyous leaves standing alone there without its
    friend near, for I knew I could not,

And I broke off a twig with a certain number of leaves upon it, and twined
    around it a little moss,
And brought it away, and I have placed it in sight in my room,
It is not needed to remind me as of my own dear friends,
(For I believe lately I think of little else than of them,)
Yet it remains to me a curious token, it makes me think of manly love;
For all that, and though the live-oak glistens there in Louisiana solitary in a
    wide flat space,
Uttering joyous leaves all its life without a friend a lover near,
I know very well I could not.

AS ADAM EARLY IN THE MORNING

As Adam early in the morning,
Walking forth from the bower refresh'd with sleep,
Behold me where I pass, hear my voice, approach,
Touch me, touch the palm of your hand to my body as I pass,
Be not afraid of my body.

CROSSING BROOKLYN FERRY

1

Flood-tide below me! I see you face to face!
Clouds of the west—sun there half an hour high—I see you also face to face.

Crowds of men and women attired in the usual costumes, how curious you are
    to me!
On the ferry-boats the hundreds and hundreds that cross, returning home, are
    more curious to me than you suppose,
And you that shall cross from shore to shore years hence are more to me, and
    more in my meditations, than you might suppose.

2

The impalpable sustenance of me from all things at all hours of the day,
The simple, compact, well-join'd scheme, myself disintegrated, every one
    disintegrated yet part of the scheme,

The similitudes of the past and those of the future,
The glories strung like beads on my smallest sights and hearings, on the walk in
     the street and the passage over the river,
The current rushing so swiftly and swimming with me far away,
The others that are to follow me, the ties between me and them,
The certainty of others, the life, love, sight, hearing of others.

Others will enter the gates of the ferry and cross from shore to shore,
Others will watch the run of the flood-tide,
Others will see the shipping of Manhattan north and west, and the heights of
     Brooklyn to the south and east,
Others will see the islands large and small;
Fifty years hence, others will see them as they cross, the sun half an hour high,
A hundred years hence, or ever so many hundred years hence, others will see
     them,
Will enjoy the sunset, the pouring-in of the flood-tide, the falling-back to the
     sea of the ebb-tide.

3

It avails not, time nor place—distance avails not,
I am with you, you men and women of a generation, or ever so many
     generations hence,
Just as you feel when you look on the river and sky, so I felt,
Just as any of you is one of a living crowd, I was one of a crowd,
Just as you are refresh'd by the gladness of the river and the bright flow, I was
     refresh'd,
Just as you stand and lean on the rail, yet hurry with the swift current, I stood
     yet was hurried,
Just as you look on the numberless masts of ships and the thick-stemm'd pipes
     of steamboats, I look'd.

I too many and many a time cross'd the river of old,
Watched the Twelfth-month sea-gulls, saw them high in the air floating with
     motionless wings, oscillating their bodies,
Saw how the glistening yellow lit up parts of their bodies and left the rest in
     strong shadow,
Saw the slow-wheeling circles and the gradual edging toward the south,
Saw the reflection of the summer sky in the water,
Had my eyes dazzled by the shimmering track of beams,
Look'd at the fine centrifugal spokes of light round the shape of my head in the
     sunlit water,
Look'd on the haze on the hills southward and south-westward,

Look'd on the vapor as it flew in fleeces tinged with violet,
Look'd toward the lower bay to notice the vessels arriving,
Saw their approach, saw aboard those that were near me,
Saw the white sails of schooners and sloops, saw the ships at anchor,
The sailors at work in the rigging or out astride the spars,
The round masts, the swinging motion of the hulls, the slender serpentine
     pennants,
The large and small steamers in motion, the pilots in their pilot-houses,
The white wake left by the passage, the quick tremulous whirl of the wheels,
The flags of all nations, the falling of them at sunset,
The scallop-edged waves in the twilight, the ladled cups, the frolicsome crests
     and glistening,
The stretch afar growing dimmer and dimmer, the gray walls of the granite
     storehouses by the docks,
On the river the shadowy group, the big steam-tug closely flank'd on each side
     by the barges, the hay-boat, the belated lighter,
On the neighboring shore the fires from the foundry chimneys burning high
     and glaringly into the night,
Casting their flicker of black contrasted with wild red and yellow light over the
     tops of houses, and down into the clefts of streets.

     4

These and all else were to me the same as they are to you,
I loved well those cities, loved well the stately and rapid river,
The men and women I saw were all near to me,
Others the same—others who look back on me because I look'd forward to
     them,
(The time will come, though I stop here to-day and to-night.)

     5

What is it then between us?
What is the count of the scores or hundreds of years between us?

Whatever it is, it avails not—distance avails not, and place avails not,
I too lived, Brooklyn of ample hills was mine,
I too walk'd the streets of Manhattan island, and bathed in the waters around it,
I too felt the curious abrupt questionings stir within me,
In the day among crowds of people sometimes they came upon me,
In my walks home late at night or as I lay in my bed they came upon me,
I too had been struck from the float forever held in solution,
I too had receiv'd identity by my body,

That I was I knew was of my body, and what I should be I knew I should be of
    my body.

6

It is not upon you alone the dark patches fall,
The dark threw its patches down upon me also,
The best I had done seem'd to me blank and suspicious,
My great thoughts as I supposed them, were they not in reality meagre?
Nor is it you alone who know what it is to be evil,
I am he who knew what it was to be evil,
I too knitted the old knot of contrariety,
Blabb'd, blush'd, resented, lied, stole, grudg'd,
Had guile, anger, lust, hot wishes I dared not speak,
Was wayward, vain, greedy, shallow, sly, cowardly, malignant,
The wolf, the snake, the hog, not wanting in me,
The cheating look, the frivolous word, the adulterous wish, not wanting,
Refusals, hates, postponements, meanness, laziness, none of these wanting,
Was one with the rest, the days, and haps of the rest,
Was call'd by my nighest name by clear loud voices of young men as they saw
    me approaching or passing,
Felt their arms on my neck as I stood, or the negligent leaning of their flesh
    against me as I sat,
Saw many I loved in the street or ferry-boat or public assembly, yet never told
    them a word,
Lived the same life with the rest, the same old laughing, gnawing, sleeping,
Play'd the part that still looks back on the actor or actress,
The same old role, the role that is what we make it, as great as we like,
Or as small as we like, or both great and small.

7

Closer yet I approach you,
What thought you have of me now, I had as much of you—I laid in my stores
    in advance,
I consider'd long and seriously of you before you were born.

Who was to know what should come home to me?
Who knows but I am enjoying this?
Who knows, for all the distance, but I am as good as looking at you now, for all
    you cannot see me?

8

Ah, what can ever be more stately and admirable to me than masthemm'd
    Manhattan?
River and sunset and scallop-edg'd waves of flood-tide?
The sea-gulls oscillating their bodies, the hay-boat in the twilight, and the
    belated lighter?
What gods can exceed these that clasp me by the hand, and with voices I love
    call me promptly and loudly by my nighest name as I approach?
What is more subtle than this which ties me to the woman or man that looks in
    my face?
Which fuses me into you now, and pours my meaning into you?

We understand then do we not?
What I promis'd without mentioning it, have you not accepted?
What the study could not teach—what the preaching could not accomplish is
    accomplish'd, is it not?

9

Flow on, river! flow with the flood-tide, and ebb with the ebb-tide!
Frolic on, crested and scallop-edg'd waves!
Gorgeous clouds of the sunset! drench with your splendor me, or the men and
    women generations after me!
Cross from shore to shore, countless crowds of passengers!
Stand up, tall masts of Mannahatta! stand up, beautiful hills of Brooklyn!
Throb, baffled and curious brain! throw out questions and answers!
Suspend here and everywhere, eternal float of solution!
Gaze, loving and thirsting eyes, in the house or street or public assembly!
Sound out, voices of young men! loudly and musically call me by my nighest
    name!
Live, old life! play the part that looks back on the actor or actress!
Play the old role, the role that is great or small according as one makes it!
Consider, you who peruse me, whether I may not in unknown ways be looking
    upon you;
Be firm, rail over the river, to support those who lean idly, yet haste with the
    hasting current;
Fly on, sea-birds! fly sideways, or wheel in large circles high in the air;
Receive the summer sky, you water, and faithfully hold it till all downcast eyes
    have time to take it from you!
Diverge, fine spokes of light, from the shape of my head, or any one's head, in
    the sunlit water!

Come on, ships from the lower bay! pass up or down, white-sail'd schooners,
     sloops, lighters!
Flaunt away, flags of all nations! be duly lower'd at sunset!
Burn high your fires, foundry chimneys! cast black shadows at nightfall! cast
     red and yellow light over the tops of the houses!
Appearances, now or henceforth, indicate what you are,
You necessary film, continue to envelop the soul,
About my body for me, and your body for you, be hung our divinest aromas,
Thrive, cities—bring your freight, bring your shows, ample and sufficient
     rivers,
Expand, being than which none else is perhaps more spiritual,
Keep your places, objects than which none else is more lasting.

You have waited, you always wait, you dumb, beautiful ministers,
We receive you with free sense at last, and are insatiate henceforward,
Not you any more shall be able to foil us, or withhold yourselves from us,
We use you, and do not cast you aside—we plant you permanently within us,
We fathom you not—we love you—there is perfection in you also,
You furnish your parts toward eternity,
Great or small, you furnish your parts toward the soul.

OUT OF THE CRADLE ENDLESSLY ROCKING

Out of the cradle endlessly rocking,
Out of the mocking-bird's throat, the musical shuttle,
Out of the Ninth-month midnight,
Over the sterile sands and the fields beyond, where the child leaving his bed
     wander'd alone, bareheaded, barefoot,
Down from the shower'd halo,
Up from the mystic play of shadows twining and twisting as if they were alive,
Out from the patches of briers and blackberries,
From the memories of the bird that chanted to me,
From your memories sad brother, from the fitful risings and fallings I heard,
From under that yellow half-moon late-risen and swollen as if with tears,
From those beginning notes of yearning and love there in the mist,
From the thousand responses of my heart never to cease,
From the myriad thence-arous'd words,
From the word stronger and more delicious than any,

From such as now they start the scene revisiting,
As a flock, twittering, rising, or overhead passing,
Borne hither, ere all eludes me, hurriedly,
A man, yet by these tears a little boy again,
Throwing myself on the sand, confronting the waves,
I, chanter of pains and joys, uniter of here and hereafter,
Taking all hints to use them, but swiftly leaping beyond them,
A reminiscence sing.

Once Paumanok,
When the lilac-scent was in the air and Fifth-month grass was growing,
Up this seashore in some briers,
Two feather'd guests from Alabama, two together,
And their nest, and four light-green eggs spotted with brown,
And every day the he-bird to and fro near at hand,
And every day the she-bird crouch'd on her nest, silent, with bright eyes,
And every day I, a curious boy, never too close, never disturbing them,
Cautiously peering, absorbing, translating.

Shine! shine! shine!
Pour down your warmth, great sun!
While we bask, we two together.

Two together!
Winds blow south, or winds blow north,
Day come white, or night come black,
Home, or rivers and mountains from home,
Singing all time, minding no time,
While we two keep together.

Till of a sudden,
May-be kill'd, unknown to her mate,
One forenoon the she-bird crouch'd not on the nest,
Nor return'd that afternoon, nor the next,
Nor ever appear'd again.

And thenceforward all summer in the sound of the sea,
And at night under the full of the moon in calmer weather,
Over the hoarse surging of the sea,
Or flitting from brier to brier by day,
I saw, I heard at intervals the remaining one, the he-bird,
The solitary guest from Alabama.

Blow! blow! blow!
Blow up sea-winds along Paumanok's shore;
I wait and I wait till you blow my mate to me.

Yes, when the stars glisten'd,
All night long on the prong of a moss-scallop'd stake,
Down almost amid the slapping waves,
Sat the lone singer wonderful causing tears.

He call'd on his mate,
He pour'd forth the meanings which I of all men know.

Yes my brother I know,
The rest might not, but I have treasur'd every note,
For more than once dimly down to the beach gliding,
Silent, avoiding the moonbeams, blending myself with the shadow,
Recalling now the obscure shapes, the echoes, the sounds and sights after their
        sorts,
The white arms out in the breakers tirelessly tossing,
I, with bare feet, a child, the wind wafting my hair,
Listen'd long and long.

Listen'd to keep, to sing, now translating the notes,
Following you my brother,

Soothe! soothe! soothe!
Close on its wave soothes the wave behind,
And again another behind embracing and lapping, every one close,
But my love soothes not me, not me.

Low hangs the moon, it rose late,
It is lagging—O I think it is heavy with love, with love.

O madly the sea pushes upon the land,
With love, with love.

O night! do I not see my love fluttering out among the breakers?
What is that little black thing I see there in the white?

Loud! loud! loud!
Loud I call to you, my love!

High and clear I shoot my voice over the waves,
Surely you must know who is here, is here,
You must know who I am, my love.

Low-hanging moon!
What is that dusky spot in your brown yellow?
O it is the shape, the shape of my mate!
O moon do not keep her from me any longer.

Land! land! O land!
Whichever way I turn, O I think you could give me my mate back again if you
    only would,
For I am almost sure I see her dimly whichever way I look.

O rising stars!
Perhaps the one I want so much will rise, will rise with some of you.

O throat! O trembling throat!
Sound clearer through the atmosphere!
Pierce the woods, the earth,
Somewhere listening to catch you must be the one I want.

Shake out carols!
Solitary here, the night's carols!
Carols of lonesome love! death's carols!
Carols under that lagging, yellow, waning moon!
O under that moon where she droops almost down into the sea!
O reckless despairing carols.

But soft! sink low!
Soft! let me just murmur,
And do you wait a moment you husky-nois'd sea,
For somewhere I believe I heard my mate responding to me,
So faint, I must be still, be still to listen,
But not altogether still, for then she might not come immediately to me.

Hither my love!
Here I am! here!
With this just-sustain'd note I announce myself to you,
This gentle call is for you my love, for you.

Do not be decoy'd elsewhere,
That is the whistle of the wind, it is not my voice,
That is the fluttering, the fluttering of the spray,
Those are the shadows of leaves.

O darkness! O in vain!
O I am very sick and sorrowful.

O brown halo in the sky near the moon, drooping upon the sea!
O troubled reflection in the sea!
O throat! O throbbing heart!
And I singing uselessly, uselessly all the night.

O past! O happy life! O songs of joy!
In the air, in the woods, over fields,
Loved! loved! loved! loved! loved!
But my mate no more, no more with me!
We two together no more.

The aria sinking,
All else continuing, the stars shining,
The winds blowing, the notes of the bird continuous echoing,
With angry moans the fierce old mother incessantly moaning,
On the sands of Paumanok's shore gray and rustling,
The yellow half-moon enlarged, sagging down, drooping, the face of the sea
    almost touching,
The boy ecstatic, with his bare feet the waves, with his hair the atmosphere
    dallying,
The love in the heart long pent, now loose, now at last tumultuously bursting,
The aria's meaning, the ears, the soul, swiftly depositing,
The strange tears down the cheeks coursing,
The colloquy there, the trio, each uttering,
The undertone, the savage old mother incessantly crying,
To the boy's soul's questions sullenly timing, some drown'd secret hissing,
To the outsetting bard.

Demon or bird! (said the boy's soul,)
Is it indeed toward your mate you sing? or is it really to me?
For I, that was a child, my tongue's use sleeping, now I have heard you,
Now in a moment I know what I am for, I awake,
And already a thousand singers, a thousand songs, clearer, louder and more
    sorrowful than yours,
A thousand warbling echoes have started to life within me, never to die.

O you singer solitary, singing by yourself, projecting me,
O solitary me listening, never more shall I cease perpetuating you,
Never more shall I escape, never more the reverberations,
Never more the cries of unsatisfied love be absent from me,
Never again leave me to be the peaceful child I was before what there in the
    night,
By the sea under the yellow and sagging moon,
The messenger there arous'd, the fire, the sweet hell within,
The unknown want, the destiny of me.

O give me the clew! (it lurks in the night here somewhere,)
O if I am to have so much, let me have more!

A word then, (for I will conquer it,)
The word final, superior to all,
Subtle, sent up—what is it?—I listen;
Are you whispering it, and have been all the time, you sea-waves?
Is that it from your liquid rims, and wet sands?

Whereto answering, the sea,
Delaying not, hurrying not,
Whisper'd me through the night, and very plainly before day-break,
Lisp'd to me the low and delicious word death,
And again death, death, death, death,
Hissing melodious, neither like the bird nor like my arous'd child's heart,
But edging near as privately for me rustling at my feet,
Creeping thence steadily up to my ears and laving me softly all over,
Death, death, death, death, death.

Which I do not forget,
But fuse the song of my dusky demon and brother,
That he sang to me in the moonlight on Paumanok's gray beach,
With the thousand responsive songs at random,
My own songs awaked from that hour,
And with them the key, the word up from the waves,
The word of the sweetest song and all songs,
That strong and delicious word which, creeping to my feet,
(Or like some old crone rocking the cradle, swathed in sweet garments, bending
    aside,)
The sea whisper'd me.

WHEN I HEARD THE LEARN'D ASTRONOMER

When I heard the learn'd astronomer,
When the proofs, the figures, were ranged in columns before me,
When I was shown the charts and diagrams, to add, divide, and measure them,
When I sitting heard the astronomer where he lectured with much applause in
        the lecture-room,
How soon unaccountable I became tired and sick,
Till rising and gliding out I wander'd off by myself,
In the mystical moist night-air, and from time to time,
Look'd up in perfect silence at the stars.

VIGIL STRANGE I KEPT
ON THE FIELD ONE NIGHT

Vigil strange I kept on the field one night;
When you my son and my comrade dropt at my side that day,
One look I but gave which your dear eyes return'd with a look I shall never forget,
One touch of your hand to mine O boy, reach'd up as you lay on the ground,
Then onward I sped in the battle, the even-contested battle,
Till late in the night reliev'd to the place at last again I made my way,
Found you in death so cold dear comrade, found your body son of responding
        kisses, (never again on earth responding,)
Bared your face in the starlight, curious the scene, cool blew the moderate
        night-wind,
Long there and then in vigil I stood, dimly around me the battle-field
        spreading,
Vigil wondrous and vigil sweet there in the fragrant silent night,
But not a tear fell, not even a long-drawn sigh, long, long I gazed,
Then on the earth partially reclining sat by your side leaning my chin in my
        hands,
Passing sweet hours, immortal and mystic hours with you dearest comrade—
        not a tear, not a word,
Vigil of silence, love and death, vigil for you my son and my soldier,
As onward silently stars aloft, eastward new ones upward stole,
Vigil final for you brave boy, (I could not save you, swift was your death,
I faithfully loved you and cared for you living, I think we shall surely meet
        again,)
Till at latest lingering of the night, indeed just as the dawn appear'd,

My comrade I wrapt in his blanket, envelop'd well his form,
Folded the blanket well, tucking it carefully over head and carefully under feet,
And there and then and bathed by the rising sun, my son in his grave, in his
     rude-dug grave I deposited,
Ending my vigil strange with that, vigil of night and battle-field dim,
Vigil for boy of responding kisses, (never again on earth responding,)
Vigil for comrade swiftly slain, vigil I never forget, how as day brighten'd,
I rose from the chill ground and folded my soldier well in his blanket,
And buried him where he fell.

THE WOUND-DRESSER

1

An old man bending I come among new faces,
Years looking backward resuming in answer to children,
Come tell us old man, as from young men and maidens that love me,
(Arous'd and angry, I'd thought to beat the alarum, and urge relentless war,
But soon my fingers fail'd me, my face droop'd and I resign'd myself,
To sit by the wounded and soothe them, or silently watch the dead;)
Years hence of these scenes, of these furious passions, these chances,
Of unsurpass'd heroes, (was one side so brave? the other was equally brave;)
Now be witness again, paint the mightiest armies of earth,
Of those armies so rapid so wondrous what saw you to tell us?
What stays with you latest and deepest? of curious panics,
Of hard-fought engagements or sieges tremendous what deepest remains?

2

O maidens and young men I love and that love me,
What you ask of my days those the strangest and sudden your talking recalls,
Soldier alert I arrive after a long march covr'd with sweat and dust,
In the nick of time I come, plunge in the fight, loudly shout in the rush of
     successful charge,
Enter the captur'd works—yet lo, like a swift-running river they fade,
Pass and are gone they fade—I dwell not on soldiers' perils or soldiers' joys,
(Both I remember well—many the hardships, few the joys, yet I was content.)

But in silence, in dreams' projections,
While the world of gain and appearance and mirth goes on,
So soon what is over forgotten, and waves wash the imprints off the sand,

With hinged knees returning I enter the doors, (while for you up there,
Whoever you are, follow without noise and be of strong heart.)

Bearing the bandages, water and sponge,
Straight and swift to my wounded I go,
Where they lie on the ground after the battle brought in,
Where their priceless blood reddens the grass the ground,
Or to the rows of the hospital tent, or under the roof'd hospital,
To the long rows of cots up and down each side I return,
To each and all one after another I draw near, not one do I miss,
An attendant follows holding a tray, he carries a refuse pail,
Soon to be fill'd with clotted rags and blood, emptied, and fill'd again.

I onward go, I stop,
With hinged knees and steady hand to dress wounds,
I am firm with each, the pangs are sharp yet unavoidable,
One turns to me his appealing eyes—poor boy! I never knew you,
Yet I think I could not refuse this moment to die for you, if that would save
    you.

        3

On, on I go, (open doors of time! open hospital doors!)
The crush'd head I dress, (poor crazed hand tear not the bandage away,)
The neck of the cavalry-man with the bullet through and through I examine,
Hard the breathing rattles, quite glazed already the eye, yet life struggles hard,
(Come sweet death! be persuaded O beautiful death!
In mercy come quickly.)

From the stump of the arm, the amputated hand,
I undo the clotted lint, remove the slough, wash off the matter and blood,
Back on his pillow the soldier bends with curv'd neck and side-falling head,
His eyes are closed, his face is pale, he dares not look on the bloody stump,
And has not yet look'd on it.

I dress a wound in the side, deep, deep,
But a day or two more, for see the frame all wasted and sinking,
And the yellow-blue countenance see.

I dress the perforated shoulder, the foot with the bullet-wound,
Cleanse the one with a gnawing and putrid gangrene, so sickening, so
    offensive,
While the attendant stands behind aside me holding the tray and pail.

I am faithful, I do not give out,
The fractur'd thigh, the knee, the wound in the abdomen,
These and more I dress with impassive hand, (yet deep in my breast a fire, a
    burning flame.)

    4

Thus in silence in dreams' projections,
Returning, resuming, I thread my way through the hospitals,
The hurt and wounded I pacify with soothing hand,
I sit by the restless all the dark night, some are so young,
Some suffer so much, I recall the experience sweet and sad,
(Many a soldier's loving arms about this neck have cross'd and rested,
Many a soldier's kiss dwells on these bearded lips.)

WHEN LILACS LAST
IN THE DOORYARD BLOOM'D

    1

When lilacs last in the dooryard bloom'd,
And the great star early droop'd in the western sky in the night,
I mourn'd, and yet shall mourn with ever-returning spring.

Ever-returning spring, trinity sure to me you bring,
Lilac blooming perennial and drooping star in the west,
And thought of him I love.

    2

O powerful western fallen star!
O shades of night—O moody, tearful night!
O great star disappear'd—O the black murk that hides the star!
O cruel hands that hold me powerless—O helpless soul of me!
O harsh surrounding cloud that will not free my soul.

    3

In the dooryard fronting an old farm-house near the white-wash'd palings,
Stands the lilac-bush tall-growing with heart-shaped leaves of rich green,

With many a pointed blossom rising delicate, with the perfume strong I love,
With every leaf a miracle—and from this bush in the dooryard,
With delicate-color'd blossoms and heart-shaped leaves of rich green,
A sprig with its flower I break.

4

In the swamp in secluded recesses,
A shy and hidden bird is warbling a song.

Solitary the thrush,
The hermit withdrawn to himself, avoiding the settlements,
Sings by himself a song.

Song of the bleeding throat,
Death's outlet song of life, (for well dear brother I know,
If thou wast not granted to sing thou would'st surely die.)

5

Over the breast of the spring, the land, amid cities,
Amid lanes and through old woods, where lately the violets peep'd from the
        ground, spotting the gray debris,
Amid the grass in the fields each side of the lanes, passing the endless grass,
Passing the yellow-spear'd wheat, every grain from its shroud in the dark-brown
        fields uprisen,
Passing the apple-tree blows of white and pink in the orchards,
Carrying a corpse to where it shall rest in the grave,
Night and day journeys a coffin.

6

Coffin that passes through lanes and streets,
Through day and night with the great cloud darkening the land,
With the pomp of the inloop'd flags with the cities draped in black,
With the show of the States themselves as of crape-veil'd women standing,
With processions long and winding and the flambeaus of the night,
With the countless torches lit, with the silent sea of faces and the unbared
        heads,
With the waiting depot, the arriving coffin, and the sombre faces,
With dirges through the night, with the thousand voices rising strong and
        solemn,
With all the mournful voices of the dirges pour'd around the coffin,

The dim-lit churches and the shuddering organs—where amid these you
    journey,
With the tolling tolling bells' perpetual clang,
Here, coffin that slowly passes,
I give you my sprig of lilac.

        7

(Nor for you, for one alone,
Blossoms and branches green to coffins all I bring,
For fresh as the morning, thus would I chant a song for you O sane and sacred
    death.

All over bouquets of roses,
O death, I cover you over with roses and early lilies,
But mostly and now the lilac that blooms the first,
Copious I break, I break the sprigs from the bushes,
With loaded arms I come, pouring for you,
For you and the coffins all of you O death.)

        8

O western orb sailing the heaven,
Now I know what you must have meant as a month since I walk'd,
As I walk'd in silence the transparent shadowy night,
As I saw you had something to tell as you bent to me night after night,
As you droop'd from the sky low down as if to my side, (while the other stars all
    look'd on,)
As we wander'd together the solemn night, (for something I know not what kept
    me from sleep,)
As the night advanced, and I saw on the rim of the west how full you were of
    woe,
As I stood on the rising ground in the breeze in the cool transparent night,
As I watch'd where you pass'd and was lost in the netherward black of the
    night,
As my soul in its trouble dissatisfied sank, as where you sad orb,
Concluded, dropt in the night, and was gone.

        9

Sing on there in the swamp,
O singer bashful and tender, I hear your notes, I hear your call,
I hear, I come presently, I understand you,

But a moment I linger, for the lustrous star has detain'd me,
The star my departing comrade holds and detains me.

10

O how shall I warble myself for the dead one there I loved?
And how shall I deck my song for the large sweet soul that has gone?
And what shall my perfume be for the grave of him I love?
Sea-winds blown from east and west,
Blown from the Eastern sea and blown from the Western sea, till there on the
     prairies meeting,
These and with these and the breath of my chant,
I'll perfume the grave of him I love.

11

O what shall I hang on the chamber walls?
And what shall the pictures be that I hang on the walls,
To adorn the burial-house of him I love?

Pictures of growing spring and farms and homes,
With the Fourth-month eve at sundown, and the gray smoke lucid and bright,
With floods of the yellow gold of the gorgeous, indolent, sinking sun, burning,
     expanding the air,
With the fresh sweet herbage under foot, and the pale green leaves of the trees
     prolific,
In the distance the flowing glaze, the breast of the river, with a wind-dapple
     here and there,
With ranging hills on the banks, with many a line against the sky, and
     shadows,
And the city at hand with dwellings so dense, and stacks of chimneys,
And all the scenes of life and the workshops, and the workmen homeward
     returning.

12

Lo, body and soul—this land,
My own Manhattan with spires, and the sparkling and hurrying tides, and the
     ships,
The varied and ample land, the South and the North in the light, Ohio's
     shores and flashing Missouri,
And ever the far-spreading prairies cover'd with grass and corn.

Lo, the most excellent sun so calm and haughty,
The violet and purple morn with just-felt breezes,
The gentle soft-born measureless light
The miracle spreading bathing all, the fulfill'd noon,
The coming eve delicious, the welcome night and the stars,
Over my cities shining all, enveloping man and land.

13

Sing on, sing on you gray-brown bird,
Sing from the swamps, the recesses, pour your chant from the bushes,
Limitless out of the dusk, out of the cedars and pines.

Sing on dearest brother, warble your reedy song,
Loud human song, with voice of uttermost woe.
O liquid and free and tender!
O wild and loose to my soul—O wondrous singer!
You only I hear—yet the star holds me, (but will soon depart,)
Yet the lilac with mastering odor holds me.

14

Now while I sat in the day and look'd forth,
In the close of the day with its light and the fields of spring, and the farmers
      preparing their crops,
In the large unconscious scenery of my land with its lakes and forests,
In the heavenly aerial beauty, (after the perturb'd winds and the storms,)
Under the arching heavens of the afternoon swift passing, and the voices of
      children and women,
The many-moving sea-tides, and I saw the ships how they sail'd,
And the summer approaching with richness, and the fields all busy with labor,
And the infinite separate houses, how they all went on, each with its meals and
      minutia of daily usages,
And the streets how their throbbings throbb'd, and the cities pent—lo, then
      and there,
Falling upon them all and among them all, enveloping me with the rest,
Appear'd the cloud, appear'd the long black trail,
And I knew death, its thought, and the sacred knowledge of death.

Then with the knowledge of death as walking one side of me,
And the thought of death close-walking the other side of me,
And I in the middle as with companions, and as holding the hands of
      companions,

I fled forth to the hiding receiving night that talks not,
Down to the shores of the water, the path by the swamp in the dimness,
To the solemn shadowy cedars and ghostly pines so still.

And the singer so shy to the rest receiv'd me,
The gray-brown bird I know receiv'd us comrades three,
And he sang the carol of death, and a verse for him I love.

From deep secluded recesses,
From the fragrant cedars and the ghostly pines so still,
Came the carol of the bird.

And the charm of the carol rapt me,
As I held as if by their hands my comrades in the night,
And the voice of my spirit tallied the song of the bird.

Come lovely and soothing death,
Undulate round the world, serenely arriving, arriving,
In the day, in the night, to all, to each,
Sooner or later delicate death.

Prais'd be the fathomless universe,
For life and joy, and for objects and knowledge curious,
And for love, sweet love—but praise! praise! praise!
For the sure-enwinding arms of cool-enfolding death.

Dark mother always gliding near with soft feet,
Have none chanted for thee a chant of fullest welcome?
Then I chant it for thee, I glorify thee above all,
I bring thee a song that when thou must indeed come, come unfalteringly.

Approach strong deliveress,
When it is so, when thou hast taken them I joyously sing the dead,
Lost in the loving floating ocean of thee,
Laved in the flood of thy bliss O death.

From me to thee glad serenades,
Dances for thee I propose saluting thee, adornments and feastings for thee,
And the sights of the open landscape and the high-spread sky are fitting,
And life and the fields, and the huge and thoughtful night.

The night in silence under many a star,
The ocean shore and the husky whispering wave whose voice I know,
And the soul turning to thee O vast and well-veil'd death,
And the body gratefully nestling close to thee.

Over the tree-tops I float thee a song,
Over the rising and sinking waves, over the myriad fields and the prairies wide,
Over the dense-pack'd cities all and the teeming wharves and ways,
I float this carol with joy, with joy to thee O death.

15

To the tally of my soul,
Loud and strong kept up the gray-brown bird,
With pure deliberate notes spreading filling the night.

Loud in the pines and cedars dim,
Clear in the freshness moist and the swamp-perfume,
And I with my comrades there in the night.

While my sight that was bound in my eyes unclosed,
As to long panoramas of visions.

And I saw askant the armies,
I saw as in noiseless dreams hundreds of battle-flags,
Borne through the smoke of the battles and pierc'd with missiles I saw them,
And carried hither and yon through the smoke, and torn and bloody,
And at last but a few shreds left on the staffs, (and all in silence,)
And the staffs all splinter'd and broken.

I saw battle-corpses, myriads of them,
And the white skeletons of young men, I saw them,
I saw the debris and debris of all the slain soldiers of the war,
But I saw they were not as was thought,
They themselves were fully at rest, they suffer'd not,
The living remain'd and suffer'd, the mother suffer'd,
And the wife and the child and the musing comrade suffer'd,
And the armies that remain'd suffer'd.

16

Passing the visions, passing the night,
Passing, unloosing the hold of my comrades' hands,
Passing the song of the hermit bird and the tallying song of my soul,
Victorious song, death's outlet song, yet varying ever-altering song,
As low and wailing, yet clear the notes, rising and falling, flooding the night,
Sadly sinking and fainting, as warning and warning, and yet again bursting
    with joy,

Covering the earth and filling the spread of the heaven,
As that powerful psalm in the night I heard from recesses,
Passing, I leave thee lilac with heart-shaped leaves,
I leave thee there in the door-yard, blooming, returning with spring.

I cease from my song for thee,
From my gaze on thee in the west, fronting the west, communing with thee,
O comrade lustrous with silver face in the night.

Yet each to keep and all, retrievements out of the night,
The song, the wondrous chant of the gray-brown bird,
And the tallying chant, the echo arous'd in my soul,
With the lustrous and drooping star with the countenance full of woe,
With the holders holding my hand nearing the call of the bird,
Comrades mine and I in the midst, and their memory ever to keep, for the
    dead I loved so well,
For the sweetest, wisest soul of all my days and lands—and this for his dear
    sake,
Lilac and star and bird twined with the chant of my soul,
There in the fragrant pines and the cedars dusk and dim.

A NOISELESS PATIENT SPIDER

A noiseless patient spider,
I mark'd where on a little promontory it stood isolated,
Mark'd how to explore the vacant vast surrounding,
It launch'd forth filament, filament, filament, out of itself,
Ever unreeling them, ever tirelessly speeding them.

And you O my soul where you stand,
Surrounded, detached, in measureless oceans of space,
Ceaselessly musing, venturing, throwing, seeking the spheres to connect them,
Till the bridge you will need be form'd, till the ductile anchor hold,
Till the gossamer thread you fling catch somewhere, O my soul.

Julia Ward Howe

(1819–1910)

THE BATTLE HYMN OF THE REPUBLIC

Mine eyes have seen the glory of the coming of the Lord:
He is trampling out the vintage where the grapes of wrath are stored;
He hath loosed the fatal lightning of His terrible swift sword:
    His truth is marching on.

I have seen Him in the watch-fires of a hundred circling camps,
They have builded Him an altar in the evening dews and damps;
I can read His righteous sentence by the dim and flaring lamps:
    His day is marching on.

I have read a fiery gospel writ in burnished rows of steel:
"As ye deal with my contemners, so with you my grace shall deal;
Let the Hero, born of woman, crush the serpent with his heel,
    Since God is marching on."

He has sounded forth the trumpet that shall never call retreat;
He is sifting out the hearts of men before His judgement seat:
Oh, be swift, my soul, to answer Him! Be jubilant, my feet!
    Our God is marching on.

In the beauty of the lilies Christ was born across the sea,
With a glory in his bosom that transfigures you and me:
As he died to make men holy, let us die to make men free,
    While God is marching on.

KOSMOS

Of dust the primal Adam came
In wondrous sequency evolved,
With speech that gave creation name,
Of art and artist never solved.

With something of a mother-pang
The Sun conceived the starry spheres
That from her burning bosom sprang,—
Immortal children of her tears.

From height of heat, and stress of span,
The measured Earth took poise and hold;
And beasts, the prophecy of man,
And man, were latent in her mould.

And hid in man a world intense,
The centre point of things that be,
With soul that conquers out of sense
Its incomplete divinity.

Around one infinite intent
All power and inspiration move,
Thrilling with light the firmament,
Lifting the heart of man with love.

A WILD NIGHT

The storm is sweeping o'er the land,
   And raging o'er the sea:
It urgeth sharp and dismal sounds,
   The Psalm of Misery.

The straining of the cordage now,
   The creaking of a spar,
The deep dumb shock the vessel feels
   When billows strike and jar,

It breathes of distant seamen's hearts
   That think upon their wives;
Of wretches clinging to the mast,
   And wrestling for their lives.

The clouds are flying through the sky
   Like spectres of affright:

Yon pale witch moon doth blast them all
  With bleared and ghastly light.

Great Demons flutter through the dark
  Flame touched, with dusky wing;
And Passion crouches out of sight
  Like a forbidden thing.

The blast doth scourge the forest through,
  Great oaks, and bushes small;
And God, the fable of the fools,
  Looks silently on all.

Oh! if He watches, as I know,
  Safe let Him keep our rest,
And give my little ones and me
  The shelter of His breast.

No harm shall come on earth, we trust;
  But, if mischance must be,
Most let Him help those weary souls
  That struggle with the sea!

Herman Melville

(1819–1891)

THE PORTENT

1859

Hanging from the beam,
   Slowly swaying (such the law),
Gaunt the shadow on your green,
   Shenandoah!
The cut is on the crown
(Lo, John Brown),
And the stabs shall heal no more.

Hidden in the cap
   Is the anguish none can draw
So your future veils its face,
   Shenandoah!
But the streaming beard is shown
(Weird John Brown),
The meteor of the war.

THE MARCH INTO VIRGINIA

Ending in the First Manassas

July 1861

Did all the lets and bars appear
   To every just or larger end,
Whence should come the trust and cheer?
   Youth must its ignorant impulse lend . . .
Age finds place in the rear.
   All wars are boyish, and are fought by boys,
The champions and enthusiasts of the state:
   Turbid ardours and vain joys
     Not barrenly abate . . .

Stimulants to the power mature,
   Preparatives of fate.

Who here forecasteth the event?
What heart but spurns at precedent
And warnings of the wise,
Contemned foreclosures of surprise?
The banners play, the bugles call,
The air is blue and prodigal.
   No berrying party, pleasure-wooed,
No picnic party in the May,
Ever went less loth than they
   Into that leafy neighbourhood.
In Bacchic glee they file toward Fate,
Moloch's uninitiate;
Expectancy, and glad surmise
Of battle's unknown mysteries.

All they feel is this: 'tis glory,
A rapture sharp, though transitory,
Yet lasting in belaurelled story.
So they gaily go to fight,
Chatting left and laughing right.
But some who this blithe mood present,
   As on in lightsome files they fare,
Shall die experienced ere three days are spent . . .
   Perish, enlightened by the volleyed glare;
Or shame survive, and, like to adamant,
   The throe of Second Manassas share.

A UTILITARIAN VIEW
OF THE MONITOR'S FIGHT

Plain be the phrase, yet apt the verse,
   More ponderous than nimble;
For since grimed War here laid aside
His Orient pomp, 'twould ill befit
   Overmuch to ply
   The rhyme's barbaric cymbal.

Hail to victory without the gaud
   Of glory; zeal that needs no fans
Of banners; plain mechanic power
Plied cogently in War now placed . . .
     Where War belongs . . .
   Among the trades and artisans.

Yet this was battle, and intense . . .
   Beyond the strife of fleets heroic;
Deadlier, closer, calm 'mid storm;
No passion; all went on by crank,
     Pivot, and screw,
   And calculations of caloric.

Needless to dwell; the story's known.
   The ringing of those plates on plates
Still ringeth round the world . . .
The clangour of that blacksmiths' fray.
     The anvil-din
   Resounds this message from the Fates:

War shall yet be, and to the end;
   But war-paint shows the streaks of weather;
War yet shall be, but warriors
Are now but operatives; War's made
     Less grand than Peace,
   And a singe runs through lace and feather.

SHILOH

A REQUIEM

April 1862

Skimming lightly, wheeling still,
   The swallows fly low
Over the field in clouded days,
   The forest-field of Shiloh—
Over the field where April rain
Solaced the parched one stretched in pain

Through the pause of night
That followed the Sunday fight
   Around the church of Shiloh—
The church so lone, the log-built one,
That echoed to many a parting groan
     And natural prayer
   Of dying foemen mingled there—
Foemen at morn, but friends at eve—
   Fame or country least their care:
(What like a bullet can undeceive!)
   But now they lie low,
While over them the swallows skim
   And all is hushed at Shiloh.

MALVERN HILL

July 1862

Ye elms that wave on Malvern Hill
   In prime of morn and May,
Recall ye how McClellan's men
     Here stood at bay?
While deep within yon forest dim
   Our rigid comrades lay . . .
Some with the cartridge in their mouth,
Others with fixed arms lifted South . . .
     Invoking so
The cypress glades? Ah wilds of woe!

The spires of Richmond, late beheld
   Through rifts in musket-haze,
Were closed from view in clouds of dust
    On leaf-walled ways,
Where streamed our wagons in caravan;
   And the Seven Nights and Days
Of march and fast, retreat and fight,
Pinched our grimed faces to ghastly plight . . .
     Does the elm wood
Recall the haggard beards of blood?

The battle-smoked flag, with stars eclipsed,
　　We followed (it never fell!) . . .
In silence husbanded our strength . . .
　　　Received their yell;
Till on this slope we patient turned
　　With cannon ordered well;
Reverse we proved was not defeat;
But ah, the sod what thousands meet! . . .
　　　Does Malvern Wood
Bethink itself, and muse and brood?

We elms of Malvern Hill
　Remember everything;
But sap the twig will fill:
Wag the world how it will,
　Leaves must be green in spring.

THE MARTYR

Indicative of the Passion of the People on the 15th of
April 1865.

Good Friday was the day
　Of the prodigy and crime,
When they killed him in his pity,
　When they killed him in his prime
Of clemency and calm . . .
　　When with yearning he was filled
　　To redeem the evil-willed,
And, though conqueror, be kind;
　But they killed him in his kindness,
　In their madness and their blindness,
And they killed him from behind.

There is sobbing of the strong,
　And a pall upon the land;
But the People in their weeping
　　Bare the iron hand:
Beware the People weeping
　When they bare the iron hand.

He lieth in his blood . . .
   The father in his face;
They have killed him, the Forgiver . . .
   The Avenger takes his place,
The Avenger wisely stern,
    Who in righteousness shall do
    What the heavens call him to,
And the parricides remand;
   For they killed him in his kindness
   In their madness and their blindness,
And his blood is on their hand.

There is sobbing of the strong,
   And a pall upon the land;
But the People in their weeping
     Bare the iron hand:
Beware the People weeping
   When they bare the iron hand.

THE MALDIVE SHARK

About the Shark, phlegmatical one,
Pale sot of the Maldive sea,
The sleek little pilot-fish, azure and slim,
How alert in attendance be.
From his saw-pit of mouth, from his charnel of maw,
They have nothing of harm to dread,
But liquidly glide on his ghastly flank
Or before his Gorgonian head;
Or lurk in the port of serrated teeth
In white triple tiers of glittering gates,
And there find a haven when peril's abroad,
An asylum in jaws of the Fates!
They are friends; and friendly they guide him to prey,
Yet never partake of the treat . . .
Eyes and brains to the dotard lethargic and dull,
Pale ravener of horrible meat.

THE BERG

A DREAM

I saw a ship of martial build
(Her standards set, her brave apparel on)
Directed as by madness mere
Against a stolid iceberg steer,
Nor budge it, though the infatuate ship went down.
The impact made huge ice-cubes fall
Sullen, in tons that crashed the deck;
But that one avalanche was all . . .
No other movement save the foundering wreck.

Along the spurs of ridges pale,
Not any slenderest shaft and frail,
A prism over glass-green gorges lone,
Toppled; nor lace of traceries fine,
Nor pendant drops in grot or mine
Were jarred, when the stunned ship went down.
Nor sole the gulls in cloud that wheeled
Circling one snow-flanked peak afar,
But nearer fowl the floes that skimmed
And crystal beaches, felt no jar.
No thrill transmitted stirred the lock
Of jack-straw needle-ice at base;
Towers undermined by waves . . . the block
Atilt impending . . . kept their place.
Seals, dozing sleek on sliddery ledges
Slipt never, when by loftier edges
Through very inertia overthrown,
The impetuous ship in bafflement went down.

Hard Berg (methought), so cold, so vast,
With mortal damps self-overcast;
Exhaling still thy dankish breath . . .
Adrift dissolving, bound for death;
Though lumpish thou, a lumbering one . . .
A lumbering lubbard loitering slow,
Impingers rue thee and go down,
Sounding thy precipice below,
Nor stir the slimy slug that sprawls
Along thy dead indifference of walls.

ART

In placid hours well pleased we dream
Of many a brave unbodied scheme.
But form to lend, pulsed life create,
What unlike things must meet and mate:
A flame to melt . . . a wind to freeze;
Sad patience . . . joyous energies;
Humility . . . yet pride and scorn;
Instinct and study; love and hate;
Audacity . . . reverence. These must mate
And fuse with Jacob's mystic heart,
To wrestle with the angel . . . Art.

Alice Cary

(1820 – 1871)

THE SEA-SIDE CAVE

"A bird of the air shall carry the voice, and that which hath
wings shall tell the matter."

At the dead of night by the side of the Sea
I met my gray-haired enemy,—
The glittering light of his serpent eye
Was all I had to see him by.

At the dead of night, and stormy weather
We went into a cave together,—
Into a cave by the side of the Sea,
And—he never came out with me!

The flower that up through the April mould
Comes like a miser dragging his gold,
Never made spot of earth so bright
As was the ground in the cave that night.

Dead of night, and stormy weather!
Who should see us going together
Under the black and dripping stone
Of the cave from whence I came alone!

Next day as my boy sat on my knee
He picked the gray hairs off from me,
And told with eyes brimful of fear
How a bird in the meadow near

Over her clay-built nest had spread
Sticks and leaves all bloody red,
Brought from a cave by the side of the Sea
Where some murdered man must be.

Frederick Goddard Tuckerman

(1 8 2 1 – 1 8 7 3)

SONNET

The starry flower, the flower-like stars that fade
And brighten with the daylight and the dark,—
The bluet in the green I faintly mark,
And glimmering crags with laurel overlaid,
Even to the Lord of light, the Lamp of shade,
Shine one to me,—the least, still glorious made
As crownèd moon, or heaven's great hierarch.
And, so, dim grassy flower, and night-lit spark,
Still move me on and upward for the True;
Seeking through change, growth, death, in new and old.
The full in few, the statelier in the less,
With patient pain; always remembering this,—
His hand, who touched the sod with showers of gold,
Stippled Orion on the midnight blue.

SONNET

And so, as this great sphere (now turning slow
Up to the light from that abyss of stars,
Now wheeling into gloom through sunset bars) —
With all its elements of form and flow,
And life in life; where crowned, yet blind, must go
The sensible king,—is but an Unity
Compressed of motes impossible to know;
Which worldlike yet in deep analogy,
Have distance, march, dimension, and degree;
So the round earth—which we the world do call—
Is but a grain in that that mightiest swells,
Whereof the stars of light are particles,

As ultimate atoms of one infinite Ball,
On which God moves, and treads beneath his feet the All!

THE QUESTION

How shall I array my love?
How should I arrange my fair?
Leave her standing white and silent
In the richness of her hair?
Motion silent, beauty bare
In the glory of her hair?
Or, for place and drapery,
Ravage land, and sack the sea?

Or from darkest summer sky,
When the white belts, riding high,
Cut the clear like ribs of pearl,
On the eastern upland's curl,
In the time of dusk and dew
Tear away a breadth of blue?
Touched from twilight's rosy bars,
With each twinkling tuft of stars,
And, shaking out the glints of gold,
Catch her softly from the cold?—
Catch, and lift her to the cloud,
Where to crown her, passing proud,
Gliding, glistening woods of June,
Reach the rain-ring from the moon?

Or—to fold her warmer-wise—
Let me try, in garb and guise
Gathered from this mortal globe;
Roll her beauty in a robe
Of the Persian lilach stain,
Purple, dim with filigrane;
Belted-in with rarer red
Than India's leaf ere figurèd,
Put a crown upon her head!
Then to lead her, high and cold,

Where, from a step of silver rolled
A crimson floweth on the floor;
Like a river riding o'er
Pearl, and priceless marbles bright,—
Onyx, myrrhine, marcasite,
And jasper green!—nor these alone,
But the famed Phengites stone,—
And leading upward to the throne.
Prop and pillar, roof and rise,
All ashake with drops and dyes,
And the diamond's precious eyes;
And she, as if a sudden storm
Had fallen upon her face and form;
Diamonds like raindrops rare,
Pearls like hailstones in her hair;
In the lamplight's ruddy stream,
Jewels crossed with jewels gleam
On jewels, jewel-circled there;
While, round her wrists and ankles bare,
Gems of jewels glimpse and gaze,—
Hyacinth, rose-stone, idocrase.

Or she stealeth, soft arrayed
Like a white Hæmonian maid
Winding under cypress shade;
Cedar shade, and paths of green,
With porch and pillar, white between;
Amaranth eyes do mine behold,
Hair like the pale marigold:
Dreamily she seems to me
Hero, or Herodice!
With a sidelong motion sweet,
Thoro' flowers she draws her feet;
This way now the ripples come,—
Shower myrtles, myrrh, and gum,
With heliochryse and ámomum!

Ah! not so, New England's flower!
Separate must her beauty be
From stars of old mythology,—
Priestesses, or Chrysophoræ,
Nor fairy garb, nor kingly dower,
May fit her in her radiant hour;

Free and bold her steps must flow,
All men see her come and go;
At her feet the planet lies,
Day and night are in her eyes,
Over her the star-flag strewn:
Lo! she standeth there alone,
Pride, in her dark glances, king!
Love, her cheek rose-colouring;
In a garden all her own,
Lo! she standeth, crownèd on
With rare roses, round her drawn
Texture like the webs of dawn
On the rose-beds lingering,
While my heart to her I bring;
Heart and garden all her own—
What, in truth, cares such a one,
Though my arm could round her throw
Gleam of gods, or crowns bestow?
Or though the old gods could confer
All godlike gifts and grace on her?
The young Medusa's locks divine,
Pelops' shoulder eburnine,
Lips that drew the Ismenean bees,
Tears of the Heliades,
Dropped into shimmering shells that be
About the indraught of the sea.
The river-riches of the sphere,
All that the dark sea-bottoms bear,
The wide earth's green convexity,
The inexhaustible blue sky,
Hold not a prize, so proud, so high,
That it could grace her, gay or grand,
By garden-gale and rose-breath fanned;
Or as to-night I saw her stand,
Lovely in the meadow-land,
With a clover in her hand.

Frances E. W. Harper

(1825–1911)

THE SLAVE AUCTION

The sale began—young girls were there,
   Defenceless in their wretchedness,
Whose stifled sobs of deep despair
   Revealed their anguish and distress.

And mothers stood with streaming eyes,
   And saw their dearest children sold;
Unheeded rose their bitter cries,
   While tyrants bartered them for gold.

And woman, with her love and truth—
   For these in sable forms may dwell—
Gaz'd on the husband of her youth,
   With anguish none may paint or tell.

And men, whose sole crime was their hue,
   The impress of their Maker's hand,
And frail and shrinking children, too,
   Were gathered in that mournful band.

Ye who have laid your love to rest,
   And wept above their lifeless clay,
Know not the anguish of that breast,
   Whose lov'd are rudely torn away.

Ye may not know how desolate
   Are bosoms rudely forced to part,
And how a dull and heavy weight
   Will press the life-drops from the heart.

BURY ME IN A FREE LAND

Make me a grave where'er you will,
In a lowly plain, or a lofty hill,
Make it among earth's humblest graves.
But not in a land where men are slaves.

I could not rest if around my grave
I heard the steps of a trembling slave;
His shadow above my silent tomb
Would make it a place of fearful gloom.

I could not rest if I heard the tread
Of a coffie gang to the shambles led,
And the mother's shriek of wild despair
Rise like a curse on the trembling air.

I could not sleep if I saw the lash
Drinking her blood at each fearful gash,
And I saw her babes torn from her breast,
Like trembling doves from their parent nest.

I'd shudder and start if I heard the bay
Of blood-hounds seizing their human prey,
And I heard the captive plead in vain
As they bound afresh his galling chain.

If I saw young girls from their mother's arms
Bartered and sold for their youthful charms,
My eye would flash with a mournful flame,
My death-paled cheek grow red with shame.

I would sleep, dear friends, where bloated might
Can rob no man of his dearest right;
My rest shall be calm in any grave
Where none can call his brother a slave.

I ask no monument, proud and high
To arrest the gaze of the passers-by;
All that my yearning spirit craves,
Is bury me not in a land of slaves.

THE SLAVE MOTHER

A Tale of the Ohio

I have but four, the treasures of my soul,
    They lay like doves around my heart;
I tremble lest some cruel hand
    Should tear my household wreaths apart.

My baby girl, with childish glance,
    Looks curious in my anxious eye,
She little knows that for her sake
    Deep shadows round my spirit lie.

My playful boys could I forget,
    My home might seem a joyous spot,
But with their sunshine mirth I blend
    The darkness of their future lot.

And thou my babe, my darling one,
    My last, my loved, my precious child,
Oh! when I think upon thy doom
    My heart grows faint and then throbs wild.

The Ohio's bridged and spanned with ice,
    The northern star is shining bright,
I'll take the nestlings of my heart
    And search for freedom by its light.

Winter and night were on the earth,
    And feebly moaned the shivering trees,
A sigh of winter seemed to run
    Through every murmur of the breeze.

She fled, and with her children all,
    She reached the stream and crossed it o'er,
Bright visions of deliverance came
    Like dreams of plenty to the poor.

Dreams! vain dreams, heroic mother,
    Give all thy hopes and struggles o'er,

The pursuer is on thy track,
    And the hunter at thy door.

Judea's refuge cities had power
    To shelter, shield and save,
E'en Rome had altars, 'neath whose shade
    Might crouch the wan and weary slave.

But Ohio had no sacred fane,
    To human rights so consecrated,
Where thou may'st shield thy hapless ones
    From their darkly gathering fate.

Then, said the mournful mother,
    If Ohio cannot save,
I will do a deed for freedom,
    Shalt find each child a grave.

I will save my precious children
    From their darkly threatened doom,
I will hew their path to freedom
    Through the portals of the tomb.

A moment in the sunlight,
    She held a glimmering knife,
The next moment she had bathed it
    In the crimson fount of life.

They snatched away the fatal knife,
    Her boys shrieked wild with dread;
The baby girl was pale and cold,
    They raised it up, the child was dead.

Sends this deed of fearful daring
    Through my country's heart no thrill,
Do the icy hands of slavery
    Every pure emotion chill?

Oh! if there is any honor,
    Truth or justice in the land,
Will ye not, us men and Christians,
    On the side of freedom stand?

Henry Timrod

(1828–1867)

CHARLESTON

Calm as that second summer which precedes
   The first fall of the snow,
In the broad sunlight of heroic deeds,
   The City bides the foe.

As yet, behind their ramparts stern and proud,
   Her bolted thunders sleep —
Dark Sumter, like a battlemented cloud,
   Looms o'er the solemn deep.

No Calpe frowns from lofty cliff or scar
   To guard the holy strand;
But Moultrie holds in leash her dogs of war
   Above the level sand.

And down the dunes a thousand guns lie couched,
   Unseen, beside the flood—
Like tigers in some Orient jungle crouched
   That wait and watch for blood.

Meanwhile, through streets still echoing with trade,
   Walk grave and thoughtful men,
Whose hands may one day wield the patriot's blade
   As lightly as the pen.

And maidens, with such eyes as would grow dim
   Over a bleeding hound,
Seem each one to have caught the strength of him
   Whose sword she sadly bound.

Thus girt without and garrisoned at home,
   Day patient following day,
Old Charleston looks from roof, and spire, and dome,
   Across her tranquil bay.

Ships, through a hundred foes, from Saxon lands
    And spicy Indian ports,
Bring Saxon steel and iron to her hands,
    And Summer to her courts.

But still, along yon dim Atlantic line,
    The only hostile smoke
Creeps like a harmless mist above the brine,
    From some frail, floating oak.

Shall the Spring dawn, and she still clad in smiles,
    And with an unscathed brow,
Rest in the strong arms of her palm-crowned isles,
    As fair and free as now?

We know not; in the temple of the Fates
    God has inscribed her doom;
And, all untroubled in her faith, she waits
    The triumph or the tomb.

ODE

Sung on the occasion of decorating the graves of the
Confederate dead, at Magnolia Cemetery,
Charleston, S.C., 1867.

1

Sleep sweetly in your humble graves,
    Sleep, martyrs of a fallen cause;
Though yet no marble column craves
    The pilgrim here to pause.

2

In seeds of laurel in the earth
    The blossom of your fame is blown,
And somewhere, waiting for its birth,
    The shaft is in the stone!

3

Meanwhile, behalf the tardy years
    Which keep in trust your storied tombs,
Behold! your sisters bring their tears,
    And these memorial blooms.

4

Small tributes! but your shades will smile
    More proudly on these wreaths to-day,
Than when some cannon-moulded pile
    Shall overlook this bay.

5

Stoop, angels, hither from the skies!
    There is no holier spot of ground
Than where defeated valor lies,
    By mourning beauty crowned!

Emily Dickinson

(1830–1886)

SUCCESS IS
COUNTED SWEETEST

Success is counted sweetest
By those who ne'er succeed.
To comprehend a nectar
Requires sorest need.

Not one of all the purple host
Who took the flag to-day
Can tell the definition,
So clear, of victory,

As he, defeated, dying,
On whose forbidden ear
The distant strains of triumph
Break, agonized and clear.

A WOUNDED DEER
LEAPS HIGHEST

A wounded deer leaps highest,
I've heard the hunter tell;
'Tis but the ecstasy of death,
And then the brake is still.

The smitten rock that gushes,
The trampled steel that springs:
A cheek is always redder
Just where the hectic stings!

Mirth is the mail of anguish,
In which it cautious arm,
Lest anybody spy the blood
And "You're hurt" exclaim!

I FELT A FUNERAL IN MY BRAIN

I felt a funeral in my brain,
    And mourners, to and fro,
Kept treading, treading, till it seemed
    That sense was breaking through.

And when they all were seated,
    A service like a drum
Kept beating, beating, till I thought
    My mind was going numb.

And then I heard them lift a box,
    And creak across my soul
With those same boots of lead, again.
    Then space began to toll

As all the heavens were a bell,
    And Being but an ear,
And I and silence some strange race,
    Wrecked, solitary, here.

THERE'S A CERTAIN SLANT OF LIGHT

There's a certain slant of light
On winter afternoons,
That oppresses, like the weight
Of cathedral tunes.

Heavenly hurt it gives us;
We can find no scar,
But internal difference
Where the meanings are.

None may teach it anything,
'Tis the seal, despair,—
An imperial affliction
Sent us of the air.

When it comes, the landscape listens,
Shadows hold their breath;
When it goes, 'tis like the distance
On the look of death.

I CAN WADE GRIEF

I can wade grief,
Whole pools of it,—
I'm used to that.
But the least push of joy
Breaks up my feet,
And I tip — drunken.
Let no pebble smile,
'Twas the new liquor,—
That was all!

Power is only pain,
Stranded, through discipline,
Till weights will hang.
Give balm to giants,
And they'll wilt, like men.
Give Himmaleh,—
They'll carry him!

PAIN HAS AN ELEMENT OF BLANK

Pain has an element of blank;
It cannot recollect
When it began, or if there were
A day when it was not.

It has no future but itself,
Its infinite realms contain
Its past, enlightened to perceive
New periods of pain.

A BIRD CAME DOWN THE WALK

A bird came down the walk:
He did not know I saw;
He bit an angle-worm in halves
And ate the fellow, raw.

And then he drank a dew
From a convenient grass,
And then hopped sidewise to the wall
To let a beetle pass.

He glanced with rapid eyes
That hurried all abroad,—
They looked like frightened beads, I thought
He stirred his velvet head

Like one in danger; cautious,
I offered him a crumb,
And he unrolled his feathers
And rowed him softer home

Than oars divide the ocean,
Too silver for a seam,
Or butterflies, off banks of noon,
Leap, plashless, as they swim.

HE FUMBLES AT YOUR SPIRIT

He fumbles at your spirit
    As players at the keys
Before they drop full music on;
    He stuns you by degrees,

Prepares your brittle substance
    For the ethereal blow,
By fainter hammers, further heard,
    Then nearer, then so slow

Your breath has time to straighten,
  Your brain to bubble cool,—
Deals one imperial thunderbolt
  That scalps your naked soul.

I HEARD A FLY BUZZ WHEN I DIED

I heard a fly buzz when I died;
  The stillness round my form
Was like the stillness in the air
  Between the heaves of storm.

The eyes beside had wrung them dry,
  And breaths were gathering sure
For that last onset, when the king
  Be witnessed in his power.

I willed my keepsakes, signed away
  What portion of me I
Could make assignable,—and then
  There interposed a fly,

With blue, uncertain, stumbling buzz,
  Between the light and me;
And then the windows failed, and then
  I could not see to see.

I STARTED EARLY, TOOK MY DOG

I started early, took my dog,
And visited the sea;
The mermaids in the basement
Came out to look at me,

And frigates in the upper floor
Extended hempen hands,
Presuming me to be a mouse
Aground, upon the sands.

But no man moved me till the tide
Went past my simple shoe,
And past my apron and my belt,
And past my bodice too,

And made as he would eat me up
As wholly as a dew
Upon a dandelion's sleeve—
And then I started too.

And he—he followed close behind;
I felt his silver heel
Upon my ankle,—then my shoes
Would overflow with pearl.

Until we met the solid town,
No man he seemed to know;
And bowing with a mighty look
At me, the sea withdrew.

BECAUSE I COULD NOT STOP FOR DEATH

Because I could not stop for Death,
He kindly stopped for me;
The carriage held but just ourselves
And immortality.

We slowly drove, he knew no haste,
And I had put away
My labor, and my leisure too,
For his civility.

We passed the school where children played
Their lessons scarcely done;
We passed the fields of gazing grain,
We passed the setting sun.

Or rather, He passed Us.
The dews grew quivering and chill;
For only gossamer, my gown,
My tippet only tulle.

We paused before a house that seemed
A swelling of the ground;
The roof was scarcely visible,
The cornice but a mound.

Since then 'tis centuries; but each
Feels shorter than the day
I first surmised the horses' heads
Were toward eternity.

A NARROW FELLOW IN THE GRASS

A narrow fellow in the grass
Occasionally rides;
You may have met him,— did you not?
His notice sudden is.

The grass divides as with a comb,
A spotted shaft is seen;
And then it closes at your feet
And opens further on.

He likes a boggy acre,
A floor too cool for corn.
Yet when a child, and barefoot,
I more than once, at morn,

Have passed, I thought, a whip-lash
Unbraiding in the sun,—
When, stooping to secure it,
It wrinkled, and was gone.

Several of nature's people
I know, and they know me;
I feel for them a transport
Of cordiality;

But never met this fellow,
Attended or alone,
Without a tighter breathing,
And zero at the bone.

THE LAST NIGHT THAT SHE LIVED

The last night that she lived,
It was a common night,
Except the dying; this to us
Made nature different.

We noticed smallest things,—
Things overlooked before,
By this great light upon our minds
Italicized, as 'twere.

That others could exist
While she must finish quite,
A jealousy for her arose
So nearly infinite.

We waited while she passed;
It was a narrow time,
Too jostled were our souls to speak,
At length the notice came.

She mentioned, and forgot;
Then lightly as a reed
Bent to the water, shivered scarce,
Consented, and was dead.

And we, we placed the hair,
And drew the head erect;
And then an awful leisure was,
Our faith to regulate.

MY LIFE CLOSED TWICE BEFORE ITS CLOSE

My life closed twice before its close;
   It yet remains to see
If immortality unveil
   A third event to me,

So huge, so hopeless to conceive,
   As these that twice befell.
Parting is all we know of heaven,
   And all we need of hell.

TELL ALL THE TRUTH BUT TELL IT SLANT

Tell all the truth but tell it slant.
Success in circuit lies
Too bright for our infirm delight,
The truth's superb surprise
As lightning to the children eased
With explanation kind.
The truth must dazzle gradually
Or every man be blind.

Helen Hunt Jackson

(1830 – 1885)

MY LIGHTHOUSES

At westward window of a palace gray,
Which its own secret still so safely keeps
That no man now its builder's name can say,
I lie and idly sun myself to-day,
Dreaming awake far more than one who sleeps,
Serenely glad, although my gladness weeps.

I look across the harbor's misty blue,
And find and lose that magic shifting line
Where sky one shade less blue meets sea, and through
The air I catch one flush as if it knew
Some secret of that meeting, which no sign
Can show to eyes so far and dim as mine.

More ships than I can count build mast by mast
Gay lattice-work with waving green and red
Across my window-panes. The voyage past,
They crowd to anchorage so glad, so fast,
Gliding like ghosts, with noiseless breath and tread,
Mooring like ghosts, with noiseless iron and lead.

"O ships and patient men who fare by sea,"
I stretch my hands and vainly questioning cry,
"Sailed ye from west? How many nights could ye
Tell by the lights just where my dear and free
And lovely land lay sleeping? Passed ye by
Some danger safe, because her fires were nigh?"

Ah me! my selfish yearning thoughts forget
How darkness but a hand's-breadth from the coast
With danger in an evil league is set!
Ah! helpless ships and men more helpless yet,
Who trust the land-lights' short and empty boast;
The lights ye bear aloft and prayers avail ye most.

But I—ah, patient men who fare by sea,
Ye would but smile to hear this empty speech,—
I have such beacon-lights to burn for me,
In that dear west so lovely, new, and free,
That evil league by day, by night, can teach
No spell whose harm my little bark can reach.

No towers of stone uphold those beacon-lights;
No distance hides them, and no storm can shake;
In valleys they light up the darkest nights,
They outshine sunny days on sunny heights;
They blaze from every house where sleep or wake
My own who love me for my own poor sake.

Each thought they think of me lights road of flame
Across the seas; no travel on it tires
My heart. I go if they but speak my name;
From Heaven I should come and go the same,
And find this glow forestalling my desires.
My darlings, do you hear me? Trim the fires!

POPPIES ON THE WHEAT

Along Ancona's hills the shimmering heat,
A tropic tide of air with ebb and flow
Bathes all the fields of wheat until they glow
Like flashing seas of green, which toss and beat
Around the vines. The poppies lithe and fleet
Seem running, fiery torchmen, to and fro
To mark the shore.
                              The farmer does not know
That they are there. He walks with heavy feet,
Counting the bread and wine by autumn's gain,
But I,—I smile to think that days remain
Perhaps to me in which, though bread be sweet
No more, and red wine warm my blood in vain,
I shall be glad remembering how the fleet,
Lithe poppies ran like torchmen with the wheat.

Sidney Lanier

(1 8 4 2 – 1 8 8 1)

SONG OF THE CHATTAHOOCHEE

Out of the hills of Habersham,
  Down the valleys of Hall,
I hurry amain to reach the plain,
Run the rapid and leap the fall,
Split at the rock and together again,
Accept my bed, or narrow or wide,
And flee from folly on every side
With a lover's pain to attain the plain
  Far from the hills of Habersham,
  Far from the valleys of Hall.

All down the hills of Habersham,
  All through the valleys of Hall,
The rushes cried *Abide, abide,*
The willful waterweeds held me thrall,
The laving laurel turned my tide,
The ferns and the fondling grass said *Stay,*
The dewberry dipped for to work delay,
And the little reeds sighed *Abide, abide,*
  Here in the hills of Habersham,
  Here in the valleys of Hall.

High o'er the hills of Habersham,
  Veiling the valleys of Hall,
The hickory told me manifold
Fair tales of shade, the poplar tall
Wrought me her shadowy self to hold,
The chestnut, the oak, the walnut, the pine,
Overleaning, with flickering meaning and sign,
Said, *Pass not, so cold, these manifold*
  Deep shades of the hills of Habersham,
  These glades in the valleys of Hall.

And oft in the hills of Habersham,
  And oft in the valleys of Hall,
The white quartz shone, and the smooth brook-stone
Did bar me of passage with friendly brawl,
And many a luminous jewel lone
— Crystals clear or a-cloud with mist,
Ruby, garnet and amethyst—
Made lures with the lights of streaming stone
  In the clefts of the hills of Habersham,
  In the beds of the valleys of Hall.

  But oh, not the hills of Habersham,
  And oh, not the valleys of Hall
Avail: I am fain for to water the plain.
Downward the voices of Duty call—
Downward, to toil and be mixed with the main,
The dry fields burn, and the mills are to turn,
And a myriad flowers mortally yearn,
And the lordly main from beyond the plain
  Calls o'er the hills of Habersham,
  Calls through the valleys of Hall.

A BALLAD OF TREES AND THE MASTER

Into the woods my Master went,
Clean forspent, forspent.
Into the woods my Master came,
Forspent with love and shame.
But the olives they were not blind to Him,
The little gray leaves were kind to Him:
The thorn-tree had a mind to Him
When into the woods He came.

Out of the woods my Master went,
And He was well content.
Out of the woods my Master came,
Content with death and shame.
When Death and Shame would woo Him last,
From under the trees they drew Him last:

'Twas on a tree they slew Him—last
When out of the woods He came.

CLOVER

Inscribed to the Memory of John Keats

Dear uplands, Chester's favorable fields,
My large unjealous Loves, many yet one—
A grave good-morrow to your Graces, all,
Fair tilth and fruitful seasons!
                          Lo, how still!
The midmorn empties you of men, save me;
Speak to your lover, meadows! None can hear.
I lie as lies yon placid Brandywine,
Holding the hills and heavens in my heart
For contemplation.
                    'Tis a perfect hour.
From founts of dawn the fluent autumn day
Has rippled as a brook right pleasantly
Half-way to noon; but now with widening turn
Makes pause, in lucent meditation locked,
And rounds into a silver pool of morn,
Bottom'd with clover-fields. My heart just hears
Eight lingering strokes of some far village-bell,
That speak the hour so inward-voiced, meseems
Time's conscience has but whispered him eight hints
Of revolution. Reigns that mild surcease
That stills the middle of each rural morn—
When nimble noises that with sunrise ran
About the farms have sunk again to rest;
When Tom no more across the horse-lot calls
To sleepy Dick, nor Dick husk-voiced upbraids
The sway-back'd roan for stamping on his foot
With sulphurous oath and kick in flank, what time
The cart-chain clinks across the slanting shaft,
And, kitchenward, the rattling bucket plumps
Souse down the well, where quivering ducks quack loud,
And Susan Cook is singing.

                              Up the sky
The hesitating moon slow trembles on,
Faint as a new-washed soul but lately up
From out a buried body. Far about,
A hundred slopes in hundred fantasies
Most ravishingly run, so smooth of curve
That I but seem to see the fluent plain
Rise toward a rain of clover-bloom, as lakes
Pout gentle mounds of plashment up to meet
Big shower-drops. Now the little winds, as bees,
Bowing the blooms come wandering where I lie
Mixt soul and body with the clover-tufts,
Light on my spirit, give from wing and thigh
Rich pollens and divine sweet irritants
To every nerve, and freshly make report
Of inmost Nature's secret autumn-thought
Unto some soul of sense within my frame
That owns each cognizance of the outlying five,
And sees, hears, tastes, smells, touches, all in one.

Tell me, dear Clover (since my soul is thine,
Since I am fain give study all the day,
To make thy ways my ways, thy service mine,
To seek me out thy God, my God to be,
And die from out myself to live in thee) —
Now, Cousin Clover, tell me in mine ear:
Go'st thou to market with thy pink and green?
Of what avail, this color and this grace?
Wert thou but squat of stem and brindle-brown,
Still careless herds would feed. A poet, thou:
What worth, what worth, the whole of all thine art?
Three-Leaves, instruct me! I am sick of price.

Framed in the arching of two clover-stems
Where-through I gaze from off my hill, afar,
The spacious fields from me to Heaven take on
Tremors of change and new significance
To th' eye, as to the ear a simple tale
Begins to hint a parable's sense beneath.
The prospect widens, cuts all bounds of blue
Where horizontal limits bend, and spreads
Into a curious-hill'd and curious-valley'd Vast,
Endless before, behind, around; which seems

Th' incalculable Up-and-Down of Time
Made plain before mine eyes. The clover-stems
Still cover all the space; but now they bear,
For clover-blooms, fair, stately heads of men
With poets' faces heartsome, dear and pale—
Sweet visages of all the souls of time
Whose loving service to the world has been
In the artist's way expressed and bodied. Oh,
In arms' reach, here be Dante, Keats, Chopin,
Raphael, Lucretius, Omar, Angelo,
Beethoven, Chaucer, Schubert, Shakspere, Bach,
And Buddha (sweetest masters! Let me lay
These arms this once, this humble once, about
Your reverend necks—the most containing clasp,
For all in all, this world e'er saw!), and there,
Yet further on, bright throngs unnamable
Of workers worshipful, nobilities
In the Court of Gentle Service, silent men,
Dwellers in woods, brooders on helpful art,
And all the press of them, the fair, the large,
That wrought with beauty.
                              Lo, what bulk is here?
Now comes the Course-of-things, shaped like an Ox,
Slow browsing, o'er my hillside, ponderously—
The huge-brawned, tame, and workful Course-of-things,
That hath his grass, if earth be round or flat,
And hath his grass, if empires plunge in pain
Or faiths flash out. This cool, unasking Ox
Comes browsing o'er my hills and vales of Time,
And thrusts me out his tongue, and curls it, sharp
And sicklewise, about my poets' heads,
And twists them in, all—Dante, Keats, Chopin,
Raphael, Lucretius, Omar, Angelo,
Beethoven, Chaucer, Schubert, Shakspere, Bach,
And Buddha, in one sheaf—and champs and chews,
With slanty-churning jaws, and swallows down;
Then slowly plants a mighty forefoot out,
And makes advance to futureward, one inch.
So: they have played their part.
                              And to this end?
This, God? This, troublous-breeding Earth? This, Sun
Of hot, quick pains? To this no-end that ends,
These Masters wrought, and wept, and sweated blood,

And burned, and loved, and ached with public shame,
And found no friends to breathe their loves to, save
Woods and wet pillows? This was all? This Ox?
"Nay," quoth a sum of voices in mine ear,
"God's clover, we, and feed His Course-of-things;
The pasture is God's pasture; systems strange
Of food and fiberment He hath, whereby
The general brawn is built for plans of His
To quality precise. Kinsman, learn this:
The artist's market is the heart of man;
The artist's price, some little good of man.
Tease not thy vision with vain search for ends.
The End of Means is art that works by love.
The End of Ends . . . in God's Beginning's lost."

Sarah Orne Jewett

(1849–1887)

AT HOME FROM CHURCH

The lilacs lift in generous bloom
    Their plumes of dear old-fashioned flowers;
Their fragrance fills the still old house
    Where left alone I count the hours.

High in the apple-trees the bees
    Are humming, busy in the sun,—
An idle robin cries for rain
    But once or twice and then is done.

The Sunday-morning quiet holds
    In heavy slumber all the street,
While from the church, just out of sight
    Behind the elms, comes slow and sweet

The organ's drone, the voices faint
    That sing the quaint long-meter hymn—
I somehow feel as if shut out
    From some mysterious temple, dim

And beautiful with blue and red
    And golden lights from windows high,
Where angels in the shadows stand
    And earth seems very near the sky.

The day-dream fades—and so I try
    Again to catch the tune that brings
No thought of temple nor of priest,
    But only of voice that sings.

A COUNTRY BOY IN WINTER

The wind may blow the snow about,
   For all I care, says Jack,
And I don't mind how cold it grows,
   For then the ice won't crack.
Old folks may shiver all day long,
   But I shall never freeze;
What cares a jolly boy like me
   For winter days like these?

Far down the long snow-covered hills
   It is such fun to coast,
So clear the road! the fastest sled
   There is in school I boast.
The paint is pretty well worn off,
   But then I take the lead;
A dandy sled's a loiterer,
   And I go in for speed.

When I go home at supper-time,
   Ki! but my cheeks are red!
They burn and sting like anything;
   I'm cross until I'm fed.
You ought to see the biscuit go,
   I am so hungry then;
And old Aunt Polly says that boys
   Eat twice as much as men.

There's always something I can do
   To pass the time away;
The dark comes quick in winter-time—
   A short and stormy day
And when I give my mind to it,
   It's just as father says,
I almost do a man's work now,
   And help him many ways.

I shall be glad when I grow up
   And get all through with school,

I'll show them by-and-by that I
    Was not meant for a fool.
I'll take the crops off this old farm,
    I'll do the best I can.
A jolly boy like me won't be
    A dolt when he's a man.

I like to hear the old horse neigh
    Just as I come in sight,
The oxen poke me with their horns
    To get their hay at night.
Somehow the creatures seem like friends,
    And like to see me come.
Some fellows talk about New York,
    But I shall stay at home.

A CAGED BIRD

High at the window in her cage
    The old canary flits and sings,
Nor sees across the curtain pass
    The shadow of a swallow's wings.

A poor deceit and copy, this,
    Of larger lives that mark their span,
Unreckoning of wider worlds
    Or gifts that Heaven keeps for man.

She gathers piteous bits and shreds,
    This solitary, mateless thing,
To patient build again the nest
    So rudely scattered spring by spring;

And sings her brief, unlistened songs,
    Her dreams of bird life wild and free,
Yet never beats her prison bars
    At sound of song from bush or tree.

But in my busiest hours I pause,
    Held by a sense of urgent speech,

Bewildered by that spark-like soul,
   Able my very soul to reach.

She will be heard; she chirps me loud,
   When I forget those gravest cares,
Her small provision to supply,
   Clear water or her seedsman's wares.

She begs me now for that chief joy
   The round great world is made to grow,—
Her wisp of greenness. Hear her chide,
   Because my answering thought is slow!

What can my life seem like to her?
   A dull, unpunctual service mine;
Stupid before her eager call,
   Her flitting steps, her insight fine.

To open wide thy prison door,
   Poor friend, would give thee to thy foes;
And yet a plaintive note I hear,
   As if to tell how slowly goes

The time of thy long prisoning.
   Bird! does some promise keep thee sane?
Will there be better days for thee?
   Will thy soul too know life again?

Ah, none of us have more than this:
   If one true friend green leaves can reach
From out some fairer, wider place,
   And understand our wistful speech!

Emma Lazarus

(1849 – 1887)

THE NEW EZEKIEL

What, can these dead bones live, whose sap is dried
    By twenty scorching centuries of wrong?
Is this the House of Israel, whose pride
    Is as a tale that's told, an ancient song?
Are these ignoble relics all that live
    Of psalmist, priest, and prophet? Can the breath
Of very heaven bid these bones revive,
    Open the graves and clothe the ribs of death?
Yea, Prophesy, the Lord hath said. Again
    Say to the wind, Come forth and breathe afresh,
Even that they may live upon these slain,
    And bone to bone shall leap, and flesh to flesh.
The Spirit is not dead, proclaim the word,
    Where lay dead bones, a host of armed men stand!
I ope your graves, my people, saith the Lord,
    And I shall place you living in your land.

THE SOUTH

Night, and beneath star-blazoned summer skies
    Behold the Spirit of the musky South,
A creole with still-burning, languid eyes,
    Voluptuous limbs and incense-breathing mouth:
            Swathed in spun gauze is she,
From fibres of her own anana tree.

Within these sumptuous woods she lies at ease.
    By rich night-breezes, dewy cool, caressed:
'Twixt cypresses and slim palmetto trees,

269

Like to the golden oriole's hanging nest,
    Her airy hammock swings,
And through the dark her mocking-bird yet sings.

How beautiful she is! A tulip-wreath
   Twines round her shadowy, free-floating hair:
Young, weary, passionate, and sad as death,
   Dark visions haunt for her the vacant air,
     While movelessly she lies
With lithe, lax, folded hands and heavy eyes.

Full well knows she how wide and fair extend
   Her groves bright-flowered, her tangled everglades,
Majestic streams that indolently wend
   Through lush savanna or dense forest shades,
     Where the brown buzzard flies
To broad bayous 'neath hazy-golden skies.

Hers is the savage splendor of the swamp,
   With pomp of scarlet and of purple bloom,
Where blow warm, furtive breezes faint and damp,
   Strange insects whir, and stalking bitterns boom—
     Where from stale waters dead
Oft looms the great-jawed alligator's head.

Her wealth, her beauty, and the blight on these,—
   Of all she is aware: luxuriant woods,
Fresh, living, sunlit, in her dream she sees;
   And ever midst those verdant solitudes
     The soldier's wooden cross,
O'ergrown by creeping tendrils and rank moss.

Was hers a dream of empire? was it sin?
   And is it well that all was borne in vain?
She knows no more than one who slow doth win.
   After fierce fever, conscious life again,
     Too tired, too weak, too sad,
By the new light to be or stirred or glad.

From rich sea-islands fringing her green shore,
   From broad plantations where swart freemen bend
Bronzed backs in willing labor, from her store

Of golden fruit, from stream, from town, ascend
      Life-currents of pure health:
Her aims shall be subserved with boundless wealth.

Yet now how listless and how still she lies,
   Like some half-savage, dusky Indian queen,
Rocked in her hammock 'neath her native skies,
   With the pathetic, passive, broken mien
      Of one who, sorely proved,
Great-souled, hath suffered much and much hath loved!

But look! along the wide-branched, dewy glade
   Glimmers the dawn: the light palmetto-trees
And cypresses reissue from the shade,
   And *she* hath wakened. Through clear air she sees
      The pledge, the brightening ray,
And leaps from dreams to hail the coming day.

Louise Imogen Guiney

(1 8 6 1 – 1 9 2 0)

THE WILD RIDE

I hear in my heart, I hear in its ominous pulses
All day, on the road, the hoofs of invisible horses,
All night, from their stalls, the importunate pawing and neighing.

Let cowards and laggards fall back! but alert to the saddle
Weather-worn and abreast, go men of our galloping legion,
With a stirrup-cup each to the lily of women that loves him.

The trail is through dolour and dread, over crags and morasses;
There are shapes by the way, there are things that appal or entice us:
What odds? We are Knights of the Grail, we are vowed to the riding.

Thought's self is a vanishing wing, and joy is a cobweb,
And friendship a flower in the dust, and glory a sunbeam:
Not here is our prize, nor, alas! after these our pursuing.

A dipping of plumes, a tear, a shake of the bridle,
A passing salute to this world and her pitiful beauty:
We hurry with never a word in the track of our fathers.

(I hear in my heart, I hear in its ominous pulses
All day, on the road, the hoofs of invisible horses,
All night, from their stalls, the importunate pawing and neighing.)

We spur to a land of no name, out-racing the storm-wind;
We leap to the infinite dark like sparks from the anvil.
Thou leadest, O God! All's well with Thy troopers that follow.

WHEN ON THE MARGE OF EVENING

When on the marge of evening the last blue light is broken,
And winds of dreamy odour are loosened from afar,
Or when my lattice opens, before the lark hath spoken,
On dim laburnum-blossoms, and morning's dying star,

I think of thee (O mine the more if other eyes be sleeping!),
Whose greater noonday splendours the many share and see,
While sacred and for ever, some perfect law is keeping
The late, the early twilight, alone and sweet for me.

Edgar Lee Masters

(1868 – 1950)

THE HILL

Where are Elmer, Herman, Bert, Tom and Charley,
The weak of will, the strong of arm, the clown, the boozer, the fighter?
All, all, are sleeping on the hill.

One passed in a fever,
One was burned in a mine,
One was killed in a brawl,
One died in a jail,
One fell from a bridge toiling for children and wife—
All, all are sleeping, sleeping, sleeping on the hill.

Where are Ella, Kate, Mag, Lizzie and Edith,
The tender heart, the simple soul, the loud, the proud, the happy one?—
All, all, are sleeping on the hill.

One died in shameful child-birth,
One of a thwarted love,
One at the hands of a brute in a brothel,
One of a broken pride, in the search for heart's desire,
One after life in far-away London and Paris
Was brought to her little space by Ella and Kate and Mag—
All, all are sleeping, sleeping, sleeping on the hill.

Where are Uncle Isaac and Aunt Emily,
And old Towny Kincaid and Sevigne Houghton,
And Major Walker who had talked
With venerable men of the revolution?—
All, all, are sleeping on the hill.

They brought them dead sons from the war,
And daughters whom life had crushed,
And their children fatherless, crying—
All, all are sleeping, sleeping, sleeping on the hill.

Where is Old Fiddler Jones
Who played with life all his ninety years,
Braving the sleet with bared breast,
Drinking, rioting, thinking neither of wife nor kin,
Nor gold, nor love, nor heaven?
Lo! he babbles of the fish-frys of long ago,
Of the horse-races of long ago at Clary's Grove,
Of what Abe Lincoln said
One time at Springfield.

PETIT, THE POET

Seeds in a dry pod, tick, tick, tick,
Tick, tick, tick, like mites in a quarrel—
Faint iambics that the full breeze wakens—
But the pine tree makes a symphony thereof.
Triolets, villanelles, rondels, rondeaus,
Ballades by the score with the same old thought:
The snows and the roses of yesterday are vanished;
And what is love but a rose that fades?
Life all around me here in the village:
Tragedy, comedy, valor and truth,
Courage, constancy, heroism, failure—
All in the loom, and oh what patterns!
Woodlands, meadows, streams and rivers—
Blind to all of it all my life long.
Triolets, villanelles, rondels, rondeaus,
Seeds in a dry pod, tick, tick, tick,
Tick, tick, tick, what little iambics,
While Homer and Whitman roared in the pines?

THE LOST ORCHARD

Loves and sorrows of those who lose an orchard
Are less seen than the shadow shells
Of butterflies whose wings are tortured

In the perilous escape of rainy dells,
In the ecstatic flight of blinding Junes.
Save for the breath dirge of the wind-rung harebells
They have no words that ever shall be known,
Neither have they speech or tone,
Save the tones when the sun with gold galloons
Trims the blue edges of the air;
And save the quiet which quells
The music of the water drop in the well's
Water far down, where vision swoons.

These are the voices and these alone
Of the lost orchard, and its vague despair.
Branches may gnarl with scale and lift their bare
Paralysis, or the withered crone
Of loneliness breed water sprouts; or frost
Heap the dull turf over the strawberry vines;
Or rust unhinge the gates; or the fallen pear
Waste like the Cretan gold of ruined shrines
In tangled grasses; or the broken share
Be sunk in leaf mould—these are noonday signs
Of the deserted, but not of the orchard that is lost.
Silver secrets speak of the lost orchard, as the shells
Of butterflies escaped whisper the vanished wings;
Or as light shaken from the field of clover tells
Of the zephyr's irised wanderings.

A lost orchard is the memory of a friend
Wronged by life to death, who lies
Lifelike, but with unseeing eyes.
It is music made a ghost, because the end
Of life has come which made the music mean
Eyes that look and lips that thrill.
Music is no breast where wounded souls may lean,
If played when hands it signified are still.
A lost orchard is the road on which we passed
Where a house was with a candle in the night;
And we must go that way still, but at last
The house is by the roadside, but no light.

Over a lost orchard I have strayed
In March when down the wooded ravine
The behemoth wind bellowed to the glade

By the sky-blue water before the rushes were green.
While yet the acorn cups crushed under feet
Against the moss mould, yellow as smoke;
And the lanterns of wild cucumbers quenched by sleet,
And gusts of winter hung by the leafless oak;
When the crow's nest was a splotch of sticks on the sky,
And burnt out torches of feasts the sumach cone.
And I have climbed till the wind was naught but a sigh
Over the stairs of stone and the seat of stone.
And there I have seen the orchard, the apple trees
Patient in loneliness, and forgotten care;
And the grass as heavy as the Sargasso Sea's
Around the trunks, grown like a dead man's hair.
And I have returned in Spring when the nebulae
Of early blossoms whitened before it was June;
And I have seen them merge in their leafy sky
Till they became the light of the full moon.
Warm is the orchard as the stalls of the sun
At midnight, when each budded stem is dewed
With a firefly and the whispering zephyrs run
From leaf to leaf, awaking the dreams that brood
Before the gray woolens of the shadows fall
From the sleeping earth, and the lights of the orchard are wooed
From sea gray to sea green in a carnival
Change of flame, in a dawning many hued.
Till the long winds come, blowing from woodlands over
The glistening water, and meadows beyond the citrine
Sand of the hill that walls the field of clover
Nod their blossoms amid a tide of green.

Edwin Arlington Robinson

(1869–1935)

JOHN EVERELDOWN

"Where are you going tonight, tonight,—
    Where are you going, John Evereldown?
There's never the sign of a star in sight,
    Nor a lamp that's nearer than Tilbury Town.
Why do you stare as a dead man might?
Where are you pointing away from the light?
And where are you going tonight, tonight,—
    Where are you going, John Evereldown?"

"Right through the forest, where none can see,
    There's where I'm going, to Tilbury Town.
The men are asleep,—or awake, may be,—
    But the women are calling John Evereldown.
Ever and ever they call for me,
And while they call can a man be free?
So right through the forest, where none can see,
    There's where I'm going, to Tilbury Town."

"But why are you going so late, so late,—
    Why are you going, John Evereldown?
Though the road may be smooth and the way be straight,
    There are two long leagues to Tilbury Town.
Come in by the fire, old man, and wait!
Why do you chatter out there by the gate?
And why are you going so late, so late,—
    Why are you going, John Evereldown?"

"I follow the women wherever they call,—
    That's why I'm going to Tilbury Town.
God knows if I pray to be done with it all,
    But God is no friend to John Evereldown.
So the clouds may come and the rain may fall,
The shadows may creep and the dead men crawl,—

But I follow the women wherever they call,
  And that's why I'm going to Tilbury Town."

RICHARD CORY

Whenever Richard Cory went down town,
We people on the pavement looked at him:
He was a gentleman from sole to crown,
Clean favored, and imperially slim.

And he was always quietly arrayed,
And he was always human when he talked;
But still he fluttered pulses when he said,
"Good-morning," and he glittered when he walked.

And he was rich—yes, richer than a king—
And admirably schooled in every grace:
In fine, we thought that he was everything
To make us wish that we were in his place.

So on we worked, and waited for the light,
And went without the meat, and cursed the bread;
And Richard Cory, one calm summer night,
Went home and put a bullet through his head.

MINIVER CHEEVY

Miniver Cheevy, child of scorn,
  Grew lean while he assailed the seasons;
He wept that he was ever born,
  And he had reasons.

Miniver loved the days of old
  When swords were bright and steeds were prancing;
The vision of a warrior bold
  Would set him dancing.

Miniver sighed for what was not,
    And dreamed, and rested from his labors;
He dreamed of Thebes and Camelot,
    And Priam's neighbors.

Miniver mourned the ripe renown
    That made so many a name so fragrant;
He mourned Romance, now on the town,
    And Art, a vagrant.

Miniver loved the Medici,
    Albeit he had never seen one;
He would have sinned incessantly
    Could he have been one.

Miniver cursed the commonplace
    And eyed a khaki suit with loathing;
He missed the mediæval grace
    Of iron clothing.

Miniver scorned the gold he sought,
    But sore annoyed was he without it;
Miniver thought, and thought, and thought,
    And thought about it.

Miniver Cheevy, born too late,
    Scratched his head and kept on thinking;
Miniver coughed, and called it fate,
    And kept on drinking.

MR. FLOOD'S PARTY

Old Eben Flood, climbing alone one night
Over the hill between the town below
And the forsaken upland hermitage
That held as much as he should ever know
On earth again of home, paused warily.
The road was his with not a native near;
And Eben, having leisure, said aloud,
For no man else in Tilbury Town to hear:

"Well, Mr. Flood, we have the harvest moon
Again, and we may not have many more;
The bird is on the wing, the poet says,
And you and I have said it here before.
Drink to the bird." He raised up to the light
The jug that he had gone so far to fill,
And answered huskily: "Well, Mr. Flood,
Since you propose it, I believe I will."

Alone, as if enduring to the end
A valiant armor of scarred hopes outworn,
He stood there in the middle of the road
Like Roland's ghost winding a silent horn.
Below him, in the town among the trees,
Where friends of other days had honored him,
A phantom salutation of the dead
Rang thinly till old Eben's eyes were dim.

Then, as a mother lays her sleeping child
Down tenderly, fearing it may awake,
He set the jug down slowly at his feet
With trembling care, knowing that most things break;
And only when assured that on firm earth
It stood, as the uncertain lives of men
Assuredly did not, he paced away,
And with his hand extended paused again:

"Well, Mr. Flood, we have not met like this
In a long time; and many a change has come
To both of us, I fear, since last it was
We had a drop together. Welcome home!"
Convivially returning with himself,
Again he raised the jug up to the light;
And with an acquiescent quaver said:
"Well, Mr. Flood, if you insist, I might.

"Only a very little, Mr. Flood—
For auld lang syne. No more, sir; that will do."
So, for the time, apparently it did,
And Eben evidently thought so too;
For soon amid the silver loneliness
Of night he lifted up his voice and sang,

Secure, with only two moons listening,
Until the whole harmonious landscape rang—

"For auld lang syne." The weary throat gave out,
The last word wavered, and the song was done.
He raised again the jug regretfully
And shook his head, and was again alone.
There was not much that was ahead of him,
And there was nothing in the town below—
Where strangers would have shut the many doors
That many friends had opened long ago.

Stephen Crane

(1871–1900)

From THE BLACK RIDERS

IN THE DESERT

In the desert
I saw a creature, naked, bestial,
Who, squatting upon the ground,
Held his heart in his hands,
And ate of it.
I said, "Is it good, friend?"
"It is bitter—bitter," he answered;
"But I like it
Because it is bitter,
And because it is my heart."

James Weldon Johnson

(1871-1938)

O BLACK AND UNKNOWN BARDS

O black and unknown bards of long ago,
How came your lips to touch the sacred fire?
How, in your darkness, did you come to know
The power and beauty of the minstrel's lyre?
Who first from midst his bonds lifted his eyes?
Who first from out the still watch, lone and long,
Feeling the ancient faith of prophets rise
Within his dark-kept soul, burst into song?

Heart of what slave poured out such melody
As "Steal away to Jesus"? On its strains
His spirit must have nightly floated free,
Though still about his hands he felt his chains.
Who heard great "Jordan roll"? Whose starward eye
Saw chariot "swing low"? And who was he
That breathed that comforting, melodic sigh,
"Nobody knows de trouble I see"?

What merely living clod, what captive thing,
Could up toward God through all its darkness grope,
And find within its deadened heart to sing
These songs of sorrow, love and faith, and hope?
How did it catch that subtle undertone,
That note in music heard not with the ears?
How sound the elusive reed so seldom blown,
Which stirs the soul or melts the heart to tears.

Not that great German master in his dream
Of harmonies that thundered amongst the stars
At the creation, ever heard a theme
Nobler than "Go down, Moses." Mark its bars
How like a mighty trumpet-call they stir
The blood. Such are the notes that men have sung

Going to valorous deeds; such tones there were
That helped make history when Time was young.

There is a wide, wide wonder in it all,
That from degraded rest and servile toil
The fiery spirit of the seer should call
These simple children of the sun and soil.
O black slave singers, gone, forgot, unfamed,
You—you alone, of all the long, long line
Of those who've sung untaught, unknown, unnamed,
Have stretched out upward, seeking the divine.

You sang not deeds of heroes or of kings;
No chant of bloody war, no exulting paean
Of arms-won triumphs; but your humble strings
You touched in chord with music empyrean.
You sang far better than you knew; the songs
That for your listeners' hungry hearts sufficed
Still live,—but more than this to you belongs:
You sang a race from wood and stone to Christ.

Paul Laurence Dunbar

(1872 – 1906)

A NEGRO LOVE SONG

Seen my lady home las' night,
  Jump back, honey, jump back.
Hel' huh han' an' sque'z it tight,
  Jump back, honey, jump back.
Hyeahd huh sigh a little sigh,
Seen a light gleam f'om huh eye,
An' a smile go flittin' by—
  Jump back, honey, jump back.

Hyeahd de win' blow thoo de pine,
  Jump back, honey, jump back.
Mockin'-bird was singin' fine,
  Jump back, honey, jump back.
An' my hea't was beatin' so,
When I reached my lady's do',
Dat I could n't ba' to go—
  Jump back, honey, jump back.

Put my ahm aroun' huh wais',
  Jump back, honey, jump back.
Raised huh lips an' took a tase,
  Jump back, honey, jump back.
Love me, honey, love me true?
Love me well ez I love you?
An' she answe'd, "Cose I do"—
  Jump back, honey, jump back.

ERE SLEEP COMES DOWN
TO SOOTHE THE WEARY EYES

Ere sleep comes down to soothe the weary eyes,
Which all the day with ceaseless care have sought
The magic gold which from the seeker flies;
Ere dreams put on the gown and cap of thought,
And make the waking world a world of lies,—
Of lies most palpable, uncouth, forlorn,
That say life's full of aches and tears and sighs—
Oh, how with more than dreams the soul is torn,
Ere sleep comes down to soothe the weary eyes.

Ere sleep comes down to soothe the weary eyes,
How all the griefs and heartaches we have known
Come up like pois'nous vapors that arise
From some base witch's caldron, when the crone,
To work some potent spell, her magic plies.
The past which held its share of bitter pain,
Whose ghost we prayed that Time might exorcise,
Comes up, is lived and suffered o'er again,
Ere sleep comes down to soothe the weary eyes.

Ere sleep comes down to soothe the weary eyes,
What phantoms fill the dimly lighted room;
What ghostly shades in awe-creating guise
Are bodied forth within the teeming gloom.
What echoes faint of sad and soul-sick cries,
And pangs of vague inexplicable pain
That pay the spirit's ceaseless enterprise,
Come thronging through the chambers of the brain,
Ere sleep comes down to soothe the weary eyes.

Ere sleep comes down to soothe the weary eyes,
Where ranges forth the spirit far and free?
Through what strange realms and unfamiliar skies
Tends her far course to lands of mystery?
To lands unspeakable—beyond surmise,
Where shapes unknowable to being spring,
Till, faint of wing, the Fancy fails and dies
Much wearied with the spirit's journeying,
Ere sleep comes down to soothe the weary eyes.

Ere sleep comes down to soothe the weary eyes,
How questioneth the soul that other soul—
The inner sense which neither cheats nor lies,
But self exposes unto self, a scroll
Full writ with all life's acts unwise or wise,
In characters indelible and known;
So, trembling with the shock of sad surprise,
The soul doth view its awful self alone,
Ere sleep comes down to soothe the weary eyes.

When sleep comes down to seal the weary eyes,
The last dear sleep whose soft embrace is balm,
And whom sad sorrow teaches us to prize
For kissing all our passions into calm,
Ah, then, no more we heed the sad world's cries,
Or seek to probe th' eternal mystery,
Or fret our souls at long-withheld replies,
At glooms through which our visions cannot see,
When sleep comes down to seal the weary eyes.

SHIPS THAT PASS IN THE NIGHT

Out in the sky the great dark clouds are massing;
    I look far out into the pregnant night,
Where I can hear a solemn booming gun
    And catch the gleaming of a random light,
That tells me that the ship I seek is passing, passing.

My tearful eyes my soul's deep hurt are glassing;
    For I would hail and check that ship of ships.
I stretch my hands imploring, cry aloud,
    My voice falls dead a foot from mine own lips,
And but its ghost doth reach that vessel, passing, passing.

O Earth, O Sky, O Ocean, both surpassing,
    O heart of mine, O soul that dreads the dark!
Is there no hope for me? Is there no way
    That I may sight and check that speeding bark
Which out of sight and sound is passing, passing?

LOVER'S LANE

Summah night an' sighin' breeze,
   'Long de lovah's lane;
Frien'ly, shadder-mekin' trees,
   'Long de lovah's lane.
White folks' wo'k all done up gran'—
Me an' 'Mandy han'-in-han'
Struttin' lak we owned de lan',
   'Long de lovah's lane.

Owl a-settin' 'side de road,
   'Long de lovah's lane,
Lookin' at us lak he knowed
   Dis uz lovah's lane.
Go on, hoot yo' mou'nful tune,
You ain' nevah loved in June,
An' come hidin' fom de moon
   Down in lovah's lane.

Bush it ben' an' nod an' sway,
   Down in lovah's lane,
Try'n' to hyeah me whut I say
   'Long de lovah's lane.
But I whispahs low lak dis,
An' my 'Mandy smile huh bliss—
Mistah Bush he shek his fis',
   Down in lovah's lane.

Whut I keer ef day is long,
   Down in lovah's lane.
I kin allus sing a song
   'Long de lovah's lane.
An' de wo'ds I hyeah an' say
Meks up fu' de weary day
W'en I's strollin' by de way,
   Down in lovah's lane.

An' dis t'ought will allus rise
   Down in lovah's lane;

Wondah whethah in de skies
   Dey's a lovah's lane.
Ef dey ain't, I tell you true,
'Ligion do look mighty blue,
'Cause I do' know whut I'd do
   'Dout a lovah's lane.

THE DEBT

This is the debt I pay
Just for one riotous day,
Years of regret and grief,
Sorrow without relief.

Pay it I will to the end—
Until the grave, my friend,
Gives me a true release—
Gives me the clasp of peace.

Slight was the thing I bought,
Small was the debt I thought,
Poor was the loan at best—
God! but the interest!

THE HAUNTED OAK

Pray why are you so bare, so bare,
   Oh, bough of the old oak-tree;
And why, when I go through the shade you throw,
   Runs a shudder over me?

My leaves were green as the best, I trow,
   And sap ran free in my veins,
But I saw in the moonlight dim and weird
   A guiltless victim's pains.

I bent me down to hear his sigh;
   I shook with his gurgling moan,
And I trembled sore when they rode away,
   And left him here alone.

They'd charged him with the old, old crime,
   And set him fast in jail:
Oh, why does the dog howl all night long,
   And why does the night wind wail?

He prayed his prayer and he swore his oath,
   And he raised his hand to the sky;
But the beat of hoofs smote on his ear,
   And the steady tread drew nigh.

Who is it rides by night, by night,
   Over the moonlit road?
And what is the spur that keeps the pace,
   What is the galling goad?

And now they beat at the prison door,
   "Ho, keeper, do not stay!
We are friends of him whom you hold within,
   And we fain would take him away

"From those who ride fast on our heels
   With mind to do him wrong;
They have no care for his innocence,
   And the rope they bear is long."

They have fooled the jailer with lying words,
   They have fooled the man with lies;
The bolts unbar, the locks are drawn,
   And the great door open flies.

Now they have taken him from the jail,
   And hard and fast they ride,
And the leader laughs low down in his throat,
   As they halt my trunk beside.

Oh, the judge, he wore a mask of black,
   And the doctor one of white,

And the minister, with his oldest son,
　　Was curiously bedight.

Oh, foolish man, why weep you now?
　　'Tis but a little space,
And the time will come when these shall dread
　　The mem'ry of your face.

I feel the rope against my bark,
　　And the weight of him in my grain,
I feel in the throe of his final woe
　　The touch of my own last pain.

And never more shall leaves come forth
　　On a bough that bears the ban;
I am burned with dread, I am dried and dead,
　　From the curse of a guiltless man.

And ever the judge rides by, rides by,
　　And goes to hunt the deer,
And ever another rides his soul
　　In the guise of a mortal fear.

And ever the man he rides me hard,
　　And never a night stays he;
For I feel his curse as a haunted bough
　　On the trunk of a haunted tree.

Trumbull Stickney

(1 8 7 4 – 1 9 0 4)

AGE IN YOUTH

From far she's come, and very old,
And very soiled with wandering.
The dust of seasons she has brought
Unbidden to this field of Spring.

She's halted at the log-barred gate.
The May-day waits, a tangled spill
Of light that weaves and moves along
The daisied margin of the hill,

Where Nature bares her bridal heart,
And on her snowy soul the sun
Languors desirously and dull,
An amorous pale vermilion.

She's halted, propped her rigid arms,
With dead big eyes she drinks the west;
The brown rags hang like clotted dust
About her, save her withered breast.

A very soilure of a dream
Runs in the furrows of her brow,
And with a crazy voice she croons
An ugly catch of long ago.

Its broken rhythm is hard and hoarse,
Its sunken soul of music toils
In precious ashes, dust of youth
And lovely faces sorrow soils.

But look! Along the molten sky
There runs strange havoc of the sun.
"What a strange sight this is," she says,
"I'll cross the field, I'll follow on."

The bars are falling from the gate.
The meshes of the meadow yield;
And trudging sunsetward she draws
A journey thro' the daisy field.

The daisies shudder at her hem.
Her dry face laughs with flowery light;
An aureole lifts her soiled gray hair:
"I'll on," she says, "to see this sight."

In the rude math her torn shoe mows
Juices of trod grass and crushed stalk
Mix with a soiled and earthy dew,
With smear of petals gray as chalk.

The Spring grows sour along her track;
The winy airs of amethyst
Turn acid. "Just beyond the ledge,"
She says, "I'll see the sun at rest."

And to the tremor of her croon,
Her old, old catch of long ago,
The newest daisies of the grass
She shreds and passes on below. . . .

The sun is gone where nothing is
And the black-bladed shadows war.
She came and passed, she passed along
That wet, black curve of scimitar.

In vain the flower-lifting morn
With golden fingers to uprear
The week Spring here shall pause awhile:
This is a scar upon the year.

PITY

An old light smoulders in her eye.
There! she looks up. They grow and glow
Like mad laughs of a rhapsody
That flickers out in woe.

An old charm slips into her sighs,
An old grace sings about her hand.
She bends: it's musically wise.
I cannot understand.

Her voice is strident; but a spell
Of fluted whisper silkens in—
The lost heart in a moss-grown bell,
Faded—but sweet—but thin.

She bows like waves—waves near the shore.
Her hair is in a vulgar knot—
Lovely, dark hair, whose curves deplore
Something she's well forgot.

She must have known the sun, the moon,
On heaven's warm throat star-jewels strung—
It's late. The gas-lights flicker on.
Young, only in years, but young!

One might remind her, say the street
Is dark and vile now day is done.
But would she care, she fear to meet—
But there she goes—is gone.

REQUIESCAM

Come to the window! You're the painter used
To shadow-in pools of light far out to sea,
Or fix it where the solitary wave
Rears with a shimmering scoop before the shore,—
A glorious wave! But now look out awhile
And love my view, from our suburban height
The squalid champaign zigzagged by the Seine.

I'm old, most of my labour done. My chisel
One of these days among the pellets of dry clay
Will lie and rust. I have immensely worked,
And hitherto seen nothing but the Form
Staring upon my eyeballs. Years and years,

Whether alone along the shining streets
O' the city or in companionship, I've looked
So long and seen away so fixedly
That space scrolled up, I seeing none the less:
Except some shape, some woman lightning-blenched,
Pinned to the ground, lay dreadful in my road.
O Labour, everlasting vanity,
That fills her cracking pitcher and falls down
Face to the earth, the water in her hair!

Into a bole of clay all my life long
I've stared my visions in, and, thumbing, seen
Materialize obscurely to a line
The long desire of Nature turning home.
So strains itself out of the sea a shape
With loads of weedy tide up to the land,
Straining to touch and taste, to lose and die,
Straining fore'er miserably unsatisfied.
Between the toad and lyre-bird, 'twixt the snail
And greyhound all is struggle: the which is vain.
For by our bases we're firm sunken-down
In the element: and whenever a little while
Yearning Illusion flutters up the sky,
She presently swings to the gasping pitch,
To fall bolt-like.

I say, all my life long close to I've stared
Into the clay, have with my chisel rasped
The marble off and stroked the lovely limbs,
The breasts of women and the lips of boys
In stone. Again, into the mould I've poured
The wretched desolation of my dreams
And bruisèd here and there the bronze. All this
I had done my life long, and not so much
As lifted up my eyes.
                              But now at last
I pleasurably look to either side.
For I would paint some landscapes ere I die,
One or two landscapes of the view you see,
The squalid plain meandered by the Seine.
There, when there's moon, thro' fumes of gray and black
The silver river curls away; beyond
It's night and vapid darkness infinite.

And sitting at this window, I suppose
A pallet on my thumb, and brushes and
The colours gently mixing with their oil:—
Leaving my marbles in imagination
For final solace in a softer art.
You, painter, have enjoyed with all your self;
You've little looked into the dark. But I
Forged in the night. It's resting-time, I'm old.
Landscape will ease me somewhat toward the end.

QUIET AFTER THE RAIN OF MORNING

Quiet after the rain of morning
Midday covers the dampened trees;
Sweet and fresh in the languid breeze
Still returning
Birds are twittering at ease.

And to me in the far and foreign
Land as further I go and come,
Sweetly over the wearisome
Endless barren
Flutter whisperings of home.

There between the two hillocks lightens
Straight and little a bluish bar:
I feel the strain of the mariner
Grows and tightens
After home and after her.

IN THE PAST

There lies a somnolent lake
Under a noiseless sky,
Where never the mornings break
Nor the evenings die.

Mad flakes of colour
Whirl on its even face
Iridescent and streaked with pallour;
And, warding the silent place,

The rocks rise sheer and gray
From the sedgeless brink to the sky
Dull-lit with the light of pale half-day
Thro' a void space and dry.

And the hours lag dead in the air
With a sense of coming eternity
To the heart of the lonely boatman there:
That boatman am I,

I, in my lonely boat,
A waif on the somnolent lake,
Watching the colours creep and float
With the sinuous track of a snake.

Now I lean o'er the side
And lazy shades in the water see,
Lapped in the sweep of a sluggish tide
Crawled in from the living sea;

And next I fix mine eyes,
So long that the heart declines,
On the changeless face of the open skies
Where no star shines;

And now to the rocks I turn,
To the rocks, around
That lie like walls of a circling urn
Wherein lie bound

The waters that feel my powerless strength
And meet my homeless oar
Labouring over their ashen length
Never to find a shore.

But the gleam still skims
At times on the somnolent lake,
And a light there is that swims
With the whirl of a snake;

And tho' dead be the hours i' the air,
And dayless the sky,
The heart is alive of the boatman there:
That boatman am I.

IN AMPEZZO

In days of summer let me go
Up over fields, at afternoon,
And, lying low against my stone
On slopes the scythe has pain to mow,
Look southward a long hour alone.

For evening there is lovelier
Than vision or enchanted tale:
When wefts of yellow vapour pale,
And green goes down to lavender
On rosy cliffs, shutting the vale

Whose smoke of violet forest seeks
The steep and rock, where crimson crawls,
And drenched with carmine fire their walls
Go thinly smouldering to the peaks,
High, while the sun now somewhere falls;

Except a cloud-caught ochre spark
In one last summit,—and away
On lazy wings of mauve and gray,
Away and near, like memory, dark
Is bluish with the filmy day,

What time the swallows flying few
Over uncoloured fields become
Small music thro' the shining dome;
And sleepy leaves are feeling dew
Above the crickets' under-hum,

In bye-tone to a savage sound
Of waters that with discord smite

The frigid wind and lurking light,
And swarm behind the gloom, and bound
Down sleepy valleys to the night:

And thoughts delicious of the whole,
Gathering over all degrees,
Yet sad for something more than these,
Across low meadow-lands of soul
Grow large, like north-lights no one sees.

I care not if the painter wrought
The tinted dream his spirit hid,
When rich with sight he saw, amid
A jarring world, one tone, and caught
The colour passing to his lid.

Be still, musician and thy choir!
Where trumpets blare and the bow stings
In symphony a thousand strings
To cry of wood-wind and desire
Of one impassioned voice that sings.

Nay, silence have the poet's mode
And southern vowels all! let die,
So ghostly-vague, the northern cry!—
This world is better than an ode
And evening more than elegy.—

Yet what shall singing do for me?
How shall a verse be crimsoned o'er?
I ever dream one art the more;
I who did never paint would see
The colour painters languish for,

And wisely use the instruments
That earlier harmony affords;
I dream a poesy of chords
Embroidered very rich in tints:
'Tis not enough, this work of words.

A wilder thing inflames our hearts.
We do refuse to sift and share.
For we would musically bear

The burden of the gathered arts
Together which divided were,

And, passing Knowledge, highly rear
Upon her iron architrave
These airy images we rave,—
Lest wholly vain and fallen sheer
Our vision dress us for the grave.

THE DEPARTURE

The skies are cold and hard; the dead lights trail
On the long hills; the bitter day is o'er.
Closer I fold my cloak against the gale:
For I return no more.

No more! the vow shall not be reconciled;
How long, how bitter was the day I bore!
Enough! and now away into the wild,
Away, to turn no more.

Surely I shadowed on the coming days
Th'embracing trust and love of childish lore;
For now, be it blame I leave behind or praise,
I may return no more.

On, on! How long the way, the time how brief!
Folly to linger round the scene of yore!
Away with memory, and the memory's grief,—
For I return no more.

I ask, can ever this dark night pale to morn,
And has yon dubious morrow aught in store?
Or shall it find me weary and forlorn,
Who can return no more?

If then the night grow blacker with black cloud,
And sink the road to nothingness before;
If break the heart; still should I say, "I vowed,
And shall return no more"?

If then I madden, if I yield, and yearn
For such past light as once the evening wore;
And if it come to *death* or to return,
Still shall I turn no more?—

Some voice shall guide me in the night that falls,
Assure that I shall reach the further shore,
And nerve the failing heart, while still it calls,
"On! for thou turnest no more."

Then on! Not much avails the will, the thought;
Abandonment the voice of reason swore.
What recks it then? The mould of Fate is wrought;
And lo! I turn no more.

Amy Lowell

(1874-1925)

MEETING-HOUSE HILL

I must be mad, or very tired,
When the curve of a blue bay beyond a railroad track
Is shrill and sweet to me like the sudden springing of a tune,
And the sight of a white church above thin trees in a city square
Amazes my eyes as though it were the Parthenon.
Clear, reticent, superbly final,
With the pillars of its portico refined to a cautious elegance,
It dominates the weak trees,
And the shot of its spire
Is cool, and candid,
Rising into an unresisting sky.
Strange meeting-house
Pausing a moment upon a squalid hill-top.
I watch the spire sweeping the sky,
I am dizzy with the movement of the sky,
I might be watching a mast
With its royals set full
Straining before a two-reef breeze.
I might be sighting a tea-clipper,
Tacking into the blue bay,
Just back from Canton
With her hold full of green and blue porcelain,
And a Chinese coolie leaning over the rail
Gazing at the white spire
With dull, sea-spent eyes.

MUSIC

The neighbour sits in his window and plays the flute.
From my bed I can hear him,
And the round notes flutter and tap about the room,

And hit against each other,
Blurring to unexpected chords.
It is very beautiful,
With the little flute-notes all about me,
In the darkness.

In the daytime,
The neighbour eats bread and onions with one hand
And copies music with the other.
He is fat and has a bald head,
So I do not look at him,
But run quickly past his window.
There is always the sky to look at,
Or the water in the well!

But when night comes and he plays his flute,
I think of him as a young man,
With gold seals hanging from his watch,
And a blue coat with silver buttons.
As I lie in my bed
The flute-notes push against my ears and lips,
And I go to sleep, dreaming.

CHINOISERIES

REFLECTIONS

When I looked into your eyes,
I saw a garden
With peonies, and tinkling pagodas,
And round-arched bridges
Over still lakes.
A woman sat beside the water
In a rain-blue, silken garment.
She reached through the water
To pluck the crimson peonies
Beneath the surface,
But as she grasped the stems,
They jarred and broke into white-green ripples;

And as she drew out her hand,
The water-drops dripping from it
Stained her rain-blue dress like tears.

FALLING SNOW

The snow whispers about me,
And my wooden clogs
Leave holes behind me in the snow.
But no one will pass this way
Seeking my footsteps,
And when the temple bell rings again
They will be covered and gone.

HOAR-FROST

In the cloud-gray mornings
I heard the herons flying;
And when I came into my garden,
My silken outer-garment
Trailed over withered leaves.
A dried leaf crumbles at a touch,
But I have seen many Autumns
With herons blowing like smoke
Across the sky.

Robert Frost

(1874 – 1963)

STORM FEAR

When the wind works against us in the dark,
And pelts with snow
The lower-chamber window on the east,
And whispers with a sort of stifled bark,
The beast,
"Come out! Come out!"—
It costs no inward struggle not to go,
Ah, no!
I count our strength,
Two and a child,
Those of us not asleep subdued to mark
How the cold creeps as the fire dies at length—
How drifts are piled,
Dooryard and road ungraded,
Till even the comforting barn grows far away,
And my heart owns a doubt
Whether 'tis in us to arise with day
And save ourselves unaided.

MOWING

There was never a sound beside the wood but one,
And that was my long scythe whispering to the ground.
What was it it whispered? I knew not well myself;
Perhaps it was something about the heat of the sun,
Something, perhaps, about the lack of sound—
And that was why it whispered and did not speak.
It was no dream of the gift of idle hours,
Or easy gold at the hand of fay or elf:
Anything more than the truth would have seemed too weak

To the earnest love that laid the swale in rows,
Not without feeble-pointed spikes of flowers
(Pale orchises), and scared a bright green snake.
The fact is the sweetest dream that labor knows.
My long scythe whispered and left the hay to make.

HOME BURIAL

He saw her from the bottom of the stairs
Before she saw him. She was starting down,
Looking back over her shoulder at some fear.
She took a doubtful step and then undid it
To raise herself and look again. He spoke
Advancing toward her: "What is it you see
From up there always?—for I want to know."
She turned and sank upon her skirts at that,
And her face changed from terrified to dull.
He said to gain time: "What is it you see?"
Mounting until she cowered under him.
"I will find out now—you must tell me, dear."
She, in her place, refused him any help,
With the least stiffening of her neck and silence.
She let him look, sure that he wouldn't see,
Blind creature; and awhile he didn't see.
But at last he murmured, "Oh," and again, "Oh."

"What is it—what?" she said.

                              "Just that I see."

"You don't," she challenged. "Tell me what it is."

"The wonder is I didn't see at once.
I never noticed it from here before.
I must be wonted to it—that's the reason.
The little graveyard where my people are!
So small the window frames the whole of it.
Not so much larger than a bedroom, is it?
There are three stones of slate and one of marble,
Broad-shouldered little slabs there in the sunlight

On the sidehill. We haven't to mind *those*.
But I understand: it is not the stones,
But the child's mound—"

"Don't, don't, don't, don't," she cried.

She withdrew, shrinking from beneath his arm
That rested on the banister, and slid downstairs;
And turned on him with such a daunting look,
He said twice over before he knew himself:
"Can't a man speak of his own child he's lost?"

"Not you!—Oh, where's my hat? Oh, I don't need it!
I must get out of here. I must get air.—
I don't know rightly whether any man can."

"Amy! Don't go to someone else this time.
Listen to me. I won't come down the stairs."
He sat and fixed his chin between his fists.
"There's something I should like to ask you, dear."

"You don't know how to ask it."

                              "Help me, then."

Her fingers moved the latch for all reply.

"My words are nearly always an offense.
I don't know how to speak of anything
So as to please you. But I might be taught,
I should suppose. I can't say I see how.
A man must partly give up being a man
With womenfolk. We could have some arrangement
By which I'd bind myself to keep hands off
Anything special you're a-mind to name.
Though I don't like such things 'twixt those that love.
Two that don't love can't live together without them.
But two that do can't live together with them."
She moved the latch a little. "Don't—don't go.
Don't carry it to someone else this time.
Tell me about it if it's something human.
Let me into your grief. I'm not so much

Unlike other folks as your standing there
Apart would make me out. Give me my chance.
I do think, though, you overdo it a little.
What was it brought you up to think it the thing
To take your mother-loss of a first child
So inconsolably—in the face of love.
You'd think his memory might be satisfied——   "

"There you go sneering now!"

                              "I'm not, I'm not!
You make me angry. I'll come down to you.
God, what a woman! And it's come to this,
A man can't speak of his own child that's dead."

"You can't because you don't know how to speak.
If you had any feelings, you that dug
With your own hand—how could you?—his little grave;
I saw you from that very window there,
Making the gravel leap and leap in air,
Leap up, like that, like that, and land so lightly
And roll back down the mound beside the hole.
I thought, Who is that man? I didn't know you.
And I crept down the stairs and up the stairs
To look again, and still your spade kept lifting.
Then you came in. I heard your rumbling voice
Out in the kitchen, and I don't know why,
But I went near to see with my own eyes.
You could sit there with the stains on your shoes
Of the fresh earth from your own baby's grave
And talk about your everyday concerns.
You had stood the spade up against the wall
Outside there in the entry, for I saw it."

"I shall laugh the worst laugh I ever laughed.
I'm cursed. God, if I don't believe I'm cursed."

"I can repeat the very words you were saying:
'Three foggy mornings and one rainy day
Will rot the best birch fence a man can build.'
Think of it, talk like that at such a time!
What had how long it takes a birch to rot

To do with what was in the darkened parlor?
You *couldn't* care! The nearest friends can go
With anyone to death, comes so far short
They might as well not try to go at all.
No, from the time when one is sick to death,
One is alone, and he dies more alone.
Friends make pretense of following to the grave,
But before one is in it, their minds are turned
And making the best of their way back to life
And living people, and things they understand.
But the world's evil. I won't have grief so
If I can change it. Oh, I won't, I won't!"

"There, you have said it all and you feel better.
You won't go now. You're crying. Close the door.
The heart's gone out of it: why keep it up?
Amy! There's someone coming down the road!"

"You—oh, you think the talk is all. I must go—
Somewhere out of this house. How can I make you——"

"If—you—do!" She was opening the door wider.
"Where do you mean to go? First tell me that.
I'll follow and bring you back by force. I *will!*——"

THE WOOD-PILE

Out walking in the frozen swamp one gray day,
I paused and said, "I will turn back from here.
No, I will go on farther—and we shall see."
The hard snow held me, save where now and then
One foot went through. The view was all in lines
Straight up and down of tall slim trees
Too much alike to mark or name a place by
So as to say for certain I was here
Or somewhere else: I was just far from home.
A small bird flew before me. He was careful
To put a tree between us when he lighted,

And say no word to tell me who he was
Who was so foolish as to think what *he* thought.
He thought that I was after him for a feather—
The white one in his tail; like one who takes
Everything said as personal to himself.
One flight out sideways would have undeceived him.
And then there was a pile of wood for which
I forgot him and let his little fear
Carry him off the way I might have gone,
Without so much as wishing him good-night.
He went behind it to make his last stand.
It was a cord of maple, cut and split
And piled—and measured, four by four by eight.
And not another like it could I see.
No runner tracks in this year's snow looped near it.
And it was older sure than this year's cutting,
Or even last year's or the year's before.
The wood was gray and the bark warping off it
And the pile somewhat sunken. Clematis
Had wound strings round and round it like a bundle.
What held it, though, on one side was a tree
Still growing, and on one a stake and prop,
These latter about to fall. I thought that only
Someone who lived in turning to fresh tasks
Could so forget his handiwork on which
He spent himself, the labor of his ax,
And leave it there far from a useful fireplace
To warm the frozen swamp as best it could
With the slow smokeless burning of decay.

FIRE AND ICE

Some say the world will end in fire,
Some say in ice.
From what I've tasted of desire
I hold with those who favor fire.
But if it had to perish twice,
I think I know enough of hate

To say that for destruction ice
Is also great
And would suffice.

STOPPING BY WOODS
ON A SNOWY EVENING

Whose woods these are I think I know.
His house is in the village, though;
He will not see me stopping here
To watch his woods fill up with snow.

My little horse must think it queer
To stop without a farmhouse near
Between the woods and frozen lake
The darkest evening of the year.

He gives his harness bells a shake
To ask if there is some mistake.
The only other sound's the sweep
Of easy wind and downy flake.

The woods are lovely, dark, and deep,
But I have promises to keep,
And miles to go before I sleep,
And miles to go before I sleep.

NOTHING GOLD CAN STAY

Nature's first green is gold,
Her hardest hue to hold.
Her early leaf's a flower;
But only so an hour.
Then leaf subsides to leaf.

So Eden sank to grief,
So dawn goes down to day.
Nothing gold can stay.

SPRING POOLS

These pools that, though in forests, still reflect
The total sky almost without defect,
And like the flowers beside them, chill and shiver,
Will like the flowers beside them soon be gone,
And yet not out by any brook or river,
But up by roots to bring dark foliage on.

The trees that have it in their pent-up buds
To darken nature and be summer woods—
Let them think twice before they use their powers
To blot out and drink up and sweep away
These flowery waters and these watery flowers
From snow that melted only yesterday.

DESIGN

I found a dimpled spider, fat and white,
On a white heal-all, holding up a moth
Like a white piece of rigid satin cloth—
Assorted characters of death and blight
Mixed ready to begin the morning right,
Like the ingredients of a witches' broth—
A snow-drop spider, a flower like a froth,
And dead wings carried like a paper kite.

What had that flower to do with being white,
The wayside blue and innocent heal-all?
What brought the kindred spider to that height,
Then steered the white moth thither in the night?

What but design of darkness to appall?—
If design govern in a thing so small.

THE GIFT OUTRIGHT

The land was ours before we were the land's.
She was our land more than a hundred years
Before we were her people. She was ours
In Massachusetts, in Virginia,
But we were England's, still colonials,
Possessing what we still were unpossessed by,
Possessed by what we now no more possessed.
Something we were withholding made us weak
Until we found out that it was ourselves
We were withholding from our land of living,
And forthwith found salvation in surrender.
Such as we were we gave ourselves outright
(The deed of gift was many deeds of war)
To the land vaguely realizing westward,
But still unstoried, artless, unenhanced,
Such as she was, such as she would become.

THE SILKEN TENT

She is as in a field a silken tent
At midday when a sunny summer breeze
Has dried the dew and all its ropes relent,
So that in guys it gently sways at ease,
And its supporting central cedar pole,
That is its pinnacle to heavenward
And signifies the sureness of the soul,
Seems to owe naught to any single cord,
But strictly held by none, is loosely bound
By countless silken ties of love and thought
To everything on earth the compass round,
And only by one's going slightly taut

In the capriciousness of summer air
Is of the slightest bondage made aware.

"OUT, OUT—"

The buzz-saw snarled and rattled in the yard
And made dust and dropped stove-length sticks of wood,
Sweet-scented stuff when the breeze drew across it.
And from there those that lifted eyes could count
Five mountain ranges one behind the other
Under the sunset far into Vermont.
And the saw snarled and rattled, snarled and rattled,
As it ran light, or had to bear a load.
And nothing happened: day was all but done.
Call it a day, I wish they might have said
To please the boy by giving him the half hour
That a boy counts so much when saved from work.
His sister stood beside them in her apron
To tell them "Supper." At the word, the saw,
As if to prove saws knew what supper meant,
Leaped out at the boy's hand, or seemed to leap—
He must have given the hand. However it was,
Neither refused the meeting. But the hand!
The boy's first outcry was a rueful laugh,
As he swung toward them holding up the hand
Half in appeal, but half as if to keep
The life from spilling. Then the boy saw all—
Since he was old enough to know, big boy
Doing a man's work, though a child at heart—
He saw all spoiled. "Don't let him cut my hand off—
The doctor, when he comes. Don't let him, sister!"
So. But the hand was gone already.
The doctor put him in the dark of ether.
He lay and puffed his lips out with his breath.
And then—the watcher at his pulse took fright.
No one believed. They listened at his heart.
Little—less—nothing!—and that ended it.
No more to build on there. And they, since they
Were not the one dead, turned to their affairs.

THE SUBVERTED FLOWER

She drew back; he was calm:
"It is this that had the power."
And he lashed his open palm
With the tender-headed flower.
He smiled for her to smile,
But she was either blind
Or willfully unkind.
He eyed her for a while
For a woman and a puzzle.
He flicked and flung the flower,
And another sort of smile
Caught up like fingertips
The corners of his lips
And cracked his ragged muzzle.
She was standing to the waist
In goldenrod and brake,
Her shining hair displaced.
He stretched her either arm
As if she made it ache
To clasp her—not to harm;
As if he could not spare
To touch her neck and hair.
"If this has come to us
And not to me alone——"
So she thought she heard him say;
Though with every word he spoke
His lips were sucked and blown
And the effort made him choke
Like a tiger at a bone.
She had to lean away.
She dared not stir a foot,
Lest movement should provoke
The demon of pursuit
That slumbers in a brute.
It was then her mother's call
From inside the garden wall
Made her steal a look of fear
To see if he could hear
And would pounce to end it all
Before her mother came.

She looked and saw the shame:
A hand hung like a paw,
An arm worked like a saw
As if to be persuasive,
An ingratiating laugh
That cut the snout in half,
An eye become evasive.
A girl could only see
That a flower had marred a man,
But what she could not see
Was that the flower might be
Other than base and fetid:
That the flower had done but part,
And what the flower began
Her own too meager heart
Had terribly completed.
She looked and saw the worst.
And the dog or what it was,
Obeying bestial laws,
A coward save at night,
Turned from the place and ran.
She heard him stumble first
And use his hands in flight.
She heard him bark outright.
And oh, for one so young
The bitter words she spit
Like some tenacious bit
That will not leave the tongue.
She plucked her lips for it,
And still the horror clung.
Her mother wiped the foam
From her chin, picked up her comb,
And drew her backward home.

DIRECTIVE

Back out of all this now too much for us,
Back in a time made simple by the loss
Of detail, burned, dissolved, and broken off
Like graveyard marble sculpture in the weather,

There is a house that is no more a house
Upon a farm that is no more a farm
And in a town that is no more a town.
The road there, if you'll let a guide direct you
Who only has at heart your getting lost,
May seem as if it should have been a quarry—
Great monolithic knees the former town
Long since gave up pretense of keeping covered.
And there's a story in a book about it:
Besides the wear of iron wagon wheels
The ledges show lines ruled southeast-northwest,
The chisel work of an enormous Glacier
That braced his feet against the Arctic Pole.
You must not mind a certain coolness from him
Still said to haunt this side of Panther Mountain.
Nor need you mind the serial ordeal
Of being watched from forty cellar holes
As if by eye pairs out of forty firkins.
As for the woods' excitement over you
That sends light rustle rushes to their leaves,
Charge that to upstart inexperience.
Where were they all not twenty years ago?
They think too much of having shaded out
A few old pecker-fretted apple trees.
Make yourself up a cheering song of how
Someone's road home from work this once was,
Who may be just ahead of you on foot
Or creaking with a buggy load of grain.
The height of the adventure is the height
Of country where two village cultures faded
Into each other. Both of them are lost.
And if you're lost enough to find yourself
By now, pull in your ladder road behind you
And put a sign up CLOSED to all but me.
Then make yourself at home. The only field
Now left's no bigger than a harness gall.
First there's the children's house of make-believe,
Some shattered dishes underneath a pine,
The playthings in the playhouse of the children.
Weep for what little things could make them glad.
Then for the house that is no more a house,
But only a belilaced cellar hole,
Now slowly closing like a dent in dough.

This was no playhouse but a house in earnest.
Your destination and your destiny's
A brook that was the water of the house,
Cold as a spring as yet so near its source,
Too lofty and original to rage.
(We know the valley streams that when aroused
Will leave their tatters hung on barb and thorn.)
I have kept hidden in the instep arch
Of an old cedar at the waterside
A broken drinking goblet like the Grail
Under a spell so the wrong ones can't find it,
So can't get saved, as Saint Mark says they mustn't.
(I stole the goblet from the children's playhouse.)
Here are your waters and your watering place.
Drink and be whole again beyond confusion.

Carl Sandburg

(1 8 7 8 – 1 9 6 7)

THE HARBOR

Passing through huddled and ugly walls
By doorways where women
Looked from their hunger-deep eyes,
Haunted with shadows of hunger-hands,
Out from the huddled and ugly walls,
I came sudden, at the city's edge,
On a blue burst of lake,
Long lake waves breaking under the sun
On a spray-flung curve of shore;
And a fluttering storm of gulls,
Masses of great gray wings
And flying white bellies
Veering and wheeling free in the open.

CHICAGO

Hog Butcher for the World,
Tool Maker, Stacker of Wheat,
Player with Railroads and the Nation's Freight Handler;
Stormy, husky, brawling,
City of the Big Shoulders:

They tell me you are wicked and I believe them, for I have seen your painted
women under the gas lamps luring the farm boys.
And they tell me you are crooked and I answer: Yes, it is true I have seen the
gunman kill and go free to kill again.
And they tell me you are brutal and my reply is: On the faces of women and
children I have seen the marks of wanton hunger.
And having answered so I turn once more to those who sneer at this my city,
and I give them back the sneer and say to them:

Come and show me another city with lifted head singing so proud to be alive
    and coarse and strong and cunning.
Flinging magnetic curses amid the toil of piling job on job, here is a tall bold
    slugger set vivid against the little soft cities;
Fierce as a dog with tongue lapping for action, cunning as a savage pitted
    against the wilderness,
    Bareheaded,
    Shoveling,
    Wrecking,
    Planning,
    Building, breaking, rebuilding,
Under the smoke, dust all over his mouth, laughing with white teeth,
Under the terrible burden of destiny laughing as a young man laughs,
Laughing even as an ignorant fighter laughs who has never lost a battle,
Bragging and laughing that under his wrist is the pulse, and under his ribs the
    heart of the people,
            Laughing!
Laughing the stormy, husky, brawling laughter of Youth, half-naked, sweating,
    proud to be Hog Butcher, Tool Maker, Stacker of Wheat, Player with
    Railroads and Freight Handler to the Nation.

LANGUAGES

There are no handles upon a language
Whereby men take hold of it
And mark it with signs for its remembrance.
It is a river, this language,
Once in a thousand years
Breaking a new course
Changing its way to the ocean.
It is mountain effluvia
Moving to valleys
And from nation to nation
Crossing borders and mixing.
Languages die like rivers.
Words wrapped round your tongue today
And broken to shape of thought
Between your teeth and lips speaking
Now and today

Shall be faded hieroglyphics
Ten thousand years from now.
Sing—and singing—remember
Your song dies and changes
And is not here tomorrow
Any more than the wind
Blowing ten thousand years ago.

BAS-RELIEF

Five geese deploy mysteriously.
Onward proudly with flagstaffs,
Hearses with silver bugles,
Bushels of plum-blossoms dropping
For ten mystic web-feet—
Each his own drum-major,
Each charged with the honour
Of the ancient goose nation,
Each with a nose-length surpassing
The nose-lengths of rival nations.
Sombrely, slowly, unimpeachably,
Five geese deploy mysteriously.

COOL TOMBS

When Abraham Lincoln was shoveled into the tombs, he forgot the
    copperheads and the assassin . . . in the dust, in the cool tombs.

And Ulysses Grant lost all thought of con men and Wall Street, cash and
    collateral turned ashes . . . in the dust, in the cool tombs.

Pocahontas' body, lovely as a poplar, sweet as a red haw in November or a
    pawpaw in May, did she wonder? does she remember? . . . in the dust, in
    the cool tombs?

Take any streetful of people buying clothes and groceries, cheering a hero or
     throwing confetti and blowing tin horns . . . tell me if the lovers are losers
     . . . tell me if any get more than the lovers . . . in the dust . . . in the cool
     tombs.

GRASS

Pile the bodies high at Austerlitz and Waterloo.
Shovel them under and let me work—
                I am the grass; I cover all.

And pile them high at Gettysburg
And pile them high at Ypres and Verdun.
Shovel them under and let me work.
Two years, ten years, and passengers ask the conductor:
                What place is this?
                Where are we now?

                I am the grass.
                Let me work.

Vachel Lindsay

(1 8 7 9 – 1 9 3 1)

GENERAL WILLIAM BOOTH
ENTERS INTO HEAVEN

To be sung to the tune of "The Blood of the Lamb"
with indicated instrument.

1

   (Bass drum beaten loudly)
Booth led boldly with his big bass drum—
(Are you washed in the blood of the Lamb?)
The Saints smiled gravely and they said: "He's come."
(Are you washed in the blood of the Lamb?)
Walking lepers followed, rank on rank,
Lurching bravos from the ditches dank,
Drabs from the alleyways and drug fiends pale—
Minds still passion-ridden, soul-powers frail:—
Vermin-eaten saints with moldy breath,
Unwashed legions with the ways of Death—
(Are you washed in the blood of the Lamb?)

   (Banjos)
Every slum had sent its half-a-score
The round world over. (Booth had groaned for more.)
Every banner that the wide world flies
Bloomed with glory and transcendent dyes.
Big-voiced lasses made their banjos bang,
Tranced, fanatical they shrieked and sang:—
"Are you washed in the blood of the Lamb?"
Hallelujah! It was queer to see
Bull-necked convicts with that land make free.
Loons with trumpets blowed a blare, blare, blare
On, on upward thro' the golden air!
(Are you washed in the blood of the Lamb?)

2

(Bass drum slower and softer)
Booth died blind and still by faith he trod,
Eyes still dazzled by the ways of God.
Booth led boldly, and he looked the chief
Eagle countenance in sharp relief,
Beard a-flying, air of high command
Unabated in that holy land.

(Sweet flute music)
Jesus came from out the court-house door,
Stretched his hands above the passing poor.
Booth saw not, but led his queer ones there
Round and round the mighty court-house square.
Then, in an instant all that blear review
Marched on spotless, clad in raiment new.
The lame were straightened, withered limbs uncurled
And blind eyes opened on a new, sweet world.

(Bass drum louder)
Drabs and vixens in a flash made whole!
Gone was the weasel-head, the snout, the jowl!
Sages and sibyls now, and athletes clean,
Rulers of empires, and of forests green!

(Grand chorus of all instruments;
  tambourines to the foreground)
The hosts were sandalled, and their wings were fire!
(Are you washed in the blood of the Lamb?)
But their noise played havoc with the angel-choir.
(Are you washed in the blood of the Lamb?)
Oh, shout Salvation! It was good to see
Kings and Princes by the Lamb set free.
The banjos rattled and the tambourines
Jing-jing-jingled in the hands of Queens.

(Reverently sung, no instruments)
And when Booth halted by the curb for prayer
He saw his Master thro' the flag-filled air.
Christ came gently with a robe and crown
For Booth the soldier, while the throng knelt down.
He saw King Jesus. They were face to face,
And he knelt a-weeping in that holy place.
Are you washed in the blood of the Lamb?

Wallace Stevens

(1879 – 1955)

THE SNOW MAN

One must have a mind of winter
To regard the frost and the boughs
Of the pine-trees crusted with snow;

And have been cold a long time
To behold the junipers shagged with ice,
The spruces rough in the distant glitter

Of the January sun; and not to think
Of any misery in the sound of the wind,
In the sound of a few leaves,

Which is the sound of the land
Full of the same wind
That is blowing in the same bare place

For the listener, who listens in the snow,
And, nothing himself, beholds
Nothing that is not there and the nothing that is.

NOMAD EXQUISITE

As the immense dew of Florida
Brings forth
The big-finned palm
And green vine angering for life,

As the immense dew of Florida
Brings forth hymn and hymn
From the beholder,

Beholding all these green sides
And gold sides of green sides,

And blessed mornings,
Meet for the eye of the young alligator,
And lightning colors
So, in me, come flinging
Forms, flames, and the flakes of flames.

OF MODERN POETRY

The poem of the mind in the act of finding
What will suffice. It has not always had
To find: the scene was set; it repeated what
Was in the script.
                    Then the theatre was changed
To something else. Its past was a souvenir.
It has to be living, to learn the speech of the place.
It has to face the men of the time and to meet
The women of the time. It has to think about war
And it has to find what will suffice. It has
To construct a new stage. It has to be on that stage
And, like an insatiable actor, slowly and
With meditation, speak words that in the ear,
In the delicatest ear of the mind, repeat,
Exactly, that which it wants to hear, at the sound
Of which, an invisible audience listens,
Not to the play, but to itself, expressed
In an emotion as of two people, as of two
Emotions becoming one. The actor is
A metaphysician in the dark, twanging
An instrument, twanging a wiry string that gives
Sounds passing through sudden rightnesses, wholly
Containing the mind, below which it cannot descend,
Beyond which it has no will to rise.
                            It must
Be the finding of a satisfaction, and may
Be of a man skating, a woman dancing, a woman
Combing. The poem of the act of the mind.

THIRTEEN WAYS OF LOOKING
AT A BLACKBIRD

1

Among twenty snowy mountains,
The only moving thing
Was the eye of the blackbird.

2

I was of three minds,
Like a tree
In which there are three blackbirds.

3

The blackbird whirled in the autumn winds.
It was a small part of the pantomime.

4

A man and a woman
Are one.
A man and a woman and a blackbird
Are one.

5

I do not know which to prefer,
The beauty of inflections
Or the beauty of innuendoes,
The blackbird whistling
Or just after.

6

Icicles filled the long window
With barbaric glass.
The shadow of the blackbird

Crossed it, to and fro.
The mood
Traced in the shadow
An indecipherable cause.

7

O thin men of Haddam,
Why do you imagine golden birds?
Do you not see how the blackbird
Walks around the feet
Of the women about you?

8

I know noble accents
And lucid, inescapable rhythms;
But I know, too,
That the blackbird is involved
In what I know.

9

When the blackbird flew out of sight,
It marked the edge
Of one of many circles.

10

At the sight of blackbirds
Flying in a green light,
Even the bawds of euphony
Would cry out sharply.

11

He rode over Connecticut
In a glass coach.
Once, a fear pierced him,
In that he mistook
The shadow of his equipage
For blackbirds.

12

The river is moving.
The blackbird must be flying.

13

It was evening all afternoon.
It was snowing
And it was going to snow.
The blackbird sat
In the cedar-limbs.

SUNDAY MORNING

1

Complacencies of the peignoir, and late
Coffee and oranges in a sunny chair,
And the green freedom of a cockatoo
Upon a rug mingle to dissipate
The holy hush of ancient sacrifice.
She dreams a little, and she feels the dark
Encroachment of that old catastrophe,
As a calm darkens among water-lights.
The pungent oranges and bright, green wings
Seem things in some procession of the dead,
Winding across wide water, without sound.
The day is like wide water, without sound,
Stilled for the passing of her dreaming feet
Over the seas, to silent Palestine,
Dominion of the blood and sepulchre.

2

Why should she give her bounty to the dead?
What is divinity if it can come
Only in silent shadows and in dreams?
Shall she not find in comforts of the sun,
In pungent fruit and bright, green wings, or else
In any balm or beauty of the earth,

Things to be cherished like the thought of heaven?
Divinity must live within herself:
Passions of rain, or moods in falling snow;
Grievings in loneliness, or unsubdued
Elations when the forest blooms; gusty
Emotions on wet roads on autumn nights;
All pleasures and all pains, remembering
The bough of summer and the winter branch.
These are the measures destined for her soul.

3

Jove in the clouds had his inhuman birth.
No mother suckled him, no sweet land gave
Large-mannered motions to his mythy mind
He moved among us, as a muttering king,
Magnificent, would move among his hinds,
Until our blood, commingling, virginal,
With heaven, brought such requital to desire
The very hinds discerned it, in a star.
Shall our blood fail? Or shall it come to be
The blood of paradise? And shall the earth
Seem all of paradise that we shall know?
The sky will be much friendlier then than now,
A part of labor and a part of pain,
And next in glory to enduring love,
Not this dividing and indifferent blue.

4

She says, "I am content when wakened birds,
Before they fly, test the reality
Of misty fields, by their sweet questionings;
But when the birds are gone, and their warm fields
Return no more, where, then, is paradise?"
There is not any haunt of prophecy,
Nor any old chimera of the grave,
Neither the golden underground, nor isle
Melodious, where spirits gat them home,
Nor visionary south, nor cloudy palm
Remote on heaven's hill, that has endured
As April's green endures; or will endure
Like her remembrance of awakened birds,

Or her desire for June and evening, tipped
By the consummation of the swallow's wings.

5

She says, "But in contentment I still feel
The need of some imperishable bliss."
Death is the mother of beauty; hence from her,
Alone, shall come fulfilment to our dreams
And our desires. Although she strews the leaves
Of sure obliteration on our paths,
The path sick sorrow took, the many paths
Where triumph rang its brassy phrase, or love
Whispered a little out of tenderness,
She makes the willow shiver in the sun
For maidens who were wont to sit and gaze
Upon the grass, relinquished to their feet.
She causes boys to pile new plums and pears
On disregarded plate. The maidens taste
And stray impassioned in the littering leaves.

6

Is there no change of death in paradise?
Does ripe fruit never fall? Or do the boughs
Hang always heavy in that perfect sky,
Unchanging, yet so like our perishing earth,
With rivers like our own that seek for seas
They never find, the same receding shores
That never touch with inarticulate pang?
Why set the pear upon those river-banks
Or spice the shores with odors of the plum?
Alas, that they should wear our colors there,
The silken weavings of our afternoons,
And pick the strings of our insipid lutes!
Death is the mother of beauty, mystical,
Within whose burning bosom we devise
Our earthly mothers waiting, sleeplessly.

7

Supple and turbulent, a ring of men
Shall chant in orgy on a summer morn

Their boisterous devotion to the sun,
Not as a god, but as a god might be,
Naked among them, like a savage source.
Their chant shall be a chant of paradise,
Out of their blood, returning to the sky;
And in their chant shall enter, voice by voice,
The windy lake wherein their lord delights,
The trees, like serafin, and echoing hills,
That choir among themselves long afterward.
They shall know well the heavenly fellowship
Of men that perish and of summer morn.
And whence they came and whither they shall go
The dew upon their feet shall manifest.

8

She hears, upon that water without sound,
A voice that cries, "The tomb in Palestine
Is not the porch of spirits lingering.
It is the grave of Jesus, where he lay."
We live in an old chaos of the sun,
Or old dependency of day and night,
Or island solitude, unsponsored, free,
Of that wide water, inescapable.
Deer walk upon our mountains, and the quail
Whistle about us their spontaneous cries;
Sweet berries ripen in the wilderness;
And, in the isolation of the sky,
At evening, casual flocks of pigeons make
Ambiguous undulations as they sink,
Downward to darkness, on extended wings.

ANECDOTE OF THE JAR

I placed a jar in Tennessee,
And round it was, upon a hill.
It made the slovenly wilderness
Surround that hill.

The wilderness rose up to it,
And sprawled around, no longer wild.
The jar was round upon the ground
And tall and of a port in air.

It took dominion everywhere.
The jar was gray and bare.
It did not give of bird or bush,
Like nothing else in Tennessee.

THE IDEA OF ORDER AT KEY WEST

She sang beyond the genius of the sea.
The water never formed to mind or voice,
Like a body wholly body, fluttering
Its empty sleeves; and yet its mimic motion
Made constant cry, caused constantly a cry,
That was not ours although we understood,
Inhuman, of the veritable ocean.

The sea was not a mask. No more was she.
The song and water were not medleyed sound
Even if what she sang was what she heard,
Since what she sang was uttered word by word.
It may be that in all her phrases stirred
The grinding water and the gasping wind;
But it was she and not the sea we heard.

For she was the maker of the song she sang.
The ever-hooded, tragic-gestured sea
Was merely a place by which she walked to sing.
Whose spirit is this? we said, because we knew
It was the spirit that we sought and knew
That we should ask this often as she sang.

If it was only the dark voice of the sea
That rose, or even colored by many waves;
If it was only the outer voice of sky
And cloud, of the sunken coral water-walled,
However clear, it would have been deep air,

The heaving speech of air, a summer sound
Repeated in a summer without end
And sound alone. But it was more than that,
More even than her voice, and ours, among
The meaningless plungings of water and the wind,
Theatrical distances, bronze shadows heaped
On high horizons, mountainous atmospheres
Of sky and sea.
                  It was her voice that made
The sky acutest at its vanishing.
She measured to the hour its solitude.
She was the single artificer of the world
In which she sang. And when she sang, the sea,
Whatever self it had, became the self
That was her song, for she was the maker. Then we,
As we beheld her striding there alone,
Knew that there never was a world for her
Except the one she sang and, singing, made.

Ramon Fernandez, tell me, if you know,
Why, when the singing ended and we turned
Toward the town, tell why the glassy lights,
The lights in the fishing boats at anchor there,
As the night descended, tilting in the air,
Mastered the night and portioned out the sea,
Fixing emblazoned zones and fiery poles,
Arranging, deepening, enchanting night.

Oh! Blessed rage for order, pale Ramon,
The maker's rage to order words of the sea,
Words of the fragrant portals, dimly-starred,
And of ourselves and of our origins,
In ghostlier demarcations, keener sounds.

From NOTES TOWARD A SUPREME FICTION

To Henry Church

And for what, except for you, do I feel love?
Do I press the extremest book of the wisest man
Close to me, hidden in me day and night?

In the uncertain light of single, certain truth,
Equal in living changingness to the light
In which I meet you, in which we sit at rest,
For a moment in the central of our being,
The vivid transparence that you bring is peace.

IT MUST BE ABSTRACT

1

Begin, ephebe, by perceiving the idea
Of this invention, this invented world,
The inconceivable idea of the sun.

You must become an ignorant man again
And see the sun again with an ignorant eye
And see it clearly in the idea of it.

Never suppose an inventing mind as source
Of this idea nor for that mind compose
A voluminous master folded in his fire.

How clean the sun when seen in its idea,
Washed in the remotest cleanliness of a heaven
That has expelled us and our images . . .

The death of one god is the death of all.
Let purple Phoebus lie in umber harvest,
Let Phoebus slumber and die in autumn umber,

Phoebus is dead, ephebe. But Phoebus was
A name for something that never could be named.
There was a project for the sun and is.

There is a project for the sun. The sun
Must bear no name, gold flourisher, but be
In the difficulty of what it is to be.

                    *   *   *

4

The first idea was not our own. Adam
In Eden was the father of Descartes
And Eve made air the mirror of herself,

Of her sons and of her daughters. They found themselves
In heaven as in a glass; a second earth;
And in the earth itself they found a green—

The inhabitants of a very varnished green.
But the first idea was not to shape the clouds
In imitation. The clouds preceded us

There was a muddy centre before we breathed.
There was a myth before the myth began,
Venerable and articulate and complete.

From this the poem springs: that we live in a place
That is not our own and, much more, not ourselves
And hard it is in spite of blazoned days.

We are the mimics. Clouds are pedagogues
The air is not a mirror but bare board,
Coulisse bright-dark, tragic chiaroscuro

And comic color of the rose, in which
Abysmal instruments make sounds like pips
Of the sweeping meanings that we add to them.

        *   *   *

7

It feels good as it is without the giant,
A thinker of the first idea. Perhaps
The truth depends on a walk around a lake,

A composing as the body tires, a stop
To see hepatica, a stop to watch
A definition growing certain and

A wait within that certainty, a rest
In the swags of pine-trees bordering the lake.
Perhaps there are times of inherent excellence,

As when the cock crows on the left and all
Is well, incalculable balances,
At which a kind of Swiss perfection comes

And a familiar music of the machine
Sets up its Schwärmerei, not balances
That we achieve but balances that happen,

As a man and woman meet and love forthwith.
Perhaps there are moments of awakening,
Extreme, fortuitous, personal, in which

We more than awaken, sit on the edge of sleep,
As on an elevation, and behold
The academies like structures in a mist.

         *   *   *

10

The major abstraction is the idea of man
And major man is its exponent, abler
In the abstract than in his singular,

More fecund as principle than particle,
Happy fecundity, flor-abundant force,
In being more than an exception, part,

Though an heroic part, of the commonal.
The major abstraction is the commonal,
The inanimate, difficult visage. Who is it?

What rabbi, grown furious with human wish,
What chieftain, walking by himself, crying
Most miserable, most victorious,

Does not see these separate figures one by one,
And yet see only one, in his old coat,
His slouching pantaloons, beyond the town,

Looking for what was, where it used to be?
Cloudless the morning. It is he. The man
In that old coat, those sagging pantaloons,

It is of him, ephebe, to make, to confect
The final elegance, not to console
Nor sanctify, but plainly to propound.

         *   *   *

Soldier, there is a war between the mind
And sky, between thought and day and night. It is
For that the poet is always in the sun,

Patches the moon together in his room
To his Virgilian cadences, up down,
Up down. It is a war that never ends.

Yet it depends on yours. The two are one.
They are a plural, a right and left, a pair,
Two parallels that meet if only in

The meeting of their shadows or that meet
In a book in a barrack, a letter from Malay.
But your war ends. And after it you return

With six meats and twelve wines or else without
To walk another room . . . Monsieur and comrade,
The soldier is poor without the poet's lines,

His petty syllabi, the sounds that stick,
Inevitably modulating, in the blood.
And war for war, each has its gallant kind.

How simply the fictive hero becomes the real;
How gladly with proper words the soldier dies,
If he must, or lives on the bread of faithful speech.

TO AN OLD PHILOSOPHER IN ROME

On the threshold of heaven, the figures in the street
Become the figures of heaven, the majestic movement
Of men growing small in the distances of space,
Singing, with smaller and still smaller sound,
Unintelligible absolution and an end—

The threshold, Rome, and that more merciful Rome
Beyond, the two alike in the make of the mind.
It is as if in a human dignity

Two parallels become one, a perspective, of which
Men are part both in the inch and in the mile.

How easily the blown banners change to wings . . .
Things dark on the horizons of perception,
Become accompaniments of fortune, but
Of the fortune of the spirit, beyond the eye,
Not of its sphere, and yet not far beyond,

The human end in the spirit's greatest reach,
The extreme of the known in the presence of the extreme
Of the unknown. The newsboys' muttering
Becomes another murmuring; the smell
Of medicine, a fragrantness not to be spoiled . . .

The bed, the books, the chair, the moving nuns,
The candle as it evades the sight, these are
The sources of happiness in the shape of Rome,
A shape within the ancient circles of shapes,
And these beneath the shadow of a shape

In a confusion on bed and books, a portent
On the chair, a moving transparence on the nuns,
A light on the candle tearing against the wick
To join a hovering excellence, to escape
From fire and be part only of that of which

Fire is the symbol: the celestial possible.
Speak to your pillow as if it was yourself.
Be orator but with an accurate tongue
And without eloquence, O, half-asleep,
Of the pity that is the memorial of this room,

So that we feel, in this illumined large,
The veritable small, so that each of us
Beholds himself in you, and hears his voice
In yours, master and commiserable man,
Intent on your particles of nether-do,

Your dozing in the depths of wakefulness,
In the warmth of your bed, at the edge of your chair, alive
Yet living in two worlds, impenitent
As to one, and, as to one, most penitent,
Impatient for the grandeur that you need

In so much misery; and yet finding it
Only in misery, the afflatus of ruin,
Profound poetry of the poor and of the dead,
As in the last drop of the deepest blood,
As it falls from the heart and lies there to be seen,

Even as the blood of an empire, it might be,
For a citizen of heaven though still of Rome.
It is poverty's speech that seeks us out the most.
It is older than the oldest speech of Rome.
This is the tragic accent of the scene.

And you—it is you that speak it, without speech,
The loftiest syllables among loftiest things,
The one invulnerable man among
Crude captains, the naked majesty, if you like,
Of bird-nest arches and of rain-stained-vaults.

The sounds drift in. The buildings are remembered.
The life of the city never lets go, nor do you
Ever want it to. It is part of the life in your room.
Its domes are the architecture of your bed.
The bells keep on repeating solemn names

In choruses and choirs of choruses,
Unwilling that mercy should be a mystery
Of silence, that any solitude of sense
Should give you more than their peculiar chords
And reverberations clinging to whisper still.

It is a kind of total grandeur at the end,
With every visible thing enlarged and yet
No more than a bed, a chair and moving nuns,
The immensest theatre, the pillared porch,
The book and candle in your ambered room,

Total grandeur of a total edifice,
Chosen by an inquisitor of structures
For himself. He stops upon this threshold,
As if the design of all his words takes form
And frame from thinking and is realized.

FINAL SOLILOQUY
OF THE INTERIOR PARAMOUR

Light the first light of evening, as in a room
In which we rest and, for small reason, think
The world imagined is the ultimate good.

This is, therefore, the intensest rendezvous.
It is in that thought that we collect ourselves,
Out of all the indifferences, into one thing:

Within a single thing, a single shawl
Wrapped tightly round us, since we are poor, a warmth,
A light, a power, the miraculous influence.

Here, now, we forget each other and ourselves.
We feel the obscurity of an order, a whole,
A knowledge, that which arranged the rendezvous.

Within its vital boundary, in the mind.
We say God and the imagination are one . . .
How high that highest candle lights the dark.

Out of this same light, out of the central mind,
We make a dwelling in the evening air,
In which being there together is enough.

William Carlos Williams

(1 8 8 3 – 1 9 6 3)

WOMAN WALKING

An oblique cloud of purple smoke
across a milky silhouette
of house sides and tiny trees—
a little village—
that ends in a saw edge
of mist-covered trees
on a sheet of grey sky.

To the right, jutting in,
a dark crimson corner of roof.
To the left, half a tree:

    —what a blessing it is
to see you in the street again,
powerful woman,
coming with swinging haunches,
breasts straight forward,
supple shoulders, full arms
and strong, soft hands (I've felt them)
carrying the heavy basket.

I might well see you oftener!
And for a different reason
than the fresh eggs
you bring us so regularly.

Yes, you, young as I,
with boney brows,
kind grey eyes and a kind mouth;
you walking out toward me
from that dead hillside!
I might well see you oftener.

IT IS A SMALL PLANT

It is a small plant
delicately branched and
tapering conically
to a point, each branch
and the peak a wire for
green pods, blind lanterns
starting upward from
the stalk each way to
a pair of prickly edged blue
flowerets: it is her regard,
a little plant without leaves,
a finished thing guarding
its secret. Blue eyes—
but there are twenty looks
in one, alike as forty flowers
on twenty stems—Blue eyes
a little closed upon a wish
achieved and half lost again,
stemming back, garlanded
with green sacks of
satisfaction gone to seed,
back to a straight stem—if
one looks into you, trumpets—!
No. It is the pale hollow of
desire itself counting
over and over the moneys of
a stale achievement. Three
small lavender imploring tips
below and above them two
slender colored arrows
of disdain with anthers
between them and
at the edge of the goblet
a white lip, to drink from—!
And summer lifts her look
forty times over, forty times
over—namelessly.

TO A POOR OLD WOMAN

munching a plum on
the street a paper bag
of them in her hand

They taste good to her
They taste good
to her. They taste
good to her

You can see it by
the way she gives herself
to the one half
sucked out in her hand

Comforted
a solace of ripe plums
seeming to fill the air
They taste good to her

THE SADNESS OF THE SEA

This is the sadness of the sea—
waves like words, all broken—
a sameness of lifting and falling mood.

I lean watching the detail
of brittle crest, the delicate
imperfect foam, yellow weed
one piece like another—

There is no hope—if not a coral
island slowly forming
to wait for birds to drop
the seeds will make it habitable

SPRING AND ALL

By the road to the contagious hospital
under the surge of the blue
mottled clouds driven from the
northeast—a cold wind. Beyond, the
waste of broad, muddy fields
brown with dried weeds, standing and fallen

patches of standing water
the scattering of tall trees

All along the road the reddish
purplish, forked, upstanding, twiggy
stuff of bushes and small trees
with dead, brown leaves under them
leafless vines —

Lifeless in appearance, sluggish
dazed spring approaches —

They enter the new world naked,
cold, uncertain of all
save that they enter. All about them
the cold, familiar wind—

Now the grass, tomorrow
the stiff curl of wildcarrot leaf
One by one objects are defined—
It quickens: clarity, outline of leaf

But now the stark dignity of
entrance—Still, the profound change
has come upon them: rooted, they
grip down and begin to awaken

THE RED WHEELBARROW

so much depends
upon

a red wheel
barrow

glazed with rain
water

beside the white
chickens.

THE YOUNG HOUSEWIFE

At ten A.M. the young housewife
moves about in negligee behind
the wooden walls of her husband's house.
I pass solitary in my car.

Then again she comes to the curb
to call the ice-man, fish-man, and stands
shy, uncorseted, tucking in
stray ends of hair, and I compare her
to a fallen leaf.

The noiseless wheels of my car
rush with a crackling sound over
dried leaves as I bow and pass smiling.

TO FORD MADOX FORD IN HEAVEN

Is it any better in Heaven, my friend Ford,
       than you found it in Provence?

I don't think so for you made Provence a
       heaven by your praise of it
to give a foretaste of what might be
       your joy in the present circumstances.
It was Heaven you were describing there

transubstantiated from its narrowness
to resemble the paths and gardens of a
        greater world where you now reside.
But, dear man, you have taken a major
        part of it from us.
                Provence that you
praised so well will never be the same
        Provence to us
                now you are gone.

A heavenly man you seem to me now, never
        having been for me a saintly one.
It lived about you, a certain grossness that
        was not like the world.
The world is cleanly, polished and well
        made but heavenly man
is filthy with his flesh and corrupt that
        loves to eat and drink and whore—
to laugh at himself and not be afraid of
        himself knowing well he has
no possessions and opinions that are worth
        caring a broker's word about
and that all he is, but one thing, he feeds
        as one will feed a pet dog.

So roust and love and dredge the belly full
        in Heaven's name!
I laugh to think of you wheezing in Heaven.
        Where is Heaven? But why
do I ask that, since you showed the way?
        I don't care a damn for it
other than for that better part lives beside
        me here so long as I
live and remember you. Thank God you
        were not delicate, you let the world in
and lied! damn it you lied grossly
        sometimes. But it was all, I
see now, a carelessness, the part of a man
        that is homeless here on earth.

Provence, the fat assed Ford will never
        again strain the chairs of your cafés

pull and pare for his dish your sacred garlic,
    grunt and sweat and lick
his lips. Gross as the world he has left to
    us he has become
a part of that of which you were the known
    part, Provence, he loved so well.

MISTS OVER THE RIVER

The river-mirror mirrors the cold sky
through mists that tangle sunlight,
the sunlight of early morning,
in their veils veiling

the dark outlines of the shores. But
the necessity, you say, cries
aloud for the adjusting—greater than
song, greater perhaps than all song

While the song, self committed, the river
a mirror swathed in sunlight,
the river in its own body cries out
also, silently

from its obscuring veils. You
insist on my unqualified endorsement.
Many years, I see, many years
of reading have not made you wise.

From PATERSON

THE FALLS

What common language to unravel?
The Falls, combed into straight lines

from that rafter of a rock's
lip. Strike in! the middle of

some trenchant phrase, some
well packed clause. Then . . .
This is my plan. 4 sections: First,
the archaic persons of the drama.

An eternity of bird and bush,
resolved. An unraveling:
the confused streams aligned, side
by side, speaking! Sound

married to strength, a strength
of falling—from a height! The wild
voice of the shirt-sleeved
Evangelist rivaling, Hear

me! I am the Resurrection
and the Life! echoing
among the bass and pickerel, slim
eels from Barbados, Sargasso

Sea, working up the coast to that
bounty, ponds and wild streams—
Third, the old town: Alexander Hamilton
working up from St. Croix,

from that sea! and a deeper, whence
he came! stopped cold
by that unmoving roar, fastened
there: the rocks silent

but the water, married to the stone,
voluble, though frozen; the water
even when and though frozen
still whispers and moans—

And in the brittle air
a factory bell clangs, at dawn, and

snow whines under their feet. Fourth,
the modern town, a

disembodied roar! the cataract and
its clamor broken apart—and from
all learning, the empty
ear struck from within, roaring . . .

Sara Teasdale

(1884 – 1933)

OPEN WINDOWS

Out of the window a sea of green trees
    Lift their soft boughs like the arms of a dancer;
They beckon and call me, "Come out in the sun!"
    But I cannot answer.

I am alone with Weakness and Pain,
    Sick abed and June is going,
I cannot keep her, she hurries by
    With the silver-green of her garments blowing.

Men and women pass in the street
    Glad of the shining sapphire weather;
But we know more of it than they,
    Pain and I together.

They are the runners in the sun,
    Breathless and blinded by the race,
But we are watchers in the shade
    Who speak with Wonder face to face.

OVER THE ROOFS

I said, "I have shut my heart,
    As one shuts an open door,
That Love may starve therein
    And trouble me no more."

But over the roofs there came
    The wet new wind of May,

And a tune blew up from the curb
   Where the street-pianos play.

My room was white with the sun
   And Love cried out in me,
"I am strong, I will break your heart
   Unless you set me free."

Ezra Pound

(1885–1972)

SESTINA: ALTAFORTE

LOQUITUR: *En* Bertrans de Born.
    Dante Alighieri put this man in hell for that he was a stirrer-
    up of strife.
    Eccovi!
    Judge ye!
    Have I dug him up again?
The scene is at his castle, Altaforte. "Papiols" is his jongleur.
"The Leopard," the *device* of Richard (Cœur de Lion).

1

Damn it all! all this our South stinks peace.
You whoreson dog, Papiols, come! Let's to music!
I have no life save when the swords clash.
But ah! when I see the standards gold, vair, purple, opposing
And the broad fields beneath them turn crimson,
Then howl I my heart nigh mad with rejoicing.

2

In hot summer have I great rejoicing
When the tempests kill the earth's foul peace,
And the light'nings from black heav'n flash crimson,
And the fierce thunders roar me their music
And the winds shriek through the clouds mad, opposing,
And through all the riven skies God's swords clash.

3

Hell grant soon we hear again the swords clash!
And the shrill neighs of destriers in battle rejoicing,
Spiked breast to spiked breast opposing!
Better one hour's stour than a year's peace

With fat boards, bawds, wine and frail music!
Bah! there's no wine like the blood's crimson!

4

And I love to see the sun rise blood-crimson.
And I watch his spears through the dark clash
And it fills all my heart with rejoicing
And pries wide my mouth with fast music
When I see him so scorn and defy peace,
His lone might 'gainst all darkness opposing.

5

The man who fears war and squats opposing
My words for stour, hath no blood of crimson
But is fit only to rot in womanish peace
Far from where worth's won and the swords clash
For the death of such sluts I go rejoicing;
Yea, I fill all the air with my music.

6

Papiols, Papiols, to the music!
There's no sound like to swords swords opposing,
No cry like the battle's rejoicing
When our elbows and swords drip the crimson
And our charges 'gainst "The Leopard's" rush clash.
May God damn for ever all who cry "Peace!"

7

And let the music of the swords make them crimson!
Hell grant soon we hear again the swords clash!
Hell blot black for alway the thought "Peace"!

A VIRGINAL

No, no! Go from me. I have left her lately.
I will not spoil my sheath with lesser brightness,
For my surrounding air has a new lightness;

Slight are her arms, yet they have bound me straitly
And left me cloaked as with a gauze of æther;
As with sweet leaves; as with a subtle clearness.
Oh, I have picked up magic in her nearness
To sheathe me half in half the things that sheathe her.

No, no! Go from me. I have still the flavour,
Soft as spring wind that's come from birchen bowers.
Green come the shoots, aye April in the branches,
As winter's wound with her sleight hand she staunches,
Hath of the trees a likeness of the savour:
As white their bark, so white this lady's hours.

THE RETURN

See, they return; ah, see the tentative
        Movements, and the slow feet,
        The trouble in the pace and the uncertain
        Wavering!

See, they return, one, and by one,
With fear, as half-awakened;
As if the snow should hesitate
And murmur in the wind,
                and half turn back;
These were the "Wing'd-with-Awe,"
                Inviolable.

Gods of the wingèd shoe!
With them the silver hounds,
                sniffing the trace of air!

Haie! Haie!
    These were the swift to harry;
    These the keen-scented;
    These were the souls of blood.

    Slow on the leash,
                pallid the leash-men!

THE RIVER-MERCHANT'S WIFE: A LETTER

While my hair was still cut straight across my forehead
I playcd about the front gate, pulling flowers.
You came by on bamboo stilts, playing horse,
You walked about my seat, playing with blue plums.
And we went on living in the village of Chokan:
Two small people, without dislike or suspicion.

At fourteen I married My Lord you.
I never laughed, being bashful.
Lowering my head, I looked at the wall.
Called to, a thousand times, I never looked back.

At fifteen I stopped scowling,
I desired my dust to be mingled with yours
Forever and forever and forever.
Why should I climb the look out?

At sixteen you departed,
You went into far Ku-to-yen, by the river of swirling eddies,
And you have been gone five months.
The monkeys make sorrowful noise overhead.

You dragged your feet when you went out.
By the gate now, the moss is grown, the different mosses,
Too deep to clear them away!
The leaves fall early this autumn, in wind.
The paired butterflies are already yellow with August
Over the grass in the West garden;
They hurt me. I grow older.
If you are coming down through the narrows of the river Kiang,
Please let me know beforehand,
And I will come out to meet you
                                As far as Cho-fu-Sa.

                                                                (*By* Rihaku)

A PACT

I make a pact with you, Walt Whitman—
I have detested you long enough.
I come to you as a grown child
Who has had a pig-headed father;
I am old enough now to make friends.
It was you that broke the new wood,
Now is a time for carving.
We have one sap and one root—
Let there be commerce between us.

IN A STATION OF THE METRO

The apparition of these faces in the crowd;
Petals on a wet, black bough.

From HUGH SELWYN MAUBERLEY

1

The tea-rose tea-gown, etc.
Supplants the mousseline of Cos,
The pianola "replaces"
Sappho's barbitos.

Christ follows Dionysus,
Phallic and ambrosial
Made way for macerations;
Caliban casts out Ariel.

All things are a flowing,
Sage Heracleitus says;
But a tawdry cheapness
Shall outlast our days.

Even the Christian beauty
Defects—after Samothrace;
We see τὸ καλόν
Decreed in the market place.

Faun's flesh is not to us,
Nor the saint's vision.
We have the Press for wafer;
Franchise for circumcision.

All men, in law, are equals.
Free of Pisistratus,
We choose a knave or an eunuch
To rule over us.

O bright Apollo,
τίν' ἄνδρα, τίν' ἥρωα, τίνα θεόν,
What god, man, or hero
Shall I place a tin wreath upon!

        2

These fought in any case,
and some believing,
                    pro domo, in any case . . .

Some quick to arm,
some for adventure,
some from fear of weakness,
some from fear of censure,
some for love of slaughter, in imagination,
learning later . . .
some in fear, learning love of slaughter;

Died some, pro patria,
                    non "dulce" non "et decor" . . .
walked eye-deep in hell
believing in old men's lies, then unbelieving
came home, home to a lie,
home to many deceits,
home to old lies and new infamy;
usury age-old and age-thick
and liars in public places.

CANTO I

And then went down to the ship,
Set keel to breakers, forth on the godly sea, and
We set up mast and sail on that swart ship,
Bore sheep aboard her, and our bodies also
Heavy with weeping, and winds from sternward
Bore us out onward with bellying canvas,
Circe's this craft, the trim-coifed goddess.
Then sat we amidships, wind jamming the tiller,
Thus with stretched sail, we went over sea till day's end.
Sun to his slumber, shadows o'er all the ocean,
Came we then to the bounds of deepest water,
To the Kimmerian lands, and peopled cities
Covered with close-webbed mist, unpierced ever
With glitter of sun-rays
Nor with stars stretched, nor looking back from heaven
Swartest night stretched over wretched men there.
The ocean flowing backward, came we then to the place
Aforesaid by Circe.
Here did they rites, Perimedes and Eurylochus,
And drawing sword from my hip
I dug the ell-square pitkin;
Poured we libations unto each the dead,
First mead and then sweet wine, water mixed with white flour.
Then prayed I many a prayer to the sickly death's-heads;
As set in Ithaca, sterile bulls of the best
For sacrifice, heaping the pyre with goods,
A sheep to Tiresias only, black and a bell-sheep.
Dark blood flowed in the fosse,
Souls out of Erebus, cadaverous dead, of brides
Of youths and of the old who had borne much;
Souls stained with recent tears, girls tender,
Men many, mauled with bronze lance heads,
Battle spoil, bearing yet dreory arms,
These many crowded about me; with shouting,
Pallor upon me, cried to my men for more beasts;
Slaughtered the herds, sheep slain of bronze;
Poured ointment, cried to the gods,
To Pluto the strong, and praised Proserpine;
Unsheathed the narrow sword,

I sat to keep off the impetuous impotent dead,
Till I should hear Tiresias.
But first Elpenor came, our friend Elpenor,
Unburied, cast on the wide earth,
Limbs that we left in the house of Circe,
Unwept, unwrapped in sepulchre, since toils urged other.
Pitiful spirit. And I cried in hurried speech:
"Elpenor, how art thou come to this dark coast?
"Cam'st thou afoot, outstripping seamen?"
              And he in heavy speech:
"Ill fate and abundant wine. I slept in Circe's ingle.
"Going down the long ladder unguarded,
"I fell against the buttress,
"Shattered the nape-nerve, the soul sought Avernus.
"But thou, O King, I bid remember me, unwept, unburied,
"Heap up mine arms, be tomb by sea-bord, and inscribed:
"*A man of no fortune, and with a name to come.*
"And set my oar up, that I swung mid fellows."

And Anticlea came, whom I beat off, and then Tiresias Theban,
Holding his golden wand, knew me, and spoke first:
"A second time? why? man of ill star,
"Facing the sunless dead and this joyless region?
"Stand from the fosse, leave me my bloody bever
"For soothsay."
              And I stepped back,
And he strong with the blood, said then: "Odysseus
"Shalt return through spiteful Neptune, over dark seas,
"Lose all companions." And then Anticlea came.
Lie quiet Divus. I mean, that is Andreas Divus,
In officina Wecheli, 1538, out of Homer.
And he sailed, by Sirens and thence outward and away
And unto Circe.
              Venerandam,
In the Cretan's phrase, with the golden crown, Aphrodite,
Cypri munimenta sortita est, mirthful, oricalchi, with golden
Girdles and breast bands, thou with dark eyelids
Bearing the golden bough of Argicida. So that:

CANTO XLV

With *Usura*

With usura hath no man a house of good stone
each block cut smooth and well fitting
that design might cover their face,
with usura
hath no man a painted paradise on his church wall
harpes et luthes
or where virgin receiveth message
and halo projects from incision,
with usura
seeth no man Gonzaga his heirs and his concubines
no picture is made to endure nor to live with
but it is made to sell and sell quickly
with usura, sin against nature,
is thy bread ever more of stale rags
is thy bread dry as paper,
with no mountain wheat, no strong flour
with usura the line grows thick
with usura is no clear demarcation
and no man can find site for his dwelling.
Stone cutter is kept from his stone
weaver is kept from his loom
WITH USURA
wool comes not to market
sheep bringeth no gain with usura
Usura is a murrain, usura
blunteth the needle in the maid's hand
and stoppeth the spinner's cunning. Pietro Lombardo
came not by usura
Duccio came not by usura
nor Pier della Francesca; Zuan Bellin' not by usura
nor was "La Calunnia" painted.
Came not by usura Angelico; came not Ambrogio Praedis,
Came no church of cut stone signed: *Adamo me fecit.*
Not by usura St. Trophime
Not by usura Saint Hilaire,
Usura rusteth the chisel

It rusteth the craft and the craftsman
It gnaweth the thread in the loom
None learneth to weave gold in her pattern;
Azure hath a canker by usura; cramoisi is unbroidered
Emerald findeth no Memling
Usura slayeth the child in the womb
It stayeth the young man's courting
It hath brought palsey to bed, lyeth
between the young bride and her bridegroom
                    CONTRA NATURAM
They have brought whores for Eleusis
Corpses are set to banquet
at behest of usura.

"H.D." (Hilda Doolittle)

(1 8 8 6 – 1 9 6 1)

PEAR TREE

Silver dust,
lifted from the earth,
higher than my arms reach,
you have mounted,
O, silver,
higher than my arms reach,
you front us with great mass;

no flower ever opened
so staunch a white leaf,
no flower ever parted silver
from such rare silver;

O, white pear,
your flower-tufts
thick on the branch
bring summer and ripe fruits
in their purple hearts.

OREAD

Whirl up, sea—
whirl your pointed pines,
splash your great pines
on our rocks,
hurl your green over us,
cover us with your pools of fir.

AT ITHACA

Over and back,
the long waves crawl
and track the sand with foam;
night darkens and the sea
takes on that desperate tone
of dark that wives put on
when all their love is done.

Over and back,
the tangled thread falls slack,
over and up and on;
over and all is sewn;
now while I bind the end,
I wish some fiery friend
would sweep impetuously
these fingers from the loom.

My weary thoughts
play traitor to my soul,
just as the toil is over;
swift while the woof is whole,
turn now my spirit, swift,
and tear the pattern there,
the flowers so deftly wrought,
the border of sea-blue,
the sea-blue coast of home.

The web was over-fair,
that web of pictures there,
enchantments that I thought
he had, that I had lost;
weaving his happiness
within the stitching frame,
I thought my work was done,
I prayed that only one
of those that I had spurned,
might stoop and conquer this
long waiting with a kiss.

But each time that I see
my work so beautifully
inwoven and would keep
the picture and the whole,
Athene steels my soul,
slanting across my brain,
I see as shafts of rain
his chariot and his shafts,
I see the arrows fall,
I see my lord who moves
like Hector, lord of love,
I see him matched with fair
bright rivals and I see
those lesser rivals flee.

THE SHRINE

"She Watches over the Sea."

1

Are your rocks shelter for ships—
have you sent galleys from your beach,
are you graded—a safe crescent—
where the tide lifts them back to port—
are you full and sweet,
tempting the quiet
to depart in their trading ships?

Nay, you are great, fierce, evil—
you are the land-blight—
you have tempted men
but they perished on your cliffs.

Your lights are but dank shoals,
slate and pebble and wet shells
and seaweed fastened to the rocks.

It was evil— evil
when they found you,
when the quiet men looked at you—

they sought a headland
shaded with ledge of cliff
from the wind-blast.

But you—you are unsheltered,
cut with the weight of wind—
you shudder when it strikes,
then lift, swelled with the blast—
you sink as the tide sinks,
you shrill under hail, and sound
thunder when thunder sounds.

You are useless—
when the tides swirl
your boulders cut and wreck
the staggering ships.

    2

You are useless,
O grave, O beautiful,
the landsmen tell it—I have heard—
you are useless.
And the wind sounds with this
and the sea
where rollers shot with blue
cut under deeper blue.
O but stay tender, enchanted
where wave-lengths cut you
apart from all the rest—
for we have found you,
we watch the splendour of you,
we thread throat on throat of freesia
for your shelf.

You are not forgot,
O plunder of lilies,
honey is not more sweet
than the salt stretch of your beach.

    3

Stay—stay—
but terror has caught us now,

we passed the men in ships,
we dared deeper than the fisher-folk
and you strike us with terror
O bright shaft.

Flame passes under us
and sparks that unknot the flesh,
sorrow, splitting bone from bone,
splendour athwart our eyes
and rifts in the splendour,
sparks and scattered light.
Many warned of this,
men said:
there are wrecks on the fore-beach,
wind will beat your ship,
there is no shelter in that headland,
it is useless waste, that edge,
that front of rock—
sea-gulls clang beyond the breakers,
none venture to that spot.

4

But hail—
as the tide slackens,
as the wind beats out,
we hail this shore—
we sing to you,
spirit between the headlands
and the further rocks.

Though oak-beams split,
though boats and sea-men flounder,
and the strait grind sand with sand
and cut boulders to sand and drift—

your eyes have pardoned our faults,
your hands have touched us—
you have leaned forward a little
and the waves can never thrust us back
from the splendour of your ragged coast.

HELEN

All Greece hates
the still eyes in the white face,
the lustre as of olives
where she stands,
and the white hands.

All Greece reviles
the wan face when she smiles,
hating it deeper still
when it grows wan and white,
remembering past enchantments
and past ills.

Greece sees, unmoved,
God's daughter, born of love,
the beauty of cool feet
and slenderest knees,
could love indeed the maid,
only if she were laid,
white ash amid funereal cypresses.

AT BAIA

I should have thought
in a dream you would have brought
some lovely, perilous thing,
orchids piled in a great sheath,
as who would say (in a dream),
"I send you this,
who left the blue veins
of your throat unkissed."

Why was it that your hands
(that never took mine),
your hands that I could see

drift over the orchid-heads
so carefully,
your hands, so fragile, sure to lift
so gently, the fragile flower-stuff—
ah, ah, how was it

You never sent (in a dream)
the very form, the very scent,
not heavy, not sensuous,
but perilous—perilous—
of orchids, piled in a great sheath,
and folded underneath on a bright scroll,
some word:

"Flower sent to flower;
for white hands, the lesser white,
less lovely of flower-leaf,"

or

"Lover to lover, no kiss,
no touch, but forever and ever this."

Robinson Jeffers

(1 8 8 7 – 1 9 6 2)

TO THE STONE-CUTTERS

Stone-cutters fighting time with marble, you foredefeated
Challengers of oblivion
Eat cynical earnings, knowing rock splits, records fall down,
The square-limbed Roman letters
Scale in the thaws, wear in the rain. The poet as well
Builds his monument mockingly;
For man will be blotted out, the blithe earth die, the brave sun
Die blind and blacken to the heart:
Yet stones have stood for a thousand years, and pained thoughts found
The honey of peace in old poems.

NIGHT

The ebb slips from the rock, the sunken
Tide-rocks lift streaming shoulders
Out of the slack, the slow west
Sombering its torch; a ship's light
Shows faintly, far out,
Over the weight of the prone ocean
On the low cloud.

Over the dark mountain, over the dark pinewood,
Down the long dark valley along the shrunken river,
Returns the splendor without rays, the shining of shadow,
Peace-bringer, the matrix of all shining and quieter of shining.
Where the shore widens on the bay she opens dark wings
And the ocean accepts her glory. O soul worshipful of her
You like the ocean have grave depths where she dwells always,
And the film of waves above that takes the sun takes also
Her, with more love. The sun-lovers have a blond favorite,

A father of lights and noises, wars, weeping and laughter,
Hot labor, lust and delight and the other blemishes. Quietness
Flows from her deeper fountain; and he will die; and she is immortal.

Far off from here the slender
Flocks of the mountain forest
Move among stems like towers
Of the old redwoods to the stream,
No twig crackling; dip shy
Wild muzzles into the mountain water
Among the dark ferns.

O passionately at peace you being secure will pardon
The blasphemies of glowworms, the lamp in my tower, the fretfulness
Of cities, the cressets of the planets, the pride of the stars.
This August night in a rift of cloud Antares reddens,
The great one, the ancient torch, a lord among lost children,
The earth's orbit doubled would not girdle his greatness, one fire
Globed, out of grasp of the mind enormous; but to you O Night
What? Not a spark? What flicker of a spark in the faint far glimmer
Of a lost fire dying in the desert, dim coals of a sand-pit the Bedouins
Wandered from at dawn . . . Ah singing prayer to what gulfs tempted
Suddenly are you more lost? To us the near-hand mountain
Be a measure of height, the tide-worn cliff at the sea-gate a measure of
    continuance.

The tide, moving the night's
Vastness with lonely voices,
Turns, the deep dark-shining
Pacific leans on the land,
Feeling his cold strength
To the outmost margins: you Night will resume
The stars in your time.

O passionately at peace when will that tide draw shoreward?
Truly the spouting fountains of light, Antares, Arcturus,
Tire of their flow, they sing one song but they think silence.
The striding winter giant Orion shines, and dreams darkness.
And life, the flicker of men and moths and the wolf on the hill,
Though furious for continuance, passionately feeding, passionately
Remaking itself upon its mates, remembers deep inward
The calm mother, the quietness of the womb and the egg,
The primal and the latter silences: dear Night it is memory

Prophesies, prophecy that remembers, the charm of the dark.
And I and my people, we are willing to love the four-score years
Heartily; but as a sailor loves the sea, when the helm is for harbor.

Have men's minds changed,
Or the rock hidden in the deep of the waters of the soul
Broken the surface? A few centuries
Gone by, was none dared not to people
The darkness beyond the stars with harps and habitations.
But now, dear is the truth. Life is grown sweeter and lonelier,
And death is no evil.

SHINE, PERISHING REPUBLIC

While this America settles in the mould of its vulgarity, heavily thickening to
    empire,
And protest, only a bubble in the molten mass, pops and sighs out, and the
    mass hardens,

I sadly smiling remember that the flower fades to make fruit, the fruit rots to
    make earth.
Out of the mother; and through the spring exultances, ripeness and decadence;
    and home to the mother.

You making haste haste on decay: not blameworthy; life is good, be it
    stubbornly long or suddenly
A mortal splendor: meteors are not needed less than mountains: shine,
    perishing republic.

HURT HAWKS

1

The broken pillar of the wing jags from the clotted shoulder,
The wing trails like a banner in defeat,
No more to use the sky forever but live with famine

And pain a few days: cat nor coyote
Will shorten the week of waiting for death, there is game without talons.
He stands under the oak-bush and waits
The lame feet of salvation; at night he remembers freedom
And flies in a dream, the dawns ruin it.
He is strong and pain is worse to the strong, incapacity is worse.
The curs of the day come and torment him
At distance, no one but death the redeemer will humble that head,
The intrepid readiness, the terrible eyes.
The wild God of the world is sometimes merciful to those
That ask mercy, not often to the arrogant.
You do not know him, you communal people, or you have forgotten him;
Intemperate and savage, the hawk remembers him;
Beautiful and wild, the hawks, and men that are dying, remember him.

        2

I'd sooner, except the penalties, kill a man than a hawk; but the great redtail
Had nothing left but unable misery
From the bone too shattered for mending, the wing that trailed under his talons
     when he moved.
We had fed him six weeks, I gave him freedom,
He wandered over the foreland hill and returned in the evening, asking for
     death,
Not like a beggar, still eyed with the old
Implacable arrogance. I gave him the lead gift in the twilight. What fell was
     relaxed,
Owl-downy, soft feminine feathers; but what
Soared: the fierce rush: the night-herons by the flooded river cried fear at its
     rising
Before it was quite unsheathed from reality.

ROCK AND HAWK

Here is a symbol in which
Many high tragic thoughts
Watch their own eyes.

This gray rock, standing tall
On the headland, where the seawind
Lets no tree grow,

Earthquake-proved, and signatured
By ages of storms: on its peak
A falcon has perched.

I think, here is your emblem
To hang in the future sky;
Not the cross, not the hive,

But this; bright power, dark peace;
Fierce consciousness joined with final
Disinterestedness;

Life with calm death; the falcon's
Realist eyes and act
Married to the massive

Mysticism of stone,
Which failure cannot cast down
Nor success make proud.

BUT I AM GROWING OLD AND INDOLENT

I have been warned. It is more than thirty years since I wrote—
Thinking of the narrative poems I made, which always
Ended in blood and pain, though beautiful enough—my pain, my blood,
They were my creatures —I understood, and wrote to myself:
"Make sacrifices once a year to magic
Horror away from the house"— for that hangs imminent
Over all men and all houses —"This little house here
You have built over the ocean with your own hands
Beside the standing sea-boulders . . ." So I listened
To my Demon warning me that evil would come
If my work ceased, if I did not make sacrifice
Of storied and imagined lives, Tamar and Cawdor

And Thurso's wife—"imagined victims be our redeemers"—
At that time I was sure of my fates and felt
My poems guarding the house, well-made watchdogs
Ready to bite.
        But time sucks out the juice,
A man grows old and indolent.

Elinor Wylie

(1887 – 1928)

WILD PEACHES

1

When the world turns completely upside down
You say we'll emigrate to the Eastern Shore
Aboard a river-boat from Baltimore;
We'll live among wild peach trees, miles from town,
You'll wear a coonskin cap, and I a gown
Homespun, dyed butternut's dark gold colour.
Lost, like your lotus-eating ancestor,
We'll swim in milk and honey till we drown.

The winter will be short, the summer long,
The autumn amber-hued, sunny and hot,
Tasting of cider and of scuppernong;
All seasons sweet, but autumn best of all.
The squirrels in their silver fur will fall
Like falling leaves, like fruit, before your shot.

2

The autumn frosts will lie upon the grass
Like bloom on grapes of purple-brown and gold.
The misted early mornings will be cold;
The little puddles will be roofed with glass.
The sun, which burns from copper into brass,
Melts these at noon, and makes the boys unfold
Their knitted mufflers; full as they can hold,
Fat pockets dribble chestnuts as they pass.

Peaches grow wild, and pigs can live in clover;
A barrel of salted herrings lasts a year;
The spring begins before the winter's over.
By February you may find the skins
Of garter snakes and water moccasins
Dwindled and harsh, dead-white and cloudy-clear.

3

When April pours the colours of a shell
Upon the hills, when every little creek
Is shot with silver from the Chesapeake
In shoals new-minted by the ocean swell,
When strawberries go begging, and the sleek
Blue plums lie open to the blackbird's beak,
We shall live well—we shall live very well.

The months between the cherries and the peaches
Are brimming cornucopias which spill
Fruits red and purple, sombre-bloomed and black;
Then, down rich fields and frosty river beaches
We'll trample bright persimmons, while you kill
Bronze partridge, speckled quail, and canvasback.

4

Down to the Puritan marrow of my bones
There's something in this richness that I hate.
I love the look, austere, immaculate,
Of landscapes drawn in pearly monotones.
There's something in my very blood that owns
Bare hills, cold silver on a sky of slate,
A thread of water, churned to milky spate
Streaming through slanted pastures fenced with stones.

I love those skies, thin blue or snowy gray,
Those fields sparse-planted, rendering meagre sheaves;
That spring, briefer than apple-blossom's breath,
Summer, so much too beautiful to stay,
Swift autumn, like a bonfire of leaves,
And sleepy winter, like the sleep of death.

LET NO CHARITABLE HOPE

Now let no charitable hope
Confuse my mind with images
Of eagle and of antelope:
I am in nature none of these.

I was, being human, born alone;
I am, being woman, hard beset;
I live by squeezing from a stone
The little nourishment I get.

In masks outrageous and austere
The years go by in single file;
But none has merited my fear,
And none has quite escaped my smile.

MALEDICTION UPON MYSELF

Now if the dull and thankless heart declare
That this fair city is no longer fair
Because the month has peopled it with shadows
And swept the quality to hills and meadows:
Yea, if it cry in its ingratitude
That holy beauty is no longer good
But that it is degraded and cast down
Because it treads the pavement of the town:
If it accept the rank ignoble rule
That beauty is no longer beautiful
Because it is not straitlaced and aloof
But sets its sandal on a London roof
And takes polluted Thames to be its mirror:
If the vile heart is guilty of this error
I here pronounce upon its inmost nerve
The malediction which it must deserve.
Loosen its strings: let it no longer be
The instrument of mortal ecstasy:
Empty its veins of rapture, and replace
The fine elixir with a foul and base
Till the true heaven never more descends
In delicate pulses to my finger ends,
Or flutters like a feather at my heel.
Bind blindness on my forehead: set a seal
On each of my two eyes which have forsworn
The light, and darken them with disks of horn.
Stop up my nostrils in default of breath
With graveyard powder and compacted death,

And stuff my mouth with ruin for a gag,
And break my ankles of a running stag:
Let the long legs of which I am so proud
Be bended, and the lifted throat be bowed:
Lower the arrogant pennon which I bear
Blown backward in the fringes of my hair
And let its silk be trampled to a skein
Of serpents knotted in corruptive pain:
Let these my words unwind the virtuous mesh
Which knits the spirit to the naughty flesh:
Let me dismember me in sacred wrath
And scatter me in pieces for a path
On which the step of that I have denied
Descends in silver to his proper bride.

CASTILIAN

Velasquez took a pliant knife
And scraped his palette clean;
He said, "I lead a dog's own life
Painting a king and queen."

He cleaned his palette with oily rags
And oakum from Seville wharves;
"I am sick of painting painted hags
And bad ambiguous dwarves.

"The sky is silver, the clouds are pearl,
Their locks are looped with rain.
I will not paint Maria's girl
For all the money in Spain."

He washed his face in water cold,
His hands in turpentine;
He squeezed out colour like coins of gold
And colour like drops of wine.

Each colour lay like a little pool
On the polished cedar wood;

Clear and pale and ivory-cool
Or dark as solitude.

He burnt the rags in the fireplace
And leaned from the window high;
He said, "I like that gentleman's face
Who wears his cap awry."

This is the gentleman, there he stands,
Castilian, sombre-caped,
With arrogant eyes, and narrow hands
Miraculously shaped.

Marianne Moore

(1887 – 1972)

THE FISH

wade
through black jade.
   Of the crow-blue mussel shells, one keeps
   adjusting the ash heaps;
      opening and shutting itself like

an
injured fan.
   The barnacles which encrust the side
   of the wave, cannot hide
      there for the submerged shafts of the

sun,
split like spun
   glass, move themselves with spotlight swiftness
   into the crevices—
      in and out, illuminating

the
turquoise sea
   of bodies. The water drives a wedge
   of iron through the iron edge
      of the cliff; whereupon the stars,

pink
rice-grains, ink-
   bespattered jellyfish, crabs like green
   lilies, and submarine
      toadstools, slide each on the other.

All
external
   marks of abuse are present on this

defiant edifice—
　　all the physical features of

ac-
cident—lack
　　of cornice, dynamite grooves, burns, and
　　hatchet strokes, these things stand
　　　　out on it; the chasm side is

dead.
Repeated
　　evidence has proved that it can live
　　on what can not revive
　　　　its youth. The sea grows old in it.

POETRY

I, too, dislike it: there are things that are important beyond all this fiddle.
　　Reading it, however, with a perfect contempt for it, one discovers in
　　it after all, a place for the genuine.
　　　　Hands that can grasp, eyes
　　　　that can dilate, hair that can rise
　　　　　　if it must, these things are important not because a

high-sounding interpretation can be put upon them but because they are
　　useful. When they become so derivative as to become unintelligible,
　　the same thing may be said for all of us, that we
　　　　do not admire what
　　　　we cannot understand: the bat
　　　　　　holding on upside down or in quest of something to

eat, elephants pushing, a wild horse taking a roll, a tireless wolf under
　　a tree, the immovable critic twitching his skin like a horse that feels a flea,
　　the base-
　　ball fan, the statistician—
　　　　nor is it valid
　　　　　　to discriminate against "business documents and

school-books"; all these phenomena are important. One must make a
    distinction
    however: when dragged into prominence by half poets, the result is not
        poetry,
    nor till the poets among us can be
        "literalists of
        the imagination"—above
            insolence and triviality and can present

for inspection, "imaginary gardens with real toads in them," shall we have
    it. In the meantime, if you demand on the one hand,
    the raw material of poetry in
        all its rawness and
        that which is on the other hand
            genuine, you are interested in poetry.

MARRIAGE

This institution,
perhaps one should say enterprise
out of respect for which
one says one need not change one's mind
about a thing one has believed in,
requiring public promises
of one's intention
to fulfil a private obligation:
I wonder what Adam and Eve
think of it by this time,
this fire-gilt steel
alive with goldenness;
how bright it shows—
"of circular traditions and impostures,
committing many spoils,"
requiring all one's criminal ingenuity
to avoid!
Psychology which explains everything
explains nothing,
and we are still in doubt.
Eve: beautiful woman—

I have seen her
when she was so handsome
she gave me a start,
able to write simultaneously
in three languages—
English, German, and French—
and talk in the meantime;
equally positive in demanding a commotion
and in stipulating quiet:
"I should like to be alone";
to which the visitor replies,
"I should like to be alone;
why not be alone together?"
Below the incandescent stars
below the incandescent fruit,
the strange experience of beauty;
its existence is too much;
it tears one to pieces
and each fresh wave of consciousness
is poison.
"See her, see her in this common world,"
the central flaw
in that first crystal-fine experiment,
this amalgamation which can never be more
than an interesting impossibility,
describing it
as "that strange paradise
unlike flesh, stones,
gold or stately buildings,
the choicest piece of my life:
the heart rising
in its estate of peace
as a boat rises
with the rising of the water";
constrained in speaking of the serpent—
shed snakeskin in the history of politeness
not to be returned to again—
that invaluable accident
exonerating Adam.
And he has beauty also;
it's distressing—the O thou
to whom from whom,
without whom nothing—Adam;

"something feline,
something colubrine"—how true!
a crouching mythological monster
in that Persian miniature of emerald mines,
raw silk—ivory white, snow white,
oyster white, and six others—
that paddock full of leopards and giraffes—
long lemon-yellow bodies
sown with trapezoids of blue.
Alive with words,
vibrating like a cymbal
touched before it has been struck,
he has prophesied correctly—
the industrious waterfall,
"the speedy stream
which violently bears all before it,
at one time silent as the air
and now as powerful as the wind."
"Treading chasms
on the uncertain footing of a spear,"
forgetting that there is in woman
a quality of mind
which as an instinctive manifestation
is unsafe,
he goes on speaking
in a formal customary strain,
of "past states, the present state,
seals, promises,
the evil one suffered,
the good one enjoys,
hell, heaven,
everything convenient
to promote one's joy."
In him a state of mind
perceives what it was not
intended that he should;
"he experiences a solemn joy
in seeing that he has become an idol."
Plagued by the nightingale
in the new leaves,
with its silence—
not its silence but its silences,

he says of it:
"It clothes me with a shirt of fire."
"He dares not clap his hands
to make it go on
lest it should fly off;
if he does nothing, it will sleep;
if he cries out, it will not understand."
Unnerved by the nightingale
and dazzled by the apple,
impelled by "the illusion of a fire
effectual to extinguish fire,"
compared with which
the shining of the earth
is but deformity—a fire
"as high as deep
as bright as broad
as long as life itself,"
he stumbles over marriage,
"a very trivial object indeed"
to have destroyed the attitude
in which he stood—
the ease of the philosopher
unfathered by a woman.
Unhelpful Hymen!
a kind of overgrown cupid
reduced to insignificance
by the mechanical advertising
parading as involuntary comment,
by that experiment of Adam's
with ways out but no way in—
the ritual of marriage,
augmenting all its lavishness;
its fiddlehead ferns,
lotus flowers, opuntias, white dromedaries,
its hippopotamus—
nose and mouth combined
in one magnificent hopper—
its snake and the potent apple.
He tells us
that "for love that will
gaze an eagle blind,
that is with Hercules

climbing the trees
in the garden of the Hesperides,
from forty-five to seventy
is the best age,"
commending it
as a fine art, as an experiment,
a duty or as merely recreation.
One must not call him ruffian
nor friction a calamity—
the fight to be affectionate:
"no truth can be fully known
until it has been tried
by the tooth of disputation."
The blue panther with black eyes,
the basalt panther with blue eyes,
entirely graceful—
one must give them the path—
the black obsidian Diana
who "darkeneth her countenance
as a bear doth,"
the spiked hand
that has an affection for one
and proves it to the bone,
impatient to assure you
that impatience is the mark of independence,
not of bondage.
"Married people often look that way"—
"seldom and cold, up and down,
mixed and malarial
with a good day and a bad."
We Occidentals are so unemotional,
self lost, the irony preserved
in "the Ahasuerus *tête-à-tête* banquet"
with its small orchids like snakes' tongues,
with its "good monster, lead the way,"
with little laughter
and munificence of humor
in that quixotic atmosphere of frankness
in which "four o'clock does not exist,
but at five o'clock
the ladies in their imperious humility
are ready to receive you";

in which experience attests
that men have power
and sometimes one is made to feel it.
He says, "What monarch would not blush
to have a wife
with hair like a shaving brush?"
The fact of woman
is "not the sound of the flute
but very poison."
She says, "Men are monopolists
of 'stars, garters, buttons
and other shining baubles'—
unfit to be the guardians
of another person's happiness."
He says, "These mummies
must be handled carefully—
'the crumbs from a lion's meal,
a couple of shins and the bit of an ear';
turn to the letter M
and you will find
that 'a wife is a coffin,'
that severe object
with the pleasing geometry
stipulating space not people,
refusing to be buried
and uniquely disappointing,
revengefully wrought in the attitude
of an adoring child
to a distinguished parent."
She says, "This butterfly,
this waterfly, this nomad
that has 'proposed
to settle on my hand for life'—
What can one do with it?
There must have been more time
in Shakespeare's day
to sit and watch a play.
You know so many artists who are fools."
He says, "You know so many fools
who are not artists."
The fact forgot
that "some have merely rights

while some have obligations,"
he loves himself so much,
he can permit himself
no rival in that love.
She loves herself so much,
she cannot see herself enough—
a statuette of ivory on ivory,
the logical last touch
to an expansive splendor
earned as wages for work done:
one is not rich but poor
when one can always seem so right.
What can one do for them—
these savages
condemned to disaffect
all those who are not visionaries
alert to undertake the silly task
of making people noble?
This model of petrine fidelity
who "leaves her peaceful husband
only because she has seen enough of him"—
that orator reminding you,
"I am yours to command."
"Everything to do with love is mystery;
it is more than a day's work
to investigate this science."
One sees that it is rare—
that striking grasp of opposites
opposed each to the other, not to unity,
which in cycloid inclusiveness
has dwarfed the demonstration
of Columbus with the egg—
a triumph of simplicity—
that charitive Euroclydon
of frightening disinterestedness
which the world hates,
admitting:

   "I am such a cow,
    if I had a sorrow
    I should feel it a long time;
    I am not one of those
    who have a great sorrow

    in the morning
    and a great joy at noon";

which says: "I have encountered it
among those unpretentious
protégés of wisdom,
where seeming to parade
as the debater and the Roman,
the statesmanship
of an archaic Daniel Webster
persists to their simplicity of temper
as the essence of the matter:

  'Liberty and union
   now and forever';

the Book on the writing table;
the hand in the breast pocket."

THE STEEPLE-JACK

Dürer would have seen a reason for living
       in a town like this, with eight stranded whales
to look at; with the sweet sea air coming into your house
on a fine day, from water etched
       with waves as formal as the scales
on a fish.

One by one in two's and three's, the seagulls keep
       flying back and forth over the town clock,
or sailing around the lighthouse without moving their wings—
rising steadily with a slight
       quiver of the body—or flock
mewing where

a sea the purple of the peacock's neck is
       paled to greenish azure as Dürer changed
the pine green of the Tyrol to peacock blue and guinea

gray. You can see a twenty-five-
     pound lobster; and fish nets arranged
to dry. The

whirlwind fife-and-drum of the storm bends the salt
     marsh grass, disturbs stars in the sky and the
star on the steeple; it is a privilege to see so
much confusion. Disguised by what
     might seem the opposite, the sea-
side flowers and

trees are favored by the fog so that you have
     the tropics at first hand: the trumpet vine,
foxglove, giant snapdragon, a salpiglossis that has
spots and stripes; morning-glories, gourds,
     or moon-vines trained on fishing twine
at the back door:

cattails, flags, blueberries and spiderwort,
     striped grass, lichens, sunflowers, asters, daisies—
yellow and crab-claw ragged sailors with green bracts—toad-plant,
petunias, ferns; pink lilies, blue
     ones, tigers; poppies; black sweet-peas.
The climate

is not right for the banyan, frangipani, or
     jack-fruit trees; or for exotic serpent
life. Ring lizard and snakeskin for the foot, if you see fit;
but here they've cats, not cobras, to
     keep down the rats. The diffident
little newt

with white pin-dots on black horizontal spaced-
     out bands lives here; yet there is nothing that
ambition can buy or take away. The college student
named Ambrose sits on the hillside
     with his not-native books and hat
and sees boats

at sea progress white and rigid as if in
     a groove. Liking an elegance of which
the source is not bravado, he knows by heart the antique

sugar-bowl shaped summerhouse of
      interlacing slats, and the pitch
of the church

spire, not true, from which a man in scarlet lets
      down a rope as a spider spins a thread;
he might be part of a novel, but on the sidewalk a
sign says C. J. Poole, Steeple Jack,
      in black and white; and one in red
and white says

Danger. The church portico has four fluted
      columns, each a single piece of stone, made
modester by whitewash. This would be a fit haven for
waifs, children, animals, prisoners,
      and presidents who have repaid
sin-driven

senators by not thinking about them. The
      place has a schoolhouse, a post-office in a
store, fish-houses, hen-houses, a three-masted schooner on
the stocks. The hero, the student,
      the steeple jack, each in his way,
is at home.

It could not be dangerous to be living
      in a town like this, of simple people,
who have a steeple-jack placing danger signs by the church
while he is gilding the solid-
      pointed star, which on a steeple
stands for hope.

IN DISTRUST OF MERITS

Strengthened to live, strengthened to die for
      medals and positioned victories?
They're fighting, fighting, fighting the blind
      man who thinks he sees,—

who cannot see that the enslaver is
enslaved; the hater, harmed. O shining O
     firm star, O tumultuous
          ocean lashed till small things go
       as they will, the mountainous
         wave makes us who look, know

depth. Lost at sea before they fought! O
     star of David, star of Bethlehem,
O black imperial lion
     of the Lord—emblem
of a risen world—be joined at last, be
joined. There is hate's crown beneath which all is
       death; there's love's without which none
         is king; the blessed deeds bless
       the halo. As contagion
         of sickness makes sickness,

contagion of trust can make trust. They're
     fighting in deserts and caves, one by
one, in battalions and squadrons;
     they're fighting that I
may yet recover from the disease, My
Self; some have it lightly; some will die. "Man's
       wolf to man" and we devour
         ourselves. The enemy could not
       have made a greater breach in our
         defenses. One pilot-

ing a blind man can escape him, but
     Job disheartened by false comfort knew
that nothing can be so defeating
     as a blind man who
can see. O alive who are dead, who are
proud not to see, O small dust of the earth
       that walks so arrogantly,
         trust begets power and faith is
       an affectionate thing. We
         vow, we make this promise

to the fighting—it's a promise—"We'll
     never hate black, white, red, yellow, Jew,

Gentile, Untouchable." We are
        not competent to
make our vows. With set jaw they are fighting,
fighting, fighting,—some we love whom we know,
        some we love but know not—that
                hearts may feel and not be numb.
        It cures me; or am I what
                I can't believe in? Some

in snow, some on crags, some in quicksands,
        little by little, much by much, they
are fighting fighting fighting that where
        there was death there may
be life. "When a man is prey to anger,
he is moved by outside things; when he holds
        his ground in patience patience
                patience, that is action or
        beauty," the soldier's defense
                and hardest armor for

the fight. The world's an orphans' home. Shall
        we never have peace without sorrow?
without pleas of the dying for
        help that won't come? O
quiet form upon the dust, I cannot
look and yet I must. If these great patient
        dyings—all these agonies
                and wound bearings and bloodshed—
        can teach us how to live, these
                dyings were not wasted.

Hate-hardened heart, O heart of iron,
        iron is iron till it is rust.
There never was a war that was
        not inward; I must
fight till I have conquered in myself what
causes war, but I would not believe it.
        I inwardly did nothing.
                O Iscariot-like crime!
        Beauty is everlasting
                and dust is for a time.

WHEN I BUY PICTURES

or what is closer to the truth,
when I look at that of which I may regard myself as the imaginary possessor,
I fix upon what would give me pleasure in my average moments:
the satire upon curiosity in which no more is discernible
than the intensity of the mood;
or quite the opposite—the old thing, the mediaeval decorated hat-box,
in which there are hounds with waists diminishing like the waist of the hour-glass
and deer and birds and seated people;
it may be no more than a square of parquetry; the literal biography perhaps,
in letters standing well apart upon a parchment-like expanse;
an artichoke in six varieties of blue; the snipe-legged hieroglyphic in three parts;
the silver fence protecting Adam's grave, or Michael taking Adam by the wrist.
Too stern an intellectual emphasis upon this quality or that detracts from one's
        enjoyment.
It must not wish to disarm anything; nor may the approved triumph easily be
        honored—
that which is great because something else is small.
It comes to this: of whatever sort it is,
it must be "lit with piercing glances into the life of things";
it must acknowledge the spiritual forces which have made it.

John Crowe Ransom

(1888 – 1974)

BELLS FOR JOHN WHITESIDE'S DAUGHTER

There was such speed in her little body,
And such lightness in her footfall,
It is no wonder her brown study
Astonishes us all.

Her wars were bruited in our high window.
We looked among orchard trees and beyond
Where she took arms against her shadow,
Or harried unto the pond

The lazy geese, like a snow cloud
Dripping their snow on the green grass,
Tricking and stopping, sleepy and proud,
Who cried in goose, Alas,

For the tireless heart within the little
Lady with rod that made them rise
From their noon apple-dreams and scuttle
Goose-fashion under the skies!

But now go the bells, and we are ready,
In one house we are sternly stopped
To say we are vexed at her brown study,
Lying so primly propped.

PIAZZA PIECE

—I am a gentleman in a dustcoat trying
To make you hear. Your ears are soft and small
And listen to an old man not at all,
They want the young men's whispering and sighing.

But see the roses on your trellis dying
And hear the spectral singing of the moon;
For I must have my lovely lady soon,
I am a gentleman in a dustcoat trying.

—I am a lady young in beauty waiting
Until my truelove comes, and then we kiss.
But what grey man among the vines is this
Whose words are dry and faint as in a dream?
Back from my trellis, Sir, before I scream!
I am a lady young in beauty waiting.

BLUE GIRLS

Twirling your blue skirts, travelling the sward
Under the towers of your seminary,
Go listen to your teachers old and contrary
Without believing a word.

Tie the white fillets then about your hair
And think no more of what will come to pass
Than bluebirds that go walking on the grass
And chattering on the air.

Practise your beauty, blue girls, before it fail;
And I will cry with my loud lips and publish
Beauty which all our power shall never establish,
It is so frail.

For I could tell you a story which is true;
I know a lady with a terrible tongue,
Blear eyes fallen from blue,
All her perfections tarnished—yet it is not long
Since she was lovelier than any of you.

JANET WAKING

Beautifully Janet slept
Till it was deeply morning. She woke then
And thought about her dainty-feathered hen,
To see how it had kept.

One kiss she gave her mother.
Only a small one gave she to her daddy
Who would have kissed each curl of his shining baby;
No kiss at all for her brother.

"Old Chucky, old Chucky!" she cried,
Running across the world upon the grass
To Chucky's house, and listening. But alas,
Her Chucky had died.

It was a transmogrifying bee
Came droning down on Chucky's old bald head
And sat and put the poison. It scarcely bled,
But how exceedingly

And purply did the knot
Swell with the venom and communicate
Its rigor! Now the poor comb stood up straight
But Chucky did not.

So there was Janet
Kneeling on the wet grass, crying her brown hen
(Translated far beyond the daughters of men)
To rise and walk upon it.

And weeping fast as she had breath
Janet implored us, "Wake her from her sleep!"
And would not be instructed in how deep
Was the forgetful kingdom of death.

T. S. Eliot

(1888 – 1965)

THE LOVE SONG OF J. ALFRED PRUFROCK

> S'io credessi che mia risposta fosse
> a persona che mai tornasse al mondo,
> questa fiamma staria senza più scosse.
> Ma perciòche giammai di questo fondo
> non tornò vivo alcun, s'i'odo il vero,
> senza tema d'infamia ti rispondo.

Let us go then, you and I,
When the evening is spread out against the sky
Like a patient etherised upon a table;
Let us go, through certain half-deserted streets,
The muttering retreats
Of restless nights in one-night cheap hotels
And sawdust restaurants with oyster-shells:
Streets that follow like a tedious argument
Of insidious intent
To lead you to an overwhelming question . . .
Oh, do not ask, "What is it?"
Let us go and make our visit.

In the room the women come and go
Talking of Michelangelo.

The yellow fog that rubs its back upon the window-panes,
The yellow smoke that rubs its muzzle on the window-panes,
Licked its tongue into the corners of the evening,
Lingered upon the pools that stand in drains,
Let fall upon its back the soot that falls from chimneys,
Slipped by the terrace, made a sudden leap,
And seeing that it was a soft October night,
Curled once about the house, and fell asleep.

And indeed there will be time
For the yellow smoke that slides along the street

Rubbing its back upon the window-panes;
There will be time, there will be time
To prepare a face to meet the faces that you meet;
There will be time to murder and create,
And time for all the works and days of hands
That lift and drop a question on your plate;
Time for you and time for me,
And time yet for a hundred indecisions,
And for a hundred visions and revisions,
Before the taking of a toast and tea.

    In the room the women come and go
Talking of Michelangelo.

    And indeed there will be time
To wonder, "Do I dare?" and, "Do I dare?"
Time to turn back and descend the stair,
With a bald spot in the middle of my hair—
(They will say: "How his hair is growing thin!")
My morning coat, my collar mounting firmly to the chin,
My necktie rich and modest, but asserted by a simple pin—
(They will say: "But how his arms and legs are thin!")
Do I dare
Disturb the universe?
In a minute there is time
For decisions and revisions which a minute will reverse.

    For I have known them all already, known them all—
Have known the evenings, mornings, afternoons,
I have measured out my life with coffee spoons;
I know the voices dying with a dying fall
Beneath the music from a farther room.
    So how should I presume?

    And I have known the eyes already, known them all—
The eyes that fix you in a formulated phrase,
And when I am formulated, sprawling on a pin,
When I am pinned and wriggling on the wall,
Then how should I begin
To spit out all the butt-ends of my days and ways?
    And how should I presume?

And I have known the arms already, known them all—
Arms that are braceleted and white and bare
(But in the lamplight, downed with light brown hair!)
Is it perfume from a dress
That makes me so digress?
Arms that lie along a table, or wrap about a shawl.
    And should I then presume?
    And how should I begin?

       *   *   *

    Shall I say, I have gone at dusk through narrow streets
And watched the smoke that rises from the pipes
Of lonely men in shirt-sleeves, leaning out of windows? . . .

    I should have been a pair of ragged claws
Scuttling across the floors of silent seas.

       *   *   *

    And the afternoon, the evening, sleeps so peacefully!
Smoothed by long fingers,
Asleep . . . tired . . . or it malingers,
Stretched on the floor, here beside you and me.
Should I, after tea and cakes and ices,
Have the strength to force the moment to its crisis?
But though I have wept and fasted, wept and prayed,
Though I have seen my head (grown slightly bald)
    brought in upon a platter,
I am no prophet—and here's no great matter;
I have seen the moment of my greatness flicker,
And I have seen the eternal Footman hold my coat, and snicker,
And in short, I was afraid.

    And would it have been worth it, after all,
After the cups, the marmalade, the tea,
Among the porcelain, among some talk of you and me,
Would it have been worth while,
To have bitten off the matter with a smile,
To have squeezed the universe into a ball
To roll it towards some overwhelming question,
To say: "I am Lazarus, come from the dead,
Come back to tell you all, I shall tell you all"—
If one, settling a pillow by her head,

Should say: "That is not what I meant at all.
That is not it, at all."

And would it have been worth it, after all,
Would it have been worth while,
After the sunsets and the dooryards and the sprinkled streets,
After the novels, after the teacups, after the skirts that trail along the floor—
And this, and so much more?—
It is impossible to say just what I mean!
But as if a magic lantern threw the nerves in patterns on a screen:
Would it have been worth while
If one, settling a pillow or throwing off a shawl,
And turning toward the window, should say:
   "That is not it at all,
   That is not what I meant, at all."

      *   *   *

No! I am not Prince Hamlet, nor was meant to be;
Am an attendant lord, one that will do
To swell a progress, start a scene or two,
Advise the prince; no doubt, an easy tool,
Deferential, glad to be of use,
Politic, cautious, and meticulous;
Full of high sentence, but a bit obtuse;
At times, indeed, almost ridiculous—
Almost, at times, the Fool.

I grow old . . . I grow old . . .
I shall wear the bottoms of my trousers rolled.

Shall I part my hair behind? Do I dare to eat a peach?
I shall wear white flannel trousers, and walk upon the beach.
I have heard the mermaids singing, each to each.

I do not think that they will sing to me.

I have seen them riding seaward on the waves
Combing the white hair of the waves blown back
When the wind blows the water white and black.

We have lingered in the chambers of the sea
By sea-girls wreathed with seaweed red and brown
Till human voices wake us, and we drown.

GERONTION

> Thou hast nor youth nor age
> But as it were an after dinner sleep
> Dreaming of both.

Here I am, an old man in a dry month,
Being read to by a boy, waiting for rain.
I was neither at the hot gates
Nor fought in the warm rain
Nor knee deep in the salt marsh, heaving a cutlass,
Bitten by flies, fought.
My house is a decayed house,
And the Jew squats on the window sill, the owner,
Spawned in some estaminet of Antwerp,
Blistered in Brussels, patched and peeled in London.

The goat coughs at night in the field overhead;
Rocks, moss, stonecrop, iron, merds.
The woman keeps the kitchen, makes tea,
Sneezes at evening, poking the peevish gutter.
                                        I an old man,
A dull head among windy spaces.

Signs are taken for wonders. "We would see a sign!"
The word within a word, unable to speak a word,
Swaddled with darkness. In the juvescence of the year
Came Christ the tiger

In depraved May, dogwood and chestnut, flowering Judas,
To be eaten, to be divided, to be drunk
Among whispers; by Mr. Silvero
With caressing hands, at Limoges
Who walked all night in the next room;
By Hakagawa, bowing among the Titians;
By Madame de Tornquist, in the dark room
Shifting the candles; Fräulein von Kulp
Who turned in the hall, one hand on the door. Vacant shuttles
Weave the wind. I have no ghosts,
An old man in a draughty house
Under a windy knob.

After such knowledge, what forgiveness? Think now
History has many cunning passages, contrived corridors
And issues, deceives with whispering ambitions,
Guides us by vanities. Think now
She gives when our attention is distracted
And what she gives, gives with such supple confusions
That the giving famishes the craving. Gives too late
What's not believed in, or if still believed,
In memory only, reconsidered passion. Gives too soon
Into weak hands, what's thought can be dispensed with
Till the refusal propagates a fear. Think
Neither fear nor courage saves us. Unnatural vices
Are fathered by our heroism. Virtues
Are forced upon us by our impudent crimes.
These tears are shaken from the wrath-bearing tree.

The tiger springs in the new year. Us he devours. Think at last
We have not reached conclusion, when I
Stiffen in a rented house. Think at last
I have not made this show purposelessly
And it is not by any concitation
Of the backward devils.
I would meet you upon this honestly.
I that was near your heart was removed therefrom
To lose beauty in terror, terror in inquisition.
I have lost my passion: why should I need to keep it
Since what is kept must be adulterated?
I have lost my sight, smell, hearing, taste and touch:
How should I use them for your closer contact?

These with a thousand small deliberations
Protract the profit of their chilled delirium,
Excite the membrane, when the sense has cooled,
With pungent sauces, multiply variety
In a wilderness of mirrors. What will the spider do,
Suspend its operations, will the weevil
Delay? De Bailhache, Fresca, Mrs. Cammel, whirled
Beyond the circuit of the shuddering Bear
In fractured atoms. Gull against the wind, in the windy straits
Of Belle Isle, or running on the Horn.
White feathers in the snow, the Gulf claims,
And an old man driven by the Trades
To a sleepy corner.

> Tenants of the house,
Thoughts of a dry brain in a dry season.

THE WASTE LAND

> "Nam Sibyllam quidem Cumis ego ipse oculis meis
> vidi in ampulla pendere, et cum illi pueri dicerent:
> Σίβυλλα τί Θέλεις; respondebat illa: ἀποθανειν Θέλω."

FOR EZRA POUND
Il miglior fabbro

1. THE BURIAL OF THE DEAD

April is the cruellest month, breeding
Lilacs out of the dead land, mixing
Memory and desire, stirring
Dull roots with spring rain.
Winter kept us warm, covering
Earth in forgetful snow, feeding
A little life with dried tubers.
Summer surprised us, coming over the Starnbergersee
With a shower of rain; we stopped in the colonnade,
And went on in sunlight, into the Hofgarten,
And drank coffee, and talked for an hour.
Bin gar keine Russin, stamm' aus Litauen, echt deutsch.
And when we were children, staying at the arch-duke's,
My cousin's, he took me out on a sled,
And I was frightened. He said, Marie,
Marie, hold on tight. And down we went.
In the mountains, there you feel free.
I read, much of the night, and go south in the winter.

What are the roots that clutch, what branches grow
Out of this stony rubbish? Son of man,
You cannot say, or guess, for you know only
A heap of broken images, where the sun beats,
And the dead tree gives no shelter, the cricket no relief,
And the dry stone no sound of water. Only
There is shadow under this red rock,
(Come in under the shadow of this red rock),

And I will show you something different from either
Your shadow at morning striding behind you
Or your shadow at evening rising to meet you;
I will show you fear in a handful of dust.
>   *Frisch weht der Wind*
>   *Der Heimat zu*
>   *Mein Irisch Kind,*
>   *Wo weilest du?*
"You gave me hyacinths first a year ago;
They called me the hyacinth girl."
—Yet when we came back, late, from the hyacinth garden,
Your arms full, and your hair wet, I could not
Speak, and my eyes failed, I was neither
Living nor dead, and I knew nothing,
Looking into the heart of light, the silence.
Oed' und leer das Meer.

  Madame Sosostris, famous clairvoyante,
Had a bad cold, nevertheless
Is known to be the wisest woman in Europe,
With a wicked pack of cards. Here, said she,
Is your card, the drowned Phoenician Sailor,
(Those are pearls that were his eyes. Look!)
Here is Belladonna, the Lady of the Rocks,
The lady of situations.
Here is the man with three staves, and here the Wheel,
And here is the one-eyed merchant, and this card,
Which is blank, is something he carries on his back,
Which I am forbidden to see. I do not find
The Hanged Man. Fear death by water.
I see crowds of people, walking round in a ring.
Thank you. If you see dear Mrs. Equitone,
Tell her I bring the horoscope myself:
One must be so careful these days.

  Unreal City,
Under the brown fog of a winter dawn,
A crowd flowed over London Bridge, so many,
I had not thought death had undone so many.
Sighs, short and infrequent, were exhaled,
And each man fixed his eyes before his feet.
Flowed up the hill and down King William Street,
To where Saint Mary Woolnoth kept the hours

With a dead sound on the final stroke of nine.
There I saw one I knew, and stopped him, crying: "Stetson!
You who were with me in the ships at Mylae!
That corpse you planted last year in your garden,
Has it begun to sprout? Will it bloom this year?
Or has the sudden frost disturbed its bed?
O keep the Dog far hence, that's friend to men,
Or with his nails he'll dig it up again!
You! hypocrite lecteur!—mon semblable,—mon frère!"

2. A GAME OF CHESS

The Chair she sat in, like a burnished throne,
Glowed on the marble, where the glass
Held up by standards wrought with fruited vines
From which a golden Cupidon peeped out
(Another hid his eyes behind his wing)
Doubled the flames of sevenbranched candelabra
Reflecting light upon the table as
The glitter of her jewels rose to meet it,
From satin cases poured in rich profusion.
In vials of ivory and coloured glass
Unstoppered, lurked her strange synthetic perfumes,
Unguent, powdered, or liquid—troubled, confused
And drowned the sense in odours; stirred by the air
That freshened from the window, these ascended
In fattening the prolonged candle-flames,
Flung their smoke into the laquearia,
Stirring the pattern on the coffered ceiling.
Huge sea-wood fed with copper
Burned green and orange, framed by the coloured stone,
In which sad light a carved dolphin swam.
Above the antique mantel was displayed
As though a window gave upon the sylvan scene
The change of Philomel, by the barbarous king
So rudely forced; yet there the nightingale
Filled all the desert with inviolable voice
And still she cried, and still the world pursues,
"Jug Jug" to dirty ears.
And other withered stumps of time
Were told upon the walls; staring forms
Leaned out, leaning, hushing the room enclosed.
Footsteps shuffled on the stair.

Under the firelight, under the brush, her hair
Spread out in fiery points
Glowed into words, then would be savagely still.

"My nerves are bad to-night. Yes, bad. Stay with me.
Speak to me. Why do you never speak. Speak.
     What are you thinking of? What thinking? What?
I never know what you are thinking. Think."

I think we are in rats' alley
Where the dead men lost their bones.
"What is that noise?"
                          The wind under the door.
"What is that noise now? What is the wind doing?"
                          Nothing again nothing.
                                                  "Do
You know nothing? Do you see nothing? Do you remember
Nothing?"

     I remember
Those are pearls that were his eyes.
"Are you alive, or not? Is there nothing in your head?"
                                                  But
O O O O that Shakespeherian Rag—
It's so elegant
So intelligent
"What shall I do now? What shall I do?"
"I shall rush out as I am, and walk the street
With my hair down, so. What shall we do tomorrow?
What shall we ever do?"
                          The hot water at ten.
And if it rains, a closed car at four.
And we shall play a game of chess,
Pressing lidless eyes and waiting for a knock upon the door.

     When Lil's husband got demobbed, I said—
I didn't mince my words, I said to her myself,
HURRY UP PLEASE ITS TIME
Now Albert's coming back, make yourself a bit smart.
He'll want to know what you done with that money he gave you
To get yourself some teeth. He did, I was there.
You have them all out, Lil, and get a nice set,
He said, I swear, I can't bear to look at you.

And no more can't I, I said, and think of poor Albert,
He's been in the army four years, he wants a good time,
And if you don't give it him, there's others will, I said.
Oh is there, she said. Something o' that, I said.
Then I'll know who to thank, she said, and give me a straight look.
HURRY UP PLEASE ITS TIME
If you don't like it you can get on with it, I said.
Others can pick and choose if you can't.
But if Albert makes off, it won't be for lack of telling.
You ought to be ashamed, I said, to look so antique.
(And her only thirty-one.)

I can't help it, she said, pulling a long face,
It's them pills I took, to bring it off, she said.
(She's had five already, and nearly died of young George.)
The chemist said it would be all right, but I've never been the same.
You *are* a proper fool, I said.
Well, if Albert won't leave you alone, there it is, I said,
What you get married for if you don't want children?
HURRY UP PLEASE ITS TIME
Well, that Sunday Albert was home, they had a hot gammon,
And they asked me in to dinner, to get the beauty of it hot—
HURRY UP PLEASE ITS TIME
HURRY UP PLEASE ITS TIME
Goonight Bill. Goonight Lou. Goonight May. Goonight.
Ta ta. Goonight. Goonight.
Good night, ladies, good night, sweet ladies, good night, good night.

3. THE FIRE SERMON

    The river's tent is broken; the last fingers of leaf
Clutch and sink into the wet bank. The wind
Crosses the brown land, unheard. The nymphs are departed.
Sweet Thames, run softly, till I end my song.
The river bears no empty bottles, sandwich papers,
Silk handkerchiefs, cardboard boxes, cigarette ends
Or other testimony of summer nights. The nymphs are departed.
And their friends, the loitering heirs of City directors;
Departed, have left no addresses.
By the waters of Leman I sat down and wept . . .
Sweet Thames, run softly till I end my song,
Sweet Thames, run softly, for I speak not loud or long.

But at my back in a cold blast I hear
The rattle of the bones, and chuckle spread from ear to ear.

A rat crept softly through the vegetation
Dragging its slimy belly on the bank
While I was fishing in the dull canal
On a winter evening round behind the gashouse
Musing upon the king my brother's wreck
And on the king my father's death before him.
White bodies naked on the low damp ground
And bones cast in a little low dry garret,
Rattled by the rat's foot only, year to year.
But at my back from time to time I hear
The sound of horns and motors, which shall bring
Sweeney to Mrs. Porter in the spring.
O the moon shone bright on Mrs. Porter
And on her daughter
They wash their feet in soda water
Et O ces voix d'enfants, chantant dans la coupole!

Twit twit twit
Jug jug jug jug jug jug
So rudely forc'd.
Tereu

   Unreal City
Under the brown fog of a winter noon
Mr. Eugenides, the Smyrna merchant
Unshaven, with a pocket full of currants
C.i.f. London: documents at sight,
Asked me in demotic French
To luncheon at the Cannon Street Hotel
Followed by a weekend at the Metropole.

   At the violet hour, when the eyes and back
Turn upward from the desk, when the human engine waits
Like a taxi throbbing waiting,
I Tiresias, though blind, throbbing between two lives,
Old man with wrinkled female breasts, can see
At the violet hour, the evening hour that strives
Homeward, and brings the sailor home from sea,
The typist home at teatime, clears her breakfast, lights

Her stove, and lays out food in tins.
Out of the window perilously spread
Her drying combinations touched by the sun's last rays,
On the divan are piled (at night her bed)
Stockings, slippers, camisoles, and stays.
I Tiresias, old man with wrinkled dugs
Perceived the scene, and foretold the rest—
I too awaited the expected guest.
He, the young man carbuncular, arrives,
A small house agent's clerk, with one bold stare,
One of the low on whom assurance sits
As a silk hat on a Bradford millionaire.

The time is now propitious, as he guesses,
The meal is ended, she is bored and tired,
Endeavours to engage her in caresses
Which still are unreproved, if undesired.
Flushed and decided, he assaults at once;
Exploring hands encounter no defence;
His vanity requires no response,
And makes a welcome of indifference.
(And I Tiresias have foresuffered all
Enacted on this same divan or bed;
I who have sat by Thebes below the wall
And walked among the lowest of the dead.)
Bestows one final patronising kiss,
And gropes his way, finding the stairs unlit . . .

    She turns and looks a moment in the glass,
Hardly aware of her departed lover;
Her brain allows one half-formed thought to pass:
"Well now that's done: and I'm glad it's over."
When lovely woman stoops to folly and
Paces about her room again, alone,
She smoothes her hair with automatic hand,
And puts a record on the gramophone.

"This music crept by me upon the waters"
And along the Strand, up Queen Victoria Street.
O City city, I can sometimes hear
Besides a public bar in Lower Thames Street,
The pleasant whining of a mandoline

And a clatter and a chatter from within
Where fishmen lounge at noon: where the walls
Of Magnus Martyr hold
Inexplicable splendour of Ionian white and gold.

    The river sweats
    Oil and tar
    The barges drift
    With the turning tide
    Red sails
    Wide
    To leeward, swing on the heavy spar.
    The barges wash
    Drifting logs
    Down Greenwich reach
    Past the Isle of Dogs.
            Weialala leia
            Wallala leialala

    Elizabeth and Leicester
    Beating oars
    The stern was formed
    A gilded shell
    Red and gold
    The brisk swell
    Rippled both shores
    Southwest wind
    Carried down stream
    The peal of bells
    White towers
            Weialala leia
            Wallala leialala

"Trams and dusty trees.
Highbury bore me. Richmond and Kew
Undid me. By Richmond I raised my knees
Supine on the floor of a narrow canoe."

"My feet are at Moorgate, and my heart
Under my feet. After the event
He wept. He promised 'a new start.'
I made no comment. What should I resent?"

"On Margate Sands.
I can connect
Nothing with nothing.
The broken fingernails of dirty hands.
My people humble people who expect
Nothing."
           la la

To Carthage then I came

Burning burning burning burning
O Lord Thou pluckest me out
O Lord Thou pluckest

burning

    4. DEATH BY WATER

Phlebas the Phoenician, a fortnight dead,
Forgot the cry of gulls, and the deep sea swell
And the profit and loss.
                      A current under sea
Picked his bones in whispers. As he rose and fell
He passed the stages of his age and youth
Entering the whirlpool.
                      Gentile or Jew
O you who turn the wheel and look to windward,
Consider Phlebas, who was once handsome and tall as you.

    5. WHAT THE THUNDER SAID

  After the torchlight red on sweaty faces
After the frosty silence in the gardens
After the agony in stony places
The shouting and the crying
Prison and palace and reverberation
Of thunder of spring over distant mountains
He who was living is now dead
We who were living are now dying
With a little patience

  Here is no water but only rock
Rock and no water and the sandy road

The road winding above among the mountains
Which are mountains of rock without water
If there were water we should stop and drink
Amongst the rock one cannot stop or think
Sweat is dry and feet are in the sand
If there were only water amongst the rock
Dead mountain mouth of carious teeth that cannot spit
Here one can neither stand nor lie nor sit
There is not even silence in the mountains
But dry sterile thunder without rain
There is not even solitude in the mountains
But red sullen faces sneer and snarl
From doors of mudcracked houses
                    If there were water
    And no rock
    If there were rock
    And also water
    And water
    A spring
    A pool among the rock
    If there were the sound of water only
    Not the cicada
    And dry grass singing
    But sound of water over a rock
    Where the hermit-thrush sings in the pine trees
    Drip drop drip drop drop drop drop
    But there is no water

    Who is the third who walks always beside you?
When I count, there are only you and I together
But when I look ahead up the white road
There is always another one walking beside you
Gliding wrapt in a brown mantle, hooded
I do not know whether a man or a woman
—But who is that on the other side of you?

    What is that sound high in the air
Murmur of maternal lamentation
Who are those hooded hordes swarming
Over endless plains, stumbling in cracked earth
Ringed by the flat horizon only
What is the city over the mountains
Cracks and reforms and bursts in the violet air

Falling towers
Jerusalem Athens Alexandria
Vienna London
Unreal

A woman drew her long black hair out tight
And fiddled whisper music on those strings
And bats with baby faces in the violet light
Whistled, and beat their wings
And crawled head downward down a blackened wall
And upside down in air were towers
Tolling reminiscent bells, that kept the hours
And voices singing out of empty cisterns and exhausted wells.

  In this decayed hole among the mountains
In the faint moonlight, the grass is singing
Over the tumbled graves, about the chapel
There is the empty chapel, only the wind's home.
It has no windows, and the door swings,
Dry bones can harm no one.
Only a cock stood on the rooftree
Co co rico co co rico
In a flash of lightning. Then a damp gust
Bringing rain

  Ganga was sunken, and the limp leaves
Waited for rain, while the black clouds
Gathered far distant, over Himavant.
The jungle crouched, humped in silence.
Then spoke the thunder
DA
Datta: what have we given?
My friend, blood shaking my heart
The awful daring of a moment's surrender
Which an age of prudence can never retract
By this, and this only, we have existed
Which is not to be found in our obituaries
Or in memories draped by the beneficent spider
Or under seals broken by the lean solicitor
In our empty room
DA
Dayadhvam: I have heard the key
Turn in the door once and turn once only

We think of the key, each in his prison
Thinking of the key, each confirms a prison
Only at nightfall, aethereal rumours
Revive for a moment a broken Coriolanus
DA
Damyata: The boat responded
Gaily, to the hand expert with sail and oar
The sea was calm, your heart would have responded
Gaily, when invited, beating obedient
To controlling hands

                      I sat upon the shore
Fishing, with the arid plain behind me
Shall I at least set my lands in order?
London Bridge is falling down falling down falling down
Poi s'ascose nel foco che gli affina
Quando fiam uti chelidon—O swallow swallow
Le Prince d' Aquintaine à la tour abolie
These fragments I have shored against my ruins
Why then Ile fit you. Hieronymo's mad againe.
Datta. Dayadhvam. Damyata.
                  Shantih shantih shantih

Conrad Aiken

(1889 – 1973)

DEAR UNCLE STRANGER

All my shortcomings, in this year of grace,
preach, and at midnight, from my mirrored face,
the arrogant, strict dishonesty, that lies
behind the animal forehead and the eyes;

the bloodstream coiling with its own intent,
never from passion or from pleasure bent;
the mouth and nostrils eager for their food,
indifferent to god, or to man's good.

Oh, how the horror rises from that look,
which is an open, and a dreadful, book!
much evil, and so little kindness, done,
selfish the loves, yes all, the selfless none;

illness and pain, ignored; the poor, forgotten;
the letters to the dying man, not written—
the many past, or passing, great or small,
from whom I took, nor ever gave at all!

Dear Uncle stranger, Cousin known too late,
sweet wife unkissed, come, we will celebrate
in this thronged mirror the uncelebrated dead,
good men and women gone too soon to bed.

HATTERAS CALLING

Southeast, and storm, and every weathervane
shivers and moans upon its dripping pin,
ragged on chimneys the cloud whips, the rain
howls at the flues and windows to get in,

the golden rooster claps his golden wings
and from the Baptist Chapel shrieks no more,
the golden arrow into the southeast sings
and hears on the roof the Atlantic Ocean roar.

Waves among wires, sea scudding over poles,
down every alley the magnificence of rain,
dead gutters live once more, the deep manholes
hollo in triumph a passage to the main.

Umbrellas, and in the Gardens one old man
hurries away along a dancing path,
listens to music on a watering-can,
observes among the tulips the sudden wrath,

pale willows thrashing to the needled lake,
and dinghies filled with water; while the sky
smashes the lilacs, swoops to shake and break,
till shattered branches shriek and railings cry.

Speak, Hatteras, your language of the sea:
scour with kelp and spindrift the stale street:
that man in terror may learn once more to be
child of that hour when rock and ocean meet.

SOLITAIRE

And in the river the nameless body sifts
through stiffening fingers and the seaweed hair
this ultimate of agony, that drifts
the will beyond the point where sense can bear:

out of its world of tracks and telegrams,
the impedimenta of a choice and aim,
the marked time-tables and the diagrams,
inherited with birth and growth and name:

at the precise point of the hour unnoted,
alone, as all at such an hour must be,

severance made, the last cry horror-throated,
and sought deliverance—again—in a strange sea.

Who would be walking still, but for that choice,
yourself, with ten cents in your pocket left,
stood by the river wall, and found a voice,
of all but will to loss of will bereft;

and in the river the nameless body only,
with the short movements of the water moving,
the eyes open, and the white face lonely,
plaintiff no more, and done with the farce of loving.

Claude McKay

(1890 – 1948)

THE LYNCHING

His spirit in smoke ascended to high heaven.
His father, by the cruelest way of pain,
Had bidden him to his bosom once again;
The awful sin remained still unforgiven.
All night a bright and solitary star
(Perchance the one that ever guided him,
Yet gave him up at last to Fate's wild whim)
Hung pitifully o'er the swinging char.
Day dawned, and soon the mixed crowds came to view
The ghastly body swaying in the sun:
The women thronged to look, but never a one
Showed sorrow in her eyes of steely blue;
And little lads, lynchers that were to be,
Danced round the dreadful thing in fiendish glee.

IF WE MUST DIE

If we must die—let it not be like hogs
Hunted and penned in an inglorious spot,
While round us bark the mad and hungry dogs,
Making their mock at our accursed lot.
If we must die—Oh, let us nobly die,
So that our precious blood may not be shed
In vain; then even the monsters we defy
Shall be constrained to honor us though dead!
Oh, Kinsmen! We must meet the common foe;
Though far outnumbered, let us show us brave,
And for their thousand blows deal one death-blow!
What though before us lies the open grave?
Like men we'll face the murderous, cowardly pack,
Pressed to the wall, dying, but fighting back!

HARLEM SHADOWS

I hear the halting footsteps of a lass
   In Negro Harlem when the night lets fall
Its veil. I see the shapes of girls who pass
   To bend and barter at desire's call.
Ah, little dark girls, who in slippered feet
   Go prowling through the night from street to street!

Through the long night until the silver break
   Of day the little gray feet know no rest;
Through the lone night until the last snow-flake
   Has dropped from heaven upon the earth's white breast,
The dusky, half-clad girls of tired feet
   Are trudging, thinly shod, from street to street.

Ah, stern harsh world, that in the wretched way
   Of poverty, dishonor and disgrace,
Has pushed the timid little feet of clay,
   The sacred brown feet of my fallen race!
Ah, heart of me, the weary, weary feet
   In Harlem wandering from street to street.

Archibald MacLeish

(1 8 9 2 – 1 9 8 3)

ARS POETICA

A poem should be palpable and mute
As a globed fruit,

Dumb
As old medallions to the thumb,

Silent as the sleeve-worn stone
Of casement ledges where the moss has grown—

A poem should be wordless
As the flight of birds.

    •

A poem should be motionless in time
As the moon climbs,

Leaving, as the moon releases
Twig by twig the night-entangled trees,

Leaving, as the moon behind the winter leaves,
Memory by memory the mind—

A poem should be motionless in time
As the moon climbs.

    •

A poem should be equal to:
Not true.

For all the history of grief
An empty doorway and a maple leaf.

For love
The leaning grasses and two lights above the sea—

A poem should not mean
But be.

YOU, ANDREW MARVELL

And here face down beneath the sun
And here upon earth's noonward height
To feel the always coming on
The always rising of the night:

To feel creep up the curving east
The earthy chill of dusk and slow
Upon those under lands the vast
And ever climbing shadow grow

And strange at Ecbatan the trees
Take leaf by leaf the evening strange
The flooding dark about their knees
The mountains over Persia change

And now at Kermanshah the gate
Dark empty and the withered grass
And through the twilight now the late
Few travelers in the westward pass

And Baghdad darken and the bridge
Across the silent river gone
And through Arabia the edge
Of evening widen and steal on

And deepen on Palmyra's street
The wheel rut in the ruined stone
And Lebanon fade out and Crete
High through the clouds and overblown

And over Sicily the air
Still flashing with the landward gulls
And loom and slowly disappear
The sails above the shadowy hulls

And Spain go under and the shore
Of Africa the gilded sand
And evening vanish and no more
The low pale light across that land

Nor now the long light on the sea:

And here face downward in the sun
To feel how swift how secretly
The shadow of the night comes on . . .

Edna St. Vincent Millay

(1892 – 1950)

RENASCENCE

All I could see from where I stood
Was three long mountains and a wood;
I turned and looked another way,
And saw three islands in a bay.
So with my eyes I traced the line
Of the horizon, thin and fine,
Straight around till I was come
Back to where I'd started from;
And all I saw from where I stood
Was three long mountains and a wood.

Over these things I could not see:
These were the things that bounded me.
And I could touch them with my hand,
Almost, I thought, from where I stand!
And all at once things seemed so small
My breath came short, and scarce at all.
But, sure, the sky is big, I said:
Miles and miles above my head.
So here upon my back I'll lie
And look my fill into the sky.
And so I looked, and after all,
The sky was not so very tall.
The sky, I said, must somewhere stop . . .
And—sure enough!—I see the top!
The sky, I thought, is not so grand;
I 'most could touch it with my hand!
And reaching up my hand to try,
I screamed, to feel it touch the sky.

I screamed, and—lo!—Infinity
Came down and settled over me;
Forced back my scream into my chest;
Bent back my arm upon my breast;

And, pressing of the Undefined
The definition on my mind,
Held up before my eyes a glass
Through which my shrinking sight did pass
Until it seemed I must behold
Immensity made manifold;
Whispered to me a word whose sound
Deafened the air for worlds around,
And brought unmuffled to my ears
The gossiping of friendly spheres,
The creaking of the tented sky,
The ticking of Eternity.

I saw and heard, and knew at last
The How and Why of all things, past,
And present, and forevermore.
The Universe, cleft to the core,
Lay open to my probing sense,
That, sickening, I would fain pluck thence
But could not,—nay! but needs must suck
At the great wound, and could not pluck
My lips away till I had drawn
All venom out.—Ah, fearful pawn:
For my omniscience paid I toll
In infinite remorse of soul.
All sin was of my sinning, all
Atoning mine, and mine the gall
Of all regret. Mine was the weight
Of every brooded wrong, the hate
That stood behind each envious thrust,
Mine every greed, mine every lust.

And all the while, for every grief,
Each suffering, I craved relief
With individual desire;
Craved all in vain! And felt fierce fire
About a thousand people crawl;
Perished with each,—then mourned for all!

A man was starving in Capri;
He moved his eyes and looked at me;
I felt his gaze, I heard his moan,
And knew his hunger as my own.

I saw at sea a great fog bank
Between two ships that struck and sank;
A thousand screams the heavens smote;
And every scream tore through my throat.

No hurt I did not feel, no death
That was not mine; mine each last breath
That, crying, met an answering cry
From the compassion that was I.
All suffering mine, and mine its rod;
Mine, pity like the pity of God.
Ah, awful weight! Infinity
Pressed down upon the finite Me!
My anguished spirit, like a bird,
Beating against my lips I heard;
Yet lay the weight so close about
There was no room for it without.
And so beneath the weight lay I
And suffered death, but could not die.

Long had I lain thus, craving death,
When quietly the earth beneath
Gave way, and inch by inch, so great
At last had grown the crushing weight,
Into the earth I sank till I
Full six feet under ground did lie,
And sank no more,—there is no weight
Can follow here, however great.
From off my breast I felt it roll,
And as it went my tortured soul
Burst forth and fled in such a gust
That all about me swirled the dust.

Deep in the earth I rested now.
Cool is its hand upon the brow
And soft its breast beneath the head
Of one who is so gladly dead.
And all at once, and over all
The pitying rain began to fall;
I lay and heard each pattering hoof
Upon my lowly, thatchèd roof,
And seemed to love the sound far more
Than ever I had done before.

For rain it hath a friendly sound
To one who's six feet under ground;
And scarce the friendly voice or face,
A grave is such a quiet place.

The rain, I said, is kind to come
And speak to me in my new home.
I would I were alive again
To kiss the fingers of the rain,
To drink into my eyes the shine
Of every slanting silver line,
To catch the freshened, fragrant breeze
From drenched and dripping apple-trees.
For soon the shower will be done,
And then the broad face of the sun
Will laugh above the rain-soaked earth
Until the world with answering mirth
Shakes joyously, and each round drop
Rolls, twinkling, from its grass-blade top.
How can I bear it, buried here,
While overhead the sky grows clear
And blue again after the storm?
O, multi-coloured, multi-form,
Belovèd beauty over me,
That I shall never, never see
Again! Spring-silver, autumn-gold,
That I shall never more behold!—
Sleeping your myriad magic through,
Close-sepulchred away from you!
O God, I cried, give me new birth,
And put me back upon the earth!
Upset each cloud's gigantic gourd
And let the heavy rain, down-poured
In one big torrent, set me free,
Washing my grave away from me!

I ceased; and through the breathless hush
That answered me, the far-off rush
Of herald wings came whispering
Like music down the vibrant string
Of my ascending prayer, and—crash!
Before the wild wind's whistling lash
The startled storm-clouds reared on high

And plunged in terror down the sky!
And the big rain in one black wave
Fell from the sky and struck my grave.

I know not how such things can be;
I only know there came to me
A fragrance such as never clings
To aught save happy living things;
A sound as of some joyous elf
Singing sweet songs to please himself,
And, through and over everything,
A sense of glad awakening.
The grass, a-tiptoe at my ear,
Whispering to me I could hear;
I felt the rain's cool finger-tips
Brushed tenderly across my lips,
Laid gently on my sealèd sight,
And all at once the heavy night
Fell from my eyes and I could see!—
A drenched and dripping apple-tree,
A last long line of silver rain,
A sky grown clear and blue again.
And as I looked a quickening gust
Of wind blew up to me and thrust
Into my face a miracle
Of orchard-breath, and with the smell,—
I know not how such things can be!—
I breathed my soul back into me.

Ah! Up then from the ground sprang I
And hailed the earth with such a cry
As is not heard save from a man
Who has been dead, and lives again.
About the trees my arms I wound;
Like one gone mad I hugged the ground;
I raised my quivering arms on high;
I laughed and laughed into the sky;
Till at my throat a strangling sob
Caught fiercely, and a great heart-throb
Sent instant tears into my eyes:
O God, I cried, no dark disguise
Can e'er hereafter hide from me

Thy radiant identity!
Thou canst not move across the grass
But my quick eyes will see Thee pass,
Nor speak, however silently,
But my hushed voice will answer Thee.
I know the path that tells Thy way
Through the cool eve of every day;
God, I can push the grass apart
And lay my finger on Thy heart!

The world stands out on either side
No wider than the heart is wide;
Above the world is stretched the sky,—
No higher than the soul is high.
The heart can push the sea and land
Farther away on either hand;
The soul can split the sky in two,
And let the face of God shine through.
But East and West will pinch the heart
That can not keep them pushed apart;
And he whose soul is flat—the sky
Will cave in on him by and by.

From SONNETS FROM AN UNGRAFTED TREE

1

So she came back into his house again
And watched beside his bed until he died,
Loving him not at all. The winter rain
Splashed in the painted butter-tub outside,
Where once her red geraniums had stood,
Where still their rotted stalks were to be seen;
The thin log snapped; and she went out for wood,
Bareheaded, running the few steps between
The house and shed; there, from the sodden eaves
Blown back and forth on ragged ends of twine,
Saw the dejected creeping-jinny vine,
(And one, big-aproned, blithe, with stiff blue sleeves

Rolled to the shoulder that warm day in spring,
Who planted seeds, musing ahead to their far blossoming).

THE BUCK IN THE SNOW

White sky, over the hemlocks bowed with snow,
Saw you not at the beginning of evening the antlered buck and his doe
Standing in the apple-orchard? I saw them. I saw them suddenly go,
Tails up, with long leaps lovely and slow,
Over the stone-wall into the wood of hemlocks bowed with snow.

Now lies he here, his wild blood scalding the snow.

How strange a thing is death, bringing to his knees, bringing to his antlers
The buck in the snow.
How strange a thing,—a mile away by now, it may be,
Under the heavy hemlocks that as the moments pass
Shift their loads a little, letting fall a feather of snow—
Life, looking out attentive from the eyes of the doe.

From FATAL INTERVIEW

36

Hearing your words, and not a word among them
Tuned to my liking, on a salty day
When inland woods were pushed by winds that flung them
Hissing to leeward like a ton of spray,
I thought how off Matinicus the tide
Came pounding in, came running through the Gut,
While from the Rock the warning whistle cried,
And children whimpered, and the doors blew shut;
There in the autumn when the men go forth,
With slapping skirts the island women stand
In gardens stripped and scattered, peering north,

With dahlia tubers dripping from the hand:
The wind of their endurance, driving south,
Flattened your words against your speaking mouth.

RAGGED ISLAND

There, there where those black spruces crowd
To the edge of the precipitous cliff,
Above your boat, under the eastern wall of the island;
And no wave breaks; as if
All had been done, and long ago, that needed
Doing; and the cold tide, unimpeded
By shoal or shelving ledge, moves up and down,
Instead of in and out;
And there is no driftwood there, because there is no beach;
Clean cliff going down as deep as clear water can reach;

No driftwood, such as abounds on the roaring shingle,
To be hefted home, for fires in the kitchen stove;
Barrels, banged ashore about the boiling outer harbour;
Lobster-buoys, on the eel-grass of the sheltered cove:

There, thought unbraids itself, and the mind becomes single.
There you row with tranquil oars, and the ocean
Shows no scar from the cutting of your placid keel;
Care becomes senseless there; pride and promotion
Remote; you only look; you scarcely feel.

Even adventure, with its vital uses,
Is aimless ardour now; and thrift is waste.

Oh, to be there, under the silent spruces,
Where the wide, quiet evening darkens without haste
Over a sea with death acquainted, yet forever chaste.

Charles Reznikoff

(1894 – 1976)

From TESTIMONY

I

The company had advertised for men to unload a steamer across the river. It
    was six o'clock in the morning, snowing and still dark.
There was a crowd looking for work on the dock;
and all the while men hurried to the dock.
The man at the wheel
kept the bow of the launch
against the dock—
the engine running slowly;
and the men kept jumping
from dock to deck,
jostling each other,
and crowding into the cabin.

Eighty or ninety men were in the cabin as the launch pulled away.
There were no lights in the cabin, and no room to turn—whoever was sitting
    down could not get up, and whoever had his hand up could not get it
    down,
as the launch ran in the darkness
through the ice,
ice cracking
against the launch,
bumping and scraping
against the launch
banging up against it,
until it struck
a solid cake of ice,
rolled to one side, and slowly
came back to an even keel.

The men began to feel water running against their feet as if from a
    hose.   "Cap," shouted one, "the boat is taking water! Put your rubbers on,
    boys!"

The man at the wheel turned.
"Shut up!" he said.
The men began to shout,
ankle-deep in water.
The man at the wheel turned
with his flashlight:
everybody was turning and pushing against each other;
those near the windows
were trying to break them,
in spite of the wire mesh
in the glass: those who had been near the door
were now in the river,
reaching for the cakes of ice,
their hands slipping off and
reaching for the cakes of ice.

II

Amelia was just fourteen and out of the orphan asylum; at her first job—in the
    bindery, and yes sir, yes ma'am, oh, so anxious to please.
She stood at the table, her blonde hair hanging about her shoulders, "knocking
    up" for Mary and Sadie, the stitchers
("knocking up" is counting books and stacking them in piles to be taken away).
There were twenty wire-stitching machines on the floor, worked by a shaft that
    ran under the table;
as each stitcher put her work through the machine,
she threw it on the table. The books were piling up fast
and some slid to the floor
(the forelady had said, Keep the work off the floor!);
and Amelia stooped to pick up the books—
three or four had fallen under the table
between the boards nailed against the legs.
She felt her hair caught gently;
put her hand up and felt the shaft going round and round
and her hair caught on it, wound and winding around it,
until the scalp was jerked from her head,
and the blood was coming down all over her face and waist.

Jean Toomer

(1 8 9 4 – 1 9 6 7)

REAPERS

Black reapers with the sound of steel on stones
Are sharpening scythes. I see them place the hones
In their hip-pockets as a thing that's done,
And start their silent swinging, one by one.
Black horses drive a mower through the weeds,
And there, a field rat, startled, squealing bleeds,
His belly close to ground. I see the blade,
Blood-stained, continue cutting weeds and shade.

NOVEMBER COTTON FLOWER

Boll-weevil's coming, and the winter's cold,
Made cotton-stalks look rusty, seasons old,
And cotton, scarce as any southern snow,
Was vanishing; the branch, so pinched and slow,
Failed in its function as the autumn rake;
Drouth fighting soil had caused the soil to take
All water from the streams; dead birds were found
In wells a hundred feet below the ground—
Such was the season when the flower bloomed.
Old folks were startled, and it soon assumed
Significance. Superstition saw
Something it had never seen before:
Brown eyes that loved without a trace of fear,
Beauty so sudden for that time of year.

e. e. cummings

(1 8 9 4 – 1 9 6 2)

you shall above all things be glad and young

you shall above all things be glad and young.
For if you're young, whatever life you wear

it will become you;and if you are glad
whatever's living will yourself become.
Girlboys may nothing more than boygirls need:
i can entirely her only love

whose any mystery makes every man's
flesh put space on;and his mind take off time

that you should ever think,may god forbid
and(in his mercy)your true lover spare:
for that way knowledge lies,the foetal grave
called progress,and negation's dead undoom.

I'd rather learn from one bird how to sing
than teach ten thousand stars how not to dance

anyone lived in a pretty how town

anyone lived in a pretty how town
(with up so floating many bells down)
spring summer autumn winter
he sang his didn't he danced his did.

Women and men(both little and small)
cared for anyone not at all
they sowed their isn't they reaped their same
sun moon stars rain

children guessed(but only a few
and down they forgot as up they grew
autumn winter spring summer)
that noone loved him more by more

when by now and tree by leaf
she laughed his joy she cried his grief
bird by snow and stir by still
anyone's any was all to her

someones married their everyones
laughed their cryings and did their dance
(sleep wake hope and then)they
said their nevers they slept their dream

stars rain sun moon
(and only the snow can begin to explain
how children are apt to forget to remember
with up so floating many bells down)

one day anyone died i guess
(and noone stooped to kiss his face)
busy folk buried them side by side
little by little and was by was

all by all and deep by deep
and more by more they dream their sleep
noone and anyone earth by april
wish by spirit and if by yes.

Women and men(both dong and ding)
summer autumn winter spring
reaped their sowing and went their came
sun moon stars rain

i sing of Olaf glad and big

i sing of Olaf glad and big
whose warmest heart recoiled at war:
a conscientious object-or

his wellbelovèd colonel(trig
westpointer most succinctly bred)
took erring Olaf soon in hand;
but—though an host of overjoyed
noncoms(first knocking on the head
him)do through icy waters roll
that helplessness which others stroke
with brushes recently employed
anent this muddy toiletbowl,
while kindred intellects evoke
allegiance per blunt instruments—
Olaf(being to all intents
a corpse and wanting any rag
upon what God unto him gave)
responds, without getting annoyed
"I will not kiss your f.ing flag"

straightway the silver bird looked grave
(departing hurriedly to shave)

but—though all kinds of officers
(a yearning nation's blueeyed pride)
their passive prey did kick and curse
until for wear their clarion
voices and boots were much the worse,
and egged the firstclassprivates on
his rectum wickedly to tease
by means of skilfully applied
bayonets roasted hot with heat—
Olaf(upon what were once knees)
does almost ceaselessly repeat
"there is some s. I will not eat"

our president,being of which
assertions duly notified
threw the yellowsonofabitch
into a dungeon,where he died

Christ(of His mercy infinite)
i pray to see;and Olaf,too

preponderatingly because
unless statistics lie he was
more brave than me:more blond than you.

my father moved through dooms of love

my father moved through dooms of love
through sames of am through haves of give,
singing each morning out of each night
my father moved through depths of height

this motionless forgetful where
turned at his glance to shining here;
that if(so timid air is firm)
under his eyes would stir and squirm

newly as from unburied which
floats the first who, his april touch
drove sleeping selves to swarm their fates
woke dreamers to their ghostly roots

and should some why completely weep
my father's fingers brought her sleep:
vainly no smallest voice might cry
for he could feel the mountains grow.

Lifting the valleys of the sea
my father moved through griefs of joy;
praising a forehead called the moon
singing desire into begin

joy was his song and joy so pure
a heart of star by him could steer
and pure so now and now so yes
the wrists of twilight would rejoice

keen as midsummer's keen beyond
conceiving mind of sun will stand,
so strictly(over utmost him
so hugely)stood my father's dream

his flesh was flesh his blood was blood:
no hungry man but wished him food;
no cripple wouldn't creep one mile
uphill to only see him smile.

Scorning the pomp of must and shall
my father moved through dooms of feel;
his anger was as right as rain
, his pity was as green as grain

septembering arms of year extend
less humbly wealth to foe and friend
than he to foolish and to wise
offered immeasurable is

proudly and(by octobering flame
beckoned)as earth will downward climb,
so naked for immortal work
his shoulders marched against the dark

his sorrow was as true as bread:
no liar looked him in the head;
if every friend became his foe
he'd laugh and build a world with snow.

My father moved through theys of we,
singing each new leaf out of each tree
(and every child was sure that spring
danced when she heard my father sing)

then let men kill which cannot share,
let blood and flesh be mud and mire,
scheming imagine,passion willed,
freedom a drug that's bought and sold

giving to steal and cruel kind,
a heart to fear,to doubt a mind,
to differ a disease of same,
conform the pinnacle of am

though dull were all we taste as bright,
bitter all utterly things sweet,
maggoty minus and dumb death
all we inherit,all bequeath

and nothing quite so least as truth
—i say though hate were why men breathe—
because my father lived his soul
love is the whole and more than all

Louise Bogan

(1897–1970)

WINTER SWAN

It is a hollow garden, under the cloud;
Beneath the heel a hollow earth is turned;
Within the mind the live blood shouts aloud;
Under the breast the willing blood is burned,
Shut with the fire passed and the fire returned.
But speak, you proud!
Where lies the leaf-caught world once thought abiding,
Now but a dry disarray and artifice?
Here, to the ripple cut by the cold, drifts this
Bird, the long throat bent back, and the eyes in hiding.

MEN LOVED WHOLLY BEYOND WISDOM

Men loved wholly beyond wisdom
Have the staff without the banner,
Like a fire in a dry thicket,
Rising within women's eyes
Is the love men must return.
Heart, so subtle now, and trembling,
What a marvel to be wise,
To love never in this manner!
To be quiet in the fern
Like a thing gone dead and still,
Listening to the prisoned cricket
Shake its terrible, dissembling
Music in the granite hill.

M., SINGING

Now, innocent, within the deep
Night of all things you turn the key
Unloosing what we know in sleep.
In your fresh voice they cry aloud
Those beings without heart or name.

Those creatures both corrupt and proud,
Upon the melancholy words
And in the music's subtlety,
Leave the long harvest which they reap
In the sunk land of dust and flame
And move to space beneath our sky.

Melvin Beaunearus Tolson

(1898–1966)

AFRICAN CHINA

I

A connoisseur of pearl
necklace phrases,
Wu Shang disdains
his laundry, lazes
among his bric-a-brac
metaphysical;
and yet dark customers,
on Harlem's rack
quizzical,
sweat and pack
the forked caldera of
his Stygian shop:
some worship God,
and some Be-Bop.

Wu Shang discovers
the diademed word to be,
on the sly,
a masterkey
to Harlem pocketbooks,
outjockeyed by
policy
and brimstone
theology
alone!

II

As bust and hips
her corset burst,
An Amazonian fantasy,
A Witness of Jehovah

by job and husband curst,
lumbers in.
A yellow mummy in a mummery
a tip-toe,
Wu Shang unsheathes a grin,
and then, his fingers sleeved,
gulps an ugh and eats his crow,
disarmed by ugliness disbelieved!

At last he takes his wits
from balls of moth,
salaams. "Dear Lady, I, for you,
wear goats' sackcloth
to mark this hour and place;
cursed be the shadow of delay
that for a trice conceals a trace
of beauty in thy face!"

Her jug of anger emptied, now he sighs:
"Her kind cannot play euchre.
The master trick belongs to him
who holds the joker."
His mind's eye sees a black hand drop
a red white poker.

III

The gingered gigolo,
vexed by the harrow of a date
and vanity torn,
goddamns the yellow sage,
four million yellow born,
and yellow fate!

The gigolo
a wayward bronco
seen but unheard,
Wu Shang applies the curb-bit word:
"Wise lovers know
that in their lottery success
belongs to him who plays a woman
with titbits of a guess."

The sweet man's sportive whack
Paralyzes Wu Shang's back.
"Say, Yellah Boy, I call yo' stuff
the hottest dope in town!
That red hot mama'll never know
she got her daddy down."

          IV

Sometimes the living dead
stalk in and sue for grace,
the tragic uncommon
in the comic commonplace,
the evil that the good
begets in love's embrace,
a Harlem melodrama
like that in Big John's face

as Wu Shang peers at him
and cudgels a theorem.
The sage says in a voice ilang-ilang,
"Do you direct the weathercock?"
And then his lash, a rackarock,
descends with a bang,
"Show me the man who has not thrown
a boomerang!"

. . . words, no longer pearls,
but drops of Gilead's balm.
Later, later, Wu Shang remarks,
"Siroccos mar the toughest palm."
The bigger thing, as always, goes unsaid:
the look behind the door of Big John's eyes,
awareness of the steps of *Is*,
the freedom of the wise.

          V

When Dixie Dixon breaks a leg
on arctic Lenox Avenue
and Wu Shang homes her, pays her fees,
old kismet knots the two
unraveled destinies.

The unperfumed
wag foot, forefinger, head;
and belly laughter waifs ghost rats
foxed by the smell of meat and bread;
and black walls blab, "Good Gawd,
China and Africa gits wed!"

VI

Wu Shang, whom nothing sears,
says Dixie is a dusky passion flower
unsoiled by envious years.
And Dixie says
her Wu Shang is a Mandarin
with seven times seven ways of love,
her very own oasis in
the desert
of Harlem men.

In dignity, Wu Shang and Dixie walk
the gauntlet, Lenox Avenue;
their son has Wu Shang's cast
and Dixie's hue.

The dusky children roll
their oyster eyes
at Wu Shang, Junior, flash
a premature surmise,
as if afraid:
in accents Carolina
on the streets they never made,
the dusky children tease,
"African China!"

DARK SYMPHONY

I ALLEGRO MODERATO

Black Crispus Attucks taught
  Us how to die

Before white Patrick Henry's bugle breath
Uttered the vertical
    Transmitting cry:
"Yea, give me liberty or give me death."

Waifs of the auction block,
    Men black and strong
The juggernauts of despotism withstood,
Loin-girt with faith that worms
    Equate the wrong
And dust is purged to create brotherhood.

No Banquo's ghost can rise
    Against us now,
Aver we hobnailed Man beneath the brute,
Squeezed down the thorns of greed
    On Labor's brow,
Garroted lands and carted off the loot.

II LENTO GRAVE

The centuries-old pathos in our voices
Saddens the great white world,
And the wizardry of our dusky rhythms
Conjures up shadow-shapes of ante-bellum years:

Black slaves singing *One More River to Cross*
In the torture tombs of slave-ships,
Black slaves singing *Steal Away to Jesus*
In jungle swamps,
Black slaves singing *The Crucifixion*
In slave-pens at midnight,
Black slaves singing *Swing Low, Sweet Chariot*
In cabins of death,
Black slaves singing *Go Down, Moses*
In the canebrakes of the Southern Pharaohs.

III ANDANTE SOSTENUTO

They tell us to forget
The Golgotha we tread . . .
We who are scourged with hate,
A price upon our head.

They who have shackled us
Require of us a song,
They who have wasted us
Bid us condone the wrong.

They tell us to forget
Democracy is spurned.
They tell us to forget
The Bill of Rights is burned.
Three hundred years we slaved,
We slave and suffer yet:
Though flesh and bone rebel,
They tell us to forget!

Oh, how can we forget
Our human rights denied?
Oh, how can we forget
Our manhood crucified?
When Justice is profaned
And plea with curse is met,
When Freedom's gates are barred,
Oh, how can we forget?

IV TEMPO PRIMO

The New Negro strides upon the continent
In seven-league boots . . .
The New Negro
Who sprang from the vigor-stout loins
Of Nat Turner, gallows-martyr for Freedom,
Of Joseph Cinquez, Black Moses of the Amistad Mutiny,
Of Frederick Douglass, oracle of the Catholic Man,
Of Sojourner Truth, eye and ear of Lincoln's legions,
Of Harriet Tubman, Saint Bernard of the Underground Railroad.

The New Negro
Breaks the icons of his detractors,
Wipes out the conspiracy of silence,
Speaks to *his* America:
"My history-moulding ancestors
Planted the first crops of wheat on these shores,
Built ships to conquer the seven seas,
Erected the Cotton Empire,

Flung railroads across a hemisphere,
Disemboweled the earth's iron and coal,
Tunneled the mountains and bridged rivers,
Harvested the grain and hewed forests,
Sentineled the Thirteen Colonies,
Unfurled Old Glory at the North Pole,
Fought a hundred battles for the Republic."

The New Negro:
His giant hands fling murals upon high chambers,
His drama teaches a world to laugh and weep,
His voice thunders the Brotherhood of Labor,
His science creates seven wonders,
His Republic of Letters challenges the Negro-baiters.

The New Negro,
Hard-muscled, Fascist-hating, Democracy-ensouled,
Strides in seven-league boots
Along the Highway of Today
Toward the Promised Land of Tomorrow!

    V LARGHETTO

None in the Land can say
To us black men Today:
You send the tractors on their bloody path,
And create Okies for *The Grapes of Wrath.*
You breed the slum that breeds a *Native Son*
To damn the good earth Pilgrim Fathers won.

None in the Land can say
To us black men Today:
You dupe the poor with rags-to-riches tales,
And leave the workers empty dinner pails.
You stuff the ballot box, and honest men
Are muzzled by your demagogic din.

None in the Land can say
To us black men Today:
You smash stock markets with your coined blitzkriegs,
And make a hundred million guinea pigs.
You counterfeit our Christianity,
And bring contempt upon Democracy.

None in the Land can say
To us black men Today:
You prowl when citizens are fast asleep,
And hatch Fifth Column plots to blast the deep
Foundations of the State and leave the Land
A vast Sahara with a Fascist brand.

VI TEMPO DI MARCIA

Out of abysses of Illiteracy,
Through labyrinths of Lies,
Across waste lands of Disease . . .
We advance!

Out of dead-ends of Poverty,
Through wildernesses of Superstition,
Across barricades of Jim Crowism . . .
We advance!

With the Peoples of the World . . .
We advance!

Hart Crane

(1899–1932)

REPOSE OF RIVERS

The willows carried a slow sound,
A sarabande the wind mowed on the mead.
I could never remember
That seething, steady leveling of the marshes
Till age had brought me to the sea.

Flags, weeds. And remembrance of steep alcoves
Where cypresses shared the noon's
Tyranny; they drew me into hades almost.
And mammoth turtles climbing sulphur dreams
Yielded, while sun-silt rippled them
Asunder . . .

How much I would have bartered! the black gorge
And all the singular nestings in the hills
Where beavers learn stitch and tooth.
The pond I entered once and quickly fled—
I remember now its singing willow rim.

And finally, in that memory all things nurse;
After the city that I finally passed
With scalding unguents spread and smoking darts
The monsoon cut across the delta
At gulf gates . . . There, beyond the dykes

I heard wind flaking sapphire, like this summer,
And willows could not hold more steady sound.

VOYAGES

I

Above the fresh ruffles of the surf
Bright striped urchins flay each other with sand.
They have contrived a conquest for shell shucks,
And their fingers crumble fragments of baked weed
Gaily digging and scattering.

And in answer to their treble interjections
The sun beats lightning on the waves,
The waves fold thunder on the sand;
And could they hear me I would tell them:

O brilliant kids, frisk with your dog,
Fondle your shells and sticks, bleached
By time and the elements; but there is a line
You must not cross nor ever trust beyond it
Spry cordage of your bodies to caresses
Too lichen-faithful from too wide a breast.
The bottom of the sea is cruel.

II

And yet this great wink of eternity,
Of rimless floods, unfettered leewardings,
Samite sheeted and processioned where
Her undinal vast belly moonward bends,
Laughing the wrapt inflections of our love;

Take this Sea, whose diapason knells
On scrolls of silver snowy sentences,
The sceptred terror of whose sessions rends
As her demeanors motion well or ill,
All but the pieties of lovers' hands.

And onward, as bells off San Salvador
Salute the crocus lustres of the stars,
In these poinsettia meadows of her tides,—
Adagios of islands, O my Prodigal,
Complete the dark confessions her veins spell.

Mark how her turning shoulders wind the hours,
And hasten while her penniless rich palms
Pass superscription of bent foam and wave,—
Hasten, while they are true,—sleep, death, desire,
Close round one instant in one floating flower.

Bind us in time, O Seasons clear, and awe.
O minstrel galleons of Carib fire,
Bequeath us to no earthly shore until
Is answered in the vortex of our grave
The seal's wide spindrift gaze toward paradise.

     III

Infinite consanguinity it bears—
This tendered theme of you that light
Retrieves from sea plains where the sky
Resigns a breast that every wave enthrones;
While ribboned water lanes I wind
Are laved and scattered with no stroke
Wide from your side, whereto this hour
The sea lifts, also, reliquary hands.

And so, admitted through black swollen gates
That must arrest all distance otherwise,—
Past whirling pillars and lithe pediments,
Light wrestling there incessantly with light,
Star kissing star through wave on wave unto
Your body rocking!

                and where death, if shed,
Presumes no carnage, but this single change,—
Upon the steep floor flung from dawn to dawn
The silken skilled transmemberment of song;

Permit me voyage, love, into your hands . . .

     IV

Whose counted smile of hours and days, suppose
I know as spectrum of the sea and pledge
Vastly now parting gulf on gulf of wings
Whose circles bridge, I know, (from palms to the severe

Chilled albatross's white immutability)
No stream of greater love advancing now
Than, singing, this mortality alone
Through clay aflow immortally to you.

All fragrance irrefragibly, and claim
Madly meeting logically in this hour
And region that is ours to wreathe again,
Portending eyes and lips and making told
The chancel port and portion of our June—

Shall they not stem and close in our own steps
Bright staves of flowers and quills to-day as I
Must first be lost in fatal tides to tell?
In signature of the incarnate word
The harbor shoulders to resign in mingling
Mutual blood, transpiring as foreknown
And widening noon within your breast for gathering
All bright insinuations that my years have caught
For islands where must lead inviolably
Blue latitudes and levels of your eyes,—

In this expectant, still exclaim receive
The secret oar and petals of all love.

                    V

Meticulous, past midnight in clear rime,
Infrangible and lonely, smooth as though cast
Together in one merciless white blade—
The bay estuaries fleck the hard sky limits.

—As if too brittle or too clear to touch!
The cables of our sleep so swiftly filed,
Already hang, shred ends from remembered stars.
One frozen trackless smile . . . What words
Can strangle this deaf moonlight? For we

Are overtaken. Now no cry, no sword
Can fasten or deflect this tidal wedge,
Slow tyranny of moonlight, moonlight loved
And changed . . . "There's

Nothing like this in the world," you say,
Knowing I cannot touch your hand and look
Too, into that godless cleft of sky
Where nothing turns but dead sands flashing.

"—And never to quite understand!" No,
In all the argosy of your bright hair I dreamed
Nothing so flagless as this piracy.

                                        But now
Draw in your head, alone and too tall here.
Your eyes already in the slant of drifting foam;
Your breath sealed by the ghosts I do not know:
Draw in your head and sleep the long way home.

        VI

Where icy and bright dungeons lift
Of swimmers their lost morning eyes,
And ocean rivers, churning, shift
Green borders under stranger skies,

Steadily as a shell secretes
Its beating leagues of monotone,
Or as many waters trough the sun's
Red kelson past the cape's wet stone;

O rivers mingling toward the sky
And harbor of the phœnix' breast—
My eyes pressed black against the prow,
—Thy derelict and blinded guest

Waiting, afire, what name, unspoke,
I cannot claim: let thy waves rear
More savage than the death of kings,
Some splintered garland for the seer.

Beyond siroccos harvesting
The solstice thunders, crept away,
Like a cliff swinging or a sail
Flung into April's inmost day—

Creation's blithe and petalled word
To the lounged goddess when she rose
Conceding dialogue with eyes
That smile unsearchable repose—

Still fervid covenant, Belle Isle,
—Unfolded floating dais before
Which rainbows twine continual hair—
Belle Isle, white echo of the oar!

The imaged Word, it is, that holds
Hushed willows anchored in its glow.
It is the unbetrayable reply
Whose accent no farewell can know.

From THE BRIDGE

TO BROOKLYN BRIDGE

How many dawns, chill from his rippling rest
The seagull's wings shall dip and pivot him,
Shedding white rings of tumult, building high
Over the chained bay waters Liberty—

Then, with inviolate curve, forsake our eyes
As apparitional as sails that cross
Some page of figures to be filed away;
—Till elevators drop us from our day . . .

I think of cinemas, panoramic sleights
With multitudes bent toward some flashing scene
Never disclosed, but hastened to again,
Foretold to other eyes on the same screen;

And Thee, across the harbor, silver-paced
As though the sun took step of thee, yet left
Some motion ever unspent in thy stride,—
Implicitly thy freedom staying thee!

Out of some subway scuttle, cell or loft
A bedlamite speeds to thy parapets,
Tilting there momently, shrill shirt ballooning,
A jest falls from the speechless caravan.

Down Wall, from girder into street noon leaks,
A rip-tooth of the sky's acetylene;
All afternoon the cloud-flown derricks turn . . .
Thy cables breathe the North Atlantic still.

And obscure as that heaven of the Jews,
Thy guerdon . . . Accolade thou dost bestow
Of anonymity time cannot raise:
Vibrant reprieve and pardon thou dost show.

O harp and altar, of the fury fused,
(How could mere toil align thy choiring strings!)
Terrific threshold of the prophet's pledge,
Prayer of pariah, and the lover's cry,—

Again the traffic lights that skim thy swift
Unfractioned idiom, immaculate sigh of stars,
Beading thy path—condense eternity:
And we have seen night lifted in thine arms.

Under thy shadow by the piers I waited;
Only in darkness is thy shadow clear.
The City's fiery parcels all undone,
Already snow submerges an iron year . . .

O Sleepless as the river under thee,
Vaulting the sea, the prairies' dreaming sod,
Unto us lowliest sometime sweep, descend
And of the curveship lend a myth to God.

TO EMILY DICKINSON

You who desired so much—in vain to ask—
Yet fed your hunger like an endless task,
Dared dignify the labor, bless the quest—
Achieved that stillness ultimately best,

Being, of all, least sought for: Emily, hear!
O sweet, dead Silencer, most suddenly clear
When singing that Eternity possessed
And plundered momently in every breast;

—Truly no flower yet withers in your hand,
The harvest you descried and understand
Needs more than wit to gather, love to bind.
Some reconcilement of remotest mind—

Leaves Ormus rubyless, and Ophir chill.
Else tears heap all within one clay-cold hill.

THE BROKEN TOWER

The bell-rope that gathers God at dawn
Dispatches me as though I dropped down the knell
Of a spent day—to wander the cathedral lawn
From pit to crucifix, feet chill on steps from hell.

Have you not heard, have you not seen that corps
Of shadows in the tower, whose shoulders sway
Antiphonal carillons launched before
The stars are caught and hived in the sun's ray?

The bells, I say, the bells break down their tower;
And swing I know not where. Their tongues engrave
Membrane through marrow, my long-scattered score
Of broken intervals. . . . And I, their sexton slave!

Oval encyclicals in canyons heaping
The impasse high with choir. Banked voices slain!
Pagodas, campaniles with reveilles outleaping—
O terraced echoes prostrate on the plain! . . .

And so it was I entered the broken world
To trace the visionary company of love, its voice
An instant in the wind (I know not whither hurled)
But not for long to hold each desperate choice.

My word I poured. But was it cognate, scored
Of that tribunal monarch of the air
Whose thigh embronzes earth, strikes crystal Word
In wounds pledged once to hope—cleft to despair?

The steep encroachments of my blood left me
No answer (could blood hold such a lofty tower
As flings the question true?)—or is it she
Whose sweet mortality stirs latent power?—

And through whose pulse I hear, counting the strokes
My veins recall and add, revived and sure
The angelus of wars my chest evokes:
What I hold healed, original now, and pure . . .

And builds, within, a tower that is not stone
(Not stone can jacket heaven)—but slip
Of pebbles—visible wings of silence sown
In azure circles, widening as they dip

The matrix of the heart, lift down the eye
That shrines the quiet lake and swells a tower . . .
The commodious, tall decorum of the sky
Unseals her earth, and lifts love in its shower.

Léonie Adams

(1899–1988)

LIGHT AT EQUINOX

A realm is here of masquing light
When struck rent wood and cornland by
The belled heaven claps the ground.
Husk, seed, pale straw, pale ear the year reposes,
And a thinned frieze of earth rims round
The whey-gleamed wet-as-dimming sky,
And whole trodden floor of light,
Where that slant limb winds with its shadowing closes.

Distant as lustrally the sun
Within that pearl of nimble play
Where traverse with rehearsing tread
Orients of prime to their all-reaping west,
Strangered from every grave glissade
Of blue enduskings or of milky day,
And wan, his silver nimbus on,
Muses his burning sojourn unprofessed.

Past barks mouse-sleek, wattled as serpent skin,
Rare acorn fall, rare squirrel flash.
Beyond, and in a silenced scene,
The wren, gamin wanderer of immense day
Can with luxuriant bendings preen,
Or in his pebble-scoopings plash,
To alarmless Eden flown,
And suddenly, for nothing, flies away.

And all are sole in the estranging day;
    Forms of all things their candour wear,
Like the undefending dead,
And forth from out that mortal stricture gaze,
Of unperspective radiance shed
Through everywhere horizoned air,

461

Tasking precising love to say,
For its dense words, the azuring periphrase.

To her own brink light glides, intent
An unsphering sense to bind
By narrowing measures in.
Sidelong as then up branching March she bade
Stiff buds into the glancing skein,
And the green reel unwind;
Now toward another pole she's leant,
And netherwards for partner draws her shade.

APRIL MORTALITY

Rebellion shook an ancient dust,
    And bones bleached dry of rottenness
Said: Heart, be bitter still, nor trust
    The earth, the sky, in their bright dress.

Heart, heart, dost thou not break to know
    This anguish thou wilt bear alone?
We sang of it an age ago,
    And traced it dimly upon stone.

With all the drifting race of men
    Thou also art begot to mourn
That she is crucified again,
    The lonely Beauty yet unborn.

And if thou dreamest to have won
    Some touch of her in permanence,
'Tis the old cheating of the sun,
    The intricate lovely play of sense.

Be bitter still, remember how
    Four petals, when a little breath
Of wind made stir the pear-tree bough,
    Blew delicately down to death.

Allen Tate

(1899–1979)

ODE TO THE CONFEDERATE DEAD

Row after row with strict impunity
The headstones yield their names to the element,
The wind whirrs without recollection;
In the riven troughs the splayed leaves
Pile up, of nature the casual sacrament
To the seasonal eternity of death;
Then driven by the fierce scrutiny
Of heaven to their election in the vast breath,
They sough the rumour of mortality.

Autumn is desolation in the plot
Of a thousand acres where these memories grow
From the inexhaustible bodies that are not
Dead, but feed the grass row after rich row.
Think of the autumns that have come and gone!—
Ambitious November with the humors of the year,
With a particular zeal for every slab,
Staining the uncomfortable angels that rot
On the slabs, a wing chipped here, an arm there:
The brute curiosity of an angel's stare
Turns you, like them, to stone,
Transforms the heaving air
Till plunged to a heavier world below
You shift your sea-space blindly
Heaving, turning like the blind crab.

  Dazed by the wind, only the wind
  The leaves flying, plunge

You know who have waited by the wall
The twilight certainty of an animal,
Those midnight restitutions of the blood
You know—the immitigable pines, the smoky frieze

Of the sky, the sudden call: you know the rage,
The cold pool left by the mounting flood,
Of muted Zeno and Parmenides.
You who have waited for the angry resolution
Of those desires that should be yours tomorrow,
You know the unimportant shrift of death
And praise the vision
And praise the arrogant circumstance
Of those who fall
Rank upon rank, hurried beyond decision—
Here by the sagging gate, stopped by the wall.

   Seeing, seeing only the leaves
   Flying, plunge and expire

Turn your eyes to the immoderate past,
Turn to the inscrutable infantry rising
Demons out of the earth—they will not last.
Stonewall, Stonewall, and the sunken fields of hemp,
Shiloh, Antietam, Malvern Hill, Bull Run.
Lost in that orient of the thick-and-fast
You will curse the setting sun.

   Cursing only the leaves crying
   Like an old man in a storm

You hear the shout, the crazy hemlocks point
With troubled fingers to the silence which
Smothers you, a mummy, in time.

               The hound bitch
Toothless and dying, in a musty cellar
Hears the wind only.

           Now that the salt of their blood
Stiffens the saltier oblivion of the sea,
Seals the malignant purity of the flood,
What shall we who count our days and bow
Our heads with a commemorial woe
In the ribboned coats of grim felicity,
What shall we say of the bones, unclean,
Whose verdurous anonymity will grow?
The ragged arms, the ragged heads and eyes
Lost in these acres of the insane green?

The gray lean spiders come, they come and go;
In a tangle of willows without light
The singular screech-owl's tight
Invisible lyric seeds the mind
With the furious murmur of their chivalry.

　　We shall say only the leaves
　　Flying, plunge and expire

We shall say only the leaves whispering
In the improbable mist of nightfall
That flies on multiple wing;
Night is the beginning and the end
And in between the ends of distraction
Waits mute speculation, the patient curse
That stones the eyes, or like the jaguar leaps
For his own image in a jungle pool, his victim.
What shall we say who have knowledge
Carried to the heart? Shall we take the act
To the grave? Shall we, more hopeful, set up the grave
In the house? The ravenous grave?

　　　　　　　　　　　　　　Leave now
The shut gate and the decomposing wall:
The gentle serpent, green in the mulberry bush,
Riots with his tongue through the hush—
Sentinel of the grave who counts us all!

MR. POPE

When Alexander Pope strolled in the city
Strict was the glint of pearl and gold sedans.
Ladies leaned out more out of fear than pity
For Pope's tight back was rather a goat's than man's.

Often one thinks the urn should have more bones
Than skeletons provide for speedy dust,
The urn gets hollow, cobwebs brittle as stones
Weave to the funeral shell a frivolous rust.

And he who dribbled couplets like a snake
Coiled to a lithe precision in the sun
Is missing. The jar is empty; you may break
It only to find that Mr. Pope is gone.

What requisitions of a verity
Prompted the wit and rage between his teeth
One cannot say. Around a crooked tree
A moral climbs whose name should be a wreath.

Yvor Winters

(1900–1968)

SUMMER NOON: 1941

With visionary care
The mind imagines Hell,
Draws fine the sound of flame
Till one can scarcely tell
The nature, or the name,
Or what the thing is for:
  Past summer bough and cry,
The sky, distended, bare,
Now whispers like a shell
Of the increase of war.
  Thus will man reach an end:
In fear of his own will,
Yet moved where it may tend,
With mind and word grown still.
  The fieldmouse and the hare,
The small snake of the garden,
Whose little muscles harden,
Whose eyes now quickened stare,
Though driven by the sound
—Too small and free to pardon!—
Will repossess this ground.

THE SLOW PACIFIC SWELL

Far out of sight forever stands the sea,
Bounding the land with pale tranquillity.
When a small child, I watched it from a hill
At thirty miles or more. The vision still
Lies in the eye, soft blue and far away:
The rain has washed the dust from April day;

Paint-brush and lupine lie against the ground;
The wind above the hill-top has the sound
Of distant water in unbroken sky;
Dark and precise the little steamers ply—
Firm in direction they seem not to stir.
That is illusion. The artificer
Of quiet, distance holds me in a vise
And holds the ocean steady to my eyes.

Once when I rounded Flattery, the sea
Hove its loose weight like sand to tangle me
Upon the washing deck, to crush the hull;
Subsiding, dragged flesh at the bone. The skull
Felt the retreating wash of dreaming hair.
Half drenched in dissolution, I lay bare.
I scarcely pulled myself erect; I came
Back slowly, slowly knew myself the same.
That was the ocean. From the ship we saw
Gray whales for miles: the long sweep of the jaw,
The blunt head plunging clean above the wave.
And one rose in a tent of sea and gave
A darkening shudder; water fell away;
The whale stood shining, and then sank in spray.

A landsman, I. The sea is but a sound.
I would be near it on a sandy mound,
And hear the steady rushing of the deep
While I lay stinging in the sand with sleep.
I have lived inland long. The land is numb.
It stands beneath the feet, and one may come
Walking securely, till the sea extends
Its limber margin, and precision ends.
By night a chaos of commingling power,
The whole Pacific hovers hour by hour.
The slow Pacific swell stirs on the sand,
Sleeping to sink away, withdrawing land,
Heaving and wrinkled in the moon, and blind;
Or gathers seaward, ebbing out of mind.

Laura Riding Jackson

(1901–1991)

PRISMS

What is beheld through glass seems glass.

The quality of what I am
Encases what I am not,
Smoothes the strange world.
I perceive it slowly,
In my time,
In my material,
As my pride,
As my possession:
The vision is love.

When life crashes like a cracked pane,
Still shall I love
Even the strange dead as the living once.
Death also sees, though distantly,
And I must trust then as now
A prism—of another kind,
Through which one may not put one's hands to touch.

HELEN'S BURNING

Her beauty, which we talk of,
Is but half her fate.
All does not come to light
Until the two halves meet
And we are silent
And she speaks,
Her whole fate saying,
She is, she is not, in one breath.

But we tell only half, fear to know all
Lest all should be to tell
And our mouths choke with flame
Of her consuming
And lose the gift of prophecy.

ALL THINGS

All things that wake enjoy the sun—
All things but one—
All things except the sun—
The sun because the sun.

An observation of my girlhood.
I now speak less equivocally
And yet more guardedly.

All things that wake enjoy the sun—
All things but one—
All things except the sun—
The sun because
All things once sun were
Which more and more was
The pride that could not be
Except looked back on
By all things become
One, one and one
Unto death's long precision.

All things that wake enjoy the sun.
All things remember not having been,
When waking was but sun to be,
And sleeping was but sun to be,
When life was life alone once—
Deathless, all-instantaneous,
Begun and done in one
Impossibility of being sun,
Death's too proud enemy—

All things enjoy to watch
The pride that could not be,
The largeness against death—
All things enjoy to watch this
From death where life is
As lasting as it little is.

An observation of my—
What shall I call such patience
To look back on nature,
Having already looked enough
To know the sun it is which was,
And the sun again which was not,
By nights removed from days,
By nights and days, by souls
Like little suns away toward
Dreams of pride that could not be—
What shall I call such patience—
An observation of my agedness—
Death's long precision while
All things undo themselves
From sunhood, living glory
That never, never was—
Because the sun.

THE WORLD AND I

This is not exactly what I mean
Any more than the sun is the sun.
But how to mean more closely
If the sun shines but approximately?
What a world of awkwardness!
What hostile implements of sense!
Perhaps this is as close a meaning
As perhaps becomes such knowing.
Else I think the world and I
Must live together as strangers and die—
A sour love, each doubtful whether

Was ever a thing to love the other.
No, better for both to be nearly sure
Each of each—exactly where
Exactly I and exactly the world
Fail to meet by a moment, and a word.

NOTHING SO FAR

Nothing so far but moonlight
Where the mind is;
Nothing in that place, this hold,
To hold;
Only their faceless shadows to announce
Perhaps they come—
Nor even do they know
Whereto they cast them.

Yet here, all that remains
When each has been the universe:
No universe, but each, or nothing.
Here is the future swell curved round
To all that was.

What were we, then,
Before the being of ourselves began?
Nothing so far but strangeness
Where the moments of the mind return.
Nearly, the place was lost
In that we went to stranger places.

Nothing so far but nearly
The long familiar pang
Of never having gone;
And words below a whisper which
If tended as the graves of live men should be
May bring their names and faces home.

It makes a loving promise to itself,
Womanly, that there

More presences are promised
Than by the difficult light appear.
Nothing appears but moonlight's morning—
By which to count were as to strew
The look of day with last night's rid of moths.

Gwendolyn B. Bennett

(1902–1981)

TO A DARK GIRL

I love you for your brownness
And the rounded darkness of your breast.
I love you for the breaking sadness in your voice
And shadows where your wayward eye-lids rest.

Something of old forgotten queens
Lurks in the lithe abandon of your walk,
And something of the shackled slave
Sobs in the rhythm of your talk.

Oh, little brown girl, born for sorrow's mate,
Keep all you have of queenliness,
Forgetting that you once were slave,
And let your full lips laugh at Fate!

HERITAGE

I want to see the slim palm-trees,
Pulling at the clouds
With little pointed fingers. . . .

I want to see lithe Negro girls,
Etched dark against the sky
While sunset lingers.

I want to hear the silent sands,
Singing to the moon
Before the Sphinx-still face. . . .

I want to hear the chanting
Around a heathen fire
Of a strange black race.

I want to breathe the Lotus flow'r,
Sighing to the stars
With tendrils drinking at the Nile. . . .

I want to feel the surging
Of my sad people's soul
Hidden by a minstrel-smile.

HATRED

I shall hate you
Like a dart of singing steel
Shot through still air
At even-tide.
Or solemnly
As pines are sober
When they stand etched
Against the sky.
Hating you shall be a game
Played with cool hands
And slim fingers.
Your heart will yearn
For the lonely splendor
Of the pine tree;
While rekindled fires
In my eyes
Shall wound you like swift arrows.
Memory will lay its hands
Upon your breast
And you will understand
My hatred.

Langston Hughes

(1 9 0 2 – 1 9 6 7)

THE WEARY BLUES

Droning a drowsy syncopated tune,
Rocking back and forth to a mellow croon,
   I heard a Negro play.
Down on Lenox Avenue the other night
By the pale dull pallor of an old gas light
   He did a lazy sway. . . .
   He did a lazy sway. . . .
To the tune o' those Weary Blues.
With his ebony hands on each ivory key
He made that poor piano moan with melody.
   O Blues!
Swaying to and fro on his rickety stool
He played that sad raggy tune like a musical fool.
   Sweet Blues!
Coming from a black man's soul.
   O Blues!
In a deep song voice with a melancholy tone
I heard that Negro sing, that old piano moan—
   "Ain't got nobody in all this world,
   Ain't got nobody but ma self.
   I's gwine to quit ma frownin'
   And put ma troubles on the shelf."
Thump, thump, thump, went his foot on the floor.
He played a few chords then he sang some more—
   "I got the Weary Blues
   And I can't be satisfied.
   Got the Weary Blues
   And can't be satisfied—
   I ain't happy no mo'
   And I wish that I had died."
And far into the night he crooned that tune.
The stars went out and so did the moon.
The singer stopped playing and went to bed

While the Weary Blues echoed through his head.
He slept like a rock or a man that's dead.

THE NEGRO SPEAKS OF RIVERS

I've known rivers:
I've known rivers ancient as the world and older than the flow of human blood
    in human veins.

My soul has grown deep like the rivers.

I bathed in the Euphrates when dawns were young.
I built my hut near the Congo and it lulled me to sleep.
I looked upon the Nile and raised the pyramids above it.
I heard the singing of the Mississippi when Abe Lincoln went down to New
    Orleans, and I've seen its muddy bosom turn all golden in the sunset.

I've known rivers:
Ancient, dusky rivers.

My soul has grown deep like rivers.

JAZZONIA

Oh, silver tree!
Oh, shining rivers of the soul!

In a Harlem cabaret
Six long-headed jazzers play.
A dancing girl whose eyes are bold
Lifts high a dress of silken gold.

Oh, singing tree!
Oh, shining rivers of the soul!

Were Eve's eyes
In the first garden
Just a bit too bold?
Was Cleopatra gorgeous
In a gown of gold?

Oh, shining tree!
Oh, silver rivers of the soul!

In a whirling cabaret
Six long-headed jazzers play.

CROSS

My old man's a white old man
And my old mother's black.
If ever I cursed my white old man
I take my curses back.

If ever I cursed my black old mother
And wished she were in hell,
I'm sorry for that evil wish
And now I wish her well.

My old man died in a fine big house.
My ma died in a shack.
I wonder where I'm gonna die,
Being neither white nor black?

PO' BOY BLUES

When I was home de
Sunshine seemed like gold.
When I was home de
Sunshine seemed like gold.
Since I come up North de
Whole damn world's turned cold.

I was a good boy,
Never done no wrong.
Yes, I was a good boy,
Never done no wrong,
But this world is weary
An' de road is hard an' long.

I fell in love with
A gal I thought was kind.
Fell in love with
A gal I thought was kind.
She made me lose ma money
An' almost lose ma mind.

Weary, weary,
Weary early in de morn.
Weary, weary,
Early, early in de morn.
I's so weary
I wish I'd never been born.

ESTHETE IN HARLEM

Strange,
That in this nigger place
I should meet life face to face;
When, for years, I had been seeking
Life in places gentler-speaking,
Until I came to this vile street
And found Life stepping on my feet!

AS I GREW OLDER

It was a long time ago.
I have almost forgotten my dream.
But it was there then,

In front of me,
Bright like a sun—
My dream.

And then the wall rose,
Rose slowly,
Slowly,
Between me and my dream.
Rose slowly, slowly,
Dimming,
Hiding,
The light of my dream.
Rose until it touched the sky—
The wall.

Shadow.
I am black.

I lie down in the shadow.
No longer the light of my dream before me,
Above me.
Only the thick wall.
Only the shadow.

My hands!
My dark hands!
Break through the wall!
Find my dream!
Help me to shatter this darkness,
To smash this night,
To break this shadow
Into a thousand lights of sun,
Into a thousand whirling dreams
Of sun!

THEME FOR ENGLISH B

The instructor said,

 Go home and write
 a page tonight.

And let that page come out of you—
Then, it will be true.

I wonder if it's that simple?
I am twenty-two, colored, born in Winston-Salem.
I went to school there, then Durham, then here
to this college on the hill above Harlem.
I am the only colored student in my class.
The steps from the hill lead down into Harlem,
through a park, then I cross St. Nicholas,
Eighth Avenue, Seventh, and I come to the Y,
the Harlem Branch Y, where I take the elevator
up to my room, sit down, and write this page:

It's not easy to know what is true for you or me
at twenty-two, my age. But I guess I'm what
I feel and see and hear, Harlem, I hear you:
hear you, hear me—we two—you, me, talk on this page.
(I hear New York, too.) Me—who?
Well, I like to eat, sleep, drink, and be in love.
I like to work, read, learn, and understand life.
I like a pipe for a Christmas present,
or records—Bessie, bop, or Bach.
I guess being colored doesn't make me *not* like
the same things other folks like who are other races.
So will my page be colored that I write?
Being me, it will not be white.
But it will be
a part of you, instructor.
You are white—
yet a part of me, as I am a part of you.
That's American.
Sometimes perhaps you don't want to be a part of me.
Nor do I often want to be a part of you.
But we are, that's true!
As I learn from you,
I guess you learn from me—
although you're older—and white—
and somewhat more free.

This is my page for English B.

Arna Bontemps

(1902 – 1973)

A BLACK MAN TALKS OF REAPING

I have sown beside all waters in my day.
I planted deep within my heart the fear
That wind or fowl would take the grain away.
I planted safe against this stark, lean year.

I scattered seed enough to plant the land
In rows from Canada to Mexico.
But for my reaping only what the hand
Can hold at once is all that I can show.

Yet what I sowed and what the orchard yields
My brother's sons are gathering stalk and root,
Small wonder then my children glean in fields
They have not sown, and feed on bitter fruit.

NOCTURNE OF THE WHARVES

All night they whine upon their ropes and boom
Against the dock with helpless prows:
These little ships that are too worn for sailing
From the wharf but do not rest at all.
Tugging at the dim gray wharf they think
No doubt of China and of bright Bombay.
And they remember islands of the East,
Formosa and the mountains of Japan.
They think of cities ruined by the sea
And they are restless, sleeping at the wharf.

Tugging at the dim gray wharf they think
No less of Africa. An east wind blows
And salt spray sweeps the unattended decks.

Shouts of dead men break upon the night.
The captain calls his crew and they respond—
The little ships are dreaming—land is near.
But mist comes up to dim the copper coast,
Mist dissembles images of the trees.
The captain and his men alike are lost
And their shouts go down in the rising sound of waves.

Ah little ships, I know your weariness!
I know the sea-green shadows of your dream.
For I have loved the cities of the sea
And desolations of the old days I
Have loved: I was a wanderer like you
And I have broken down before the wind.

BLIGHT

I have seen a lovely thing
Stark before a whip of weather:
The tree that was so wistful after spring
Beating barren twigs together.

The birds that came there one by one,
The sensuous leaves that used to sway
And whisper there at night, all are gone,
Each has vanished in its way.

And this whip is on my heart;
There is no sound that it allows,
No little song that I may start
But I hear the beating of dead boughs.

GOD GIVE TO MEN

God give the yellow man
An easy breeze at blossom time.
Grant his eager, slanting eyes to cover

Every land and dream
Of afterwhile.

Give blue-eyed men their swivel chairs
To whirl in tall buildings.
Allow them many ships at sea,
And on land, soldiers
And policemen.

For black man, God,
No need to bother more
But only fill afresh his meed
Of laughter,
His cup of tears.

God suffer little men
The taste of soul's desire.

Countee Cullen

(1903 – 1946)

HERITAGE

What is Africa to me:
Copper sun or scarlet sea,
Jungle star or jungle track,
Strong bronzed men, or regal black
Women from whose loins I sprang
When the birds of Eden sang?
One three centuries removed
From the scenes his fathers loved,
Spicy grove, cinnamon tree,
What is Africa to me?

So I lie, who all day long
Want no sound except the song
Sung by wild barbaric birds
Goading massive jungle herds,
Juggernauts of flesh that pass
Trampling tall defiant grass
Where young forest lovers lie,
Plighting troth beneath the sky.
So I lie, who always hear,
Though I cram against my ear
Both my thumbs, and keep them there,
Great drums throbbing through the air.
So I lie, whose fount of pride,
Dear distress, and joy allied,
Is my somber flesh and skin,
With the dark blood dammed within
Like great pulsing tides of wine
That, I fear, must burst the fine
Channels of the chafing net
Where they surge and foam and fret.

Africa? A book one thumbs
Listlessly, till slumber comes.

Unremembered are her bats
Circling through the night, her cats
Crouching in the river reeds,
Stalking gentle flesh that feeds
By the river brink; no more
Does the bugle-throated roar
Cry that monarch claws have leapt
From the scabbards where they slept.
Silver snakes that once a year
Doff the lovely coats you wear,
Seek no covert in your fear
Lest a mortal eye should see;
What's your nakedness to me?
Here no leprous flowers rear
Fierce corollas in the air;
Here no bodies sleek and wet,
Dripping mingled rain and sweat,
Tread the savage measures of
Jungle boys and girls in love.
What is last year's snow to me,
Last year's anything? The tree
Budding yearly must forget
How its past arose or set—
Bough and blossom, flower, fruit,
Even what shy bird with mute
Wonder at her travail there,
Meekly labored in its hair.
One three centuries removed
From the scenes his fathers loved,
Spicy grove, cinnamon tree,
What is Africa to me?

So I lie, who find no peace
Night or day, no slight release
From the unremittent beat
Made by cruel padded feet
Walking through my body's street.
Up and down they go, and back,
Treading out a jungle track.
So I lie, who never quite
Safely sleep from rain at night—
I can never rest at all

When the rain begins to fall;
Like a soul gone mad with pain
I must match its weird refrain;
Ever must I twist and squirm,
Writhing like a baited worm,
While its primal measures drip
Through my body, crying, "Strip!
Doff this new exuberance.
Come and dance the Lover's Dance!"
In an old remembered way
Rain works on me night and day.

Quaint, outlandish heathen gods
Black men fashion out of rods,
Clay, and brittle bits of stone,
In a likeness like their own,
My conversion came high-priced;
I belong to Jesus Christ,
Preacher of humility;
Heathen gods are naught to me.

Father, Son, and Holy Ghost,
So I make an idle boast;
Jesus of the twice-turned cheek,
Lamb of God, although I speak
With my mouth thus, in my heart
Do I play a double part.
Ever at Thy glowing altar
Must my heart grow sick and falter,
Wishing He I served were black,
Thinking then it would not lack
Precedent of pain to guide it,
Let who would or might deride it;
Surely then this flesh would know
Yours had borne a kindred woe.
Lord, I fashion dark gods, too,
Daring even to give You
Dark despairing features where,
Crowned with dark rebellious hair,
Patience wavers just so much as
Mortal grief compels, while touches
Quick and hot, of anger, rise

To smitten cheek and weary eyes.
Lord, forgive me if my need
Sometimes shapes a human creed.

All day long and all night through,
One thing only must I do:
Quench my pride and cool my blood,
Lest I perish in the flood.
Lest a hidden ember set
Timber that I thought was wet
Burning like the dryest flax,
Melting like the merest wax,
Lest the grave restore its dead.
Not yet has my heart or head
In the least way realized
They and I are civilized.

FROM THE DARK TOWER

We shall not always plant while others reap
The golden increment of bursting fruit,
Not always countenance, abject and mute,
That lesser men should hold their brothers cheap;
Not everlastingly while others sleep
Shall we beguile their limbs with mellow flute,
Not always bend to some more subtle brute;
We were not made eternally to weep.

The night whose sable breast relieves the stark,
White stars is no less lovely being dark,
And there are buds that cannot bloom at all
In light, but crumple, piteous, and fall;
So in the dark we hide the heart that bleeds,
And wait, and tend our agonizing seeds.

TIMID LOVER

I who employ a poet's tongue,
Would tell you how
You are a golden damson hung
Upon a silver bough.

I who adore exotic things
Would shape a sound
To be your name, a word that sings
Until the head goes round.

I who am proud with other folk
Would grow complete
In pride on bitter words you spoke,
And kiss your petaled feet.

But never past the frail intent
My will may flow,
Though gentle looks of yours are bent
Upon me where I go.

So must I, starved for love's delight,
Affect the mute,
When love's divinest acolyte
Extends me holy fruit.

Louis Zukofsky

(1904–1978)

"A" – 11

For Celia and Paul

River that must turn full after I stop dying
Song, my song, raise grief to music
Light as my loves' thought, the few sick
So sick of wrangling: thus weeping,
Sounds of light, stay in her keeping
And my son's face—this much for honor.

Freed by their praises who make honor dearer
Whose losses show them rich and you no poorer
Take care, song, that what stars' imprint you mirror
Grazes their tears; draw speech from their nature or
Love in you—faced to your outer stars—purer
Gold than tongues make without feeling
Art new, hurt old: revealing
The slackened bow as the stinging
Animal dies, thread gold stringing
The fingerboard pressed in my honor.

Honor, song, sang the blest is delight knowing
We overcome ills by love. Hurt, song, nourish
Eyes, think most of whom you hurt. For the flowing
River   's poison where what rod blossoms. Flourish
By love's sweet lights and sing *in them I flourish.*
No, song, not any one power
May recall or forget, our
Love to see your love flows into
Us. If Venus lights, your words spin, to
Live our desires lead us to honor.

Graced, your heart in nothing less than in death, go—
I, dust—raise the great hem of the extended
World that nothing can leave; having had breath go

Face my son, say: "If your father offended
You with mute wisdom, my words have not ended
His second paradise where
His love was in her eyes where
They turn, quick for you two—sick
Or gone cannot make music
You set less than all. Honor

His voice in me, the river's turn that finds the
Grace in you, four notes first too full for talk, leaf
Lighting stem, stems bound to the branch that binds the
Tree, and then as from the same root we talk, leaf
After leaf of your mind's music, page, walk leaf
Over leaf of his thought, sounding
His happiness: song sounding
The grace that comes from knowing
Things, her love our own showing
Her love in all her honor."

Richard Eberhart

(1904–)

FOR A LAMB

I saw on the slant hill a putrid lamb,
Propped with daisies. The sleep looked deep,
The face nudged in the green pillow
But the guts were out for crows to eat.

Where's the lamb? whose tender plaint
Said all for the mute breezes.
Say he's in the wind somewhere,
Say, there's a lamb in the daisies.

THE FURY OF AERIAL BOMBARDMENT

You would think the fury of aerial bombardment
Would rouse God to relent; the infinite spaces
Are still silent. He looks on shock-pried faces.
History, even, does not know what is meant.

You would feel that after so many centuries
God would give man to repent; yet he can kill
As Cain could, but with multitudinous will,
No farther advanced than in his ancient furies.

Was man made stupid to see his own stupidity?
Is God by definition indifferent, beyond us all?
Is the eternal truth man's fighting soul
Wherein the Beast ravens in its own avidity?

Of Van Wettering I speak, and Averill,
Names on a list, whose faces I do not recall
But they are gone to early death, who late in school
Distinguished the belt feed lever from the belt holding paw.

A LOON CALL

Rowing between Pond and Western Islands
As the tide was coming in
Creating, for so long, two barred islands,
At the end of August, fall nip in the air,
I sensed something beyond me,
Everywhere I felt it in my flesh
As I beheld the sea and sky, the day,
The wordless immanence of the eternal,
And as I was rowing backward
To see directly where I was going,
Harmonious in the freedom of the oars.
A solitary loon cry locked the waters.

Barbaric, indivisible, replete with rack,
Somewhere off where seals were on half-tide rocks,
A loon's cry from beyond the human
Shook my sense to wordlessness.

Perfect cry, ununderstandable essence
Of sound from aeons ago, a shriek,
Strange, palpable, ebullient, wavering,
A cry that I cannot understand.
Praise to the cry that I cannot understand.

Stanley Kunitz

(1 9 0 5 –   )

THE SCIENCE OF THE NIGHT

I touch you in the night, whose gift was you,
My careless sprawler,
And I touch you cold, unstirring, star-bemused,
That have become the land of your self-strangeness.
What long seduction of the bone has led you
Down the imploring roads I cannot take
Into the arms of ghosts I never knew,
Leaving my manhood on a rumpled field
To guard you where you lie so deep
In absent-mindedness,
Caught in the calcium snows of sleep?

And even should I track you to your birth
Through all the cities of your mortal trial,
As in my jealous thought I try to do,
You would escape me—from the brink of earth
Take off to where the lawless auroras run,
You with your wild and metaphysic heart.
My touch is on you, who are light-years gone.
We are not souls but systems, and we move
In clouds of our unknowing
                                        like great nebulae.
Our very motives swirl and have their start
With father lion and with mother crab.

Dreamer, my own lost rib,
Whose planetary dust is blowing
Past archipelagoes of myth and light,
What far Magellans are you mistress of
To whom you speed the pleasure of your art?
As through a glass that magnifies my loss
I see the lines of your spectrum shifting red,
The universe expanding, thinning out,
Our worlds flying, oh flying, fast apart.

From hooded powers and from abstract flight
I summon you, your person and your pride.
Fall to me now from outer space,
Still fastened desperately to my side;
Through gulfs of streaming air
Bring me the mornings of the milky ways
Down to my threshold in your drowsy eyes;
And by the virtue of your honeyed word
Restore the liquid language of the moon,
That in gold mines of secrecy you delve.
Awake!
        My whirling hands stay at the noon,
Each cell within my body holds a heart
And all my hearts in unison strike twelve.

THE SNAKES OF SEPTEMBER

All summer I heard them
rustling in the shrubbery,
outracing me from tier
to tier in my garden,
a whisper among the viburnums,
a signal flashed from the hedgerow,
a shadow pulsing
in the barberry thicket.
Now that the nights are chill
and the annuals spent,
I should have thought them gone,
in a torpor of blood
slipped to the nether world
before the sickle frost.
Not so. In the deceptive balm
of noon, as if defiant of the curse
that spoiled another garden,
these two appear on show
through a narrow slit
in the dense green brocade
of a north-country spruce,
dangling head-down, entwined

in a brazen love-knot.
I put out my hand and stroke
the fine, dry grit of their skins.
After all,
we are partners in this land,
co-signers of a covenant.
At my touch the wild
braid of creation
trembles.

Robert Penn Warren

(1 9 0 5 – 1 9 8 9)

BEARDED OAKS

The oaks, how subtle and marine,
Bearded, and all the layered light
Above them swims; and thus the scene,
Recessed, awaits the positive night.

So, waiting, we in the grass now lie
Beneath the languorous tread of light:
The grasses, kelp-like, satisfy
The nameless motions of the air.

Upon the floor of light, and time,
Unmurmuring, of polyp made,
We rest; we are, as light withdraws,
Twin atolls on a shelf of shade.

Ages to our construction went,
Dim architecture, hour by hour:
And violence, forgot now, lent
The present stillness all its power.

The storm of noon above us rolled,
Of light the fury, furious gold,
The long drag troubling us, the depth:
Dark is unrocking, unrippling, still.

Passion and slaughter, ruth, decay
Descend, minutely whispering down,
Silted down swaying streams, to lay
Foundation for our voicelessness.

All our debate is voiceless here,
As all our rage, the rage of stone;
If hope is hopeless, then fearless is fear,
And history is thus undone.

Our feet once wrought the hollow street
With echo when the lamps were dead
At windows, once our headlight glare
Disturbed the doe that, leaping, fled.

I do not love you less that now
The caged heart makes iron stroke,
Or less that all that light once gave
The graduate dark should now revoke.

We live in time so little time
And we learn all so painfully,
That we may spare this hour's term
To practice for eternity.

BLOW, WEST WIND

I know, I know—though the evidence
Is lost, and the last who might speak are dead.
Blow, west wind, blow, and the evidence, O,

Is lost, and wind shakes the cedar, and O,
I know how the kestrel hung over Wyoming,
Breast reddened in sunset, and O, the cedar

Shakes, and I know how cold
Was the sweat on my father's mouth, dead.
Blow, west wind, blow, shake the cedar, I know

How once I, a boy, crouching at creekside,
Watched, in the sunlight, a handful of water
Drip, drip, from my hand. The drops—they were bright!

But you believe nothing, with the evidence lost.

EVENING HAWK

From plane of light to plane, wings dipping through
Geometries and orchids that the sunset builds,

Out of the peak's black angularity of shadow, riding
The last tumultuous avalanche of
Light above pines and the guttural gorge,
The hawk comes.

        His wing
Scythes down another day, his motion
Is that of the honed steel-edge, we hear
The crashless fall of stalks of Time.

The head of each stalk is heavy with the gold of our error.

Look! Look! he is climbing the last light
Who knows neither Time nor error, and under
Whose eye, unforgiving, the world, unforgiven, swings
Into shadow.

        Long now,
The last thrush is still, the last bat
Now cruises in his sharp hieroglyphics. His wisdom
Is ancient, too, and immense. The star
Is steady, like Plato, over the mountain.

If there were no wind we might, we think, hear
The earth grind on its axis, or history
Drip in darkness like a leaking pipe in the cellar.

HEART OF AUTUMN

Wind finds the northwest gap, fall comes.
Today, under gray cloud-scud and over gray
Wind-flicker of forest, in perfect formation, wild geese
Head for a land of warm water, the *boom*, the lead pellet.

Some crumple in air, fall. Some stagger, recover control,
Then take the last glide for a far glint of water. None
Knows what has happened. Now, today, watching
How tirelessly V upon V arrows the season's logic,

Do I know my own story? At least, they know
When the hour comes for the great wing-beat. Sky-strider,

Star-strider—they rise, and the imperial utterance,
Which cries out for distance, quivers in the wheeling sky.

That much they know, and in their nature know
The path of pathlessness, with all the joy
Of destiny fulfilling its own name.
I have known time and distance, but not why I am here.

Path of logic, path of folly, all
The same—and I stand, my face lifted now skyward,
Hearing the high beat, my arms outstretched in the tingling
Process of transformation, and soon tough legs,

With folded feet, trail in the sounding vacuum of passage,
And my heart is impacted with a fierce impulse
To unwordable utterance—
Toward sunset, at a great height.

AMAZING GRACE IN THE BACK COUNTRY

In the season of late August star-fall,
When the first crickets crinkled the dark,
There by woods, where oaks of the old forest-time
Yet swaggered and hulked over upstarts, the tent
Had been pitched, no bigger than one of
Some half-bankrupt carnival come
To town with fat lady, human skeleton, geek,
Man-woman and moth-eaten lion, and one
Boa constrictor for two bits seen
Fed a young calf or what; plus a brace
Of whores to whom menopause now
Was barely a memory, one with gold teeth and one
With game gam, but both
With aperture ready to serve
Any late-lingerers, and leave
A new and guaranteed brand of syphilis handy—yes,

The tent old and yellowed and patched,
Lit inside by three wire-hung gasoline lamps

That outside, through threadbare canvas, were muted to gold.
Here no carnival now—the tabernacle
To the glory of God the Most High, for now corn
Was laid by, business slack, such business as was, and
The late-season pain gnawing deep at the human bone
As the season burned on to its end.

God's Word and His glory—and I, aged twelve,
Sat there while an ex-railroad engineer
Turned revivalist shouted the Threat and the Promise, with sweat
On his brow, shirt plastered to belly, and
Eyes a-glaze with the mania of joy.

And now by my knees crouched some old-fool dame
In worn-out black silk, there crouching with tears
In her eyes as she tugged me to kneel
And save my pore twelve-year-old soul
Before too late. She wept.
She wept and she prayed, and I knew I was damned,
Who was guilty of all short of murder,
At least in my heart and no alibi there, and once
I had walked down a dark street, lights out in houses,
Uttering, "Lust—lust—lust,"
Like an invocation, out loud—and the word
So lovely, fresh-minted.

I saw others fall as though stricken. I heard
The shout of salvation. I stared
In the red-rimmed, wet eyes of the crazy old dame,
Whose name I never remembered, but knew
That she loved me—the Pore Little Lamb—and I thought
How old bones now creaked in God's name.

But the Pore Little Lamb, he hardened his heart,
Like a flint nigger-head rounded slick in a creek-bed
By generations of flood, and suddenly
I found myself standing, then
Ran down an aisle, and outside,
Where cool air and dark filled my lungs, and fifty
Yards off, with my brow pressed hard
On the scaly bark of a hickory tree,
Vomited. Fumbling

In darkness, I found the spring
And washed my mouth. Humped there,

And knowing damnation, I stared
Through interstices of black brush to the muted gold glow
Of God's canvas, till in
The last hymn of triumph rose voices, and hearts
Burst with joy at amazing grace so freely given,
And moving on into darkness,

Voices sang of amazing grace, singing as they
Straggled back to the village, where voice after voice died away,
As singer by singer, in some dark house,
Found bed and lay down,
And tomorrow would rise and do all the old things to do,
Until that morning they would not rise, not ever.

And now, when all voices were stilled and the lamps
Long out in the tent, and stars
Had changed place in the sky, I yet lay
By the spring with one hand in cold black water
That showed one star in reflection, alone—and lay
Wondering and wondering how many
A morning would I rise up to greet,
And what grace find.

But that was long years ago. I was twelve years old then.

WHAT VOICE AT MOTH-HOUR

What voice at moth-hour did I hear calling
As I stood in the orchard while the white
Petals of apple blossoms were falling,
Whiter than moth-wing in that twilight?

What voice did I hear as I stood by the stream,
Bemused in the murmurous wisdom there uttered,
While ripples at stone, in their steely gleam,
Caught last light before it was shuttered?

What voice did I hear as I wandered alone
In a premature night of cedar, beech, oak,
Each foot set soft, then still as stone
Standing to wait while the first owl spoke?

The voice that I heard once at dew-fall, I now
Can hear by a simple trick. If I close
My eyes, in that dusk I again know
The feel of damp grass between bare toes,

Can see the last zigzag, sky-skittering, high,
Of a bullbat, and even hear, far off, from
Swamp-cover, the whip-o-will, and as I
Once heard, hear the voice: *It's late! Come home.*

VERMONT BALLAD: CHANGE OF SEASON

All day the fitful rain
Had wrought new traceries,
New quirks, new love-knots, down the pane.

And what do I see beyond
That fluctuating gray
But a world that seems to be God-abandoned—

Last leaf, rain-soaked, from my high
Birch falling, the spruce wrapped in thought,
And the mountain dissolving rain-gray to gray sky.

In the gorge, like a maniac
In sleep, the stream grinds its teeth,
As I lay a new log at the fireplace-back.

It is not that I am cold:
But that I think how the flux,
Three quarters now of a century old,

Has faithfully swollen and ebbed,
In life's brilliantly flashing red
Through all flesh, in vein and artery webbed.

But now it feels viscous and gray
As I watch the gray of the world,
And that thought seems soaked in my brain to stay.

But who is master here?
The turn of the season, or I?
What lies in the turn of the season to fear?

If I set muzzle to forehead
And pull the trigger, I'll see
The world in a last flood of vital red—

Not gray—that cataracts down.
No, I go to the windowpane
That rain's blurring tracery claims as its own,

And stare up the mountain track
Till I see in the rain-dusk, trudging
With stolid stride, his bundle on back,

A man with no name, in the gloom,
On an errand I cannot guess.
No sportsman—no! Just a man in his doom.

In this section such a man is not an uncommon sight.
In rain or snow, you pass, and he says: "Kinda rough tonight."

Theodore Roethke

(1908 – 1963)

CUTTINGS

Sticks-in-a-drowse droop over sugary loam,
Their intricate stem-fur dries;
But still the delicate slips keep coaxing up water;
The small cells bulge;

One nub of growth
Nudges a sand-crumb loose,
Pokes through a musty sheath
Its pale tendrilous horn.

CUTTINGS

(Later)

This urge, wrestle, resurrection of dry sticks,
Cut stems struggling to put down feet,
What saint strained so much,
Rose on such lopped limbs to a new life?

I can hear, underground, that sucking and sobbing,
In my veins, in my bones I fee it,—
The small waters seeping upward,
The tight grains parting at last.
When sprouts break out,
Slippery as fish,
I quail, lean to beginnings, sheath-wet.

ROOT CELLAR

Nothing would sleep in that cellar, dank as a ditch,
Bulbs broke out of boxes hunting for chinks in the dark,
Shoots dangled and drooped,
Lolling obscenely from mildewed crates,
Hung down long yellow evil necks, like tropical snakes.
And what a congress of stinks!—
Roots ripe as old bait,
Pulpy stems, rank, silo-rich,
Leaf-mold, manure, lime, piled against slippery planks.
Nothing would give up life:
Even the dirt kept breathing a small breath.

ORCHIDS

They lean over the path,
Adder-mouthed,
Swaying close to the face,
Coming out, soft and deceptive,
Limp and damp, delicate as a young bird's tongue;
Their fluttery fledgling lips
Move slowly,
Drawing in the warm air.

And at night,
The faint moon falling through whitewashed glass,
The heat going down
So their musky smell comes even stronger,
Drifting down from their mossy cradles:
So many devouring infants!
Soft luminescent fingers,
Lips neither dead nor alive,
Loose ghostly mouths
Breathing.

BIG WIND

Where were the greenhouses going,
Lunging into the lashing
Wind driving water
So far down the river
All the faucets stopped?—
So we drained the manure-machine
For the steam plant,
Pumping the stale mixture
Into the rusty boilers,
Watching the pressure gauge
Waver over to red,
As the seams hissed
And the live steam
Drove to the far
End of the rose-house,
Where the worst wind was,
Creaking the cypress window-frames,
Cracking so much thin glass
We stayed all night,
Stuffing the holes with burlap;
But she rode it out,
That old rose-house,
She hove into the teeth of it,
The core and pith of that ugly storm,
Ploughing with her stiff prow,
Bucking into the wind-waves
That broke over the whole of her,
Flailing her sides with spray,
Flinging long strings of wet across the roof-top,
Finally veering, wearing themselves out, merely
Whistling thinly under the wind-vents;
She sailed until the calm morning,
Carrying her full cargo of roses.

MY PAPA'S WALTZ

The whiskey on your breath
Could make a small boy dizzy;
But I hung on like death:
Such waltzing was not easy.

We romped until the pans
Slid from the kitchen shelf;
My mother's countenance
Could not unfrown itself.

The hand that held my wrist
Was battered on one knuckle;
At every step you missed
My right ear scraped a buckle.

You beat time on my head
With a palm caked hard by dirt,
Then waltzed me off to bed
Still clinging to your shirt.

ELEGY FOR JANE

My Student, Thrown by a Horse

I remember the neckcurls, limp and damp as tendrils;
And her quick look, a sidelong pickerel smile;
And how, once startled into talk, the light syllables leaped for her,
And she balanced in the delight of her thought,
A wren, happy, tail into the wind,
Her song trembling the twigs and small branches.
The shade sang with her;
The leaves, their whispers turned to kissing;
And the mold sang in the bleached valleys under the rose.

Oh, when she was sad, she cast herself down into such a pure depth,
Even a father could not find her:

Scraping her cheek against straw;
Stirring the clearest water.

My sparrow, you are not here,
Waiting like a fern, making a spiny shadow.
The sides of wet stones cannot console me,
Nor the moss, wound with the last light.

If only I could nudge you from this sleep,
My maimed darling, my skittery pigeon.
Over this damp grave I speak the words of my love:
I, with no rights in this matter,
Neither father nor lover.

THE FAR FIELD

1

I dream of journeys repeatedly:
Of flying like a bat deep into a narrowing tunnel,
Of driving alone, without luggage, out a long peninsula,
The road lined with snow-laden second growth,
A fine dry snow ticking the windshield,
Alternate snow and sleet, no on-coming traffic,
And no lights behind, in the blurred side-mirror,
The road changing from glazed tarface to a rubble of stone,
Ending at last in a hopeless sand-rut,
Where the car stalls,
Churning in a snowdrift
Until the headlights darken.

2

At the field's end, in the corner missed by the mower,
Where the turf drops off into a grass-hidden culvert,
Haunt of the cat-bird, nesting-place of the field-mouse,
Not too far away from the ever-changing flower-dump,
Among the tin cans, tires, rusted pipes, broken machinery,—
One learned of the eternal;
And in the shrunken face of a dead rat, eaten by rain and ground-beetles
(I found it lying among the rubble of an old coal bin)

And the tom-cat, caught near the pheasant-run,
Its entrails strewn over the half-grown flowers,
Blasted to death by the night watchman.

I suffered for birds, for young rabbits caught in the mower,
My grief was not excessive.
For to come upon warblers in early May
Was to forget time and death:
How they filled the oriole's elm, a twittering restless cloud, all one morning,
And I watched and watched till my eyes blurred from the bird shapes,—
Cape May, Blackburnian, Cerulean,—
Moving, elusive as fish, fearless,
Hanging, bunched like young fruit, bending the end branches,
Still for a moment,
Then pitching away in half-flight,
Lighter than finches,
While the wrens bickered and sang in the half-green hedgerows,
And the flicker drummed from his dead tree in the chicken-yard.

—Or to lie naked in sand,
In the silted shallows of a slow river,
Fingering a shell,
Thinking:
Once I was something like this, mindless,
Or perhaps with another mind, less peculiar;
Or to sink down to the hips in a mossy quagmire;
Or, with skinny knees, to sit astride a wet log,
Believing:
I'll return again,
As a snake or a raucous bird,
Or, with luck, as a lion.

I learned not to fear infinity,
The far field, the windy cliffs of forever,
The dying of time in the white light of tomorrow,
The wheel turning away from itself,
The sprawl of the wave,
The on-coming water.

       3

The river turns on itself,
The tree retreats into its own shadow.
I feel a weightless change, a moving forward

As of water quickening before a narrowing channel
When banks converge, and the wide river whitens;
Or when two rivers combine, the blue glacial torrent
And the yellowish-green from the mountainy upland,—
At first a swift rippling between rocks,
Then a long running over flat stones
Before descending to the alluvial plain,
To the clay banks, and the wild grapes hanging from the elmtrees.
The slightly trembling water
Dropping a fine yellow silt where the sun stays;
And the crabs bask near the edge,
The weedy edge, alive with small snakes and bloodsuckers,—
I have come to a still, but not a deep center,
A point outside the glittering current;
My eyes stare at the bottom of a river,
At the irregular stones, iridescent sandgrains,
My mind moves in more than one place,
In a country half-land, half-water.

I am renewed by death, thought of my death,
The dry scent of a dying garden in September,
The wind fanning the ash of a low fire.
What I love is near at hand,
Always, in earth and air.

        4

The lost self changes,
Turning toward the sea,
A sea-shape turning around,—
An old man with his feet before the fire,
In robes of green, in garments of adieu.

A man faced with his own immensity
Wakes all the waves, all their loose wandering fire.
The murmur of the absolute, the why
Of being born fails on his naked ears.
His spirit moves like monumental wind
That gentles on a sunny blue plateau.
He is the end of things, the final man.

All finite things reveal infinitude:
The mountain with its singular bright shade

Like the blue shine on freshly frozen snow,
The after-light upon ice-burdened pines;
Odor of basswood on a mountain-slope,
A scent beloved of bees;
Silence of water above a sunken tree:
The pure serene of memory in one man,—
A ripple widening from a single stone
Winding around the waters of the world.

Charles Olson

(1910–1970)

From THE MAXIMUS POEMS, BOOK III

POEM 143: THE FESTIVAL ASPECT

The World
has become divided
from the Universe. Put the three Towns
together

The Individual
has become divided
from the Absolute, it is the times promised
by the poets. They shall drop delta
and lingam, all forms
of symbol
and mystery. As well as all
naturalism. And literalness. The truth

is fingers holding it all up
underneath, the Lotus
is a cusp, and its stalk
holds up it all.
It isn't even a burning point, it is a bow
of fingers shooting
a single arrow. The three Towns
are to be destroyed, as well as
that they are to be made known,
that they are to be known,
that there is no three Towns
now, that without three Towns
there is no Society, there is no
known
Absolute: we shall stand on our heads and hands
truly, kicking
all false form off
the surface

of the still, or active,
water-surface. There is no image
which is a reflection. Or a condition. There is solely
the Lotus
upside down. When the World is one again
with the Universal the Flower
will grow down, the Sun
will be stamped
on the leather
like a growing
Coin, the earth
will be the light, the air and the dust
of the air will be the perfume
of sense, the *gloire*
will have returned
of the body seen
against the window. The flesh
will glow.
                    The three Towns
will have become populated
again. In the first Town
somebody will have addressed
themselves
to someone else. There will be no need
of the explicit. In the second Town
the earth
will have replaced
the sun. In the third Town the man
shall have arisen, he shall have concluded
any use of reason, the Dialogue
will have re-begun. The earth
shall have preceded love. The sun
shall have given back its deadly
rays, there shall be no longer any
need to be so careful. The third Town
shall have revealed
itself.

The third Town
is the least known. The third Town
is the one which is the most interesting—and is overpopulated—
behind the Western
sun. It shall only come forth

from underneath. The foot of the Lotus
is not its face, but the roots
of its stalk. The Elephant
moves easily
through any trees. He is Ganesh
with the big Hands. His hands alone
offer all. Through the mountain
through the bole
of any tree through the adamantine
he passes
as though it were nothing. Only the God Himself
of whom he is the frazzled stalk
in each of the coolness, and ease, of his power
is more than water. Water is not equal
          to the
          Flower. The three Towns
          are the fairest
          which the Flower
          is. Only when the Flower—only when the uproar
          has driven the Soul
          out of me, only then shall the God
          strike
          the three Towns. The three Towns
          shall first
          be born again. The Flower shall
          grow down. The mud of the bottom
          is the floor
          of the Upside Down. The present
          is an uproar, the present
          is the times of the re-birth of
          the Lotus. Ganesh
          is walking
          through anything. There is no obs-
          tacle. There will be no more
          anger. There is only one
          anyway. It is too early
          for anger. The third Town
          has only just
          begun.

Josephine Miles

(1 9 1 1 – 1 9 8 5)

BELIEF

Mother said to call her if the H bomb exploded
And I said I would, and it about did
When Louis my brother robbed a service station
And lay cursing on the oily cement in handcuffs.

But by that time it was too late to tell Mother,
She was too sick to worry the life out of her
Over *why why*. Causation is sequence
And everything is one thing after another.

Besides, my other brother, Eddie, had got to be President,
And you can't ask too much of one family.
The chances were as good for a good future
As bad for a bad one.

Therefore it was surprising that, as we kept the newspapers from
                                                    Mother,
She died feeling responsible for a disaster unverified,
Murmuring, in her sleep as it seemed, the ancient slogan
Noblesse oblige.

CONCEPTION

Death did not come to my mother
Like an old friend.
She was a mother, and she must
Conceive him.

Up and down the bed she fought crying
Help me, but death

Was a slow child
Heavy. He
Waited. When he was born
We took and tired him, now he is ready
To do his good in the world.

He has my mother's features.
He can go among strangers
To save lives.

ALBUM

This is a hard life you are living
While you are young,
My father said,
As I scratched my casted knees with a paper knife.
By laws of compensation
Your old age should be grand.

Not grand, but of a terrible
Compensation, to perceive
Past the energy of survival
In its sadness
The hard life of the young.

Elizabeth Bishop

(1911 – 1979)

SEASCAPE

This celestial seascape, with white herons got up as angels,
flying as high as they want and as far as they want sidewise
in tiers and tiers of immaculate reflections;
the whole region, from the highest heron
down to the weightless mangrove island
with bright green leaves edged neatly with bird-droppings
like illumination in silver,
and down to the suggestively Gothic arches of the mangrove roots
and the beautiful pea-green back-pasture
where occasionally a fish jumps, like a wild-flower
in an ornamental spray of spray;
this cartoon by Raphael for a tapestry for a Pope:
it does look like heaven.
But a skeletal lighthouse standing there
in black and white clerical dress,
who lives on his nerves, thinks he knows better.
He thinks that hell rages below his iron feet,
that that is why the shallow water is so warm,
and he knows that heaven is not like this.
Heaven is not like flying or swimming,
but has something to do with blackness and a strong glare
and when it gets dark he will remember something
strongly worded to say on the subject.

A COLD SPRING

For Jane Dewey, Maryland

> Nothing is so beautiful as spring.
> Hopkins

A cold spring:
the violet was flawed on the lawn.

For two weeks or more the trees hesitated;
the little leaves waited,
carefully indicating their characteristics.
Finally a grave green dust
settled over your big and aimless hills.
One day, in a chill white blast of sunshine,
on the side of one a calf was born.
The mother stopped lowing
and took a long time eating the after-birth,
a wretched flag,
but the calf got up promptly
and seemed inclined to feel gay.

The next day
was much warmer.
Greenish-white dogwood infiltrated the wood,
each petal burned, apparently, by a cigarette-butt;
and the blurred redbud stood
beside it, motionless, but almost more
like movement than any placeable color.
Four deer practised leaping over your fences.
The infant oak-leaves swung through the sober oak.
Song-sparrows were wound up for the summer,
and in the maple the complementary cardinal
cracked a whip, and the sleeper awoke,
stretching miles of green limbs from the south.
In his cap the lilacs whitened,
then one day they fell like snow.
Now, in the evening,
a new moon comes.
The hills grow softer. Tufts of long grass show
where each cow-flop lies.
The bull-frogs are sounding,
slack strings plucked by heavy thumbs.
Beneath the light, against your white front door,
the smallest moths, like Chinese fans,
flatten themselves, silver and silver-gilt
over pale yellow, orange, or gray.
Now, from the thick grass, the fireflies
begin to rise:
up, then down, then up again:
lit on the ascending flight,
drifting simultaneously to the same height,

—exactly like the bubbles in champagne.
—Later on they rise much higher.
And your shadowy pastures will be able to offer
these particular glowing tributes
every evening now throughout the summer.

THE MAP

Land lies in water; it is shadowed green.
Shadows, or are they shallows, at its edges
showing the line of long sea-weeded ledges
where weeds hang to the simple blue from green.
Or does the land lean down to lift the sea from under,
drawing it unperturbed around itself?
Along the fine tan sandy shelf
is the land tugging at the sea from under?

The shadow of Newfoundland lies flat and still.
Labrador's yellow, where the moony Eskimo
has oiled it. We can stroke these lovely bays,
under a glass as if they were expected to blossom,
or as if to provide a clean cage for invisible fish.
The names of seashore towns run out to sea,
the names of cities cross the neighboring mountains
—the printer here experiencing the same excitement
as when emotion too far exceeds its cause.
These peninsulas take the water between thumb and finger
like women feeling for the smoothness of yard-goods.

Mapped waters are more quiet than the land is,
lending the land their waves' own conformation:
and Norway's hare runs south in agitation,
profiles investigate the sea, where land is.
Are they assigned, or can the countries pick their colors?
—What suits the character or the native waters best.
Topography displays no favorites; North's as near as West.
More delicate than the historians' are the map-makers' colors.

LITTLE EXERCISE

Think of the storm roaming the sky uneasily
like a dog looking for a place to sleep in,
listen to it growling.

Think how they must look now, the mangrove keys
lying out there unresponsive to the lightning
in dark, coarse-fibred families,

where occasionally a heron may undo his head,
shake up his feathers, make an uncertain comment
when the surrounding water shines.

Think of the boulevard and the little palm trees
all stuck in rows, suddenly revealed
as fistfuls of limp fish-skeletons.

It is raining there. The boulevard
and its broken sidewalks with weeds in every crack,
are relieved to be wet, the sea to be freshened.

Now the storm goes away again in a series
of small, badly lit battle-scenes,
each in "Another part of the field."

Think of someone sleeping in the bottom of a row-boat
tied to a mangrove root or the pile of a bridge;
think of him as uninjured, barely disturbed.

IN THE WAITING ROOM

In Worcester, Massachusetts,
I went with Aunt Consuelo
to keep her dentist's appointment
and sat and waited for her
in the dentist's waiting room.

It was winter. It got dark
early. The waiting room
was full of grown-up people,
arctics and overcoats,
lamps and magazines.
My aunt was inside
what seemed like a long time
and while I waited I read
the *National Geographic*
(I could read) and carefully
studied the photographs:
The inside of a volcano,
black, and full of ashes;
then it was spilling over
in rivulets of fire.
Osa and Martin Johnson
dressed in riding breeches,
laced boots, and pith helmets.
A dead man slung on a pole
—"Long Pig," the caption said.
Babies with pointed heads
wound round and round with string;
black, naked women with necks
wound round and round with wire
like the necks of light bulbs.
Their breasts were horrifying.
I read it right straight through.
I was too shy to stop.
And then I looked at the cover:
the yellow margins, the date.

Suddenly, from inside,
came an *oh!* of pain
—Aunt Consuelo's voice—
not very loud or long.
I wasn't at all surprised;
even then I knew she was
a foolish, timid woman.
I might have been embarrassed,
but wasn't. What took me
completely by surprise
was that it was *me*:
my voice, in my mouth.

Without thinking at all
I was my foolish aunt,
I—we—were falling, falling,
our eyes glued to the cover
of the *National Geographic*,
February, 1918.

I said to myself: three days
and you'll be seven years old.
I was saying it to stop
the sensation of falling off
the round, turning world
into cold, blue-black space.
But I felt: you are an *I*,
you are an *Elizabeth*,
you are one of *them*.
Why should you be one, too?
I scarcely dared to look
to see what it was I was.
I gave a sidelong glance
—I couldn't look any higher—
at shadowy gray knees,
trousers and skirts and boots
and different pairs of hands
lying under the lamps.
I knew that nothing stranger
had ever happened, that nothing
stranger could ever happen.

THE ARMADILLO

For Robert Lowell

This is the time of year
when almost every night
the frail, illegal fire balloons appear.
Climbing the mountain height,

rising toward a saint
still honored in these parts,

the paper chambers flush and fill with light
that comes and goes, like hearts.

Once up against the sky it's hard
to tell them from the stars—
planets, that is—the tinted ones:
Venus going down, or Mars,

or the pale green one. With a wind,
they flare and falter, wobble and toss;
but if it's still they steer between
the kite sticks of the Southern Cross,

receding, dwindling, solemnly
and steadily forsaking us,
or, in the downdraft from a peak,
suddenly turning dangerous.

Last night another big one fell.
It splattered like an egg of fire
against the cliff behind the house.
The flame ran down. We saw the pair

of owls who nest there flying up
and up, their whirling black-and-white
stained bright pink underneath, until
they shrieked up out of sight.

The ancient owls' nest must have burned.
Hastily, all alone,
a glistening armadillo left the scene,
rose-flecked, head down, tail down,

and then a baby rabbit jumped out,
short-eared, to our surprise.
So soft!—a handful of intangible ash
with fixed, ignited eyes.

Too pretty, dreamlike mimicry!
O falling fire and piercing cry
and panic, and a weak mailed fist
clenched ignorant against the sky!

QUESTIONS OF TRAVEL

There are too many waterfalls here; the crowded streams
hurry too rapidly down to the sea,
and the pressure of so many clouds on the mountaintops
makes them spill over the sides in soft slow-motion,
turning to waterfalls under our very eyes.
—For if those streaks, those mile-long, shiny, tearstains,
aren't waterfalls yet,
in a quick age or so, as ages go here,
they probably will be.
But if the streams and clouds keep travelling, travelling,
the mountains look like the hulls of capsized ships,
slime-hung and barnacled.

Think of the long trip home.
Should we have stayed at home and thought of here?
Where should we be today?
Is it right to be watching strangers in a play
in this strangest of theatres?
What childishness is it that while there's a breath of life
in our bodies, we are determined to rush
to see the sun the other way around?
The tiniest green hummingbird in the world?
To stare at some inexplicable old stonework,
inexplicable and impenetrable,
at any view,
instantly seen and always, always delightful?
Oh, must we dream our dreams
and have them, too?
And have we room
for one more folded sunset, still quite warm?

But surely it would have been a pity
not to have seen the trees along this road,
really exaggerated in their beauty,
not to have seen them gesturing
like noble pantomimists, robed in pink.
—Not to have had to stop for gas and heard
the sad, two-noted, wooden tune

of disparate wooden clogs
carelessly clacking over
a grease-stained filling-station floor.
(In another country the clogs would all be tested.
Each pair there would have identical pitch.)
—A pity not to have heard
the other, less primitive music of the fat brown bird
who sings above the broken gasoline pump
in a bamboo church of Jesuit baroque:
three towers, five silver crosses.
—Yes, a pity not to have pondered,
blurr'dly and inconclusively,
on what connection can exist for centuries
between the crudest wooden footwear
and, careful and finicky,
the whittled fantasies of wooden cages.
—Never to have studied history in
the weak calligraphy of songbird's cages.
—And never to have had to listen to rain
so much like politicians' speeches:
two hours of unrelenting oratory
and then a sudden golden silence
in which the traveller takes a notebook, writes:

"Is it lack of imagination that makes us come
to imagined places, not just stay at home?
Or could Pascal have been not entirely right
about just sitting quietly in one's room?

Continent, city, country, society:
the choice is never wide and never free.
And here, or there .. No. Should we have stayed at home,
wherever that may be?"

Muriel Rukeyser

(1913–1980)

IRIS

I

Middle of May, when the iris blows,
blue below blue, the bearded patriarch-
face on the green flute body of a boy
Poseidon   torso of Eros
blue
sky below sea
day over daybreak violet behind twilight
the May iris
midnight on midday

II

Something is over and under this deep blue.
Over and under this movement, *etwas*
before and after, *alguna cosa*
blue before blue
is it
       perhaps
              death?
That may be the wrong word.

The iris stands in the light.

III

Death is here, death is guarded by swords.
No. By shapes of swords
flicker of green leaves
under all the speaking and crying
shadowing the words the eyes   here they all die
racing withering   blue evening
my sister death the iris
stands clear in light.

IV

In the water-cave
ferocious needles of teeth
the green morays
in blue water   rays
a maleficence   ribbon of green   the flat look of
eyes staring   fatal mouth staring
the rippling potent force
curving into any hole
death finding his way.

V

Depth of petals, May iris
transparent   infinitely deep they are
petal-thin   with light behind them
and you, death,
and you
behind them
blue under blue.
What I cannot say
in adequate music
something being born
transparency   blue of
light standing on light
this stalk of
(among mortal petals-and-leaves)
light

THEN I SAW WHAT THE CALLING WAS

All the voices of the wood called "Muriel!"
but it was soon solved; it was nothing, it was not for me.
The words were a little like Mortal and More and Endure
and a word like Real, a sound like Health or Hell.
Then I saw what the calling was   :   it was the road I traveled,
                                                            the clear
time and these colors of orchards, gold behind gold and the full
shadow behind each tree and behind each slope.   Not to me

the calling, but to anyone, and at last I saw   :   where
the road lay through sunlight and many voices and the marvel
orchards, not for me, not for me, not for me.
I came into my clear being;   uncalled, alive, and sure.
Nothing was speaking to me, but I offered and all was well.

And then I arrived at the powerful green hill.

Robert Hayden

(1913 – 1980)

NIGHT, DEATH, MISSISSIPPI

I

A quavering cry. Screech-owl?
Or one of them?
The old man in his reek
and gauntness laughs—

One of them, I bet—
and turns out the kitchen lamp,
limping to the porch to listen
in the windowless night.

Be there with Boy and the rest
if I was well again.
Time was. Time was.
White robes like moonlight

In the sweetgum dark.
Unbucked that one then
and him squealing bloody Jesus
as we cut it off.

Time was. A cry?
A cry all right.
He hawks and spits,
fevered as by groinfire.

Have us a bottle,
Boy and me—
he's earned him a bottle—
when he gets home.

II

Then we beat them, he said,
beat them till our arms was tired

and the big old chains
messy and red.

O Jesus burning on the lily cross

Christ, it was better
than hunting bear
which don't know why
you want him dead.

O night, rawhead and bloodybones night

You kids fetch Paw
some water now so's he
can wash that blood
off him, she said.

O night betrayed by darkness not its own

A ROAD IN KENTUCKY

And when that ballad lady went
        to ease the lover whose life she broke,
oh surely this is the road she took,
        road all hackled through barberry fire,
through cedar and alder and sumac and thorn.

Red clay stained her flounces
        and stones cut her shoes
and the road twisted on to his loveless house
        and his cornfield dying
in the scarecrow's arms.

And when she had left her lover lying
        so stark and so stark, with the Star-of-Hope
drawn over his eyes, oh this is the road
        that lady walked in the cawing light,
so dark and so dark in the briary light.

THOSE WINTER SUNDAYS

Sundays too my father got up early
and put his clothes on in the blueblack cold,
then with cracked hands that ached
from labor in the weekday weather made
banked fires blaze. No one ever thanked him.

I'd wake and hear the cold splintering, breaking.
When the rooms were warm, he'd call,
and slowly I would rise and dress,
fearing the chronic angers of that house,

Speaking indifferently to him,
who had driven out the cold
and polished my good shoes as well.
What did I know, what did I know
of love's austere and lonely offices?

MIDDLE PASSAGE

I

Jesús, Estrella, Esperanza, Mercy:

      Sails flashing to the wind like weapons,
      sharks following the moans the fever and the dying;
      horror the corposant and compass rose.

Middle Passage:
          voyage through death
                    to life upon these shores.

      "10 April 1800—
      Blacks rebellious. Crew uneasy. Our linguist says
      their moaning is a prayer for death,
      ours and their own. Some try to starve themselves.
      Lost three this morning leaped with crazy laughter
      to the waiting sharks, sang as they went under."

Desire, Adventure, Tartar, Ann:

> Standing to America, bringing home
> black gold, black ivory, black seed.

>> *Deep in the festering hold thy father lies,*
>> *of his bones New England pews are made,*
>> *those are altar lights that were his eyes.*

Jesus   Saviour   Pilot   Me
Over   Life's   Tempestuous   Sea

We pray that Thou wilt grant, O Lord,
safe passage to our vessels bringing
heathen souls unto Thy chastening.

Jesus   Saviour

> "8 bells. I cannot sleep, for I am sick
> with fear, but writing eases fear a little
> since still my eyes can see these words take shape
> upon the page & so I write, as one
> would turn to exorcism. 4 days scudding,
> but now the sea is calm again. Misfortune
> follows in our wake like sharks (our grinning
> tutelary gods). Which one of us
> has killed an albatross? A plague among
> our blacks—Ophthalmia: blindness—& we
> have jettisoned the blind to no avail.
> It spreads, the terrifying sickness spreads.
> Its claws have scratched sight from the Capt.'s eyes
> & there is blindness in the fo'c'sle
> & we must sail 3 weeks before we come
> to port."

>> *What port awaits us, Davy Jones'*
>> *or home? I've heard of slavers drifting, drifting,*
>> *playthings of wind and storm and chance, their crews*
>> *gone blind, the jungle hatred*
>> *crawling up on deck.*

Thou   Who   Walked   On   Galilee

"Deponent further sayeth *The Bella J*
left the Guinea Coast
with cargo of five hundred blacks and odd
for the barracoons of Florida:

"That there was hardly room 'tween-decks for half
the sweltering cattle stowed spoon-fashion there;
that some went mad of thirst and tore their flesh
and sucked the blood:

"That Crew and Captain lusted with the comeliest
of the savage girls kept naked in the cabins;
that there was one they called The Guinea Rose
and they cast lots and fought to lie with her:

"That when the Bo's'n piped all hands, the flames
spreading from starboard already were beyond
control, the negroes howling and their chains
entangled with the flames:

"That the burning blacks could not be reached,
that the Crew abandoned ship,
leaving their shrieking negresses behind,
that the Captain perished drunken with the wenches:

"Further Deponent sayeth not."

Pilot   Oh   Pilot   Me

          II

Aye, lad, and I have seen those factories,
Gambia, Rio Pongo, Calabar;
have watched the artful mongos baiting traps
of war wherein the victor and the vanquished

Were caught as prizes for our barracoons.
Have seen the nigger kings whose vanity
and greed turned wild black hides of Fellatah,
Mandingo, Ibo, Kru to gold for us.

And there was one—King Anthracite we named him—
fetish face beneath French parasols

of brass and orange velvet, impudent mouth
whose cups were carven skulls of enemies:

He'd honor us with drum and feast and conjo
and palm-oil-glistening wenches deft in love,
and for tin crowns that shone with paste,
red calico and German-silver trinkets

Would have the drums talk war and send
his warriors to burn the sleeping villages
and kill the sick and old and lead the young
in coffles to our factories.

Twenty years a trader, twenty years,
for there was wealth aplenty to be harvested
from those black fields, and I'd be trading still
but for the fevers melting down my bones.

    III

Shuttles in the rocking loom of history,
the dark ships move, the dark ships move,
their bright ironical names
like jests of kindness on a murderer's mouth;
plough through thrashing glister toward
fata morgana's lucent melting shore,
weave toward New World littorals that are
mirage and myth and actual shore.

Voyage through death,
                      voyage whose chartings are unlove.

A charnel stench, effluvium of living death
spreads outward from the hold,
where the living and the dead, the horribly dying,
lie interlocked, lie foul with blood and excrement.

Deep in the festering hold thy father lies,
the corpse of mercy rots with him,
rats eat love's rotten gelid eyes.

But, oh, the living look at you
with human eyes whose suffering accuses you,

whose hatred reaches through the swill of dark
to strike you like a leper's claw.

You cannot stare that hatred down
or chain the fear that stalks the watches
and breathes on you its fetid scorching breath;
cannot kill the deep immortal human wish,
the timeless will.

> "But for the storm that flung up barriers
> of wind and wave, *The Amistad*, señores,
> would have reached the port of Príncipe in two,
> three days at most; but for the storm we should
> have been prepared for what befell.
> Swift as the puma's leap it came. There was
> that interval of moonless calm filled only
> with the water's and the rigging's usual sounds,
> then sudden movement, blows and snarling cries
> and they had fallen on us with machete
> and marlinspike. It was as though the very
> air, the night itself were striking us.
> Exhausted by the rigors of the storm,
> we were no match for them. Our men went down
> before the murderous Africans. Our loyal
> Celestino ran from below with gun
> and lantern and I saw, before the cane-
> knife's wounding flash, Cinquez,
> that surly brute who calls himself a prince,
> directing, urging on the ghastly work.
> He hacked the poor mulatto down, and then
> he turned on me. The decks were slippery
> when daylight finally came. It sickens me
> to think of what I saw, of how these apes
> threw overboard the butchered bodies of
> our men, true Christians all, like so much jetsam.
> Enough, enough. The rest is quickly told:
> Cinquez was forced to spare the two of us
> you see to steer the ship to Africa,
> and we like phantoms doomed to rove the sea
> voyaged east by day and west by night,
> deceiving them, hoping for rescue,
> prisoners on our own vessel, till
> at length we drifted to the shores of this

your land, America, where we were freed
from our unspeakable misery. Now we
demand, good sirs, the extradition of
Cinquez and his accomplices to La
Havana. And it distresses us to know
there are so many here who seem inclined
to justify the mutiny of these blacks.
We find it paradoxical indeed
that you whose wealth, whose tree of liberty
are rooted in the labor of your slaves
should suffer the august John Quincy Adams
to speak with so much passion of the right
of chattel slaves to kill their lawful masters
and with his Roman rhetoric weave a hero's
garland for Cinquez. I tell you that
we are determined to return to Cuba
with our slaves and there see justice done. Cinquez—
or let us say 'the Prince'—Cinquez shall die."

The deep immortal human wish,
the timeless will:

    Cinquez its deathless primaveral image,
    life that transfigures many lives.

Voyage through death
                 to life upon these shores.

Delmore Schwartz

(1913–1966)

THE HEAVY BEAR WHO GOES WITH ME

The Withness of the Body

The heavy bear who goes with me,
A manifold honey to smear his face,
Clumsy and lumbering here and there,
The central ton of every place,
The hungry beating brutish one
In love with candy, anger, and sleep,
Crazy factotum, dishevelling all,
Climbs the building, kicks the football,
Boxes his brother in the hate-ridden city.

Breathing at my side, that heavy animal,
That heavy bear who sleeps with me,
Howls in his sleep for a world of sugar,
A sweetness intimate as the water's clasp,
Howls in his sleep because the tight-rope
Trembles and shows the darkness beneath.
—The strutting show-off is terrified,
Dressed in his dress-suit, bulging his pants,
Trembles to think that his quivering meat
Must finally wince to nothing at all.

That inescapable animal walks with me,
Has followed me since the black womb held,
Moves where I move, distorting my gesture,
A caricature, a swollen shadow,
A stupid clown of the spirit's motive,
Perplexes and affronts with his own darkness,
The secret life of belly and bone,
Opaque, too near, my private, yet unknown,
Stretches to embrace the very dear
With whom I would walk without him near,
Touches her grossly, although a word

Would bare my heart and make me clear,
Stumbles, flounders, and strives to be fed
Dragging me with him in his mouthing care,
Amid the hundred million of his kind,
The scrimmage of appetite everywhere.

William Stafford

(1914 – 1993)

TRAVELING THROUGH THE DARK

Traveling through the dark I found a deer
dead on the edge of the Wilson River road.
It is usually best to roll them into the canyon:
that road is narrow; to swerve might make more dead.

By glow of the tail-light I stumbled back of the car
and stood by the heap, a doe, a recent killing;
she had stiffened already, almost cold.
I dragged her off; she was large in the belly.

My fingers touching her side brought me the reason—
her side was warm; her fawn lay there waiting,
alive, still, never to be born.
Beside that mountain road I hesitated.

The car aimed ahead its lowered parking lights;
under the hood purred the steady engine.
I stood in the glare of the warm exhaust turning red;
around our group I could hear the wilderness listen.

I thought hard for us all—my only swerving—,
then pushed her over the edge into the river.

THE RESCUED YEAR

Take a model of the world so big
it is the world again, pass your hand,
press back that area in the west where no one lived,
the place only your mind explores. On your thumb
that smudge becomes my ignorance, a badge

the size of Colorado: toward that state by train
we crossed our state like birds and lodged—
the year my sister gracefully
grew up—against the western boundary
where my father had a job.

Time should go the way it went
that year: we weren't at war; we had
each day a treasured unimportance;
the sky existed, so did our town;
the library had books we hadn't read;
every day at school we learned and sang,
or at least hummed and walked in the hall.

In church I heard the preacher; he said
"Honor!" with a sound like empty silos
repeating the lesson. For a minute I held
Kansas Christian all along the Santa Fe.
My father's mean attention, though, was busy—this
I knew—and going home his wonderfully level gaze
would hold the state I liked, where little happened
and much was understood. I watched my father's finger
mark off huge eye-scans of what happened in the creed.

Like him, I tried. I still try,
send my sight like a million pickpockets
up rich people's drives; it is time
when I pass for every place I go to be alive.
Around any corner my sight is a river,
and I let it arrive: rich by those brooks
his thought poured for hours
into my hand. His creed: the greatest ownership
of all is to glance around and understand.

That Christmas Mother made paper
presents; we colored them with crayons
and hung up a tumbleweed for a tree.
A man from Hugoton brought my sister
a present (his farm was tilted near oil
wells; his car ignored the little
bumps along our drive: nothing
came of all this—it was just part of the year).

I walked out where a girl I knew would be;
we crossed the plank over the ditch
to her house. There was popcorn on the stove,
and her mother recalled the old days, inviting me back.
When I walked home in the cold evening,
snow that blessed the wheat had roved
along the highway seeking furrows,
and all the houses had their lights—
oh, that year did not escape me: I rubbed
the wonderful old lamp of our dull town.

That spring we crossed the state again,
my father soothing us with stories:
the river lost in Utah, underground—
"They've explored only the ones they've found!"—
and that old man who spent his life knowing,
unable to tell how he knew—
"I've been sure by smoke, persuaded
by mist, or a cloud, or a name:
once the truth was ready"—my father smiled
at this—"it didn't care how it came."

In all his ways I hold that rescued year—
comes that smoke like love into the broken
coal, that forms to chunks again and lies
in the earth again in its dim folds, and comes a sound,
then shapes to make a whistle fade,
and in the quiet I hold no need, no hurry:
any day the dust will move, maybe settle;
the train that left will roll back into our station,
the name carved on the platform unfill with rain,
and the sound that followed the couplings back
will ripple forward and hold the train.

AT THE BOMB TESTING SITE

At noon in the desert a panting lizard
waited for history, its elbows tense,
watching the curve of a particular road
as if something might happen.

It was looking for something farther off
than people could see, an important scene
acted in stone for little selves
at the flute end of consequences.

There was just a continent without much on it
under a sky that never cared less.

John Berryman

(1914 – 1972)

From HOMAGE TO MISTRESS BRADSTREET [42–57]

When by me in the dusk my child sits down
I am myself. Simon, if that's loose,
let me wiggle it out.
You'll get a bigger one there, and bite.
How they loft, how their sizes delight and grate.
The proportioned, spiritless poems accumulate.
And they publish them
away in brutish London, for a hollow crown.

Father is not himself. He keeps his bed,
and threw a saffron scum Thursday. God-forsaken words
escaped him raving. Save,
Lord, thy servant zealous & just.
Sam he saw back from Harvard. He did scold
his secting enemies. His stomach is cold
while we drip, while
my baby John breaks out. O far from where he bred!

Bone of moaning: sung Where he has gone
a thousand summers by truth-hallowed souls;
be still. Agh, he is gone!
Where? I know. Beyond the shoal.
Still-all a Christian daughter grinds her teeth
a little. This our land has ghosted with
our dead: I am at home.
Finish, Lord, in me this work thou hast begun.

And they tower, whom the pear-tree lured
to let them fall, fierce mornings they reclined
down the brook-bank to the east
fishing for shiners with a crookt pin,
wading, dams massing, well, and Sam's to be
a doctor in Boston. After the divisive sea,

544

and death's first feast,
and the galled effort on the wilderness endured,

Arminians, and the King bore against us;
of an "inward light" we hear with horror.
Whose fan is in his hand
and he will throughly purge his floor,
come towards mé. I have what licks the joints
and bites the heart, which winter more appoints.
Iller I, oftener.
Hard at the outset; in the ending thus hard, thus?

Sacred & unutterable Mind
flashing thorough the universe one thought,
I do wait without peace.
In the article of death I budge.
Eat my sore breath, Black Angel. Let me die.
Body a-drain, when will you be dry
and countenance my speed
to Heaven's springs? lest stricter writhings have me declined.

"What are those pictures in the air at night,
Mother?" Mercy did ask. Space charged with faces
day & night! I place
a goatskin's fetor, and sweat: fold me
in savoury arms. Something is shaking, wrong.
He smells the musket and lifts it. It is long.
It points at my heart.
Missed he must have. In the gross storm of sunlight

I sniff a fire burning without outlet,
consuming acrid its own smoke. It's me.
Ruined laughter sounds
outside. Ah but I waken, free.
And so I am about again. I hagged
a fury at the short maid, whom tongues tagged,
and I am sorry. Once
less I was anxious when more passioned to upset

the mansion & the garden & the beauty of God.
Insectile unreflective busyness
blunts & does amend.

Hangnails, piles, fibs, life's also.
But we are that from which draws back a thumb.
The seasons stream and, somehow, I am become
an old woman. It's so:
I look. I bear to look. Strokes once more his rod.

My window gives on the graves, in our great new house
(how many burned?) upstairs, among the elms.
I lie, & endure, & wonder.
A haze slips sometimes over my dreams
and holiness on horses' bells shall stand.
Wandering pacemaker, unsteadying friend,
in a redskin calm I wait:
beat when you will our end. Sinkings & droopings drowse.

They say thro' the fading winter Dorothy fails,
my second, who than I bore one more, nine;
and I see her inearthed. I linger.
Seaborn she wed knelt before Simon;
Simon I, and linger. Black-yellow seething, vast
it lies fròm me, mine: all they look aghast.
It will be a glorious arm.
Docile I watch. My wreckt chest hurts when Simon pales.

In the yellowing days your faces wholly fail,
at Fall's onset. Solemn voices fade.
I feel no coverlet.
Light notes leap, a beckon, swaying
the tilted sickening ear within. I'll—I'll—
I am closed & coming. Somewhere! I defile
wide as a cloud, in a cloud,
unfit, desirous, glad—even the singings veil—

—You are not ready? You are ready. Pass,
as shadow gathers shadow in the welling night.
Fireflies of childhood torch
you down. We commit our sister down.
One candle mourn by, which a lover gave,
the use's edge and order of her grave.
Quiet? Moisture shoots.
Hungry throngs collect. They sword into the carcass.

Headstones stagger under great draughts of time
after heads pass out, and their world must reel

speechless, blind in the end
about its chilling star: thrift tuft,
whin cushion—nothing. Already with the wounded flying
dark air fills, I am a closet of secrets dying,
races murder, foxholes hold men,
reactor piles wage slow upon the wet brain rime.

I must pretend to leave you. Only you draw off
a benevolent phantom. I say you seem to me
drowned towns off England,
featureless as those myriads
who what bequeathed save fire-ash, fossils, burled
in the open river-drifts of the Old World?
Simon lived on for years.
I renounce not even ragged glances, small teeth, nothing,

O all your ages at the mercy of my loves
together lie at once, forever or
so long as I happen.
In the rain of pain & departure, still
Love has no body and presides the sun,
and elfs from silence melody. I run.
Hover, utter, still,
a sourcing whom my lost candle like the firefly loves.

From THE DREAM SONGS

1

Huffy Henry hid the day,
unappeasable Henry sulked.
I see his point,—a trying to put things over.
It was the thought that they thought
they could *do* it made Henry wicked & away.
But he should have come out and talked.

All the world like a woolen lover
once did seem on Henry's side.
Then came a departure.
Thereafter nothing fell out as it might or ought.

I don't see how Henry, pried
open for all the world to see, survived.

What he has now to say is a long
wonder the world can bear & be.
Once in a sycamore I was glad
all at the top, and I sang.
Hard on the land wears the strong sea
and empty grows every bed.

     4

Filling her compact & delicious body
with chicken páprika, she glanced at me
twice.
Fainting with interest, I hungered back
and only the fact of her husband & four other people
kept me from springing on her

or falling at her little feet and crying
"You are the hottest one for years of night
Henry's dazed eyes
have enjoyed, Brilliance." I advanced upon
(despairing) my spumoni.—Sir Bones: is stuffed,
de world, wif feeding girls.

—Black hair, complexion Latin, jewelled eyes
downcast . . . The slob beside her feasts . . . What wonders is
she sitting on, over there?
The restaurant buzzes. She might as well be on Mars.
Where did it all go wrong? There ought to be a law against Henry.
—Mr. Bones: there is.

     5

Henry sats in de bar & was odd,
off in the glass from the glass,
at odds wif de world & its god,
his wife is a complete nothing,
St Stephen
getting even.

Henry sats in de plane & was gay.
Careful Henry nothing said aloud

but where a Virgin out of cloud
to her Mountain dropt in light,
his thought made pockets & the plane buckt.
"Parm me, lady." "Orright."

Henry lay in de netting, wild,
while the brainfever bird did scales;
Mr. Heartbreak, the New Man,
come to farm a crazy land;
an image of the dead on the fingernail
of a newborn child.

14

Life, friends, is boring. We must not say so.
After all, the sky flashes, the great sea yearns,
we ourselves flash and yearn,
and moreover my mother told me as a boy
(repeatingly) "Ever to confess you're bored
means you have no

Inner Resources." I conclude now I have no
inner resources, because I am heavy bored.
Peoples bore me,
literature bores me, especially great literature,
Henry bores me, with his plights & gripes
as bad as achilles,

who loves people and valiant art, which bores me.
And the tranquil hills, & gin, look like a drag
and somehow a dog
has taken itself & its tail considerably away
into mountains or sea or sky, leaving
behind: me, wag.

HENRY'S FATE

All projects failed, in the August afternoon
he lay & cursed himself & cursed his lot
like Housman's lad forsooth.

A breeze sometimes came by. His sunburn itcht.
His wife was out on errands. He sighed & scratcht.
The little girls were fiddling with the telephone.

They wanted candy, the which he gave them.
His entire soul contorted with the phlegm.
The sun burned down.
Photos of him in despair flooded the town
or city. Mourned his many friends, or so.
The little girls were fiddling with the piano.

He crusht a cigarette out. Crusht him out
surprising God, at last, in a wink of time.
His soul was forwarded.
Adressat unbekannt. The little girls with a shout
welcomed the dazzling package. 'n official rime
the official verdict was: dead.

Randall Jarrell

(1 9 1 4 – 1 9 6 5)

THE DEATH OF THE BALL TURRET GUNNER

From my mother's sleep I fell into the State,
And I hunched in its belly till my wet fur froze.
Six miles from earth, loosed from its dream of life,
I woke to black flak and the nightmare fighters.
When I died they washed me out of the turret with a hose.

THE KNIGHT, DEATH, AND THE DEVIL

Cowhorn-crowned, shockheaded, cornshuck-bearded,
Death is a scarecrow—his death's-head a teetotum
That tilts up toward man confidentially
But trimmed with adders; ringlet-maned, rope-bridled,
The mare he rides crops herbs beside a skull.
He holds up, warning, the crossed cones of time:
Here, narrowing into now, the Past and Future
Are quicksand.
            A hoofed pikeman trots behind.
His pike's claw-hammer mocks—in duplicate, inverted—
The pocked, ribbed, soaring crescent of his horn.
A scapegoat aged into a steer; boar-snouted;
His great limp ears stuck sidelong out in air;
A dewlap bunched at his breast; a ram's-horn wound
Beneath each ear; a spur licked up and out
From the hide of his forehead; bat-winged, but in bone;
His eye a ring inside a ring inside a ring
That leers up, joyless, vile, in meek obscenity—
This is the devil. Flesh to flesh, he bleats
The herd back to the pit of being.
In fluted mail; upon his lance the bush
Of that old fox; a sheep-dog bounding at his stirrup,

In its eyes the cast of faithfulness (our help,
Our foolish help); his dun war-horse pacing
Beneath in strength, in ceremonious magnificence;
His castle—some man's castle—set on every crag:
So, companioned so, the knight moves through this world.
The fiend moos in amity, Death mouths, reminding:
He listens in assurance, has no glance
To spare for them, but looks past steadily
At—at—
           a man's look completes itself.

The death of his own flesh, set up outside him;
The flesh of his own soul, set up outside him—
Death and the devil, what are these to him?
His being accuses him—and yet his face is firm
In resolution, in absolute persistence;
The folds of smiling do for steadiness;
The face is its own fate—*a man does what he must*—
And the body underneath it says: *I am.*

THE WOMAN AT THE WASHINGTON ZOO

The saris go by me from the embassies.

Cloth from the moon. Cloth from another planet.
They look back at the leopard like the leopard.

And I. . . .
              this print of mine, that has kept its color
Alive through so many cleanings; this dull null
Navy I wear to work, and wear from work, and so
To my bed, so to my grave, with no
Complaints, no comment: neither from my chief,
The Deputy Chief Assistant, nor his chief—
Only I complain. . . . this serviceable
Body that no sunlight dyes, no hand suffuses
But, dome-shadowed, withering among columns,
Wavy beneath fountains—small, far-off, shining
In the eyes of animals, these beings trapped

As I am trapped but not, themselves, the trap,
Aging, but without knowledge of their age,
Kept safe here, knowing not of death, for death—
Oh, bars of my own body, open, open!

The world goes by my cage and never sees me.
And there come not to me, as come to these,
The wild beasts, sparrows pecking the llamas' grain,
Pigeons settling on the bears' bread, buzzards
Tearing the meat the flies have clouded. . . .
                                        Vulture,
When you come for the white rat that the foxes left,
Take off the red helmet of your head, the black
Wings that have shadowed me, and step to me as man:
The wild brother at whose feet the white wolves fawn,
To whose hand of power the great lioness
Stalks, purring. . . .
                        You know what I was,
You see what I am: change me, change me!

Robert Lowell

(1917–1977)

THE QUAKER GRAVEYARD IN NANTUCKET

For Warren Winslow, Dead at Sea

> Let man have dominion over the fishes of the sea and the
> fowls of the air and the beasts of the whole earth, and every
> creeping creature that moveth upon the earth.

I

A brackish reach of shoal off Madaket—
The sea was still breaking violently and night
Had steamed into our North Atlantic Fleet,
When the drowned sailor clutched the drag-net. Light
Flashed from his matted head and marble feet,
He grappled at the net
With the coiled, hurdling muscles of his thighs:
The corpse was bloodless, a botch of reds and whites,
Its open, staring eyes
Were lustreless dead-lights
Or cabin-windows on a stranded hulk
Heavy with sand. We weight the body, close
Its eyes and heave it seaward whence it came,
Where the heel-headed dogfish barks its nose
On Ahab's void and forehead; and the name
Is blocked in yellow chalk.
Sailors, who pitch this portent at the sea
Where dreadnaughts shall confess
Its hell-bent deity,
When you are powerless
To sand-bag this Atlantic bulwark, faced
By the earth-shaker, green, unwearied, chaste
In his steel scales: ask for no Orphean lute
To pluck life back. The guns of the steeled fleet
Recoil and then repeat
The hoarse salute.

II

Whenever winds are moving and their breath
Heaves at the roped-in bulwarks of this pier,
The terns and sea-gulls tremble at your death
In these home waters. Sailor, can you hear
The Pequod's sea wings, beating landward, fall
Headlong and break on our Atlantic wall
Off 'Sconset, where the yawing S-boats splash
The bellbuoy, with ballooning spinnakers,
As the entangled, screeching mainsheet clears
The blocks: off Madaket, where lubbers lash
The heavy surf and throw their long lead squids
For blue-fish? Sea-gulls blink their heavy lids
Seaward. The winds' wings beat upon the stones,
Cousin, and scream for you and the claws rush
At the sea's throat and wring it in the slush
Of this old Quaker graveyard where the bones
Cry out in the long night for the hurt beast
Bobbing by Ahab's whaleboats in the East.

III

All you recovered from Poseidon died
With you, my cousin, and the harrowed brine
Is fruitless on the blue beard of the god,
Stretching beyond us to the castles in Spain,
Nantucket's westward haven. To Cape Cod
Guns, cradled on the tide,
Blast the eelgrass about a waterclock
Of bilge and backwash, roil the salt and sand
Lashing earth's scaffold, rock
Our warships in the hand
Of the great God, where time's contrition blues
Whatever it was these Quaker sailors lost
In the mad scramble of their lives. They died
When time was open-eyed,
Wooden and childish; only bones abide
There, in the nowhere, where their boats were tossed
Sky-high, where mariners had fabled news
Of IS, the whited monster. What it cost
Them is their secret. In the sperm-whale's slick

I see the Quakers drown and hear their cry:
"If God himself had not been on our side,
If God himself had not been on our side,
When the Atlantic rose against us, why,
Then it had swallowed us up quick."

     I V

This is the end of the whaleroad and the whale
Who spewed Nantucket bones on the thrashed swell
And stirred the troubled waters to whirlpools
To send the Pequod packing off to hell:
This is the end of them, three-quarters fools,
Snatching at straws to sail
Seaward and seaward on the turntail whale,
Spouting out blood and water as it rolls,
Sick as a dog to these Atlantic shoals:
Clamavimus, O depths. Let the sea-gulls wail

For water, for the deep where the high tide
Mutters to its hurt self, mutters and ebbs.
Waves wallow in their wash, go out and out,
Leave only the death-rattle of the crabs,
The beach increasing, its enormous snout
Sucking the ocean's side.
This is the end of running on the waves;
We are poured out like water. Who will dance
The mast-lashed master of Leviathans
Up from this field of Quakers in their unstoned graves?

     V

When the whale's viscera go and the roll
Of its corruption overruns this world
Beyond tree-swept Nantucket and Woods Hole
And Martha's Vineyard, Sailor, will your sword
Whistle and fall and sink into the fat?
In the great ash-pit of Jehoshaphat
The bones cry for the blood of the white whale,
The fat flukes arch and whack about its ears,
The death-lance churns into the sanctuary, tears
The gun-blue swingle, heaving like a flail,
And hacks the coiling life out: it works and drags

And rips the sperm-whale's midriff into rags,
Gobbets of blubber spill to wind and weather,
Sailor, and gulls go round the stoven timbers
Where the morning stars sing out together
And thunder shakes the white surf and dismembers
The red flag hammered in the mast-head. Hide,
Our steel, Jonas Messias, in Thy side.

VI

OUR LADY OF WALSINGHAM

There once the penitents took off their shoes
And then walked barefoot the remaining mile;
And the small trees, a stream and hedgerows file
Slowly along the munching English lane,
Like cows to the old shrine, until you lose
Track of your dragging pain.
The stream flows down under the druid tree,
Shiloah's whirlpools gurgle and make glad
The castle of God. Sailor, you were glad
And whistled Sion by that stream. But see:

Our Lady, too small for her canopy,
Sits near the altar. There's no comeliness
At all or charm in that expressionless
Face with its heavy eyelids. As before,
This face, for centuries a memory,
Non est species, neque decor,
Expressionless, expresses God: it goes
Past castled Sion. She knows what God knows,
Not Calvary's Cross nor crib at Bethlehem
Now, and the world shall come to Walsingham.

VII

The empty winds are creaking and the oak
Splatters and splatters on the cenotaph,
The boughs are trembling and a gaff
Bobs on the untimely stroke
Of the greased wash exploding on a shoal-bell
In the old mouth of the Atlantic. It's well;
Atlantic, you are fouled with the blue sailors,

Sea-monsters, upward angel, downward fish:
Unmarried and corroding, spare of flesh
Mart once of supercilious, wing'd clippers,
Atlantic, where your bell-trap guts its spoil
You could cut the brackish winds with a knife
Here in Nantucket, and cast up the time
When the Lord God formed man from the sea's slime
And breathed into his face the breath of life,
And blue-lung'd combers lumbered to the kill.
The Lord survives the rainbow of His will.

MR. EDWARDS AND THE SPIDER

I saw the spiders marching through the air,
Swimming from tree to tree that mildewed day
   In latter August when the hay
   Came creaking to the barn. But where
      The wind is westerly,
Where gnarled November makes the spiders fly
Into the apparitions of the sky,
They purpose nothing but their ease and die
Urgently beating east to sunrise and the sea;

What are we in the hands of the great God?
It was in vain you set up thorn and briar
   In battle array against the fire
   And treason crackling in your blood;
      For the wild thorns grow tame
And will do nothing to oppose the flame;
Your lacerations tell the losing game
You play against a sickness past your cure.
How will the hands be strong? How will the heart endure?

A very little thing, a little worm,
Or hourglass-blazoned spider, it is said,
   Can kill a tiger. Will the dead
   Hold up his mirror and affirm
      To the four winds the smell
And flash of his authority? It's well

If God who holds you to the pit of hell,
   Much as one holds a spider, will destroy,
Baffle and dissipate your soul. As a small boy

   On Windsor Marsh, I saw the spider die
   When thrown into the bowels of fierce fire:
      There's no long struggle, no desire
      To get up on its feet and fly—
         It stretches out its feet
   And dies. This is the sinner's last retreat;
   Yes, and no strength exerted on the heat
   Then sinews the abolished will, when sick
And full of burning, it will whistle on a brick.

   But who can plumb the sinking of that soul?
   Josiah Hawley, picture yourself cast
      Into a brick-kiln where the blast
      Fans your quick vitals to a coal—
         If measured by a glass,
   How long would it seem burning! Let there pass
   A minute, ten, ten trillion; but the blaze
   Is infinite, eternal: this is death,
To die and know it. This is the Black Widow, death.

GRANDPARENTS

They're altogether otherworldly now,
those adults champing for their ritual Friday spin
to pharmacist and five-and-ten in Brockton.
Back in my throw-away and shaggy span
of adolescence, Grandpa still waves his stick
like a policeman;
Grandmother, like a Mohammedan, still wears her thick
lavender mourning and touring veil;
the Pierce Arrow clears its throat in a horse stall.
Then the dry road dust rises to whiten
the fatigued elm leaves—
the nineteenth century, tired of children, is gone.
They're all gone into a world of light; the farm's my own.

The farm's my own!
Back there alone,
I keep indoors, and spoil another season.
I hear the rattly little country gramophone
racking its five foot horn:
"O Summer Time!"
Even at noon here the formidable
Ancien Régime still keeps nature at a distance. Five
green shaded light bulbs spider the billiards-table;
no field is greener than its cloth,
where Grandpa, dipping sugar for us both,
once spilled his demitasse.
His favorite ball, the number three,
still hides the coffee stain.
Never again
to walk there, chalk our cues,
insist on shooting for us both.
Grandpa! Have me, hold me, cherish me!
Tears smut my fingers. There
half my life-lease later,
I hold an Illustrated London News—;
disloyal still,
I doodle handlebar
mustaches on the last Russian Czar.

MAN AND WIFE

Tamed by Miltown, we lie on Mother's bed;
the rising sun in war paint dyes us red;
in broad daylight her gilded bed-posts shine,
abandoned, almost Dionysian.
At last the trees are green on Marlborough Street,
blossoms on our magnolia ignite
the morning with their murderous five days' white.
All night I've held your hand,
as if you had
a fourth time faced the kingdom of the mad—
its hackneyed speech, its homicidal eye—
and dragged me home alive. . . . Oh my Petite,
clearest of all God's creatures, still all air and nerve:

you were in your twenties, and I,
once hand on glass
and heart in mouth,
outdrank the Rahvs in the heat
of Greenwich Village, fainting at your feet—
too boiled and shy
and poker-faced to make a pass,
while the shrill verve
of your invective scorched the traditional South.

Now twelve years later, you turn your back.
Sleepless, you hold
your pillow to your hollows like a child;
your old-fashioned tirade—
loving, rapid, merciless—
breaks like the Atlantic Ocean on my head.

SKUNK HOUR

For Elizabeth Bishop

Nautilus Island's hermit
heiress still lives through winter in her Spartan cottage;
her sheep still graze above the sea.
Her son's a bishop. Her farmer
is first selectman in our village;
she's in her dotage.

Thirsting for
the hierarchic privacy
of Queen Victoria's century,
she buys up all
the eyesores facing her shore,
and lets them fall.

The season's ill—
we've lost our summer millionaire,
who seemed to leap from an L. L. Bean
catalogue. His nine-knot yawl
was auctioned off to lobstermen.
A red fox stain covers Blue Hill.

And now our fairy
decorator brightens his shop for fall;
his fishnet's filled with orange cork,
orange, his cobbler's bench and awl;
there is no money in his work,
he'd rather marry.

One dark night,
my Tudor Ford climbed the hill's skull;
I watched for love-cars. Lights turned down,
they lay together, hull to hull,
where the graveyard shelves on the town. . . .
My mind's not right.

A car radio bleats,
"Love, O careless Love. . . ." I hear
my ill-spirit sob in each blood cell,
as if my hand were at its throat. . . .
I myself am hell;
nobody's here—

only skunks, that search
in the moonlight for a bite to eat.
They march on their soles up Main Street:
white stripes, moonstruck eyes' red fire
under the chalk-dry and spar spire
of the Trinitarian Church.

I stand on top
of our back steps and breathe the rich air—
a mother skunk with her column of kittens swills the garbage pail.
She jabs her wedge-head in a cup
of sour cream, drops her ostrich tail,
and will not scare.

FOR THE UNION DEAD

"Relinquunt Omnia Servare Rem Publicam."

The old South Boston Aquarium stands
in a Sahara of snow now. Its broken windows are boarded.

The bronze weathervane cod has lost half its scales.
The airy tanks are dry.

Once my nose crawled like a snail on the glass;
my hand tingled
to burst the bubbles
drifting from the noses of the cowed, compliant fish.

My hand draws back. I often sigh still
for the dark downward and vegetating kingdom
of the fish and reptile. One morning last March,
I pressed against the new barbed and galvanized

fence on the Boston Common. Behind their cage,
yellow dinosaur steamshovels were grunting
as they cropped up tons of mush and grass
to gouge their underworld garage.

Parking spaces luxuriate like civic
sandpiles in the heart of Boston.
A girdle of orange, Puritan-pumpkin colored girders
braces the tingling Statehouse,

shaking over the excavations, as it faces Colonel Shaw
and his bell-cheeked Negro infantry
on St. Gaudens' shaking Civil War relief,
propped by a plank splint against the garage's earthquake.

Two months after marching through Boston,
half the regiment was dead;
at the dedication,
William James could almost hear the bronze Negroes breathe.

Their monument sticks like a fishbone
in the city's throat.
Its Colonel is as lean
as a compass-needle.

He has an angry wrenlike vigilance,
a greyhound's gentle tautness;
he seems to wince at pleasure,
and suffocate for privacy.

He is out of bounds now. He rejoices in man's lovely,
peculiar power to choose life and die—
when he leads his black soldiers to death,
he cannot bend his back.

On a thousand small town New England greens,
the old white churches hold their air
of sparse, sincere rebellion; frayed flags
quilt the graveyards of the Grand Army of the Republic.

The stone statues of the abstract Union Soldier
grow slimmer and younger each year—
wasp-waisted, they doze over muskets
and muse through their sideburns . . .

Shaw's father wanted no monument
except the ditch,
where his son's body was thrown
and lost with his "niggers."

The ditch is nearer.
There are no statues for the last war here;
on Boylston Street, a commercial photograph
shows Hiroshima boiling

over a Mosler Safe, the "Rock of Ages"
that survived the blast. Space is nearer.
When I crouch to my television set,
the drained faces of Negro school-children rise like balloons.

Colonel Shaw
is riding on his bubble,
he waits
for the blessèd break.

The Aquarium is gone. Everywhere,
giant finned cars nose forward like fish;
a savage servility
slides by on grease.

HISTORY

History has to live with what was here,
clutching and close to fumbling all we had—
it is so dull and gruesome how we die,
unlike writing, life never finishes.
Abel was finished; death is not remote,
a flash-in-the-pan electrifies the skeptic,
his cows crowding like skulls against high-voltage wire,
his baby crying all night like a new machine.
As in our Bibles, white-faced, predatory,
the beautiful, mist-drunken hunter's moon ascends—
a child could give it a face: two holes, two holes,
my eyes, my mouth, between them a skull's no-nose—
O there's a terrifying innocence in my face
drenched with the silver salvage of the mornfrost.

Gwendolyn Brooks

(1 9 1 7 –   )

NEGRO HERO

To Suggest Dorie Miller

I had to kick their law into their teeth in order to save them.
However I have heard that sometimes you have to deal
Devilishly with drowning men in order to swim them to shore.
Or they will haul themselves and you to the trash and the fish beneath.
(When I think of this, I do not worry about a few
Chipped teeth.)

It is good I gave glory, it is good I put gold on their name.
Or there would have been spikes in the afterward hands.
But let us speak only of my success and the pictures in the Caucasian dailies
As well as the Negro weeklies. For I am a gem.
(They are not concerned that it was hardly The Enemy my fight was against
But them.)

It was a tall time. And of course my blood was
Boiling about in my head and straining and howling and singing me on.
Of course I was rolled on wheels of my boy itch to get at the gun.
Of course all the delicate rehearsal shots of my childhood massed in mirage
        before me.
Of course I was child
And my first swallow of the liquor of battle bleeding black air dying and demon
        noise
Made me wild.

It was kinder than that, though, and I showed like a banner my kindness.
I loved. And a man will guard when he loves.
Their white-gowned democracy was my fair lady.
With her knife lying cold, straight, in the softness of her sweet-flowing sleeve.
But for the sake of the dear smiling mouth and the stuttered promise I toyed
        with my life.
I threw back!—I would not remember
Entirely the knife.

Still—am I good enough to die for them, is my blood bright enough to be
    spilled,
Was my constant back-question—are they clear
On this? Or do I intrude even now?
Am I clean enough to kill for them, do they wish me to kill
For them or is my place while death licks his lips and strides to them
In the galley still?

(In a southern city a white man said
Indeed, I'd rather be dead;
Indeed, I'd rather be shot in the head
Or ridden to waste on the back of a flood
Than saved by the drop of a black man's blood.)

Naturally, the important thing is, I helped to save them, them and a part of
    their democracy.
Even if I had to kick their law into their teeth in order to do that for them.
And I am feeling well and settled in myself because I believe it was a good job,
Despite this possible horror: that they might prefer the
Preservation of their law in all its sick dignity and their knives
To the continuation of their creed
And their lives.

NOTES FROM THE CHILDHOOD
AND THE GIRLHOOD

THE PARENTS: PEOPLE LIKE OUR MARRIAGE
MAXIE AND ANDREW

Clogged and soft and sloppy eyes
Have lost the light that bites or terrifies.

There are no swans and swallows any more.
The people settled for chicken and shut the door.

But one by one
They got things done:
Watch for porches as you pass
And prim low fencing pinching in the grass.

Pleasant custards sit behind
The white Venetian blind.

SUNDAY CHICKEN

Chicken, she chided early, should not wait
Under the cranberries in after-sermon state.
Who had been beaking about the yard of late.

Elite among the speckle-gray, wild white
On blundering mosaic in the night.
Or lovely baffle-brown. It was not right.

You could not hate the cannibal they wrote
Of, with the nostril bone-thrust, who could dote
On boiled or roasted fellow thigh and throat.

Nor hate the handsome tiger, call him devil
To man-feast, manifesting Sunday evil.

OLD RELATIVE

After the baths and bowel-work, he was dead.
Pillows no longer mattered, and getting fed
And anything that anybody said.

Whatever was his he never more strictly had,
Lying in long hesitation. Good or bad,
Hypothesis, traditional and fad.

She went in there to muse on being rid
Of relative beneath the coffin lid.
No one was by. She stuck her tongue out; slid.

Since for a week she must not play "Charmaine"
Or "Honey Bunch," or "Singing in the Rain."

THE BALLAD OF LATE ANNIE

Late Annie in her bower lay,
Though sun was up and spinning.

The blush-brown shoulder was so bare,
Blush-brown lip was winning.

Out then shrieked the mother-dear,
"Be I to fetch and carry?
Get a broom to whish the doors
Or get a man to marry."

"Men there were and men there be
But never men so many
Chief enough to marry me,"
Thought the proud late Annie.

"Whom I raise my shades before
Must be gist and lacquer.
With melted opals for my milk,
Pearl-leaf for my cracker."

THROWING OUT THE FLOWERS

The duck fats rot in the roasting pan,
And it's over and over and all,
The fine fraught smiles, and spites that began
Before it was over and all.

The Thanksgiving praying's away with the silk.
It's over and over and all.
The broccoli, yams and the bead-buttermilk
Are dead with the hail in the hall,
   All
Are dead with the hail in the hall.

The three yellow 'mums and the one white 'mum
Bear to such brusque burial
With pity for little encomium
Since it's over and over and all.

Forgotten and stinking they stick in the can.
And the vase breath's better and all, and all.
And so for the end of our life to a man,
Just over, just over and all.

"DO NOT BE AFRAID OF NO"

"Do not be afraid of no,
Who has so far so very far to go":

New caution to occur
To one whose inner scream set her to cede, for softer lapping and smooth fur!

Whose esoteric need
Was merely to avoid the nettle, to not-bleed.

Stupid, like a street
That beats into a dead end and dies there, with nothing left to reprimand or
       meet.

And like a candle fixed
Against dismay and countershine of mixed

Wild moon and sun. And like
A flying furniture, or bird with lattice wing; or gaunt thing, a-stammer down a
       nightmare neon peopled with condor, hawk and shrike.

To say yes is to die
A lot or a little. The dead wear capably their wry

Enameled emblems. They smell.
But that and that they do not altogether yell is all that we know well.

It is brave to be involved,
To be not fearful to be unresolved.

Her new wish was to smile
When answers took no airships, walked a while.

"PYGMIES ARE PYGMIES STILL, THOUGH PERCHT ON ALPS"

Edward Young

But can see better there, and laughing there
Pity the giants wallowing on the plain.
Giants who bleat and chafe in their small grass,
Seldom to spread the palm; to spit; come clean.

Pygmies expand in cold impossible air,
Cry fie on giantshine, poor glory which
Pounds breast-bone punily, screeches, and has
Reached no Alps: or, knows no Alps to reach.

JESSIE MITCHELL'S MOTHER

Into her mother's bedroom to wash the ballooning body.
"My mother is jelly-hearted and she has a brain of jelly:
Sweet, quiver-soft, irrelevant. Not essential.
Only a habit would cry if she should die.
A pleasant sort of fool without the least iron. . . .
Are you better, mother, do you think it will come today?"
The stretched yellow rag that was Jessie Mitchell's mother
Reviewed her. Young, and so thin, and so straight.
So straight! as if nothing could ever bend her.
But poor men would bend her, and doing things with poor men,
Being much in bed, and babies would bend her over,
And the rest of things in life that were for poor women,
Coming to them grinning and pretty with intent to bend and to kill.
Comparisons shattered her heart, ate at her bulwarks:
The shabby and the bright: she, almost hating her daughter,
Crept into an old sly refuge: "Jessie's black
And her way will be black, and jerkier even than mine.
Mine, in fact, because I was lovely, had flowers
Tucked in the jerks, flowers were here and there. . . ."
She revived for the moment settled and dried-up triumphs,
Forced perfume into old petals, pulled up the droop,
Refueled
Triumphant long-exhaled breaths.
Her exquisite yellow youth . . .

OF ROBERT FROST

There is a little lightning in his eyes.
Iron at the mouth.
His brows ride neither too far up nor down.

He is splendid. With a place to stand.

Some glowing in the common blood.
Some specialness within.

LANGSTON HUGHES

       is merry glory.
Is saltatory.
Yet grips his right of twisting free.

Has a long reach,
Strong speech,
Remedial fears.
Muscular tears.

Holds horticulture
In the eye of the vulture
Infirm profession.
In the Compression—
In mud and blood and sudden death—
In the breath
Of the holocaust he
Is helmsman, hatchet, headlight.
See
One restless in the exotic time! and ever,
Till the air is cured of its fever.

Robert Duncan

(1919–1988)

OFTEN I AM PERMITTED TO RETURN TO A MEADOW

as if it were a scene made-up by the mind,
that is not mine, but is a made place,

that is mine, it is so near to the heart,
an eternal pasture folded in all thought
so that there is a hall therein

that is a made place, created by light
wherefrom the shadows that are forms fall.

Wherefrom fall all architectures I am
I say are likenesses of the First Beloved
whose flowers are flames lit to the Lady.

She it is Queen Under The Hill
whose hosts are a disturbance of words within words
that is a field folded.

It is only a dream of the grass blowing
east against the source of the sun
in an hour before the sun's going down

whose secret we see in a children's game
of ring a round of roses told.

Often I am permitted to return to a meadow
as if it were a given property of the mind
that certain bounds hold against chaos,

that is a place of first permission,
everlasting omen of what is.

PASSAGE OVER WATER

We have gone out in boats upon the sea at night,
lost, and the vast waters close traps of fear about us.
The boats are driven apart, and we are alone at last
under the incalculable sky, listless, diseased with stars.

Let the oars be idle, my love, and forget at this time
our love like a knife between us
defining the boundaries that we can never cross
nor destroy as we drift into the heart of our dream,
cutting the silence, slyly, the bitter rain in our mouths
and the dark wound closed in behind us.

Forget depth-bombs, death and promises we made,
gardens laid waste, and, over the wastelands westward,
the rooms where we had come together bombd.

But even as we leave, your love turns back. I feel
your absence like the ringing of bells silenced. And salt
over your eyes and the scales of salt between us. Now,
you pass with ease into the destructive world.
There is a dry crash of cement. The light fails,
falls into the ruins of cities upon the distant shore
and within the indestructible night I am alone.

Howard Nemerov

(1920–1991)

BLUE SUBURBAN

Out in the elegy country, summer evenings,
It used to be always six o'clock, or seven,
Where the fountain of the willow always wept
Over the lawn, where the shadows crept longer
But came no closer, where the talk was brilliant,
The laughter friendly, where they all were young
And taken by the darkness in surprise
That night should come and the small lights go on
In the lonely house down in the elegy country,
Where the bitter things were said and the drunken friends
Steadied themselves away in their courses
For industrious ruin or casual disaster
Under a handful of pale, permanent stars.

THE WESTERN APPROACHES

As long as we look forward, all seems free,
Uncertain, subject to the Laws of Chance,
Though strange that chance should lie subject to laws,
But looking back on life it is as if
Our Book of Changes never let us change.

Stories already told a time ago
Were waiting for us down the road, our lives
But filled them out; and dreams about the past
Show us the world is post meridian
With little future left to dream about.

Old stories none but scholars seem to tell
Among us any more, they hide the ways,

Old tales less comprehensible than life
Whence nonetheless we know the things we do
And do the things they say the fathers did.

When I was young I flew past Skerryvore
Where the Nine Maidens still grind Hamlet's meal,
The salt and granite grain of bitter earth,
But knew it not for twenty years and more.
My chances past their changes now, I know

How a long life grows ghostly towards the close
As any man dissolves in Everyman
Of whom the story, as it always did, begins
In a far country, once upon a time,
There lived a certain man and he had three sons . . .

THE WAR IN THE AIR

For a saving grace, we didn't see our dead,
Who rarely bothered coming home to die
But simply stayed away out there
In the clean war, the war in the air.

Seldom the ghosts came back bearing their tales
Of hitting the earth, the incompressible sea,
But stayed up there in the relative wind,
Shades fading in the mind,

Who had no graves but only epitaphs
Where never so many spoke for never so few:
Per ardua, said the partisans of Mars,
Per aspera, to the stars.

That was the good war, the war we won
As if there were no death, for goodness' sake,
With the help of the losers we left out there
In the air, in the empty air.

Amy Clampitt

(1920 – 1994)

A BAROQUE SUNBURST

struck through such a dome
as might await a groaning Michelangelo,
finding only alders and barnacles
and herring gulls at their usual squabbles,
sheds on the cove's voluted
silver the aloof skin tones
of a Crivelli angel: a region,
a weather and a point of view
as yet unsettled, save for the lighthouse
like a Venetian campanile, from whose nightlong
reflected angelus you might suppose
the coast of Maine had Europe
on the brain or in its bones, as though
it were a kind of sickness.

Mona Van Duyn

(1921 –)

MOOSE IN THE MORNING, NORTHERN MAINE

At six A.M. the log cabins
nose an immense cow-pie of mist
that lies on the lake.
Nineteen pale goldfinches perch
side by side on the telephone wire
that runs to shore,
and under them the camp cow,
her bones pointing this way and that,
is collapsed like a badly-constructed
pup tent in the dark weeds.
Inside, I am building a fire
in the old woodstove with its rod overhead
for hunters' clothes to steam on.
I am hunting for nothing—
perhaps the three cold pencils
that lie on the table like kindling
could go in to start the logs.
I remember Ted Weiss saying,
"At the exhibition I suddenly realized
Picasso had to re-make everything he laid his eyes on
into an art object.
He couldn't let the world alone.
Since then I don't write every morning."

The world is warming and lightening
and mist on the pond
dissolves into bundles and ribbons.
At the end of my dock there comes clear,
bared by the gentle burning,
a monstrous hulk with thorny head,
up to his chest in the water,
mist wreathing round him.
Grander and grander grows the sun

until he gleams, his brown coat
glistens, the great rack,
five feet wide, throws sparks
of light. A ton of monarch,
munching, he stands spotlit.
Then slowly, gravely, the great neck lowers
head and forty pounds of horn
to sip the lake.
The sun stains the belittled
cow's hide amber.
She heaves her bones and bag
and her neckbell gongs
as she gets to her feet
in yellow blooms of squaw-weed.
On the telephone wire
all the little golden bells are ringing
as that compulsive old scribbler, the universe,
jots down another day.

Richard Wilbur

(1921–)

A BAROQUE WALL-FOUNTAIN
IN THE VILLA SCIARRA

For Dore and Adja

    Under the bronze crown
Too big for the head of the stone cherub whose feet
    A serpent has begun to eat,
Sweet water brims a cockle and braids down

    Past spattered mosses, breaks
On the tipped edge of a second shell, and fills
    The massive third below. It spills
In threads then from the scalloped rim, and makes

    A scrim or summery tent
For a faun-ménage and their familiar goose.
    Happy in all that ragged, loose
Collapse of water, its effortless descent

    And flatteries of spray,
The stocky god upholds the shell with ease,
    Watching, about his shaggy knees,
The goatish innocence of his babes at play;

    His fauness all the while
Leans forward, slightly, into a clambering mesh
    Of water-lights, her sparkling flesh
In a saecular ecstasy, her blinded smile

    Bent on the sand floor
Of the trefoil pool, where ripple-shadows come
    And go in swift reticulum,
More addling to the eye than wine, and more

    Interminable to thought
Than pleasure's calculus. Yet since this all

Is pleasure, flash, and waterfall,
Must it not be too simple? Are we not

   More intricately expressed
In the plain fountains that Maderna set
   Before St. Peter's—the main jet
Struggling aloft until it seems at rest

   In the act of rising, until
The very wish of water is reversed,
   That heaviness borne up to burst
In a clear, high, cavorting head, to fill

   With blaze, and then in gauze
Delays, in a gnatlike shimmering, in a fine
   Illumined version of itself, decline,
And patter on the stones its own applause?

   If that is what men are
Or should be, if those water-saints display
   The pattern of our areté,
What of these showered fauns in their bizarre,

   Spangled, and plunging house?
They are at rest in fulness of desire
   For what is given, they do not tire
Of the smart of the sun, the pleasant water-douse

   And riddled pool below,
Reproving our disgust and our ennui
   With humble insatiety.
Francis, perhaps, who lay in sister snow

   Before the wealthy gate
Freezing and praising, might have seen in this
   No trifle, but a shade of bliss—
That land of tolerable flowers, that state

   As near and far as grass
Where eyes become the sunlight, and the hand
   Is worthy of water: the dreamt land
Toward which all hungers leap, all pleasures pass.

STILL, CITIZEN SPARROW

Still, citizen sparrow, this vulture which you call
Unnatural, let him but lumber again to air
Over the rotten office, let him bear
The carrion ballast up, and at the tall

Tip of the sky lie cruising. Then you'll see
That no more beautiful bird is in heaven's height,
No wider more placid wings, no watchfuller flight;
He shoulders nature there, the frightfully free,

The naked-headed one. Pardon him, you
Who dart in the orchard aisles, for it is he
Devours death, mocks mutability,
Has heart to make an end, keeps nature new.

Thinking of Noah, childheart, try to forget
How for so many bedlam hours his saw
Soured the song of birds with its wheezy gnaw,
And the slam of his hammer all the day beset

The people's ears. Forget that he could bear
To see the towns like coral under the keel,
And the fields so dismal deep. Try rather to feel
How high and weary it was, on the waters where

He rocked his only world, and everyone's.
Forgive the hero, you who would have died
Gladly with all you knew; he rode that tide
To Ararat; all men are Noah's sons.

LOVE CALLS US TO THE THINGS
OF THIS WORLD

   The eyes open to a cry of pulleys,
And spirited from sleep, the astounded soul
Hangs for a moment bodiless and simple
As false dawn.

Outside the open window
The morning air is all awash with angels.

Some are in bed-sheets, some are in blouses,
Some are in smocks: but truly there they are.
Now they are rising together in calm swells
Of halcyon feeling, filling whatever they wear
With the deep joy of their impersonal breathing;

Now they are flying in place, conveying
The terrible speed of their omnipresence, moving
And staying like white water; and now of a sudden
They swoon down into so rapt a quiet
That nobody seems to be there.
                              The soul shrinks

From all that it is about to remember,
From the punctual rape of every blessèd day,
And cries,
            "Oh, let there be nothing on earth but laundry,
Nothing but rosy hands in the rising steam
And clear dances done in the sight of heaven."

Yet, as the sun acknowledges
With a warm look the world's hunks and colors,
The soul descends once more in bitter love
To accept the waking body, saying now
In a changed voice as the man yawns and rises,

"Bring them down from their ruddy gallows;
Let there be clean linen for the backs of thieves;
Let lovers go fresh and sweet to be undone,
And the heaviest nuns walk in a pure floating
Of dark habits,
                keeping their difficult balance."

MIND

Mind in its purest play is like some bat
That beats about in caverns all alone,
Contriving by a kind of senseless wit
Not to conclude against a wall of stone.

It has no need to falter or explore;
Darkly it knows what obstacles are there,
And so may weave and flitter, dip and soar
In perfect courses through the blackest air.

And has this simile a like perfection?
The mind is like a bat. Precisely. Save
That in the very happiest intellection
A graceful error may correct the cave.

James Dickey

(1923–)

THE HEAVEN OF ANIMALS

Here they are. The soft eyes open.
If they have lived in a wood
It is a wood.
If they have lived on plains
It is grass rolling
Under their feet forever.

Having no souls, they have come,
Anyway, beyond their knowing.
Their instincts wholly bloom
And they rise.
The soft eyes open.

To match them, the landscape flowers,
Outdoing, desperately
Outdoing what is required:
The richest wood,
The deepest field.

For some of these,
It could not be the place
It is, without blood.
These hunt, as they have done,
But with claws and teeth grown perfect,

More deadly than they can believe.
They stalk more silently,
And crouch on the limbs of trees,
And their descent
Upon the bright backs of their prey

May take years
In a sovereign floating of joy.
And those that are hunted

Know this as their life,
Their reward: to walk

Under such trees in full knowledge
Of what is in glory above them,
And to feel no fear,
But acceptance, compliance.
Fulfilling themselves without pain

At the cycle's center,
They tremble, they walk
Under the tree,
They fall, they are torn,
They rise, they walk again.

THE DUSK OF HORSES

Right under their noses, the green
Of the field is paling away
Because of something fallen from the sky.

They see this, and put down
Their long heads deeper in grass
That only just escapes reflecting them

As the dream of a millpond would.
The color green flees over the grass
Like an insect, following the red sun over

The next hill. The grass is white.
There is no cloud so dark and white at once;
There is no pool at dawn that deepens

Their faces and thirsts as this does.
Now they are feeding on solid
Cloud, and, one by one,

With nails as silent as stars among the wood
Hewed down years ago and now rotten,
The stalls are put up around them.

Now if they lean, they come
On wood on any side. Not touching it, they sleep.
No beast ever lived who understood

What happened among the sun's fields,
Or cared why the color of grass
Fled over the hill while he stumbled,

Led by the halter to sleep
On his four taxed, worthy legs.
Each thinks he awakens where

The sun is black on the rooftop,
That the green is dancing in the next pasture,
And that the way to sleep

In a cloud, or in a risen lake,
Is to walk as though he were still
In the drained field standing, head down,

To pretend to sleep when led,
And thus to go under the ancient white
Of the meadow, as green goes

And whiteness comes up through his face
Holding stars and rotten rafters,
Quiet, fragrant, and relieved.

CHERRYLOG ROAD

Off Highway 106
At Cherrylog Road I entered
The '34 Ford without wheels,
Smothered in kudzu,
With a seat pulled out to run
Corn whiskey down from the hills,

And then from the other side
Crept into an Essex

With a rumble seat of red leather
And then out again, aboard
A blue Chevrolet, releasing
The rust from its other color,

Reared up on three building blocks.
None had the same body heat;
I changed with them inward, toward
The weedy heart of the junkyard,
For I knew that Doris Holbrook
Would escape from her father at noon

And would come from the farm
To seek parts owned by the sun
Among the abandoned chassis,
Sitting in each in turn
As I did, leaning forward
As in a wild stock-car race

In the parking lot of the dead.
Time after time, I climbed in
And out the other side, like
An envoy or movie star
Met at the station by crickets.
A radiator cap raised its head,

Become a real toad or a kingsnake
As I neared the hub of the yard,
Passing through many states,
Many lives, to reach
Some grandmother's long Pierce-Arrow
Sending platters of blindness forth

From its nickel hubcaps
And spilling its tender upholstery
On sleepy roaches,
The glass panel in between
Lady and colored driver
Not all the way broken out,

The back-seat phone
Still on its hook.
I got in as though to exclaim,

"Let us go to the orphan asylum,
John; I have some old toys
For children who say their prayers."

I popped with sweat as I thought
I heard Doris Holbrook scrape
Like a mouse in the southern-state sun
That was eating the paint in blisters
From a hundred car tops and hoods.
She was tapping like code,

Loosening the screws,
Carrying off headlights,
Sparkplugs, bumpers,
Cracked mirrors and gear-knobs,
Getting ready, already,
To go back with something to show

Other than her lips' new trembling
I would hold to me soon, soon,
Where I sat in the ripped back seat
Talking over the interphone,
Praying for Doris Holbrook
To come from her father's farm

And to get back there
With no trace of me on her face
To be seen by her red-haired father
Who would change, in the squalling barn,
Her back's pale skin with a strop,
Then lay for me

In a bootlegger's roasting car
With a string-triggered 12-gauge shotgun
To blast the breath from the air.
Not cut by the jagged windshields,
Through the acres of wrecks she came
With a wrench in her hand,

Through dust where the blacksnake dies
Of boredom, and the beetle knows
The compost has no more life.
Someone outside would have seen

The oldest car's door inexplicably
Close from within:

I held her and held her and held her,
Convoyed at terrific speed
By the stalled, dreaming traffic around us,
So the blacksnake, stiff
With inaction, curved back
Into life, and hunted the mouse

With deadly overexcitement,
The beetles reclaimed their field
As we clung, glued together,
With the hooks of the seat springs
Working through to catch us red-handed
Amidst the gray breathless batting

That burst from the seat at our backs.
We left by separate doors
Into the changed, other bodies
Of cars, she down Cherrylog Road
And I to my motorcycle
Parked like the soul of the junkyard

Restored, a bicycle fleshed
With power, and tore off
Up Highway 106, continually
Drunk on the wind in my mouth,
Wringing the handlebar for speed,
Wild to be wreckage forever.

Anthony Hecht

(1923-)

JASON

> And from America the golden fleece.
> Marlowe

The room is full of gold.
Is it a chapel? Is that the genuine buzz
Of cherubim, the wingèd goods?
Is it no more than sun that floods
To pool itself at her uncovered breast?
O lights, o numina, behold
How we are gifted. He who never was,
Is, and her fingers bless him and are blessed.

That blessedness is tossed
In a wild, dodging light. Suddenly clear
And poised in heavenly desire
Prophets and eastern saints take fire
And fuse with gold in windows across the way,
And turn to liquid, and are lost.
And now there deepens over lakes of air
A remembered stillness of the seventh day

Borne in on the soft cruise
And sway of birds. Slowly the ancient seas,
Those black, predestined waters rise
Lisping and calm before my eyes,
And Massachusetts rises out of foam
A state of mind in which by twos
All beasts browse among barns and apple trees
As in their earliest peace, and the dove comes home.

Tonight, my dear, when the moon
Settles the radiant dust of every man,
Powders the bedsheets and the floor
With lightness of those gone before,
Sleep then, and dream the story as foretold:

Dream how a little boy alone
With a wooden sword and the top of a garbage can
Triumphs in gardens full of marigold.

THE GARDENS OF THE VILLA D'ESTE

This is Italian. Here
Is cause for the undiminished bounce
Of sex, cause for the lark, the animal spirit
To rise, aerated, but not beyond our reach, to spread
Friction upon the air, cause to sing loud for the bed
Of jonquils, the linen bed, and established merit
Of love, and grandly to pronounce
Pleasure without peer.

Goddess, be with me now;
Commend my music to the woods.
There is no garden to the practiced gaze
Half so erotic: here the sixteenth century thew
Rose to its last perfection, this being chiefly due
To the provocative role the water plays.
Tumble and jump, the fountains' moods
Teach the world how.

But, ah, who ever saw
Finer proportion kept. The sum
Of intersecting limbs was something planned.
Ligorio, the laurel! Every turn and quirk
Weaves in this waving green and liquid world to work
Its formula, binding upon the gland,
Even as molecules succumb
To Avogadro's law.

The intricate mesh of trees,
Sagging beneath a lavender snow
Of wisteria, wired by creepers, perfectly knit
A plot to capture alive the migrant, tourist soul
In its corporeal home with all the deft control
And artifice of an Hephaestus' net.

Sunlight and branch rejoice to show
 Sudden interstices.

 The whole garden inclines
 The flesh as water falls, to seek
For depth. Consider the top balustrade,
Where twinned stone harpies, with domed and virgin breasts,
Spurt from their nipples that no pulse or hand has pressed
 Clear liquid arcs of benefice and aid
  To the chief purpose. They are Greek
  Versions of valentines

 And spend themselves to fill
 The celebrated flumes that skirt
The horseshoe stairs. Triumphant then to a sluice,
With Brownian movement down the giggling water drops
Past haunches, over ledges, out of mouths, and stops
 In a still pool, but, by a plumber's ruse,
  Rises again to laugh and squirt
  At heaven, and is still

 Busy descending. White
 Ejaculations leap to teach
How fertile are these nozzles; the streams run
Góngora through the garden, channel themselves, and pass
To lily-padded ease, where insubordinate lass
 And lad can cool their better parts, where sun
  Heats them again to furnace pitch
  To prove his law is light.

 Marble the fish that puke
 Eternally, marble the lips
Of gushing naiads, pleased to ridicule
Adonis, marble himself, and larger than life-sized,
Untouched by Venus, posthumously circumcised
 Patron of Purity; and any fool
  Who feels no flooding at the hips
  These spendthrift stones rebuke.

 It was in such a place
 That Mozart's Figaro contrived
The totally expected. This is none
Of your French topiary, geometric works,

Based on God's rational, wrist-watch universe; here lurks
   The wood louse, the night crawler, the homespun
      Spider; here are they born and wived
         And bedded, by God's grace.

      Actually, it is real
    The way the world is real: the horse
  Must turn against the wind, and the deer feed
Against the wind, and finally the garden must allow
For the recalcitrant; a style can teach us how
   To know the world in little where the weed
      Has license, where by dint of force
         D'Estes have set their seal.

      Their spirit entertains.
    And we are honorable guests
  Come by imagination, come by night,
Hearing in the velure of darkness impish strings
Mincing Tartini, hearing the hidden whisperings:
   "*Carissima*, the moon gives too much light,"
      Though by its shining it invests
         Her bodice with such gains

      As show their shadowed worth
    Deep in the cleavage. Lanterns, lamps
  Of pumpkin-colored paper dwell upon
The implications of the skin-tight silk, allude
Directly to the body; under the subdued
   Report of corks, whisperings, the *chaconne*,
      Boisterous water runs its ramps
         Out, to the end of mirth.

      Accommodating plants
    Give umbrage where the lovers delve
  Deeply for love, give way to their delight,
As Pliny's pregnant mouse, bearing unborn within her
Lewd sons and pregnant daughters, hears the adept beginner:
   "*Cor mio*, your supports are much too tight,"
      While overhead the stars resolve
         Every extravagance.

      Tomorrow, before dawn,
    Gardeners will come to resurrect

Downtrodden iris, dispose of broken glass,
Return the diamond earrings to the villa, but
As for the moss upon the statue's shoulder, not
        To defeat its green invasion, but to pass
            Over the liberal effect
                Caprice and cunning spawn.

        For thus it was designed:
            Controlled disorder at the heart
        Of everything, the paradox, the old
Oxymoronic itch to set the formal strictures
Within a natural context, where the tension lectures
        Us on our mortal state, and by controlled
            Disorder, labors to keep art
                From being too refined.

        Susan, it had been once
            My hope to see this place with you,
        See it as in the hour of thoughtless youth.
For age mocks all diversity, its genesis,
And whispers to the heart, "*Cor mio*, beyond all this
        Lies the unchangeable and abstract truth,"
            Claims of the grass, it is not true,
                And makes our youth its dunce.

        Therefore, some later day
            Recall these words, let them be read
        Between us, let them signify that here
Are more than formulas, that age sees no more clearly
For its poor eyesight, and philosophy grows surly,
        That falling water and the blood's career
            Lead down the garden path to bed
                And win us both to May.

Denise Levertov

(1923 –)

THE ACHE OF MARRIAGE

The ache of marriage:

thigh and tongue, beloved,
are heavy with it,
it throbs in the teeth

We look for communion
and are turned away, beloved,
each and each

It is leviathan and we
in its belly
looking for joy, some joy
not to be known outside it

two by two in the ark of
the ache of it.

Donald Justice

(1 9 2 5 –   )

ON THE DEATH OF FRIENDS IN CHILDHOOD

We shall not ever meet them bearded in heaven,
Nor sunning themselves among the bald of hell;
If anywhere, in the deserted schoolyard at twilight,
Forming a ring, perhaps, or joining hands
In games whose very names we have forgotten.
Come, memory, let us seek them there in the shadows.

SONATINA IN YELLOW

> Du schnell vergehendes Daguerrotyp
> In meinen langsamer vergehenden Händen.
> > Rilke

The pages of the album,
As they are turned, turn yellow; a word,
Once spoken, obsolete,
No longer what was meant. Say it.
The meanings come, or come back later,
Unobtrusive, taking their places.
Think of the past. Think of forgetting the past.
It was an exercise requiring further practice;
A difficult exercise, played through by someone else.
Overheard from another room, now,
It seems full of mistakes.
                    So the voice of your father,
Rising as from the next room still
With all the remote but true affection of the dead,
Repeats itself, insists,
Insisting you must listen, rises
In the familiar pattern of reproof
For some childish error, a nap disturbed,

597

Or vase, broken or overturned;
Rises and subsides. And you do listen.
Listen and forget. Practice forgetting.
Forgotten sunlight still
Blinds the eyes of faces in the album.
The faces fade, and there is only
A sort of meaning that comes back.

A. R. Ammons

(1926–)

CORSONS INLET

I went for a walk over the dunes again this morning
to the sea,
then turned right along
   the surf
         rounded a naked headland
         and returned

  along the inlet shore:

it was muggy sunny, the wind from the sea steady and high,
crisp in the running sand,
     some breakthroughs of sun
   but after a bit

continuous overcast:

the walk liberating, I was released from forms,
from the perpendiculars,
     straight lines, blocks, boxes, binds
of thought
into the hues, shadings, rises, flowing bends and blends
        of sight:

               I allow myself eddies of meaning:
yield to a direction of significance
running
like a stream through the geography of my work:
  you can find
in my sayings
            swerves of action
            like the inlet's cutting edge:
       there are dunes of motion,
organizations of grass, white sandy paths of remembrance
in the overall wandering of mirroring mind:

but Overall is beyond me: is the sum of these events
I cannot draw, the ledger I cannot keep, the accounting
beyond the account:

in nature there are few sharp lines: there are areas of
primrose
        more or less dispersed;
disorderly orders of bayberry; between the rows
of dunes,
irregular swamps of reeds,
though not reeds alone, but grass, bayberry, yarrow, all . . .
predominantly reeds:

I have reached no conclusions, have erected no boundaries,
shutting out and shutting in, separating inside
        from outside: I have
        drawn no lines:
        as

manifold events of sand
change the dune's shape that will not be the same shape
tomorrow,
so I am willing to go along, to accept
the becoming
thought, to stake off no beginnings or ends, establish
        no walls:

by transitions the land falls from grassy dunes to creek
to undercreek: but there are no lines, though
        change in that transition is clear
        as any sharpness: but "sharpness" spread out,
allowed to occur over a wider range
than mental lines can keep:

the moon was full last night: today, low tide was low:
black shoals of mussels exposed to the risk
of air
and, earlier, of sun,
waved in and out with the waterline, waterline inexact,
caught always in the event of change:
        a young mottled gull stood free on the shoals
        and ate

to vomiting: another gull, squawking possession, cracked a crab,
picked out the entrails, swallowed the soft-shelled legs, a ruddy
turnstone running in to snatch leftover bits:

risk is full: every living thing in
siege: the demand is life, to keep life: the small
white blacklegged egret, how beautiful, quietly stalks and spears
            the shallows, darts to shore
                  to stab—what? I couldn't
        see against the black mudflats—a frightened
        fiddler crab?

        the news to my left over the dunes and
reeds and bayberry clumps was
            fall: thousands of tree swallows
            gathering for flight:
            an order held
            in constant change: a congregation
rich with entropy: nevertheless, separable, noticeable
        as one event,
                not chaos: preparations for
flight from winter,
cheet, cheet, cheet, cheet, wings rifling the green clumps,
beaks
at the bayberries
    a perception full of wind, flight, curve,
    sound:
    the possibility of rule as the sum of rulelessness:
the "field" of action
with moving, incalculable center:

in the smaller view, order tight with shape:
blue tiny flowers on a leafless weed: carapace of crab:
snail shell:
        pulsations of order
        in the bellies of minnows: orders swallowed,
broken down, transferred through membranes
to strengthen larger orders: but in the large view, no
lines or changeless shapes: the working in and out, together
        and against, of millions of events: this,
                so that I make
                no form
                formlessness:

orders as summaries, as outcomes of actions override
or in some way result, not predictably (seeing me gain
the top of a dune,
the swallows
could take flight—some other fields of bayberry
could enter fall
berryless) and there is serenity:

no arranged terror: no forcing of image, plan,
or thought:
no propaganda, no humbling of reality to precept:

terror pervades but is not arranged, all possibilities
of escape open: no route shut, except in
the sudden loss of all routes:

I see narrow orders, limited tightness, but will
not run to that easy victory:
still around the looser, wider forces work:
I will try
to fasten into order enlarging grasps of disorder, widening
scope, but enjoying the freedom that
Scope eludes my grasp, that there is no finality of vision,
that I have perceived nothing completely,
that tomorrow a new walk is a new walk.

SO I SAID I AM EZRA

So I said I am Ezra
and the wind whipped my throat
gaming for the sounds of my voice
I listened to the wind
go over my head and up into the night
Turning to the sea I said
I am Ezra
but there were no echoes from the waves
The words were swallowed up
in the voice of the surf
or leaping over swells

lost themselves oceanward
    Over the bleached and broken fields
I moved my feet and turning from the wind
    that ripped sheets of sand
    from the beach and threw them
    like seamists across the dunes
swayed as if the wind were taking me away
and said
    I am Ezra
As a word too much repeated
falls out of being
so I Ezra went out into the night
like a drift of sand
and splashed among the windy oats
that clutch the dunes
of unremembered seas

TRIPHAMMER BRIDGE

I wonder what to mean by *sanctuary*, if a real or
apprehended place, as of a bell rung in a gold
surround, or as of silver roads along the beaches

of clouds seas don't break or black mountains
overspill; jail: ice here's shapelier than anything,
on the eaves massive, jawed along gorge ledges, solid

in the plastic blue boat fall left water in: if I
think the bitterest thing I can think of that seems like
reality, slickened back, hard, shocked by rip-high wind:

sanctuary, sanctuary, I say it over and over and the
word's sound is the one place to dwell: that's it, just
the sound, and the imagination of the sound—a place.

Robert Creeley

(1926–   )

THE RAIN

All night the sound had
come back again,
and again falls
this quiet, persistent rain.

What am I to myself
that must be remembered,
insisted upon
so often? Is it

that never the ease,
even the hardness,
of rain falling
will have for me

something other than this,
something not so insistent—
am I to be locked in this
final uneasiness.

Love, if you love me,
lie next to me.
Be for me, like rain,
the getting out

of the tiredness, the fatuousness, the semi-
lust of intentional indifference.
Be wet
with a decent happiness.

Frank O'Hara

(1926 – 1966)

IN MEMORY OF MY FEELINGS

To Grace Hartigan

    1

My quietness has a man in it, he is transparent
and he carries me quietly, like a gondola, through the streets.
He has several likenesses, like stars and years, like numerals.

My quietness has a number of naked selves,
so many pistols I have borrowed to protect myselves
from creatures who too readily recognize my weapons
and have murder in their heart!
                       though in winter
they are warm as roses, in the desert
taste of chilled anisette.
              At times, withdrawn,
I rise into the cool skies
and gaze on at the imponderable world with the simple identification
of my colleagues, the mountains. Manfred climbs to my nape,
speaks, but I do not hear him,
                 I'm too blue.
An elephant takes up his trumpet,
money flutters from the windows of cries, silk stretching its mirror
across shoulder blades. A gun is "fired."
                  One of me rushes
to window #13 and one of me raises his whip and one of me
flutters up from the center of the track amidst the pink flamingoes,
and underneath their hooves as they round the last turn my lips
are scarred and brown, brushed by tails, masked in dirt's lust,
definition, open mouths gasping for the cries of the bettors for the lungs
of earth.

      So many of my transparencies could not resist the race!
Terror in earth, dried mushrooms, pink feathers, tickets,
a flaking moon drifting across the muddied teeth,

the imperceptible moan of covered breathing,
                                                    love of the serpent!
I am underneath its leaves as the hunter crackles and pants
and bursts, as the barrage balloon drifts behind a cloud
and animal death whips out its flashlight,
                                              whistling
and slipping the glove off the trigger hand. The serpent's eyes
redden at sight of those thorny fingernails, he is so smooth!
                                        My transparent selves
flail about like vipers in a pail, writhing and hissing
without panic, with a certain justice of response
and presently the aquiline serpent comes to resemble the Medusa.

　　　2

The dead hunting
and the alive, ahunted.
                              My father, my uncle,
my grand-uncle and the several aunts. My
grand-aunt dying for me, like a talisman, in the war,
before I had even gone to Borneo
her blood vessels rushed to the surface
and burst like rockets over the wrinkled
invasion of the Australians, her eyes aslant
like the invaded, but blue like mine.
An atmosphere of supreme lucidity,
                              humanism,
the mere existence of emphasis,
                              a rusted barge
painted orange against the sea
full of Marines reciting the Arabian ideas
which are a proof in themselves of seasickness
which is a proof in itself of being hunted.
A hit? *ergo* swim.
                    My 10   my 19,
my 9,   and the several years. My
12 years since they all died, philosophically speaking.
And now the coolness of a mind
like a shuttered suite in the Grand Hotel
where mail arrives for my incognito,
                              whose façade
has been slipping into the Grand Canal for centuries;

rockets splay over a *sposalizio*,
                              fleeing into night
from their Chinese memories, and it is a celebration,
the trying desperately to count them as they die.
But who will stay to be these numbers
when all the lights are dead?

          3

The most arid stretch is often richest,
the hand lifting towards a fig tree from hunger
                              digging
and there is water, clear, supple, or there
deep in the sand where death sleeps, a murmurous bubbling
proclaims the blackness that will ease and burn.
You preferred the Arabs? but they didn't stay to count
their inventions, racing into sands, converting themselves into
so many,
          embracing, at Ramadan, the tenderest effigies of
themselves with penises shorn by the hundreds, like a camel
ravishing a goat.
                   And the mountainous-minded Greeks could speak
of time as a river and step across it into Persia, leaving the pain
at home to be converted into statuary. I adore the Roman copies.
And the stench of the camel's spit I swallow,
and the stench of the whole goat. For we have advanced, France,
together into a new land, like the Greeks, where one feels nostalgic
for mere ideas, where truth lies on its deathbed like an uncle
and one of me has a sentimental longing for number,
as has another for the ball gowns of the Directoire and yet
another for "Destiny, Paris, destiny!"
                              or "Only a king may kill a king."

How many selves are there in a war hero asleep in names? under
a blanket of platoon and fleet, orderly. For every seaman
with one eye closed in fear and twitching arm at a sigh for Lord Nelson,
he is all dead; and now a meek subaltern writhes in his bedclothes
with the fury of a thousand, violating an insane mistress
who has only herself to offer his multitudes.
                              Rising,
he wraps himself in the burnoose of memories against the heat of life
and over the sands he goes to take an algebraic position *in re*
a sun of fear shining not too bravely. He will ask himself to

vote on fear before he feels a tremor,
                                        as runners arrive from the mountains
bearing snow, proof that the mind's obsolescence is still capable
of intimacy. His mistress will follow him across the desert
like a goat, towards a mirage which is something familiar about
one of his innumerable wrists,
                            and lying in an oasis one day,
playing catch with coconuts, they suddenly smell oil.

        4

Beneath these lives
the ardent lover of history hides,
                            tongue out
leaving a globe of spit on a taut spear of grass
and leaves off rattling his tail a moment
to admire this flag.
                I'm looking for my Shanghai Lil.
Five years ago, enamored of fire-escapes, I went to Chicago,
an eventful trip: the fountains! the Art Institute, the Y
for both sexes, absent Christianity.
                        At 7, before Jane
was up, the copper lake stirred against the sides
of a Norwegian freighter; on the deck a few dirty men,
tired of night, watched themselves in the water
as years before the German prisoners on the *Prinz Eugen*
dappled the Pacific with their sores, painted purple
by a Naval doctor.
                    Beards growing, and the constant anxiety
over looks. I'll shave before she wakes up. Sam Goldwyn
spent $2,000,000 on Anna Sten, but Grushenka left America.
One of me is standing in the waves, an ocean bather,
or I am naked with a plate of devils at my hip.
                                    Grace
to be born and live as variously as possible. The conception
of the masque barely suggests the sordid identifications.
I am a Hittite in love with a horse. I don't know what blood's
in me I feel like an African prince I am a girl walking downstairs
in a red pleated dress with heels I am a champion taking a fall
I am a jockey with a sprained ass-hole I am the light mist
                                    in which a face appears
and it is another face of blonde I am a baboon eating a banana
I am a dictator looking at his wife I am a doctor eating a child

and the child's mother smiling I am a Chinaman climbing a mountain
I am a child smelling his father's underwear I am an Indian
sleeping on a scalp
                and my pony is stamping in the birches,
and I've just caught sight of the *Niña*, the *Pinta* and the *Santa María*.
           What land is this, so free?
                       I watch
the sea at the back of my eyes, near the spot where I think
in solitude as pine trees groan and support the enormous winds,
they are humming *L'Oiseau de feu!*
              They look like gods, these whitemen,
and they are bringing me the horse I fell in love with on the frieze.

     5

And now it is the serpent's turn.
I am not quite you, but almost, the opposite of visionary.
You are coiled around the central figure,
                  the heart
that bubbles with red ghosts, since to move is to love
and the scrutiny of all things is syllogistic,
the startled eyes of the dikdik, the bush full of white flags
fleeing a hunter,
         which is our democracy
               but the prey
is always fragile and like something, as a seashell can be
a great Courbet, if it wishes. To bend the ear of the outer world.
                When you turn your head
can you feel your heels, undulating? that's what it is
to be a serpent. I haven't told you of the most beautiful things
in my lives, and watching the ripple of their loss disappear
along the shore, underneath ferns,
            face downward in the ferns
my body, the naked host to my many selves, shot
by a guerrilla warrior or dumped from a car into ferns
which are themselves *journalières*.
          The hero, trying to unhitch his parachute,
stumbles over me. It is our last embrace.
             And yet
I have forgotten my loves, and chiefly that one, the cancerous
statue which my body could no longer contain,
                 against my will
                 against my love

become art,
          I could not change it into history
and so remember it,
              and I have lost what is always and everywhere
present, the scene of my selves, the occasion of these ruses,
which I myself and singly must now kill
              and save the serpent in their midst.

CHEZ JANE

The white chocolate jar full of petals
swills odds and ends around in a dizzying eye
of four o'clocks now and to come. The tiger,
marvellously striped and irritable, leaps
on the table and without disturbing a hair
of the flowers' breathless attention, pisses
into the pot, right down its delicate spout.
A whisper of steam goes up from that porcelain
urethra. "Saint-Saëns!" it seems to be whispering,
curling unerringly around the furry nuts
of the terrible puss, who is mentally flexing.
Ah be with me always, spirit of noisy
contemplation in the studio, the Garden
of Zoos, the eternally fixed afternoons!
There, while music scratches its scrofulous
stomach, the brute beast emerges and stands,
clear and careful, knowing always the exact peril
at this moment caressing his fangs with
a tongue given wholly to luxurious usages;
which only a moment before dropped aspirin
in this sunset of roses, and now throws a chair
in the air to aggravate the truly menacing.

James Merrill

(1926–1995)

AN URBAN CONVALESCENCE

Out for a walk, after a week in bed,
I find them tearing up part of my block
And, chilled through, dazed and lonely, join the dozen
In meek attitudes, watching a huge crane
Fumble luxuriously in the filth of years.
Her jaws dribble rubble. An old man
Laughs and curses in her brain,
Bringing to mind the close of *The White Goddess*.

As usual in New York, everything is torn down
Before you have had time to care for it.
Head bowed, at the shrine of noise, let me try to recall
What building stood here. Was there a building at all?
I have lived on this same street for a decade.

Wait. Yes. Vaguely a presence rises
Some five floors high, of shabby stone
—Or am I confusing it with another one
In another part of town, or of the world?—
And over its lintel into focus vaguely
Misted with blood (my eyes are shut)
A single garland sways, stone fruit, stone leaves,
Which years of grit had etched until it thrust
Roots down, even into the poor soil of my seeing.
When did the garland become part of me?
I ask myself, amused almost,
Then shiver once from head to toe,

Transfixed by a particular cheap engraving of garlands
Bought for a few francs long ago,
All calligraphic tendril and cross-hatched rondure,
Ten years ago, and crumpled up to stanch
Boughs dripping, whose white gestures filled a cab,
And thought of neither then nor since.

611

Also, to clasp them, the small, red-nailed hand
Of no one I can place. Wait. No. Her name, her features
Lie toppled underneath that year's fashions.
The words she must have spoken, setting her face
To fluttering like a veil, I cannot hear now,
Let alone understand.

So that I am already on the stair,
As it were, of where I lived,
When the whole structure shudders at my tread
And soundlessly collapses, filling
The air with motes of stone.
Onto the still erect building next door
Are pressed levels and hues—
Pocked rose, streaked greens, brown whites.
Who drained the pousse-café?
Wires and pipes, snapped off at the roots, quiver.

Well, that is what life does. I stare
A moment longer, so. And presently
The massive volume of the world
Closes again.

Upon that book I swear
To abide by what it teaches:
Gospels of ugliness and waste,
Of towering voids, of soiled gusts,
Of a shrieking to be faced
Full into, eyes astream with cold—

With cold?
All right then. With self-knowledge.

Indoors at last, the pages of *Time* are apt
To open, and the illustrated mayor of New York,
Given a glimpse of how and where I work,
To note yet one more house that can be scrapped.

Unwillingly I picture
My walls weathering in the general view.
It is not even as though the new
Buildings did very much for architecture.

Suppose they did. The sickness of our time requires
That these as well be blasted in their prime.
You would think the simple fact of having lasted
Threatened our cities like mysterious fires.

There are certain phrases which to use in a poem
Is like rubbing silver with quicksilver. Bright
But facile, the glamour deadens overnight.
For instance, how "the sickness of our time"

Enhances, then debases, what I feel.
At my desk I swallow in a glass of water
No longer cordial, scarcely wet, a pill
They had told me not to take until much later.

With the result that back into my imagination
The city glides, like cities seen from the air,
Mere smoke and sparkle to the passenger
Having in mind another destination

Which now is not that honey-slow descent
Of the Champs-Elysées, her hand in his,
But the dull need to make some kind of house
Out of the life lived, out of the love spent.

AFTER GREECE

Light into the olive entered
And was oil. Rain made the huge pale stones
Shine from within. The moon turned his hair white
Who next stepped from between the columns,
Shielding his eyes. All through
The countryside were old ideas
Found lying open to the elements.
Of the gods' houses only
A minor premise here and there
Would be balancing the heaven of fixed stars

Upon a Doric capital. The rest
Lay spilled, their fluted drums half sunk in cyclamen
Or deep in water's biting clarity
Which just barely upheld me
The next week, when I sailed for home.
But where is home—these walls?
These limbs? The very spaniel underfoot
Races in sleep, toward what?
It is autumn. I did not invite
Those guests, windy and brittle, who drink my liquor.
Returning from a walk I find
The bottles filled with spleen, my room itself
Smeared by reflection onto the far hemlocks.
I some days flee in dream
Back to the exposed porch of the maidens
Only to find my great-great-grandmothers
Erect there, peering
Into a globe of red Bohemian glass.
As it swells and sinks, I call up
Graces, Furies, Fates, removed
To my country's warm, lit halls, with rivets forced
Through drapery, and nothing left to bear.
They seem anxious to know
What holds up heaven nowadays.
I start explaining how in that vast fire
Were other irons—well, Art, Public Spirit,
Ignorance, Economics, Love of Self,
Hatred of Self, a hundred more,
Each burning to be felt, each dedicated
To sparing us the worst; how I distrust them
As I should have done those ladies; how I want
Essentials: salt, wine, olive, the light, the scream—
No! I have scarcely named you,
And look, in a flash you stand full-grown before me,
Row upon row, Essentials,
Dressed like your sister caryatids
Or tombstone angels jealous of their dead,
With undulant coiffures, lips weathered, cracked by grime,
And faultless eyes gone blank beneath the immense
Zinc and gunmetal northern sky . . .
Stay then. Perhaps the system
Calls for spirits. This first glass I down

To the last time
I ate and drank in that old world. May I
Also survive its meanings, and my own.

CHILDLESSNESS

The weather of this winter night, my mistress
Ranting and raining, wakes me. Her cloak blown back
To show the lining's dull lead foil
Sweeps along asphalt. Houses
Look blindly on; one glimmers through a blind.
Outside, I hear her tricklings
Arraign my little plot:
Had it or not agreed
To transplantation for the common good
Of certain rare growths yielding guaranteed
Gold pollen, gender of suns, large, hardy,
Enviable blooms? But in my garden
Nothing is planted. Neither
Is that glimmering window mine.
I lie and think about the rain,
How it has been drawn up from the impure ocean,
From gardens lightly, deliberately tainted;
How it falls back, time after time,
Through poisons visible at sunset
When the enchantress, masked as friend, unfurls
Entire bolts of voluminous pistachio,
Saffron, and rose.
These, as I fall back to sleep,
And other slow colours clothe me, glide
To rest, then burst along my limbs like buds,
Like bombs from the navigator's vantage,
Waking me, lulling me. Later I am shown
The erased metropolis reassembled
On sampans, freighted each
With toddlers, holy dolls, dead ancestors.
One tiny monkey puzzles over fruit.
The vision rises and falls, the garland

Gently takes root
In the sea's coma. Hours go by
Before I can stand to own
A sky stained red, a world
Clad only in rags, threadbare,
Dabbling the highway's ice with blood.
A world. The cloak thrown down for it to wear
In token of past servitude
Has fallen onto the shoulders of my parents
Whom it is eating to the bone.

SWIMMING BY NIGHT

A light going out in the forehead
Of the house by the ocean,
Into warm black its feints of diamond fade.
Without clothes, without caution

Plunging past gravity—
Wait! Where before
Had been floating nothing, is a gradual body
Half remembered, astral with phosphor,

Yours, risen from its tomb
In your own mind,
Haunting nimbleness, glimmerings a random
Spell has kindled. So that, new-limned

By this weak lamp
The evening's alcohol will feed
Until the genie chilling bids you limp
Heavily over stones to bed,

You wear your master's robe
One last time, the far break
Of waves, their length and sparkle, the spinning globe
You wear, and the star running down his cheek.

THE BROKEN HOME

Crossing the street,
I saw the parents and the child
At their window, gleaming like fruit
With evening's mild gold leaf.

In a room on the floor below,
Sunless, cooler—a brimming
Saucer of wax, marbly and dim—
I have lit what's left of my life.

I have thrown out yesterday's milk
And opened a book of maxims.
The flame quickens. The word stirs.

Tell me, tongue of fire,
That you and I are as real
At least as the people upstairs.

My father, who had flown in World War I,
Might have continued to invest his life
In cloud banks well above Wall Street and wife.
But the race was run below, and the point was to win.

Too late now, I make out in his blue gaze
(Through the smoked glass of being thirty-six)
The soul eclipsed by twin black pupils, sex
And business; time was money in those days.

Each thirteenth year he married. When he died
There were already several chilled wives
In sable orbit—rings, cars, permanent waves.
We'd felt him warming up for a green bride.

He could afford it. He was "in his prime"
At three score ten. But money was not time.

When my parents were younger this was a popular act:
A veiled woman would leap from an electric, wine-dark car

To the steps of no matter what—the Senate or the Ritz Bar—
And bodily, at newsreel speed, attack

No matter whom—Al Smith or José Maria Sert
Or Clemenceau—veins standing out on her throat
As she yelled *War mongerer! Pig! Give us the vote!*,
And would have to be hauled away in her hobble skirt.

What had the man done? Oh, made history.
Her business (he had implied) was giving birth,
Tending the house, mending the socks.

Always that same old story—
Father Time and Mother Earth,
A marriage on the rocks.

One afternoon, red, satyr-thighed
Michael, the Irish setter, head
Passionately lowered, led
The child I was to a shut door. Inside,

Blinds beat sun from the bed.
The green-gold room throbbed like a bruise.
Under a sheet, clad in taboos
Lay whom we sought, her hair undone, outspread,

And of a blackness found, if ever now, in old
Engravings where the acid bit.
I must have needed to touch it
Or the whiteness—was she dead?
Her eyes flew open, startled strange and cold.
The dog slumped to the floor. She reached for me. I fled.

Tonight they have stepped out onto the gravel.
The party is over. It's the fall
Of 1931. They love each other still.

She: Charlie, I can't stand the pace.
He: Come on, honey—why, you'll bury us all!

A lead soldier guards my windowsill:
Khaki rifle, uniform, and face.
Something in me grows heavy, silvery, pliable.

How intensely people used to feel!
Like metal poured at the close of a proletarian novel,
Refined and glowing from the crucible,
I see those two hearts, I'm afraid,
Still. Cool here in the graveyard of good and evil,
They are even so to be honored and obeyed.

. . . Obeyed, at least, inversely. Thus
I rarely buy a newspaper, or vote.
To do so, I have learned, is to invite
The tread of a stone guest within my house.

Shooting this rusted bolt, though, against him,
I trust I am no less time's child than some
Who on the heath impersonate Poor Tom
Or on the barricades risk life and limb.

Nor do I try to keep a garden, only
An avocado in a glass of water—
Roots pallid, gemmed with air. And later,

When the small gilt leaves have grown
Fleshy and green, I let them die, yes, yes,
And start another. I am earth's no less.

A child, a red dog roam the corridors,
Still, of the broken home. No sound. The brilliant
Rag runners halt before wide-open doors.
My old room! Its wallpaper—cream, medallioned
With pink and brown—brings back the first nightmares,
Long summer colds, and Emma, sepia-faced,
Perspiring over broth carried upstairs
Aswim with golden fats I could not taste.

The real house became a boarding school.
Under the ballroom ceiling's allegory
Someone at last may actually be allowed
To learn something; or, from my window, cool
With the unstiflement of the entire story,
Watch a red setter stretch and sink in cloud.

THE KIMONO

When I returned from lovers' lane
My hair was white as snow.
Joy, incomprehension, pain
I'd seen like seasons come and go.
How I got home again
Frozen half dead, perhaps you know.

You hide a smile and quote a text:
Desires ungratified
Persist from one life to the next.
Hearths we strip ourselves beside
Long, long ago were x'd
On blueprints of "consuming pride."

Times out of mind, the bubble-gleam
To our charred level drew
April back. A sudden beam . . .
—Keep talking while I change into
The pattern of a stream
Bordered with rushes white on blue.

W. D. Snodgrass

(1926–   )

APRIL INVENTORY

The green catalpa tree has turned
All white; the cherry blooms once more.
In one whole year I haven't learned
A blessed thing they pay you for.
The blossoms snow down in my hair;
The trees and I will soon be bare.

The trees have more than I to spare.
The sleek, expensive girls I teach,
Younger and pinker every year,
Bloom gradually out of reach.
The pear tree lets its petals drop
Like dandruff on a tabletop.

The girls have grown so young by now
I have to nudge myself to stare.
This year they smile and mind me how
My teeth are falling with my hair.
In thirty years I may not get
Younger, shrewder, or out of debt.

The tenth time, just a year ago,
I made myself a little list
Of all the things I'd ought to know,
Then told my parents, analyst,
And everyone who's trusted me
I'd be substantial, presently.

I haven't read one book about
A book or memorized one plot.
Or found a mind I did not doubt.
I learned one date. And then forgot.
And one by one the solid scholars
Get the degrees, the jobs, the dollars.

And smile above their starchy collars.
I taught my classes Whitehead's notions;
One lovely girl, a song of Mahler's.
Lacking a source-book or promotions,
I showed one child the colors of
A luna moth and how to love.

I taught myself to name my name,
To bark back, loosen love and crying;
To ease my woman so she came,
To ease an old man who was dying.
I have not learned how often I
Can win, can love, but choose to die.

I have not learned there is a lie
Love shall be blonder, slimmer, younger;
That my equivocating eye
Loves only by my body's hunger;
That I have forces, true to feel,
Or that the lovely world is real.

While scholars speak authority
And wear their ulcers on their sleeves,
My eyes in spectacles shall see
These trees procure and spend their leaves.
There is a value underneath
The gold and silver in my teeth.

Though trees turn bare and girls turn wives,
We shall afford our costly seasons;
There is a gentleness survives
That will outspeak and has its reasons.
There is a loveliness exists,
Preserves us, not for specialists.

Allen Ginsberg

(1 9 2 6 –)

TO AUNT ROSE

Aunt Rose—now—might I see you
with your thin face and buck tooth smile and pain
        of rheumatism—and a long black heavy shoe
                for your bony left leg
        limping down the long hall in Newark on the running carpet
                past the black grand piano
                        in the day room
                                where the parties were
                and I sang Spanish loyalist songs
                in a high squeaky voice
                        (hysterical) the committee listening
                while you limped around the room
                        collected the money—
        Aunt Honey, Uncle Sam, a stranger with a cloth arm
                in his pocket
                        and huge young bald head
                                of Abraham Lincoln Brigade

—your long sad face
        your tears of sexual frustration
                (what smothered sobs and bony hips
                        under the pillows of Osborne Terrace)
        —the time I stood on the toilet seat naked
                and you powdered my thighs with Calomine
                        against the poison ivy—my tender
                                and shamed first black curled hairs
        what were you thinking in secret heart then
                knowing me a man already-
        and I an ignorant girl of family silence on the thin pedestal
                of my legs in the bathroom—Museum of Newark.
                        Aunt Rose
        Hitler is dead, Hitler is in Eternity; Hitler is with
                Tamburlane and Emily Brontë

Though I see you walking still, a ghost on Osborne Terrace
     down the long dark hall to the front door
       limping a little with a pinched smile
         in what must have been a silken
           flower dress
   welcoming my father, the Poet, on his visit to Newark
       —see you arriving in the living room
         dancing on your crippled leg
        and clapping hands his book
          had been accepted by Liveright

Hitler is dead and Liveright's gone out of business
The Attic of the Past and *Everlasting Minute* are out of print
       Uncle Harry sold his last silk stocking
         Claire quit interpretive dancing school
           Buba sits a wrinkled monument in Old
           Ladies Home blinking at new babies
    last time I saw you was the hospital
      pale skull protruding under ashen skin
         blue veined unconscious girl
           in an oxygen tent
     the war in Spain has ended long ago
       Aunt Rose

WALES VISITATION

White fog lifting & falling on mountain-brow
    Trees moving in rivers of wind
         The clouds arise
  as on a wave, gigantic eddy lifting mist
    above teeming ferns exquisitely swayed
             along a green crag
    glimpsed thru mullioned glass in valley raine—

Bardic, O Self, Visitacione, tell naught
    but what seen by one man in a vale in Albion,
      of the folk, whose physical sciences end in Ecology,
         the wisdom of earthly relations,

of mouths & eyes interknit ten centuries visible
        orchards of mind language manifest human,
of the satanic thistle that raises its horned symmetry
    flowering above sister grass-daisies' pink tiny
            bloomlets angelic as lightbulbs—

Remember 160 miles from London's symmetrical thorned tower
    & network of TV pictures flashing bearded your Self
the lambs on the tree-nooked hillside this day bleating
heard in Blake's old ear, & the silent thought of Wordsworth in eld
                                                    Stillness
clouds passing through skeleton arches of Tintern Abbey—
        Bard Nameless as the Vast, babble to Vastness!

All the Valley quivered, one extended motion, wind
            undulating on mossy hills
a giant wash that sank white fog delicately down red runnels
            on the mountainside
whose leaf-branch tendrils moved asway
            in granitic undertow down—
and lifted the floating Nebulous upward, and lifted the arms of the trees
    and lifted the grasses an instant in balance
        and lifted the lambs to hold still
        and lifted the green of the hill, in one solemn wave
A solid mass of Heaven, mist-infused, ebbs thru the vale,
    a wavelet of Immensity, lapping gigantic through Llanthony Valley,
the length of all England, valley upon valley under Heaven's ocean
            tonned with cloud-hang,
        —Heaven balanced on a grassblade.
Roar of the mountain wind slow, sigh of the body,
    One Being on the mountainside stirring gently
        Exquisite scales trembling everywhere in balance,
    one motion thru the cloudy sky-floor shifting on the million feet of daisies,
one Majesty the motion that stirred wet grass quivering
    to the farthest tendril of white fog poured down
            through shivering flowers on the mountain's head—

No imperfection in the budded mountain,
    Valleys breathe, heaven and earth move together,
    daisies push inches of yellow air, vegetables tremble,
            grass shimmers green

sheep speckle the mountainside, revolving their jaws with empty eyes,
                    horses dance in the warm rain,
          tree-lined canals network live farmland,
                              blueberries fringe stone walls on hawthorn'd hills,
          pheasants croak on meadows haired with fern—
Out, out on the hillside, into the ocean sound, into delicate gusts of wet air,
Fall on the ground, O great Wetness, O Mother, No harm on your body!
Stare close, no imperfection in the grass,
                    each flower Buddha-eye, repeating the story,
                              myriad-formed—
Kneel before the foxglove raising green buds, mauve bells drooped
          doubled down the stem trembling antennae,
     & look in the eyes of the branded lambs that stare
          breathing stockstill under dripping hawthorn—
I lay down mixing my beard with the wet hair of the mountainside,
          smelling the brown vagina-moist ground, harmless,
               tasting the violet thistle-hair, sweetness—
One being so balanced, so vast, that its softest breath
          moves every floweret in the stillness on the valley floor,
     trembles lamb-hair hung gossamer rain-beaded in the grass,
lifts trees on their roots, birds in the great draught
          hiding their strength in the rain, bearing same weight,

Groan thru breast and neck, a great Oh! to earth heart
                    Calling our Presence together
     The great secret is no secret
               Senses fit the winds,
                    Visible is visible,
          rain-mist curtains wave through the bearded vale,
                    gray atoms wet the wind's kabbala
Crosslegged on a rock in dusk rain,
          rubber booted in soft grass, mind moveless,
breath trembles in white daisies by the roadside,
                    Heaven breath and my own symmetric
          Airs wavering thru antlered green fern
drawn in my navel, same breath as breathes thru Capel-Y-Ffn,
               Sounds of Aleph and Aum
                    through forests of gristle,
          my skull and Lord Hereford's Knob equal,
                    All Albion one.

What did I notice? Particulars! The
          vision of the great One is myriad—

smoke curls upward from ashtray,
house fire burned low,
The night, still wet & moody black heaven
starless
upward in motion with wet wind.

John Ashbery

(1927-   )

SOME TREES

These are amazing: each
Joining a neighbor, as though speech
Were a still performance.
Arranging by chance

To meet as far this morning
From the world as agreeing
With it, you and I
Are suddenly what the trees try

To tell us we are:
That their merely being there
Means something; that soon
We may touch, love, explain.

And glad not to have invented
Such comeliness, we are surrounded:
A silence already filled with noises,
A canvas on which emerges

A chorus of smiles, a winter morning.
Placed in a puzzling light, and moving,
Our days put on such reticence
These accents seem their own defense.

A BLESSING IN DISGUISE

Yes, they are alive and can have those colors,
But I, in my soul, am alive too.
I feel I must sing and dance, to tell
Of this in a way, that knowing you may be drawn to me.

And I sing amid despair and isolation
Of the chance to know you, to sing of me
Which are you. You see,
You hold me up to the light in a way

I should never have expected, or suspected, perhaps
Because you always tell me I am you,
And right. The great spruces loom.
I am yours to die with, to desire.

I cannot ever think of me, I desire you
For a room in which the chairs ever
Have their backs turned to the light
Inflicted on the stone and paths, the real trees

That seem to shine at me through a lattice toward you.
If the wild light of this January day is true
I pledge me to be truthful unto you
Whom I cannot ever stop remembering.

Remembering to forgive. Remember to pass beyond you into the day
On the wings of the secret you will never know.
Taking me from myself, in the path
Which the pastel girth of the day has assigned to me.

I prefer "you" in the plural, I want "you,"
You must come to me, all golden and pale
Like the dew and the air.
And then I start getting this feeling of exaltation.

SPRING DAY

The immense hope, and forbearance
Trailing out of night, to sidewalks of the day
Like air breathed into a paper city, exhaled
As night returns bringing doubts

That swarm around the sleeper's head
But are fended off with clubs and knives, so that morning

Installs again in cold hope
The air that was yesterday, is what you are,

In so many phases the head slips from the hand.
The tears ride freely, laughs or sobs:
What do they matter? There is free giving and taking;
The giant body relaxed as though beside a stream

Wakens to the force of it and has to recognize
The secret sweetness before it turns into life—
Sucked out of many exchanges, torn from the womb,
Disinterred before completely dead—and heaves

Its mountain-broad chest. "They were long in coming,
Those others, and mattered so little that it slowed them
To almost nothing. They were presumed dead,
Their names honorably grafted on the landscape

To be a memory to men. Until today
We have been living in their shell.
Now we break forth like a river breaking through a dam,
Pausing over the puzzled, frightened plain,

And our further progress shall be terrible,
Turning fresh knives in the wounds
In that gulf of recreation, that bare canvas
As matter-of-fact as the traffic and the day's noise."

The mountain stopped shaking; its body
Arched into its own contradiction, its enjoyment,
As far from us lights were put out, memories of boys and girls
Who walked here before the great change,

Before the air mirrored us,
Taking the opposite shape of our effort,
Its inseparable comment and corollary
But casting us farther and farther out.

Wha—what happened? You are with
The orange tree, so that its summer produce
Can go back to where we got it wrong, then drip gently
Into history, if it wants to. A page turned; we were

Just now floundering in the wind of its colossal death.
And whether it is Thursday, or the day is stormy,
With thunder and rain, or the birds attack each other,
We have rolled into another dream.

No use charging the barriers of that other:
It no longer exists. But you,
Gracious and growing thing, with those leaves like stars,
We shall soon give all our attention to you.

TRAIN RISING OUT OF THE SEA

It is written in the Book of Usable Minutes
That all things have their center in their dying,
That each is discrete and diaphanous and
Has pointed its prow away from the sand for the next trillion years.

After that we may be friends,
Recognizing in each other the precedents that make us truly social.
Do you hear the wind? It's not dying,
It's singing, weaving a song about the president saluting the trust,

The past in each of us, until so much memory becomes an institution,
Through sheer weight, the persistence of it, no,
Not the persistence: that makes it seem a deliberate act
Of duration, much too deliberate for this ingenuous being

Like an era that refuses to come to an end or be born again.
We need more night for the sky, more blue for the daylight
That inundates our remarks before we can make them
Taking away a little bit of us each time

To be deposited elsewhere
In the place of our involvement
With the core that brought excessive flowering this year
Of enormous sunsets and big breezes

That left you feeling too simple
Like an island just off the shore, one of many, that no one

Notices, though it has a certain function, though an abstract one
Built to prevent you from being towed to shore.

CRAZY WEATHER

It's this crazy weather we've been having:
Falling forward one minute, lying down the next
Among the loose grasses and soft, white, nameless flowers.
People have been making a garment out of it,
Stitching the white of lilacs together with lightning
At some anonymous crossroads. The sky calls
To the deaf earth. The proverbial disarray
Of morning corrects itself as you stand up.
You are wearing a text. The lines
Droop to your shoelaces and I shall never want or need
Any other literature than this poetry of mud
And ambitious reminiscences of times when it came easily
Through the then woods and ploughed fields and had
A simple unconscious dignity we can never hope to
Approximate now except in narrow ravines nobody
Will inspect where some late sample of the rare,
Uninteresting specimen might still be putting out shoots, for all we know.

AT NORTH FARM

Somewhere someone is traveling furiously toward you,
At incredible speed, traveling day and night,
Through blizzards and desert heat, across torrents, through narrow passes.
But will he know where to find you,
Recognize you when he sees you,
Give you the thing he has for you?

Hardly anything grows here,
Yet the granaries are bursting with meal,
The sacks of meal piled to the rafters.

The streams run with sweetness, fattening fish;
Birds darken the sky. Is it enough
That the dish of milk is set out at night,
That we think of him sometimes,
Sometimes and always, with mixed feelings?

DARLENE'S HOSPITAL

The hospital: it wasn't her idea
That the colors should slide muddy from the brush
And spew their random evocations everywhere,
Provided that things should pick up next season.
It was a way of living, to her way of thinking.
She took a job, it wasn't odd.
But then, backing through the way many minds had been made up,
It came again, the color, always a color
Climbing the apple of the sky, often
A secret lavender place you weren't supposed to look into.
And then a sneeze would come along
Or soon we'd be too far out from shore, on a milky afternoon
Somewhere in late August with the paint flaking off,
The lines of traffic flowing like mucus.
And they won't understand its importance, it's too bad,
Not even when it's too late.

Now we're often happy. The dark car
Moves heftily away along low bluffs,
And if we don't have our feelings, what
Good are we, but whose business is it?
Beware the happy man: once she perched light
In the reading space of my room, a present joy
For all time to come, whatever happens;
And still we rotate, gathering speed until
Nothing is there but more speed in the light ahead.
Such moments as we prized in life:
The promise of a new day, living with lots of people
All headed in more or less the same direction, the sound of this
In the embracing stillness, but not the brutality,

And lists of examples of lots of things, and shit—
What more could we conceivably be satisfied with, it is
Joy, and undaunted
She leaves the earth at that point,
Intersecting all our daydreams of breakfast and lunch.
The Lady of Shalott's in hot water again.

This and the dreams of any of the young
Were not her care. The river flowed
Hard by the hospital from whose gilded
Balconies and turrets fair spirits waved,
Lonely, like us. Here be no pursuers,
Only imagined animals and cries
In the wilderness, which made it "the wilderness,"
And suddenly the lonesomeness becomes a pleasant city
Fanning out around a lake; you get to meet
Precisely the person who would have been here now,
A dream no longer, and are polished and directed
By his deliberate grasp, back
To the reality that was always there despairing
Of your return as months and years went by,
Now silent again forever, the perfect space,
Attuned to your wristwatch
As though time would never go away again.

His dirty mind
Produced it all, an oratorio based on love letters
About our sexual habits in the early 1950s.
It wasn't that these stories weren't true,
Only that a different kind of work
Of the imagination had grown up around them, taller
Than redwoods, and not
Wanting to embarrass them, effaced itself
To the extent that a colossus could, and so you looked
And saw nothing, but suddenly felt better
Without wondering why. And the serial continues:
Pain, expiation, delight, more pain,
A frieze that lengthens continually, in the lucky way
Friezes do, and no plot is produced,
Nothing you could hang an identifying question on.
It's an imitation of pleasure; it may not work
But at least we'll know then that we'll have done
What we could, and chalk it up to virtue

Or just plain laziness. And if she glides
Backwards through us, a finger hooked
Out of death, we shall not know where the mystery began:
Inaccurate dreamers of our state,
Sodden from sitting in the rain too long.

William S. Merwin

(1927–   )

FOR THE ANNIVERSARY OF MY DEATH

Every year without knowing it I have passed the day
When the last fires will wave to me
And the silence will set out
Tireless traveller
Like the beam of a lightless star

Then I will no longer
Find myself in life as in a strange garment
Surprised at the earth
And the love of one woman
And the shamelessness of men
As today writing after three days of rain
Hearing the wren sing and the falling cease
And bowing not knowing to what

RAIN TRAVEL

I wake in the dark and remember
it is the morning when I must start
by myself on the journey
I lie listening to the black hour
before dawn and you are
still asleep beside me while
around us the trees full of night lean
hushed in their dream that bears
us up asleep and awake then I hear
drops falling one by one into
the sightless leaves and I
do not know when they began but
all at once there is no sound but rain
and the stream below us roaring
away into the rushing darkness

Galway Kinnell

(1 9 2 7 –   )

THE BEAR

1

In late winter
I sometimes glimpse bits of steam
coming up from
some fault in the old snow
and bend close and see it is lung-colored
and put down my nose
and know
the chilly, enduring odor of bear.

2

I take a wolf's rib and whittle
it sharp at both ends
and coil it up
and freeze it in blubber and place it out
on the fairway of the bears.

And when it has vanished
I move out on the bear tracks,
roaming in circles
until I come to the first, tentative, dark
splash on the earth.

And I set out
running, following the splashes
of blood wandering over the world.
At the cut, gashed resting places
I stop and rest,
at the crawl-marks
where he lay out on his belly
to overpass some stretch of bauchy ice

I lie out
dragging myself forward with bear-knives in my fists.

3

On the third day I begin to starve,
at nightfall I bend down as I knew I would
at a turd sopped in blood,
and hesitate, and pick it up,
and thrust it in my mouth, and gnash it down,
and rise
and go on running.

4

On the seventh day,
living by now on bear blood alone,
I can see his upturned carcass far out ahead, a scraggled,
steamy hulk,
the heavy fur riffling in the wind.

I come up to him
and stare at the narrow-spaced, petty eyes,
the dismayed
face laid back on the shoulder, the nostrils
flared, catching
perhaps the first taint of me as he
died.

I hack
a ravine in his thigh, and eat and drink,
and tear him down his whole length
and open him and climb in
and close him up after me, against the wind,
and sleep.

5

And dream
of lumbering flatfooted
over the tundra,
stabbed twice from within,
splattering a trail behind me,
splattering it out no matter which way I lurch,

no matter which parabola of bear transcendence,
which dance of solitude I attempt,
which gravity-clutched leap,
which trudge, which groan.

6

Until one day I totter and fall—
fall on this
stomach that has tried so hard to keep up,
to digest the blood as it leaked in,
to break up
and digest the bone itself: and now the breeze
blows over me, blows off
the hideous belches of ill-digested bear blood
and rotted stomach
and the ordinary, wretched odor of bear,

blows across
my sore, lolled tongue a song
or screech, until I think I must rise up
and dance. And I lie still.

7

I awaken I think. Marshlights
reappear, geese
come trailing again up the flyway.
In her ravine under old snow the dam-bear
lies, licking
lumps of smeared fur
and drizzly eyes into shapes
with her tongue. And one
hairy-soled trudge stuck out before me,
the next groaned out,
the next,
the next,
the rest of my days I spend
wandering: wondering
what, anyway,
was that sticky infusion, that rank flavor of blood, that poetry,
    by which I lived?

AFTER MAKING LOVE WE HEAR FOOTSTEPS

For I can snore like a bullhorn
or play loud music
or sit up talking with any reasonably sober Irishman
and Fergus will only sink deeper
into his dreamless sleep, which goes by all in one flash,
but let there be that heavy breathing
or a stifled come-cry anywhere in the house
and he will wrench himself awake
and make for it on the run—as now, we lie together,
after making love, quiet, touching along the length of our bodies,
familiar touch of the long-married,
and he appears—in his baseball pajamas, it happens,
the neck opening so small
he has to screw them on, which one day may make him wonder
about the mental capacity of baseball players—
and flops down between us and hugs us and snuggles himself to sleep,
his face gleaming with satisfaction at being this very child.

In the half darkness we look at each other
and smile
and touch arms across his little, startlingly muscled body—
this one whom habit of memory propels to the ground of his making,
sleeper only the mortal sounds can sing awake,
this blessing love gives again into our arms.

James Wright

(1 9 2 7 – 1 9 8 0   )

SPARROWS IN A HILLSIDE DRIFT

Pitiful dupes of old illusion, lost
And fallen in the white, they glitter still
Sprightly as when they bathed in summer dust,
Then fade among the crystals on the hill.

Lonely for warm days when the season broke,
Alert to wing and fire, they must have flown
To rest among those toughened boughs of oak
That brood above us, now the fire is gone.

Walking around to breathe, I kick aside
The soft brown feather and the brittle beak.
All flesh is fallen snow. The days deride
The wings of these deluded, once they break.

Somewhere the race of wittier birds survive,
Southering slowly with the cooling days.
They pause to quiver in the wind alive
Like some secure felicity of phrase.

But these few blunderers below my hands
Assault the ear with silence on the wind.
I lose their words, though winter understands.
Man is the listener gone deaf and blind.

The oak above us shivers in the bleak
And lucid winter day; and, far below
Our gathering of the cheated and the weak,
A chimney whispers to a cloud of snow.

MILKWEED

While I stood here, in the open, lost in myself,
I must have looked a long time
Down the corn rows, beyond grass,
The small house,
White walls, animals lumbering toward the barn.
I look down now. It is all changed.
Whatever it was I lost, whatever I wept for
Was a wild, gentle thing, the small dark eyes
Loving me in secret.
It is here. At a touch of my hand,
The air fills with delicate creatures
From the other world.

AUTUMN BEGINS IN MARTINS FERRY, OHIO

In the Shreve High football stadium,
I think of Polacks nursing long beers in Tiltonsville,
And gray faces of Negroes in the blast furnace at Benwood,
And the ruptured night watchman of Wheeling Steel,
Dreaming of heroes.

All the proud fathers are ashamed to go home.
Their women cluck like starved pullets,
Dying for love.

Therefore,
Their sons grow suicidally beautiful
At the beginning of October,
And gallop terribly against each other's bodies.

LYING IN A HAMMOCK AT
WILLIAM DUFFY'S FARM
IN PINE ISLAND, MINNESOTA

Over my head, I see the bronze butterfly,
Asleep on the black trunk,
Blowing like a leaf in green shadow.
Down the ravine behind the empty house,
The cowbells follow one another
Into the distances of the afternoon.
To my right,
In a field of sunlight between two pines,
The droppings of last year's horses
Blaze up into golden stones.
I lean back, as the evening darkens and comes on.
A chicken hawk floats over, looking for home.
I have wasted my life.

BEGINNING

The moon drops one or two feathers into the field.
The dark wheat listens.
Be still.
Now.
There they are, the moon's young, trying
Their wings.
Between trees, a slender woman lifts up the lovely shadow
Of her face, and now she steps into the air, now she is gone
Wholly, into the air.
I stand alone by an elder tree, I do not dare breathe
Or move.
I listen.
The wheat leans back toward its own darkness,
And I lean toward mine.

Anne Sexton

(1928–1974)

MUSIC SWIMS BACK TO ME

Wait Mister. Which way is home?
They turned the light out
and the dark is moving in the corner.
There are no sign posts in this room,
four ladies, over eighty,
in diapers every one of them.
La la la, Oh music swims back to me
and I can feel the tune they played
the night they left me
in this private institution on a hill.

Imagine it. A radio playing
and everyone here was crazy.
I liked it and danced in a circle.
Music pours over the sense
and in a funny way
music sees more than I.
I mean it remembers better;
remembers the first night here.
It was the strangled cold of November;
even the stars were strapped in the sky
and that moon too bright
forking through the bars to stick me
with a singing in the head.
I have forgotten all the rest.

They lock me in this chair at eight a.m.
and there are no signs to tell the way,
just the radio beating to itself
and the song that remembers
more than I. Oh, la la la,
this music swims back to me.
The night I came I danced a circle
and was not afraid.
Mister?

THE TRUTH THE DEAD KNOW

For my mother, born March 1902, died March 1959, and my
father, born February 1900, died June 1959

Gone, I say and walk from church,
refusing the stiff procession to the grave,
letting the dead ride alone in the hearse.
It is June. I am tired of being brave.

We drive to the Cape. I cultivate
myself where the sun gutters from the sky,
where the sea swings in like an iron gate
and we touch. In another country people die.

My darling, the wind falls in like stones
from the whitehearted water and when we touch
we enter touch entirely. No one's alone.
Men kill for this, or for as much.

And what of the dead? They lie without shoes
in their stone boats. They are more like stone
than the sea would be if it stopped. They refuse
to be blessed, throat, eye and knucklebone.

THE STARRY NIGHT

> That does not keep me from having a terrible need of—shall I say
> the word—religion. Then I go out at night to paint the stars.
> Vincent Van Gogh in a letter to his brother

The town does not exist
except where one black-haired tree slips
up like a drowned woman into the hot sky.
The town is silent. The night boils with eleven stars.
Oh starry starry night! This is how
I want to die.

It moves. They are all alive.
Even the moon bulges in its orange irons

to push children, like a god, from its eye.
The old unseen serpent swallows up the stars.
Oh starry starry night! This is how
I want to die:

into that rushing beast of the night,
sucked up by that great dragon, to split
from my life with no flag,
no belly,
no cry.

WANTING TO DIE

Since you ask, most days I cannot remember.
I walk in my clothing, unmarked by that voyage.
Then the almost unnameable lust returns.

Even then I have nothing against life.
I know well the grass blades you mention,
the furniture you have placed under the sun.

But suicides have a special language.
Like carpenters they want to know *which tools*.
They never ask *why build*.

Twice I have so simply declared myself,
have possessed the enemy, eaten the enemy,
have taken on his craft, his magic.

In this way, heavy and thoughtful,
warmer than oil or water,
I have rested, drooling at the mouth-hole.

I did not think of my body at needle point.
Even the cornea and the leftover urine were gone.
Suicides have already betrayed the body.

Still-born, they don't always die,
but dazzled, they can't forget a drug so sweet
that even children would look on and smile.

To thrust all that life under your tongue!—
that, all by itself, becomes a passion.
Death's a sad bone; bruised, you'd say,

and yet she waits for me, year after year,
to so delicately undo an old wound,
to empty my breath from its bad prison.

Balanced there, suicides sometimes meet,
raging at the fruit, a pumped-up moon,
leaving the bread they mistook for a kiss,

leaving the page of the book carelessly open,
something unsaid, the phone off the hook
and the love, whatever it was, an infection.

February 3, 1964

Peter Davison

(1928–   )

CROSS CUT

Slumped on a pallet of winter-withered grass
you lie dead at my feet, in age not quite
a century, perhaps, but twice as old as I am,
in a pose your twisted trunk and dwindling leaves
had never hinted, even at your sickest.
How many stubs your gangrened upper branches
had turned into sockets and armpits
for squirrel, coon and starling
to burrow in! You thrust erect as stiff
as the memory of my oldest neighbor who watches
each new spring for your fluttering bloom
and every August for a pride of pears—
green to the eye, woody to the tooth,
taut and cidery to the fumbling tongue.
For years we've watched you dying from the top,
a peril to climbing children and seekers of shade,
but knew that, pear-like, you could stand for years,
heart eaten out, just fingering your life.
Perhaps I could have helped you out of the air
with some shreds of your stature left intact,
but now I've failed you. You lie invisible
behind the wall, your most disgraceful branches
lopped and hauled for firewood, resting scarred,
beyond your element, crushed by your own weight,
shapeless and pitiful as a beachbound whale.
Only inches above the nourishing ground
a cross-cut stump, stark white, reveals at bottom
you're still as lively as the day you bloomed.
The hearts of your leaves shone out in valentines
and your windborne, lilting, sinewy boughs
heaped proudly up toward the waning sun
those glowing, softly tinted, bumper bushels.

Philip Levine

(1928–   )

ANIMALS ARE PASSING FROM OUR LIVES

It's wonderful how I jog
on four honed-down ivory toes
my massive buttocks slipping
like oiled parts with each light step.

I'm to market. I can smell
the sour, grooved block, I can smell
the blade that opens the hole
and the pudgy white fingers

that shake out the intestines
like a hankie. In my dreams
the snouts drool on the marble,
suffering children, suffering flies,

suffering the consumers
who won't meet their steady eyes
for fear they could see. The boy
who drives me along believes

that any moment I'll fall
on my side and drum my toes
like a typewriter or squeal
and shit like a new housewife

discovering television,
or that I'll turn like a beast
cleverly to hook his teeth
with my teeth. No. Not this pig.

ANGEL BUTCHER

At sun up I am up
hosing down the outdoor abattoir
getting ready. The water
steams and hisses on the white stones
and the air pales to a
thin blue.
                    Today it is
Christophe. I don't see him
come up the long climb or
know he's here until I hear
my breathing double
and he's beside me smiling
like a young girl.
                        He asks
me the names of all
the tools and all
their functions, he lifts
and weighs and
balances, and runs a long
forefinger down the tongue
of each blade.
                    He asks
me how I came to this place and
this work, and I tell him how
I began with animals, and
he tells me how
he began with animals. We
talk about growing up and losing
the strange things we never
understood and settling.
                        I help
him with his robes; he
has a kind of modesty and sits
on the stone table with
the ends of the gown crossed
in his lap.
                    He wants to die
like a rabbit, and he wants me
to help him. I hold

his wrist; it's small, like
the throat of a young hen, but
cool and dry. He holds
mine and I can feel the
blood thudding in the ring
his fingers make.
                    He helps me, he
guides my hand at first. I can
feel my shoulders settle and
the bones take the weight, I can
feel my lungs flower as the
swing begins. He smiles again
with only one side of his mouth
and looks down to the
dark valley where the cities
burn. When I hit
him he comes apart like a
perfect puzzle or an
old flower.
                    And my legs
dance and twitch for hours.

LATER STILL

Two sons are gone.
The end of winter, and the almond blooms
near the back fence. The plum, slower,
unfolds under a streaked sky. The words become,
like prayer, a kind of nonsense
which becomes the thought of our lives.

In middle age we came
to the nine years war, the stars raged
in our horoscopes and the land
turned inwards biting for its heart.

Now in February the pussy willow
furs in the chill wind. In March
the sudden peach, cherry, lilac, in summer

the drumming gourd, corn, grape, and later still
the ghostly milkweed and the last laugh.

BELLE ISLE, 1949

We stripped in the first warm spring night
and ran down into the Detroit River
to baptize ourselves in the brine
of car parts, dead fish, stolen bicycles,
melted snow. I remember going under
hand in hand with a Polish highschool girl
I'd never seen before, and the cries
our breath made caught at the same time
on the cold, and rising through the layers
of darkness into the final moonless atmosphere
that was this world, the girl breaking
the surface after me and swimming out
on the starless waters towards the lights
of Jefferson Ave. and the stacks
of the old stove factory unwinking.
Turning at last to see no island at all
but a perfect calm dark as far
as there was sight, and then a light
and another riding low out ahead
to bring us home, ore boats maybe, or smokers
walking alone. Back panting
to the gray coarse beach we didn't dare
fall on, the damp piles of clothes,
and dressing side by side in silence
to go back where we came from.

SNOW

Today the snow is drifting
on Belle Isle, and the ducks
are searching for some opening

to the filthy waters of their river.
On Grand River Avenue, which is not
in Venice but in Detroit, Michigan,
the traffic has slowed to a standstill
and yet a sober man has hit a parked car
and swears to the police he was
not guilty. The bright squads of children
on their way to school howl
at the foolishness of the world
they will try not to inherit.
Seen from inside a window,
even a filthy one like those
at Automotive Supply Company, the snow
which has been falling for hours
is more beautiful than even the spring
grass which once unfurled here
before the invention of steel and fire,
for spring grass is what the earth sang
in answer to the new sun, to
melting snow, and the dark rain
of spring nights. But snow is nothing.
It has no melody or form, it
is as though the tears of all
the lost souls rose to heaven
and were finally heard and blessed
with substance and the power of flight
and given their choice chose then
to return to earth, to lay their
great pale cheek against the burning
cheek of earth and say, There, there, child.

BELIEF

No one believes in the calm
of the North Wind after a time
of rage and depression.
No one believes the sea cares nothing
for the shore or that
the long black volcanic reefs

that rise and fall from sight
each day are the hands
of some forgotten creature
trying to touch the unknowable
heart of water. No one believes
that the lost breath of a man
who died in 1821 is my breath
and that I will live until
I no longer want to, and then
I will write my name
in water, as he did, and pass
this breath to anyone who can
believe that life comes back
again and again without end
and always with the same face—
the face that broke in daylight
before the waves at Depot Bay
curling shoreward over and over
just after dawn as the sky cracked
into long slender fingers of light
and I heard your breath beside me
calm and sweet as you returned
to the dark crowded harbor of sleep.
That man will never return. He ate
the earth and the creatures of the sea
and the air, and so it is time he fed
the small tough patches of grass
that fight for water and air
between the blocks on the long walk
to and from school, it is time
that whatever he said began
first to echo and then fade
in the mind of no one
who listened, and that the bed
that moaned under his weight
be released, and that his shoes curl
upward at last and die, for they too
were only the skins of other animals,
not the bear or tiger he prayed to be
before he knew he too was animal,
but the slow ox that sheds his flesh
so that we might grow to our full height—
the beasts no one yearns to become

as young men dream of the sudden fox
threading his way up the thick hillside
and the old of the full-bellied seal,
whiskered and wisely playful. At the beach
at Castelldefels in 1965 a stout man
in his bare socks stood
above two young women stretched out
and dressed in almost nothing.
In one hand he held his vest,
his shoes, and his suit jacket
and with the other he pointed to those
portions of them he most admired,
and he named them in the formal,
guttural Spanish of the Catalan gentleman.
He went away with specks of fine sand
caught on his socks to remind him
that to enter the fire is to be burned
and that the finger he pointed would
blacken in time and probe the still earth,
root-like, stubborn, and find its life
in darkness. No one believes he
knew all this and dared the sea
to rise that moment and take him
away on a journey without end
or that the bodies of the drowned collect
light from the farthest stars and rise
at night to glow without song.
No one believes that to die
is beautiful, that after the hard pain
of the last unsaid word I am swept
in a calm out from shore
and hang in the silence of millions
for the first time among all my family
and that the magic of water
which has filled me becomes me
and I flow into every crack and crevice
where light can enter. Even my oak
takes me to heart. I shadow the yard
where you come in the evening
to talk while the light rises slowly
skyward, and you shiver a moment
before you go in, not believing
my voice in your ear and that the tall trees

blowing in the wind are sea sounds.
No one believes that tonight is the journey
across dark water to the lost continent
no one named. Do you hear the wind
rising all around you? That comes
only after this certain joy. Do you hear
the waves breaking, even in the darkness,
radiant and full? Close your eyes, close
them and follow us toward the first light.

John Hollander

(1 9 2 9 –   )

THE GREAT BEAR

Even on clear nights, lead the most supple children
Out onto hilltops, and by no means will
They make it out. Neither the gruff round image
From a remembered page nor the uncertain
Finger tracing that image out can manage
To mark the lines of what ought to be there,
Passing through certain bounding stars, until
The whole massive expanse of bear appear
Swinging, across the ecliptic; and, although
The littlest ones say nothing, others respond,
Making us thankful in varying degrees
For what we would have shown them: "There it is!"
"I see it now!" Even "Very like a bear!"
Would make us grateful. Because there is no bear

We blame our memory of the picture: trudging
Up the dark, starlit path, stooping to clutch
An anxious hand, perhaps the outline faded
Then; perhaps could we have retained the thing
In mind ourselves, with it we might have staged
Something convincing. We easily forget
The huge, clear, homely dipper that is such
An event to reckon with, an object set
Across the space the bear should occupy;
But even so, the trouble lies in pointing
At any stars. For one's own finger aims
Always elsewhere: the man beside one seems
Never to get the point. "No! The bright star
Just above my fingertip." The star,

If any, that he sees beyond one's finger
Will never be the intended one. To bring
Another's eye to bear in such a fashion
On any single star seems to require

Something very like a constellation
That both habitually see at night;
Not in the stars themselves, but in among
Their scatter, perhaps, some old familiar sight
Is always there to take a bearing from.
And if the smallest child of all should cry
Out on the wet, black grass because he sees
Nothing but stars, though claiming that there is
Some bear not there that frightens him, we need
Only reflect that we ourselves have need

Of what is fearful (being really nothing)
With which to find our way about the path
That leads back down the hill again, and with
Which to enable the older children standing
By us to follow what we mean by "This
Star," "That one," or "The other one beyond it."
But what of the tiny, scared ones?—Such a bear,
Who needs it? We can still make do with both
The dipper that we always knew was there
And the bright, simple shapes that suddenly
Emerge on certain nights. To understand
The signs that stars compose, we need depend
Only on stars that are entirely there
And the apparent space between them. There

Never need be lines between them, puzzling
Our sense of what is what. What a star does
Is never to surprise us as it covers
The center of its patch of darkness, sparkling
Always, a point in one of many figures.
One solitary star would be quite useless,
A frigid conjecture, true but trifling;
And any single sign is meaningless
If unnecessary. Crab, bull, and ram,
Or frosty, irregular polygons of our own
Devising, or finally the Great Dark Bear
That we can never quite believe is there—
Having the others, any one of them
Can be dispensed with. The bear, of all of them,

Is somehow most like any one, taken
At random, in that we always tend to say

That just because it might be there; because
Some Ancients really traced it out, a broken
And complicated line, webbing bright stars
And fainter ones together; because a bear
Habitually appeared—then even by day
It is for us a thing that should be there.
We should not want to train ourselves to see it.
The world is everything that happens to
Be true. The stars at night seem to suggest
The shapes of what might be. If it were best,
Even, to have it there (such a great bear!
All hung with stars!), there still would be no bear.

MORNING IN THE ISLANDS

We had sat up all night hearing it roar, the mere
Sea, roaring out of the large darkness that was full
Of the only idea of ocean, overarched
Higher above our listening than what we heard
Was itself above the roaring. Then afterwards,
Day came toward us wearing an argument of light:
It turned us to the brightness of our deceptions,
The rightness of our wrongings of the visible
Sky, in all its various state of mind. It was
To get the point of some pediment, supported
By studied columns above a deeply read sea,
That we ourselves had kept on being part of the
Picture for so long. Behind us, intent on far
Distances, were clear-headed cliffs; below, what we
Had been ignoring sang in the heart of the rock.

THE MAD POTTER

Now at the turn of the year this coil of clay
Bites its own tail: a New Year starts to choke
On the old one's ragged end. I bite my tongue

As the end of me—of my rope of stuff and nonsense
(The nonsense held, it was the stuff that broke),
Of bones and light, of levity and crime,
Of reddish clay and hope—still bides its time.

        •

Each of my pots is quite unusable,
Even for contemplating as an object
Of gross unuse. In its own mode of being
Useless, though, each of them remains unique,
Subject to nothing, and themselves unseeing,
Stronger by virtue of what makes them weak.

        •

I pound at all my clay. I pound the air.
This senseless lump, slapped into something like
Something, sits bound around by my despair.
For even as the great Creator's free
Hand shapes the forms of life, so—what? This pot,
Unhollowed solid, too full of itself,
Runneth over with incapacity.
I put it with the others on the shelf.

        •

These tiny cups will each provide one sip
Of what's inside them, aphoristic prose
Unwilling, like full arguments, to make
Its points, then join them in extended lines
Like long draughts from the bowl of a deep lake.
The honey of knowledge, like my milky slip,
Firms slowly up against what merely flows.

        •

Some of my older pieces bore inscriptions
That told a story only when you'd learned
How not to read them: LIVE reverted to EVIL,
EROS kept running backwards into SORE.
Their words, all fired up for truth, got burned.
I'll not write on weak vessels any more.

        •

My juvenilia? I gave them names
In those days: Hans was all handles and no spout;
Bernie believed the whole world turned about
Himself alone; Sadie was close to James
(But Herman touched her bottom when he could);
Paul fell to pieces; Peter wore away
To nothing; Len was never any good;

Alf was a flat, random pancake, May
An opened blossom; Bud was an ash-tray.
Even their names break off, though: Whatsisface,
That death-mask of Desire, and—you know!—
The smaller version of that (Oh, what was it?—
You know . . .) All of my pots now have to go
By number only. Which is no disgrace.

     ●

Begin with being—in an anagram
Of unending—conclude in some dark den;
This is no matter. What I've been, I am:
What I will be is what I make of all
This clay, this moment. Now begin again . . .
Poured out of emptiness, drop by slow drop,
I start up at the quarreling sounds of water.
Pots cry out silently at me to stop.

     ●

What are we like? A barrelfull of this
Oozy wet substance, shadow-crammed, whose smudges
Of darkness lurk within but rise to kiss
The fingers that disturb the gentle edges
Of their bland world of shapelessness and bliss.

     ●

The half-formed cup cries out in agony,
The lump of clay suffers a silent pain.
I heard the cup, though, full of feeling, say
"O clay be true, O clay keep constant to
Your need to take, again and once again,
This pounding from your mad creator who
Only stops hurting when he's hurting you."

     ●

What will I then have left behind me? Over
The years I have originated some
Glazes that wear away at what they cover
And weep for what they never can become.
My Deadware, widely imitated; blue
Skyware of an amazing lightness; tired
Hopeware that I abandoned for my own
Good reasons; Hereware; Thereware; ware that grew
Weary of everything that earth desired;
Hellware that dances while it's being fired,
Noware that vanishes while being thrown.

     ●

Appearing to be silly, wisdom survives
Like tribes of superseded gods who go
Hiding in caves of triviality
From which they laughingly control our lives.
So with my useless pots: safe from the blow
Of carelessness, or outrage at their flaws,
They brave time's lion and his smashing paws.
—All of which tempts intelligence to call
Pure uselessness one more commodity.
The Good-for-Nothing once became our Hero,
But images of him, laid-back, carelessly
Laughing, were upright statues after all.
From straight above, each cup adds up to zero.

     •

Clay to clay: Soon I shall indeed become
Dumb as these solid cups of hardened mud
(Dull *terra cruda* colored like our blood);
Meanwhile the slap and thump of palm and thumb
On wet mis-shapenness begins to hum
With meaning that was silent for so long.
The words of my wheel's turning come to ring
Truer than Truth itself does, my great *Ding
Dong-an-sich* that echoes everything
(Against it even lovely bells ring wrong):
Its whole voice gathers up the purest parts
Of all our speech, the vowels of the earth,
The aspirations of our hopeful hearts
Or the prophetic sibillance of song.

Robert Pack

(1 9 2 9 –   )

THE THRASHER IN THE WILLOW BY THE LAKE

Now I can tell you. Hearing the shrill leaves
Swishing with your hair, I can recall
Just how it happened: the air was thick and still,
Like now, and I could see the lake reflect
The thrasher in the willow tree. I paused,
Knowing that I could never make her change.

I told her that I thought no simple change
Could help—it was too late for help—but still
The thrasher in the willow tree had paused
As if it were an omen to reflect
What the lake desired so that I could recall
Myself in the stirred wind and fish-like leaves.

I stared at her among the willow leaves;
If she looked young or old or if some change
Showed rippling in her face, I can't recall.
I know the thrasher saw her when he paused
Over the lake as if he could reflect
Upon his past, stop it and keep it still.

Like this I held her—she would not stay still.
I watched, just like the thrasher, as the leaves
Stirred in the willow tree, and then I paused,
Groping for breath, to see the lake reflect
The blurring wind. Her face refused to change
Enough because she knew I would recall

That moment always, that I would recall
When her eye met the thrasher's eye—and paused,
And might have, but never did, let me change.
Her lake sounds gurgled with the fish-like leaves,
And if you listen, you can hear them still.
Listen, they call in the willow, they reflect

663

The crying of the lake, and they reflect
The words she might have said to make me change.
Maybe she said them, but I can't recall
Ever hearing them in the willow leaves
When the thrasher blinked and her eye went still.
You know now why I brought you here and paused,

And since I could not change when the sun paused
To reflect the thrasher's eye among the leaves,
The willow will recall your face when the lake goes still.

PROTON DECAY

> Most visible matter—stars, galaxies, and gas clouds—is made of
> hydrogen, and the nucleus of the hydrogen atom is a single
> proton. If protons decay, then the very substance of the universe
> is slowly rotting away like a cancer that infects matter itself. This
> rotting away of matter will, according to these unified [field]
> theories, take about a thousand billion billion (10^{21}) times the
> present age of the universe. We will have lots of time to explore
> the universe before it vanishes.
>
> Heinz R. Pagels, *The Cosmic Code*

From where I stand, Professor Pagels,
pausing in the tall grass as I climb the pathless hill
back to my house, picking wild asters for
the red vase on my window sill,

I say to you out loud *how much*—
how much I wish to dwell within the dwindling harvest
of my life a longer while,
how much our universe is blessed

simply by being here,
where nothing might have been, with still to go some
thousand billion billion times the age
we have already come

if matter is infected with such cancerous
but slow proton decay.
I greet your greeting to explore our universe
before time radiates away,

although, Professor, stranger, your
field theory estimate of crabbing time's disease
             stretches the earthbound scale
of my mere mankind-measuring anxieties.

             And yet I know that my wild asters
from the umbering, September valley hold
             their glow for three days
in my house, their yellow centers tarnish into gold—

             then they're forever gone,
partaking of disaster matter must at last
             experience. Right now there are
more species than *this* griever in the parting grass

             can keep at heart, in mind,
like Aromatic, Bushy, Calico, with purple blue,
             and through the alphabet to Showy,
Upland White, and Willow, my thought-gifts to you,

             my fellow mourner. So, let us
             be bound by flowing grace
of words that cherish, words that touch across
             what mortal time and space

remain, though even if we two could live to name
             each single flower and each leaf,
those billions of last years before the end
             would seem too sad, too brief,

             when, inescapably, the end did come.
Always, in thought, the end nears now—death in our minds
             outlives our lives, it's part of us,
it's always what our wakeful searching finds,

             and every flowered star we love
             is brief as azure nightfall on this hill,
brief as companionable breath that lengthens into words
             and then goes still.

Adrienne Rich

(1 9 2 9 –   )

AUNT JENNIFER'S TIGERS

Aunt Jennifer's tigers prance across a screen,
Bright topaz denizens of a world of green.
They do not fear the men beneath the tree;
They pace in sleek chivalric certainty.

Aunt Jennifer's fingers fluttering through her wool
Find even the ivory needle hard to pull.
The massive weight of Uncle's wedding band
Sits heavily upon Aunt Jennifer's hand.

When Aunt is dead, her terrified hands will lie
Still ringed with ordeals she was mastered by.
The tigers in the panel that she made
Will go on prancing, proud and unafraid.

IN THE EVENING

Three hours chain-smoking words
and you move on. We stand in the porch,
two archaic figures: a woman and a man.

The old masters, the old sources,
haven't a clue what we're about,
shivering here in the half-dark 'sixties.

Our minds hover in a famous impasse
and cling together. Your hand
grips mine like a railing on an icy night.

The wall of the house is bleeding. Firethorn!
The moon, cracked every-which-way,
pushes steadily on.

DIVING INTO THE WRECK

First having read the book of myths,
and loaded the camera,
and checked the edge of the knife-blade,
I put on
the body-armor of black rubber
the absurd flippers
the grave and awkward mask.
I am having to do this
not like Cousteau with his
assiduous team
aboard the sun-flooded schooner
but here alone.

There is a ladder.
The ladder is always there
hanging innocently
close to the side of the schooner.
We know what it is for,
we who have used it.
Otherwise
it's a piece of maritime floss
some sundry equipment.

I go down.
Rung after rung and still
the oxygen immerses me
the blue light
the clear atoms
of our human air.
I go down.
My flippers cripple me,
I crawl like an insect down the ladder
and there is no one
to tell me when the ocean
will begin.

First the air is blue and then
it is bluer and then green and then
black I am blacking out and yet
my mask is powerful

it pumps my blood with power
the sea is another story
the sea is not a question of power
I have to learn alone
to turn my body without force
in the deep element.

And now: it is easy to forget
what I came for
among so many who have always
lived here
swaying their crenellated fans
between the reefs
and besides
you breathe differently down here.

I came to explore the wreck.
The words are purposes.
The words are maps.
I came to see the damage that was done
and the treasures that prevail.
I stroke the beam of my lamp
slowly along the flank
of something more permanent
than fish or weed

the thing I came for:
the wreck and not the story of the wreck
the thing itself and not the myth
the drowned face always staring
toward the sun
the evidence of damage
worn by salt and sway into this threadbare beauty
the ribs of the disaster
curving their assertion
among the tentative haunters.

This is the place.
And I am here, the mermaid whose dark hair
streams black, the merman in his armored body
We circle silently
about the wreck
we dive into the hold.
I am she: I am he

whose drowned face sleeps with open eyes
whose breasts still bear the stress
whose silver, copper, vermeil cargo lies
obscurely inside barrels
half-wedged and left to rot
we are the half-destroyed instruments
that once held to a course
the water-eaten log
the fouled compass

We are, I am, you are
by cowardice or courage
the one who find our way
back to this scene
carrying a knife, a camera
a book of myths
in which
our names do not appear.

POWER

Living   in the earth-deposits   of our history

Today a backhoe divulged   out of a crumbling flank of earth
one bottle   amber   perfect   a hundred-year-old
cure for fever   or melancholy   a tonic
for living on this earth   in the winters of this climate

Today I was reading about Marie Curie:
she must have known she suffered   from radiation sickness
her body bombarded for years   by the element
she had purified
It seems she denied to the end
the source of the cataracts on her eyes
the cracked and suppurating skin   of her finger-ends
till she could no longer hold   a test-tube or a pencil

She died   a famous woman   denying
her wounds
denying
her wounds   came   from the same source as her power

INTEGRITY

> The quality or state of being complete; unbroken condition;
> entirety.
>
> Webster

A wild patience has taken me this far

as if I had to bring to shore
a boat with a spasmodic outboard motor
old sweaters, nets, spray-mottled books
tossed in the prow
some kind of sun burning my shoulder-blades.
Splashing the oarlocks. Burning through.
Your fore-arms can get scalded, licked with pain
in a sun blotted like unspoken anger
behind a casual mist.

The length of daylight
this far north, in this
forty-ninth year of my life
is critical.

The light is critical: of me, of this
long-dreamed, involuntary landing
on the arm of an inland sea.
The glitter of the shoal
depleting into shadow
I recognize: the stand of pines
violet-black really, green in the old postcard
but really I have nothing but myself
to go by; nothing
stands in the realm of pure necessity
except what my hands can hold.

Nothing but myself? . . . My selves.
After so long, this answer.
As if I had always known
I steer the boat in, simply.
The motor dying on the pebbles
cicadas taking up the hum
dropped in the silence.

Anger and tenderness: my selves.
And now I can believe they breathe in me
as angels, not polarities.
Anger and tenderness: the spider's genius
to spin and weave in the same action
from her own body, anywhere—
even from a broken web.

The cabin in the stand of pines
is still for sale. I know this. Know the print
of the last foot, the hand that slammed and locked that door,
then stopped to wreathe the rain-smashed clematis
back on the trellis
for no one's sake except its own.
I know the chart nailed to the wallboards
the icy kettle squatting on the burner.
The hands that hammered in those nails
emptied that kettle one last time
are these two hands
and they have caught the baby leaping
from between trembling legs
and they have worked the vacuum aspirator
and stroked the sweated temples
and steered the boat here through this hot
misblotted sunlight, critical light
imperceptibly scalding
the skin these hands will also salve.

TATTERED KADDISH

Taurean reaper of the wild apple field
messenger from earthmire gleaning
transcripts of fog
in the nineteenth year and the eleventh month
speak your tattered Kaddish for all suicides:

Praise to life though it crumbled in like a tunnel
on ones we knew and loved

Praise to life though its windows blew shut
on the breathing-room of ones we knew and loved

Praise to life though ones we knew and loved
loved it badly, too well, and not enough

Praise to life though it tightened like a knot
on the hearts of ones we thought we knew loved us

Praise to life giving room and reason
to ones we knew and loved who felt unpraisable

Praise to them, how they loved it, when they could.

Gary Snyder

(1 9 3 0 –   )

MID-AUGUST AT
SOURDOUGH MOUNTAIN LOOKOUT

Down valley a smoke haze
Three days heat, after five days rain
Pitch glows on the fir-cones
Across rocks and meadows
Swarms of new flies.

I cannot remember things I once read
A few friends, but they are in cities.
Drinking cold snow-water from a tin cup
Looking down for miles
Through high still air.

AXE HANDLES

One afternoon the last week in April
Showing Kai how to throw a hatchet
One-half turn and it sticks in a stump.
He recalls the hatchet-head
Without a handle, in the shop
And go gets it, and wants it for his own.
A broken-off axe handle behind the door
Is long enough for a hatchet,
We cut it to length and take it
With the hatchet head
And working hatchet, to the wood block.
There I begin to shape the old handle
With the hatchet, and the phrase
First learned from Ezra Pound
Rings in my ears!

"When making an axe handle
      the pattern is not far off."
And I say this to Kai
"Look: We'll shape the handle
By checking the handle
Of the axe we cut with—"
And he sees. And I hear it again:
It's in Lu Ji's *Wên Fu*, fourth century
A.D. "Essay on Literature"—in the
Preface: "In making the handle
Of an axe
By cutting wood with an axe
The model is indeed near at hand."
My teacher Shih-hsiang Chen
Translated that and taught it years ago
And I see: Pound was an axe,
Chen was an axe, I am an axe
And my son a handle, soon
To be shaping again, model
And tool, craft of culture,
How we go on.

THE SNOW ON SADDLE MOUNTAIN

The only thing that can be relied on
is the snow on Kurakake Mountain.
fields and woods
thawing, freezing, and thawing,
totally untrustworthy.
it's true, a great fuzzy windstorm
like yeast up there today, still
the only faint source of hope
is the snow on Kurakake mountain.

(*By* Miyazawa Kenji;
translated by Gary Snyder)

Sylvia Plath

(1932–1963)

MORNING SONG

Love set you going like a fat gold watch.
The midwife slapped your footsoles, and your bald cry
Took its place among the elements.

Our voices echo, magnifying your arrival. New statue.
In a drafty museum, your nakedness
Shadows our safety. We stand round blankly as walls.

I'm no more your mother
Than the cloud that distills a mirror to reflect its own slow
Effacement at the wind's hand.

All night your moth-breath
Flickers among the flat pink roses. I wake to listen:
A far sea moves in my ear.

One cry, and I stumble from bed, cow-heavy and floral
In my Victorian nightgown.
Your mouth opens clean as a cat's. The window square

Whitens and swallows its dull stars. And now you try
Your handful of notes;
The clear vowels rise like balloons.

DADDY

You do not do, you do not do
Any more, black shoe
In which I have lived like a foot
For thirty years, poor and white,
Barely daring to breathe or Achoo.

675

Daddy, I have had to kill you.
You died before I had time——
Marble-heavy, a bag full of God,
Ghastly statue with one gray toe
Big as a Frisco seal

And a head in the freakish Atlantic
Where it pours bean green over blue
In the waters off beautiful Nauset.
I used to pray to recover you.
Ach, du.

In the German tongue, in the Polish town
Scraped flat by the roller
Of wars, wars, wars.
But the name of the town is common.
My Polack friend

Says there are a dozen or two.
So I never could tell where you
Put your foot, your root,
I never could talk to you.
The tongue stuck in my jaw.

It stuck in a barb wire snare.
Ich, ich, ich, ich,
I could hardly speak.
I thought every German was you.
And the language obscene

An engine, an engine
Chuffing me off like a Jew.
A Jew to Dachau, Auschwitz, Belsen.
I began to talk like a Jew.
I think I may well be a Jew.

The snows of the Tyrol, the clear beer of Vienna
Are not very pure or true.
With my gipsy ancestress and my weird luck
And my Taroc pack and my Taroc pack
I may be a bit of a Jew.

I have always been scared of *you*,
With your Luftwaffe, your gobbledygoo.
And your neat mustache
And your Aryan eye, bright blue.
Panzer-man, panzer-man, O You——

Not God but a swastika
So black no sky could squeak through.
Every woman adores a Fascist,
The boot in the face, the brute
Brute heart of a brute like you.

You stand at the blackboard, daddy,
In the picture I have of you,
A cleft in your chin instead of your foot
But no less a devil for that, no not
Any less the black man who

Bit my pretty red heart in two.
I was ten when they buried you.
At twenty I tried to die
And get back, back, back to you.
I thought even the bones would do.

But they pulled me out of the sack,
And they stuck me together with glue.
And then I knew what to do.
I made a model of you,
A man in black with a Meinkampf look

And a love of the rack and the screw.
And I said I do, I do.
So daddy, I'm finally through.
The black telephone's off at the root,
The voices just can't worm through.

If I've killed one man, I've killed two——
The vampire who said he was you
And drank my blood for a year,
Seven years, if you want to know.
Daddy, you can lie back now.

There's a stake in your fat black heart
And the villagers never liked you.
They are dancing and stamping on you.
They always *knew* it was you.
Daddy, daddy, you bastard, I'm through.

FEVER 103°

Pure? What does it mean?
The tongues of hell
Are dull, dull as the triple

Tongues of dull, fat Cerberus
Who wheezes at the gate. Incapable
Of licking clean

The aguey tendon, the sin, the sin.
The tinder cries.
The indelible smell

Of a snuffed candle!
Love, love, the low smokes roll
From me like Isadora's scarves, I'm in a fright

One scarf will catch and anchor in the wheel.
Such yellow sullen smokes
Make their own element. They will not rise,

But trundle round the globe
Choking the aged and the meek,
The weak

Hothouse baby in its crib,
The ghastly orchid
Hanging its hanging garden in the air,

Devilish leopard!
Radiation turned it white
And killed it in an hour.

Greasing the bodies of adulterers
Like Hiroshima ash and eating in.
The sin. The sin.

Darling, all night
I have been flickering, off, on, off, on.
The sheets grow heavy as a lecher's kiss.

Three days. Three nights.
Lemon water, chicken
Water, water make me retch.

I am too pure for you or anyone.
Your body
Hurts me as the world hurts God. I am a lantern——

My head a moon
Of Japanese paper, my gold beaten skin
Infinitely delicate and infinitely expensive.

Does not my heat astound you. And my light.
All by myself I am a huge camellia
Glowing and coming and going, flush on flush.

I think I am going up,
I think I may rise——
The beads of hot metal fly, and I, love, I

Am a pure acetylene
Virgin
Attended by roses,

By kisses, by cherubim,
By whatever these pink things mean.
Not you, nor him

Not him, nor him
(My selves dissolving, old whore petticoats)——
To Paradise.

ARIEL

Stasis in darkness.
Then the substanceless blue
Pour of tor and distances.

God's lioness,
How one we grow,
Pivot of heels and knees!—The furrow

Splits and passes, sister to
The brown arc
Of the neck I cannot catch,

Nigger-eye
Berries cast dark
Hooks——

Black sweet blood mouthfuls,
Shadows.
Something else

Hauls me through air——
Thighs, hair;
Flakes from my heels.

White
Godiva, I unpeel——
Dead hands, dead stringencies.

And now I
Foam to wheat, a glitter of seas.
The child's cry

Melts in the wall.
And I
Am the arrow,

The dew that flies
Suicidal, at one with the drive
Into the red

Eye, the cauldron of morning.

Anne Stevenson

(1 9 3 3 –   )

THE SPIRIT IS TOO BLUNT AN INSTRUMENT

The spirit is too blunt an instrument
to have made this baby.
Nothing so unskilful as human passions
could have managed the intricate
exacting particulars: the tiny
blind bones with their manipulating tendons,
the knee and the knucklebones, the resilient
fine meshings of ganglia and vertebrae
in the chain of the difficult spine.

Observe the distinct eyelashes and sharp crescent
fingernails, the shell-like complexity
of the ear with its firm involutions
concentric in miniature to the minute
ossicles. Imagine the
infinitesimal capillaries, the flawless connections
of the lungs, the invisible neural filaments
through which the completed body
already answers to the brain.

Then name any passion or sentiment
possessed of the simplest accuracy.
No. No desire or affection could have done
with practice what habit
has done perfectly, indifferently,
through the body's ignorant precision.
It is left to the vagaries of the mind to invent
love and despair and anxiety
and their pain.

IN THE ORCHARD

Black bird, black voice,
almost the shadow of a voice,
so kind to this tired summer sky,
a rim of night around it,
yet almost an echo of today,
all the days since that first
soft guttural disaster
gave us "apple" and "tree"
and all that transpired thereafter
in the city of the tongue.

Blackbird, so old, so young,
happy to be stricken with a song
you can never choose away from.

Imamu Amiri Baraka

(1934 –)

RETURN OF THE NATIVE

Harlem is vicious
modernism. BangClash.
Vicious the way its made.
Can you stand such beauty?
So violent and transforming.
The trees blink naked, being
so few. The women stare
and are in love with them
selves. The sky sits awake
over us. Screaming
at us. No rain.
Sun, hot cleaning sun
drives us under it.

The place, and place
meant of
black people. Their heavy Egypt.
(Weird word!) Their minds, mine,
the black hope mine. In Time.
We slide along in pain or too
happy. So much love
for us. All over, so much of
what we need. Can you sing
yourself, your life, your place
on the warm planet earth.
And look at the stones

the hearts, the gentle hum
of meaning. Each thing, life
we have, or love, is meant
for us in a world like this.
Where we may see ourselves

all the time. And suffer
in joy, that our lives
are so familiar.

LEGACY

For Blues People

In the south, sleeping against
the drugstore, growling under
the trucks and stoves, stumbling
through and over the cluttered eyes
of early mysterious night. Frowning
drunk waving moving a hand or lash.
Dancing kneeling reaching out, letting
a hand rest in shadows. Squatting
to drink or pee. Stretching to climb
pulling themselves onto horses near
where there was sea (the old songs
lead you to believe). Riding out
from this town, to another, where
it is also black. Down a road
where people are asleep. Towards
the moon or the shadows of houses.
Towards the songs' pretended sea.

Mark Strand

(1 9 3 4 –   )

THE KITE

For Bill and Sandy Bailey

It rises over the lake, the farms,
The edge of the woods,
And like a body without arms
Or legs it swings
Blind and blackening in the moonless air.
The wren, the vireo, the thrush
Make way. The rush
And flutter of wings
Fall through the dark
Like a mild rain.
We cover our heads and ponder
The farms and woods that rim
The central lake.
A barred owl sits on a limb
Silent as bark.
An almost invisible
Curtain of rain seems to come nearer.
The muffled crack and drum
Of distant thunder
Blunders against our ears.

A row of hills appears.
It sinks into a valley
Where farms and woods surround a lake.
There is no rain.
It is impossible to say what form
The weather will take.
We blow on our hands,
Trying to keep them warm,
Hoping it will not snow.
Birds fly overhead.
A man runs by

Holding the kite string.
He does not see us standing dark
And still as mourners under the sullen sky.
The wind cries in his lapels. Leaves fall
As he moves by them.
His breath blooms in the chill
And for a time it seems that small
White roses fill the air,
Although we are not sure.

Inside the room
The curtains fall like rain.
Darkness covers the flower-papered walls,
The furniture and floors,
Like a mild stain.
The mirrors are emptied, the doors
Quietly closed. The man, asleep
In the heavy arms of a chair,
Does not see us
Out in the freezing air
Of the dream he is having.
The beating of wings and the wind
Move through the deep,
Echoing valley. The kite
Rises over the lake,
The farms, the edge of the woods
Into the moonless night
And disappears.
And the man turns in his chair,
Slowly beginning to wake.

THE GARDEN

For Robert Penn Warren

It shines in the garden,
in the white foliage of the chestnut tree,
in the brim of my father's hat
as he walks on the gravel.

In the garden suspended in time
my mother sits in a redwood chair;
light fills the sky,
the folds of her dress,
the roses tangled beside her.

And when my father bends
to whisper in her ear,
when they rise to leave
and the swallows dart
and the moon and stars
have drifted off together, it shines.

Even as you lean over this page,
late and alone, it shines; even now
in the moment before it disappears.

SHOOTING WHALES

For Judith and Leon Major

When the shoals of plankton
swarmed into St. Margaret's Bay,
turning the beaches pink,
we saw from our place on the hill
the sperm whales feeding,
fouling the nets
in their play,
and breaching clean
so the humps of their backs
rose over the wide sea meadows.

Day after day
we waited inside
for the rotting plankton to disappear.
The smell stilled even the wind,
and the oxen looked stunned,
pulling hay on the slope
of our hill.
But the plankton kept coming in
and the whales would not go.

That's when the shooting began.
The fishermen got in their boats
and went after the whales,
and my father and uncle
and we children went, too.
The froth of our wake sank fast
in the wind-shaken water.

The whales surfaced close by.
Their foreheads were huge,
the doors of their faces were closed.
Before sounding, they lifted
their flukes into the air
and brought them down hard.
They beat the sea into foam,
and the path that they made
shone after them.

Though I did not see their eyes,
I imagined they were
like the eyes of mourning,
glazed with rheum,
watching us, sweeping along
under the darkening sheets of salt.

When we cut our engine and waited
for the whales to surface again,
the sun was setting,
turning the rock-strewn barrens a gaudy salmon.
A cold wind flailed at our skin.
When finally the sun went down
and it seemed like the whales had gone,
my uncle, no longer afraid,
shot aimlessly into the sky.

Three miles out
in the rolling dark
under the moon's astonished eyes,
our engine would not start
and we headed home in the dinghy.
And my father, hunched over the oars,
brought us in. I watched him,
rapt in his effort, rowing against the tide,

his blond hair glistening with salt.
I saw the slick spillage of moonlight
being blown over his shoulders,
and the sea and spindrift
suddenly silver.

He did not speak the entire way.
At midnight
when I went to bed,
I imagined the whales
moving beneath me,
sliding over the weed-covered hills of the deep;
they knew where I was;
they were luring me
downward and downward
into the murmurous
waters of sleep.

N. Scott Momaday

(1934–)

CARRIERS OF THE DREAM WHEEL

This is the Wheel of Dreams
Which is carried on their voices,
By means of which their voices turn
And center upon being.
It encircles the First World,
This powerful wheel.
They shape their songs upon the wheel
And spin the names of the earth and sky,
The aboriginal names.
They are old men, or men
Who are old in their voices,
And they carry the wheel among the camps,
Saying: Come, come,
Let us tell the old stories,
Let us sing the sacred songs.

WINTER HOLDING
OFF THE COAST OF NORTH AMERICA

This dread is like a calm,
And colorless. Nothing
Lies in the stricken palm
But the dead cold coming.

Out there, beyond the flocs,
On the thin, pewter plane,
The polar currents close,
And stiffen, and remain.

Audre Lorde

(1 9 3 4 – 1 9 9 2)

THE NIGHT-BLOOMING JASMINE

Lady of the Night star-breathed
blooms along the searoad
between my house and the tasks before me
calls down a flute
carved from the legbone of a gull.

Through the core of me
a fine rigged wire
upon which pain will not falter
nor predict
I was no stranger to this arena
at high noon
beyond was not an enemy
to be avoided
but a challenge
against which my neck grew strong
against which my metal struck
and I rang like fire in the sun.

I still patrol that line
sword drawn
lighting red-glazed candles of petition
along the scar
the surest way of knowing
death is a fractured border
through the center of my days.
Bees seek their need
until flowers beckon
beyond the limit of their wings
then they drop where they fly
pollen baskets laden
the sweet work done.

They do not know the Lady of the Night
blossoms
between my house and the searoad
calling down a flute
carved from the legbone of a gull
your rich voice
riding the shadows of conqucring air.

Mary Oliver

(1935–)

SOME QUESTIONS YOU MIGHT ASK

Is the soul solid, like iron?
Or is it tender and breakable, like
the wings of a moth in the beak of the owl?
Who has it, and who doesn't?
I keep looking around me.
The face of the moose is as sad
as the face of Jesus.
The swan opens her white wings slowly.
In the fall, the black bear carries leaves into the darkness.
One question leads to another.
Does it have a shape? Like an iceberg?
Like the eye of a hummingbird?
Does it have one lung, like the snake and the scallop?
Why should I have it, and not the anteater
who loves her children?
Why should I have it, and not the camel?
Come to think of it, what about the maple trees?
What about the blue iris?
What about all the little stones, sitting alone in the moonlight?
What about roses, and lemons, and their shining leaves?
What about the grass?

WHEN DEATH COMES

I want to step through the door full of curiosity, wondering:
what is it going to be like, that cottage of darkness?

And therefore I look upon everything
as a brotherhood and a sisterhood,

and I look upon time as no more than an idea,
and I consider eternity as another possibility,

and I think of each life as a flower, as common
as a field daisy, as singular,
and each name a comfortable music in the mouth,
tending, as all music does, toward silence,

and each body a lion of courage, and something
precious to the earth.

Charles Wright

(1 9 3 5 –   )

VIRGO DESCENDING

Through the viridian (and black of the burnt match),
Through ox-blood and ochre, the ham-colored clay,
Through plate after plate, down
Where the worm and the mole will not go,
Through ore-seam and fire-seam,
My grandmother, senile and 89, crimpbacked, stands
Like a door ajar on her soft bed,
The open beams and bare studs of the hall
Pink as an infant's skin in the floating dark:
Shavings and curls swing down like snowflakes across her face.

My aunt and I walk past. As always, my father
Is planning rooms, dragging his lame leg.
Stroke-straightened and foreign, behind him,
An aberrant 2-by-4 he can't fit snug.
I lay my head on my aunt's shoulder, feeling
At home, and walk on.
Through arches and door jambs, the spidery wires
And coiled cables, the blueprint takes shape:
My mother's room to the left, the door closed;
My father's room to the left, the door closed—

Ahead, my brother's room, unfinished;
Behind, my sister's room, also unfinished.
Buttresses, winches, block-and-tackle: the scale of everything
Is enormous. We keep on walking. And pass
My aunt's room, almost complete, the curtains up,
The lamp and the medicine arranged
In their proper places, in arm's reach of where the bed will go . . .
The next one is mine, now more than half done,
Cloyed by the scent of jasmine,
White-gummed and anxious, their mouths sucking the air dry.

Home is what you lie in, or hang above, the house
Your father made, or keeps on making,
The dirt you moisten, the sap you push up and nourish . . .
I enter the living room, it, too, unfinished, its far wall
Not there, opening on to a radiance
I can't begin to imagine, a light
My father walks from, approaching me,
Dragging his right leg, rolling his plans into a perfect curl.
That light, he mutters, that damned light.
We can't keep it out. It keeps on filling your room.

SNOW

If we, as we are, are dust, and dust, as it will, rises,
Then we will rise, and recongregate
In the wind, in the cloud, and be their issue,

Things in a fall in a world of fall, and slip
Through the spiked branches and snapped joints of the evergreens,
White ants, white ants and the little ribs.

STONE CANYON NOCTURNE

Ancient of Days, old friend, no one believes you'll come back.
No one believes in his own life anymore.

The moon, like a dead heart, cold and unstartable, hangs by a thread
At the earth's edge,
Unfaithful at last, splotching the ferns and the pink shrubs.

In the other world, children undo the knots in their tally strings.
They sing songs, and their fingers blear.

And here, where the swan hums in his socket, where bloodroot
And belladonna insist on our comforting,
Where the fox in the canyon wall empties our hands, ecstatic for more,

Like a bead of clear oil the Healer revolves through the night wind,
Part eye, part tear, unwilling to recognize us.

SITTING AT NIGHT ON THE FRONT PORCH

I'm here, on the dark porch, restyled in my mother's chair.
10:45 and no moon.
Below the house, car lights
Swing down, on the canyon floor, to the sea.

In this they resemble us,
Dropping like match flames through the great void
Under our feet.
In this they resemble her, burning and disappearing.

Everyone's gone
And I'm here, sizing the dark, saving my mother's seat.

PORTRAIT OF THE ARTIST
WITH LI PO

The "high heavenly priest of the White Lake" is now
A small mound in an endless plain of grass,
His pendants clicking and pearls shading his eyes.
He never said anything about the life after death,
Whose body is clothed in a blue rust and the smoke of dew.

He liked flowers and water most.
Everyone knows the true story of how he would write his verses and float them,
Like paper boats, downstream
                          just to watch them drift away.
Death never entered his poems, but rowed, with its hair down, far out on the
     lake,
Laughing and looking up at the sky.

Over a 1000 years later, I write out one of his lines in a notebook,
The peach blossom follows the moving water,
And watch the October darkness gather against the hills.
All night long the river of heaven will move westward while no one notices.
The distance between the dead and the living
                    is more than a heart beat and a breath.

CALIFORNIA SPRING

At dawn the dove croons.
A hawk hangs over the field.
The liquidambar rinses its hundred hands.

And the light comes on in the pepper trees.
Under its flat surfaces horns and noises are starting up.
The dew drops begin to shrink.

How sad the morning is.
There is a tree which rains down in the field.
There is a spider that swings back and forth on his thin strings in the heart.

How cold the wind is.
And the sun is, caught like a kite in the drooped limbs of the tree.
The apricot blossoms scatter across the ice plant.

One angel dangles his wing.
The grass edges creak and the tide pools begin to shine.
Nothing forgives.

Nancy Willard

(1 9 3 6 –   )

ANGELS IN WINTER

Mercy is whiter than laundry,
great baskets of it, packed like snowmen.
In the cellar I fold and sort and watch
through a squint in the dirty window
the plain bright snow.

Unlike the earth, snow is neuter.
Unlike the moon, it stays.
It falls, not from grace, but a silence
which nourishes crystals.
My son catches them on his tongue.

Whatever I try to hold perishes.
My son and I lie down in white pastures
of snow and flap like the last survivors
of a species that couldn't adapt to the air.
Jumping free, we look back at

angels, blurred fossils of majesty and justice
from the time when a ladder of angels
joined the house of the snow
to the houses of those whom it covered
with a dangerous blanket or a healing sleep.

As I lift my body from the angel's,
I remember the mad preacher of Indiana
who chose for the site of his kingdom
the footprint of an angel and named the place
New Harmony. Nothing of it survives.

The angels do not look backward
to see how their passing changes the earth,

the way I do, watching the snow,
and the waffles our boots print on its unleavened face,
and the nervous alphabet of the pheasant's feet,

and the five-petaled footprint of the cat,
and the shape of snowshoes, white and expensive as tennis,
and the deep ribbons tied and untied by the sleds.
I remember the millions who left the earth;
it holds no trace of them,

as it holds of us, tracking through snow,
so tame and defenseless
even the air could kill us.

Charles Simic

(1938–)

FORK

This strange thing must have crept
Right out of hell.
It resembles a bird's foot
Worn around the cannibal's neck.

As you hold it in your hand,
As you stab with it into a piece of meat,
It is possible to imagine the rest of the bird:
Its head which like your fist
Is large, bald, beakless and blind.

AGAINST WHATEVER IT IS THAT'S ENCROACHING

Best of all is to be idle,
And especially on a Thursday,
And to sip wine while studying the light:
The way it ages, yellows, turns ashen
And then hesitates forever
On the threshold of the night
That could be bringing the first frost.

It's good to have a woman around just then,
And two is even better.
Let them whisper to each other
And eye you with a smirk.
Let them roll up their sleeves and unbotton their shirts a bit
As this fine old twilight deserves,

And the small schoolboy
Who has come home to a room almost dark
And now watches wide-eyed
The grownups raise their glasses to him,
The giddy-headed, red-haired woman
With eyes tightly shut,
As if she were about to cry or sing.

ANCIENT AUTUMN

Is that foolish youth still sawing
The good branch he's sitting on?
Do the orchard and hill wheeze because of it,
And the few remaining apples sway?
Can he see the village and the valley
The way a chicken hawk would?

Already wood-smoke scatters its pale plumes;
The days are getting short and chilly.
Even he must rest from time to time,
So he's lit a long-stemmed pipe
And watches a chimney-sweep at work,
And a woman pin diapers on the line
And then go behind some bushes,
Hike her skirt so that a bit of whiteness shows,
While on the commons, humpbacked men
Roll a barrel of hard cider or beer—
And still beyond, past grazing sheep
Children play soldiers and march in step.

He figures, if the wind changes direction
He'll hear their crisp commands—
But it doesn't, so the black horseman
On the cobble of the road remains inaudible.
One instant he seems to be coming,
In the next to be leaving forever . . .

It's these dumbshows with their vague lessons
That make him thoughtful and melancholy.

He's not even aware that he has resumed sawing,
That the big red sun is beginning to set.

CLOUDS GATHERING

It seemed the kind of life we wanted.
Wild strawberries and cream in the morning.
Sunlight in every room.
The two of us walking by the sea naked.

Some evenings, however, we found ourselves
Unsure of what comes next.
Like tragic actors in a theater on fire,
With birds circling over our heads,
The dark pines strangely still,
Each rock we stepped on bloodied by the sunset.

We were back on our terrace sipping wine.
Why always this hint of an unhappy ending?
Clouds of almost human appearance
Gathering on the horizon, but the rest lovely
With the air so mild and the sea untroubled.

The night suddenly upon us, a starless night.
You lighting a candle, carrying it naked
Into our bedroom and blowing it out quickly.
The dark pines and grasses strangely still.

Robert Pinsky

(1 9 4 0 –   )

FIRST EARLY MORNINGS TOGETHER

Waking up over the candy store together
We hear birds waking up below the sill
And slowly recognize ourselves, the weather,
The time, and the birds that rustle there until

Down to the street as fog and quiet lift
The pigeons from the wrinkled awning flutter
To reconnoiter, mutter, stare and shift
Pecking by ones or twos the rainbowed gutter.

SERPENT KNOWLEDGE

In something you have written in school, you say
That snakes are born (or hatched) already knowing
Everything they will ever need to know—
Weazened and prematurely shrewd, like Merlin;
Something you read somewhere, I think, some textbook
Coy on the subject of the reptile brain.
(Perhaps the author half-remembered reading
About the Serpent of Experience
That changes manna to gall.) I don't believe it;
Even a snake's horizon must expand,
Inwardly, when an instinct is confirmed
By some new stage of life: to mate, kill, die.

Like angels, who have no genitals or place
Of national origin, however, snakes
Are not historical creatures; unlike chickens,
Who teach their chicks to scratch the dust for food—
Or people, who teach ours how to spell their names:

Not born already knowing all we need,
One generation differing from the next
In what it needs, and knows.
                    So what I know,
What you know, what your sister knows (approaching
The age you were when I began this poem)
All differ, like different overlapping stretches
Of the same highway: with different lacks, and visions.
The words—"*Vietnam*"—that I can't use in poems
Without the one word threatening to gape
And swallow and enclose the poem, for you
May grow more finite; able to be touched.

The actual highway—snake's-back where it seems
That any strange thing may be happening, now,
Somewhere along its endless length—once twisted
And straightened, and took us past a vivid place:
Brave in the isolation of its profile,
"Ten miles from nowhere" on the rolling range,
A family graveyard on an Indian mound
Or little elevation above the grassland. . . .
Fenced in against the sky's huge vault at dusk
By a waist-high iron fence with spear-head tips,
The grass around and over the mound like surf.

A mile more down the flat fast road, the homestead:
Regretted, vertical, and unadorned
As its white gravestones on their lonely mound—
Abandoned now, the paneless windows breathing
Easily in the wind, and no more need
For courage to survive the open range
With just the graveyard for a nearest neighbor;
The sones of Limit—comforting and depriving.

Elsewhere along the highway, other limits—
Hanging in shades of neon from dusk to dusk,
The signs of people who know how to take
Pleasure in places where it seems unlikely:
New kinds of places, the "overdeveloped" strips
With their arousing, vacant-minded jumble;
Or garbagey lake-towns, and the tourist-pits
Where crimes unspeakably bizarre come true
To astonish countries older, or more savage . . .

As though the rapes and murders of the French
Or Indonesians were less inventive than ours,
Less goofy than those happenings that grow
Like air-plants—out of nothing, and alone.

They make us parents want to keep our children
Locked up, safe even from the daily papers
That keep the grisly record of that frontier
Where things unspeakable happen along the highways.

In today's paper, you see the teen-aged girl
From down the street; camping in Oregon
At the far point of a trip across the country,
Together with another girl her age,
They suffered and survived a random evil.

An unidentified, youngish man in jeans
Aimed his car off the highway, into the park
And at their tent (apparently at random)
And drove it over them once, and then again;
And then got out, and struck at them with a hatchet
Over and over, while they struggled; until
From fear, or for some other reason, or none,
He stopped; and got back into his car again
And drove off down the night-time highway. No rape,
No robbery, no "motive." Not even words,
Or any sound from him that they remember.
The girl still conscious, by crawling, reached the road
And even some way down it; where some people
Drove by and saw her, and brought them both to help,
So doctors could save them—barely marked.
                                                           You see
Our neighbor's picture in the paper: smiling,
A pretty child with a kerchief on her head
Covering where the surgeons had to shave it.
You read the story, and in a peculiar tone—
Factual, not unfeeling, like two policemen—
Discuss it with your sister. You seem to feel
Comforted that it happened far away,
As in a crazy place, in *Oregon*:
For me, a place of wholesome reputation;
For you, a highway where strangers go amok,
As in the universal provincial myth

That sees, in every stranger, a mad attacker . . .
(And in one's victims, it may be, a stranger).

Strangers: the Foreign who, coupling with their cousins
Or with their livestock, or even with wild beasts,
Spawn children with tails, or claws and spotted fur,
Ugly—and though their daughters are beautiful
seen dancing from the front, behind their backs
Or underneath their garments are the tails
Of reptiles, or teeth of bears.
                        So one might feel—
Thinking about the people who cross the mountains
And oceans of the earth with separate legends,
To die inside the squalor of sod huts,
Shanties, or tenements; and leave behind
Their legends, or the legend of themselves,
Broken and mended by the generations:
Their alien, orphaned, and disconsolate spooks,
Earth-trolls or Kallikaks or Snopes or golems,
Descended of Hessians, runaway slaves and Indians,
Legends confused and loose on the roads at night . . .
The Alien or Creature of the movies.

As people die, their monsters grow more tame;
So that the people who survived Saguntum,
Or in the towns that saw the Thirty Years' War,
Must have felt that the wash of blood and horror
Changed something, inside. Perhaps they came to see
The state or empire as a kind of Whale
Or Serpent, in whose body they must live—
Not that mere suffering could make us wiser,
Or nobler, but only older, and more ourselves. . . .

On television, I used to see, each week,
Americans descending in machines
With wasted bravery and blood; to spread
Pain and vast fires amid a foreign place,
Among the strangers to whom we were new—
Americans: a spook or golem, there.
I think it made our country older, forever.
I don't mean better or not better, but merely
As though a person should come to a certain place
And have his hair turn gray, that very night.

Someday, the War in Southeast Asia, somewhere—
Perhaps for you and your people younger than you—
Will be the kind of history and pain
Saguntum is for me; but never tamed
Or "history" for me, I think. I think
That I may always feel as if I lived
In a time when the country aged itself:
More lonely together in our common strangeness . . .
As if we were a family, and some members
Had done an awful thing on a road at night,
And all of us had grown white hair, or tails:
And though the tails or white hair would afflict
Only that generation then alive
And of a certain age, regardless whether
They were the ones that did or planned the thing—
Or even heard about it—nevertheless
The members of that family ever after
Would bear some consequence or demarcation,
Forgotten maybe, taken for granted, a trait,
A new syllable buried in their name.

THE QUESTIONS

What about the people who came to my father's office
For hearing aids and glasses—chatting with him sometimes

A few extra minutes while I swept up in the back,
Addressed packages, cleaned the machines; if he was busy

I might sell them batteries, or tend to their questions:
The tall overloud old man with a tilted, ironic smirk

To cover the gaps in his hearing; a woman who hummed one
Prolonged note constantly, we called her "the hummer"—how

Could her white fat husband (he looked like Rev. Peale)
Bear hearing it day and night? And others: a coquettish old lady

In a bandeau, a European. She worked for refugees who ran
Gift shops or booths on the boardwalk in the summer;

She must have lived in winter on Social Security. One man
Always greeted my father in Masonic gestures and codes.

Why do I want them to be treated tenderly by the world, now
Long after they must have slipped from it one way or another,

While I was dawdling through school at that moment—or driving,
Reading, talking to Ellen. Why this new superfluous caring?

I want for them not to have died in awful pain, friendless.
Though many of the living are starving, I still pray for these,

Dead, mostly anonymous (but Mr. Monk, Mrs. Rose Vogel)
And barely remembered: that they had a little extra, something

For pleasure, a good meal, a book or a decent television set.
Of whom do I pray this rubbery, low-class charity? I saw

An expert today, a nun—wearing a regular skirt and blouse,
But the hood or headdress navy and white around her plain

Probably Irish face, older than me by five or ten years.
The Post Office clerk told her he couldn't break a twenty

So she got change next door and came back to send her package.
As I came out she was driving off—with an air, it seemed to me,

Of annoying, demure good cheer, as if the reasonableness
Of change, mail, cars, clothes was a pleasure in itself: veiled

And dumb like the girls I thought enjoyed the rules too much
In grade school. She might have been a grade school teacher;

But she reminded me of being there, aside from that—as a name
And person there, a Mary or John who learns that the janitor

Is Mr. Woodhouse; the principal is Mr. Ringleven; the secretary
In the office is Mrs. Apostolacos; the bus driver is Ray.

SHIRT

The back, the yoke, the yardage. Lapped seams,
The nearly invisible stitches along the collar
Turned in a sweatshop by Koreans or Malaysians

Gossiping over tea and noodles on their break
Or talking money or politics while one fitted
This armpiece with its overseam to the band

Of cuff I button at my wrist. The presser, the cutter,
The wringer, the mangle. The needle, the union,
The treadle, the bobbin. The code. The infamous blaze

At the Triangle Factory in nineteen-eleven.
One hundred and forty-six died in the flames
On the ninth floor, no hydrants, no fire escapes—

The witness in a building across the street
Who watched how a young man helped a girl to step
Up to the windowsill, then held her out

Away from the masonry wall and let her drop.
And then another. As if he were helping them up
To enter a streetcar, and not eternity.

A third before he dropped her put her arms
Around his neck and kissed him. Then he held
Her into space, and dropped her. Almost at once

He stepped to the sill himself, his jacket flared
And fluttered up from his shirt as he came down,
Air filling up the legs of his gray trousers—

Like Hart Crane's Bedlamite, "shrill shirt ballooning."
Wonderful how the pattern matches perfectly
Across the placket and over the twin bar-tacked

Corners of both pockets, like a strict rhyme
Or a major chord. Prints, plaids, checks,
Houndstooth, Tattersall, Madras. The clan tartans

Invented by mill-owners inspired by the hoax of Ossian,
To control their savage Scottish workers, tamed
By a fabricated heraldry: MacGregor,

Bailey, MacMartin. The kilt, devised for workers
To wear among the dusty clattering looms.
Weavers, carders, spinners. The loader,

The docker, the navvy. The planter, the picker, the sorter
Sweating at her machine in a litter of cotton
As slaves in calico headrags sweated in fields:

George Herbert, your descendant is a Black
Lady in South Carolina, her name is Irma
And she inspected my shirt. Its color and fit

And feel and its clean smell have satisfied
Both her and me. We have culled its cost and quality
Down to the buttons of simulated bone,

The buttonholes, the sizing, the facing, the characters
Printed in black on neckband and tail. The shape,
The label, the labor, the color, the shade. The shirt.

Erica Jong

(1941–)

THE BUDDHA IN THE WOMB

Bobbing in the waters of the womb,
little godhead, ten toes, ten fingers
& infinite hope,
sails upside down through the world.

My bones, I know, are only a cage
for death.
Meditating, I can see my skull,
a death's head,
lit from within
by candles
which are possibly the suns
of other galaxies.

I know that death
is a movement toward light,
a happy dream
from which you are loath to awaken,
a lover left
in a country
to which you have no visa,
& I know that the horses of the spirit
are galloping, galloping, galloping
out of time
& into the moment called NOW.

Why then do I care
for this upside-down Buddha
bobbling through the world,
his toes, his fingers
alive with blood
that will only sing & die?

There is a light in my skull
& a light in his.
We meditate on our bones only
to let them blow away
with fewer regrets.

Flesh is merely a lesson.
We learn it
& pass on.

Robert Hass

(1941–)

MEDITATION AT LAGUNITAS

All the new thinking is about loss.
In this it resembles all the old thinking.
The idea, for example, that each particular erases
the luminous clarity of a general idea. That the clown-
faced woodpecker probing the dead sculpted trunk
of that black birch is, by his presence,
some tragic falling off from a first world
of undivided light. Or the other notion that,
because there is in this world no one thing
to which the bramble of *blackberry* corresponds,
a word is elegy to what it signifies.
We talked about it late last night and in the voice
of my friend, there was a thin wire of grief, a tone
almost querulous. After a while I understood that,
talking this way, everything dissolves: *justice,
pine, hair, woman, you* and *I.* There was a woman
I made love to and I remembered how, holding
her small shoulders in my hands sometimes,
I felt a violent wonder at her presence
like a thirst for salt, for my childhood river
with its island willows, silly music from the pleasure boat,
muddy places where we caught the little orange-silver fish
called *pumpkinseed.* It hardly had to do with her.
Longing, we say, because desire is full
of endless distances. I must have been the same to her.
But I remember so much, the way her hands dismantled bread,
the thing her father said that hurt her, what
she dreamed. There are moments when the body is as numinous
as words, days that are the good flesh continuing.
Such tenderness, those afternoons and evenings,
saying *blackberry, blackberry, blackberry.*

Simon J. Ortiz

(1941 –   )

THE CREATION: ACCORDING TO COYOTE

"First of all, it's all true."
Coyote, he says this, this way,
humble yourself, motioning and meaning
what he says.

You were born when you came
from that body, the earth;
your black head burst from granite,
the ashes cooling

until it began to rain.
It turned muddy then,
and then green and brown things
came without legs.

They looked strange.
Everything was strange.
There was nothing to know then,

until later, Coyote told me this,
and he was bullshitting probably,
two sons were born,
Uyuyayeh and Masawe.

They were young then
and then later on they were older.

And then the people were wondering
what was above.
They had heard rumors.

But, you know, Coyote,
he was mainly bragging

when he said (I think),
"My brothers, the Twins then said,
'Let's lead these poor creatures
and save them.' "

And later on, they came to light
after many exciting
and colorful and tragic things
having to do with adventure,
and this is the life, all these, all these.

My uncle told me all this, that time.
Coyote told me too, but you know
how he is, always talking to the gods,
and mountains, the stone all around

And you know, I believe him.

THE SERENITY IN STONES

I am holding this turquoise
in my hands.
My hands hold the sky
wrought in this little stone.
There is a cloud
at the furthest boundary.
The world is somewhere underneath.

I turn the stone, and there is more sky.
This is the serenity possible in stones,
the place of a feeling to which one belongs.
I am happy as I hold this sky
in my hands, in my eyes, and in myself.

Dave Smith

(1942–)

THE ROUNDHOUSE VOICES

In full glare of sunlight I came here, man-tall but thin
as a pinstripe, and stood outside the rusted fence
with its crown of iron thorns while
the soot cut into our lungs with tiny diamonds.
I walked through houses with my grain-lovely slugger
from Louisville that my uncle bought and stood
in the sun that made its glove soft on my hand
until I saw my chance to crawl under and get past
anyone who would demand a badge and a name.

The guard hollered that I could get the hell from there quick
when I popped in his face like a thief. All I ever wanted
to steal was life and you can't get that easy
in the grind of a railyard. *You can't catch me,
lardass, I can go left or right as good as the Mick,*
I hummed to him, holding my slugger by the neck
for a bunt laid smooth where the coal cars
jerked and let me pass between tracks
until, in a slide on ash, I fell safe and heard
the wheeze of his words: *Who the hell are you, kid?*

I hear them again tonight, Uncle, hard as big brakeshoes,
when I lean over your face in the box of silk. The years
you spent hobbling from room to room alone crawl
up my legs and turn this house to another
house, round and black as defeat, where slugging
comes easy when you whip the gray softball over
the glass diesel globe. Footsteps thump on the stairs
like that fat ball against bricks and when I miss
I hear you warn me to watch the timing, to keep
my eyes on your hand and forget the fence,
hearing also that other voice that keeps me out and away
from you on a day worth playing good ball. Hearing
Who the hell . . . I see myself like a burning speck

of cinder come down the hill and through a tunnel
of porches like stands, running on deep ash,
and I give him the finger, whose face still gleams
clear as a B&O headlight, just to make him get up
and chase me into a dream of scoring at your feet.
At Christmas that guard staggered home sobbing,
the thing in his chest tight as a torque wrench.
In the summer I did not have to run and now
who is the one who dreams of a drink as he leans over
tools you kept bright as a first-girl's promise? I
have no one to run from or to, nobody to give
my finger to as I steal his peace. Uncle, the light
bleeds on your gray face like the high barbed-wire
shadows I had to get through and maybe you don't remember
you said to come back, to wait and you'd show me
the right way to take a hard pitch
in the sun that shudders on the ready man. I'm here

though this is a day I did not want to see. In the roundhouse
the rasp and heel-click of compressors is still,
soot lies deep in every greasy fingerprint.
I called you from the pits and you did not come up
and I felt the fear when I stood on the tracks
that are like stars which never lead us
into any kind of light and I don't know who'll
tell me now when the guard sticks his blind snoot
between us: take off and beat the bastard out.
Can you hear him over the yard, grabbing his chest,
cry out, *Who the goddamn hell are you, kid?*

I gave him every name in the book, Uncle, but he caught us
and what good did all those hours of coaching do?
You lie on your back, eyeless forever, and I think
how once I climbed to the top of a diesel and stared
into that gray roundhouse glass where, in anger,
you threw up the ball and made a star
to swear at greater than the Mick ever dreamed.
It has been years but now I know what followed there
every morning the sun came up, not light
but the puffing bad-bellied light of words.

All day I have held your hand, trying to say back that life,
to get under that fence with words I lined

and linked up and steamed into a cold room
where the illusion of hope means skin torn in boxes
of tools. The footsteps come pounding into words
and even the finger I give death is words
that won't let us be what we wanted, each one
chasing and being chased by dreams in the dark.
Words are all we ever were and they did us
no damn good. Do you hear that?

Do you hear the words that, in oiled gravel, you gave me
when you set my feet in the right stance to swing?
They are coal-hard and they come in wings
and loops like despair not even the Mick
could knock out of this room, words softer
than the centers of hearts in guards or uncles,
words skinned and numbed by too many bricks.
I have had enough of them and bring them back here
where the tick and creak of everything dies
in your tiny starlight and I stand down
on my knees to cry, *Who the hell are you, kid?*

AUGUST, ON THE RENTED FARM

For Jeddie

In this season, through the clear tears
of discovery, my son calls me
to an abandoned barn. Among
spiders' goldspinning and the small
eulogies of crickets, he has entered
the showering secret of our lives,
and the light fur of something
half-eaten mats his hands.
Later, on a rotting length
of pine, we sit
under the star-brilliance
of birds fretting
the hollow light.
Under them, dreamless,
we have come to cast

our lot with songs
of celebration.
All afternoon we sit and become
lovers, his hand in mine
like a bird's delicate wing.
Everywhere the sparrows go down
to the river for the sweet
tears of communion. Soon,
in the yellow last light,
we will begin again to speak
of that light in the house
that is not ours, that is only
what we come to out of the fields
in the slow-plunging knowledge
of words trying to find a way home.

Marilyn Hacker

(1942–)

RONDEAU AFTER A TRANSATLANTIC TELEPHONE CALL

Love, it was good to talk to you tonight.
You lather me like summer though. I light
up, sip smoke. Insistent through walls comes
the downstairs neighbor's double-bass. It thrums
like toothache. I will shower away the sweat,

smoke, summer, sound. Slick, soapy, dripping wet,
I scrub the sharp edge off my appetite.
I want: crisp toast, cold wine prickling my gums,
love. It was good

imagining around your voice, you, late-
awake there. (It isn't midnight yet
here.) This last glass washes down the crumbs.
I wish that I could lie down in your arms
and, turned toward sleep there (later), say, "Goodnight,
love. It was good."

James Tate

(1942 –)

THE LOST PILOT

For my father, 1922–1944

Your face did not rot
like the others—the co-pilot,
for example, I saw him

yesterday. His face is corn-
mush: his wife and daughter,
the poor ignorant people, stare

as if he will compose soon.
He was more wronged than Job.
But your face did not rot

like the others—it grew dark,
and hard like ebony;
the features progressed in their

distinction. If I could cajole
you to come back for an evening,
down from your compulsive

orbiting, I would touch you,
read your face as Dallas,
your hoodlum gunner, now,

with the blistered eyes, reads
his braille editions. I would
touch your face as a disinterested

scholar touches an original page.
However frightening, I would
discover you, and I would not

turn you in; I would not make
you face your wife, or Dallas,
or the co-pilot, Jim. You

could return to your crazy
orbiting, and I would not try
to fully understand what

it means to you. All I know
is this: when I see you,
as I have seen you at least

once every year of my life,
spin across the wilds of the sky
like a tiny, African god,

I feel dead. I feel as if I were
the residue of a stranger's life,
that I should pursue you.

My head cocked toward the sky,
I cannot get off the ground,
and, you, passing over again,

fast, perfect, and unwilling
to tell me that you are doing
well, or that it was mistake

that placed you in that world,
and me in this; or that misfortune
placed these worlds in us.

Louise Glück

(1943–)

THE POND

Night covers the pond with its wing.
Under the ringed moon I can make out
your face swimming among minnows and the small
echoing stars. In the night air
the surface of the pond is metal.

Within, your eyes are open. They contain
a memory I recognize, as though
we had been children together. Our ponies
grazed on the hill, they were gray
with white markings. Now they graze
with the dead who wait
like children under their granite breastplates,
lucid and helpless:

The hills are far away. They rise up
blacker than childhood.
What do you think of, lying so quietly
by the water? When you look that way I want
to touch you, but do not, seeing
as in another life we were of the same blood.

THE SCHOOL CHILDREN

The children go forward with their little satchels.
And all morning the mothers have labored
to gather the late apples, red and gold,
like words of another language.

And on the other shore
are those who wait behind great desks
to receive these offerings.

How orderly they are—the nails
on which the children hang
their overcoats of blue or yellow wool.

And the teachers shall instruct them in silence
and the mothers shall scour the orchards for a way out,
drawing to themselves the gray limbs of the fruit trees
bearing so little ammunition.

MESSENGERS

You have only to wait, they will find you.
The geese flying low over the marsh,
glittering in black water.
They find you.

And the deer—
how beautiful they are,
as though their bodies did not impede them.
Slowly they drift into the open
through bronze panels of sunlight.

Why would they stand so still
if they were not waiting?
Almost motionless, until their cages rust,
the shrubs shiver in the wind,
squat and leafless.

You have only to let it happen:
that cry—*release, release*—like the moon
wrenched out of earth and rising
full in its circle of arrows

until they come before you
like dead things, saddled with flesh,
and you above them, wounded and dominant.

MOUNT ARARAT

Nothing's sadder than my sister's grave
unless it's the grave of my cousin, next to her.
To this day, I can't bring myself to watch
my aunt and my mother,
though the more I try to escape
seeing their suffering, the more it seems
the fate of our family:
each branch donates one girl child to the earth.

In my generation, we put off marrying, put off having children.
When we did have them, we each had one;
for the most part, we had sons, not daughters.

We don't discuss this ever.
But it's always a relief to bury an adult,
someone remote, like my father.
It's a sign that maybe the debt's finally been paid.

In fact, no one believes this.
Like the earth itself, every stone here
is dedicated to the Jewish god
who doesn't hesitate to take
a son from a mother.

THE WILD IRIS

At the end of my suffering
there was a door.

Hear me out: that which you call death
I remember.

Overhead, noises, branches of the pine shifting.
Then nothing. The weak sun
flickered over the dry surface.

It is terrible to survive
as consciousness
buried in the dark earth.

Then it was over: that which you fear, being
a soul and unable
to speak, ending abruptly, the stiff earth
bending a little. And what I took to be
birds darting in low shrubs.

You who do not remember
passage from the other world
I tell you I could speak again: whatever
returns from oblivion returns
to find a voice:

from the center of my life came
a great fountain, deep blue
shadows on azure seawater.

ACKNOWLEDGMENTS

For permission to reprint the poems in this book, the publisher gratefully thanks the following poets, copyright holders, and publishers. Any omissions or errors are completely unintentional.

ALFRED A. KNOPF

Clampitt, Amy: "A Baroque Sunburst," from *What the Light Was Like*, by Amy Clampitt. Copyright © 1985 by Amy Clampitt.

Davison, Peter: "Cross Cut," from *A Voice in the Mountains*. Reprinted by permission of Peter Davison and Alfred A. Knopf.

Hecht, Anthony: "Jason," "The Gardens of the Villa D'Este," from *Collected Earlier Poems*, by Anthony Hecht. Copyright © 1990 by Anthony E. Hecht.

Hollander, John: "Morning in the Islands," "The Mad Potter," from *Harp Lake*, by John Hollander. Copyright © 1988 by John Hollander. "The Great Bear," from *Selected Poetry*, by John Hollander. Copyright © 1993 by John Hollander.

Hughes, Langston: "As I Grew Older," "Cross," "Esthete in Harlem," "Jazzonia," "The Negro Speaks of Rivers," "The Weary Blues." Copyright © 1926 by Alfred A. Knopf and renewed 1954 by Langston Hughes. "Po' Boy Blues," from *Selected Poems*, by Langston Hughes. Copyright © 1927 by Alfred A. Knopf and renewed 1955 by Langston Hughes.

Levine, Philip: "Angel Butcher," "Animals Are Passing from Our Lives," "Belief," "Belle Isle, 1949," "Later Still," "Snow," from *New and Selected Poems*, by Philip Levine. Copyright © 1991 by Philip Levine.

Merrill, James: "After Greece," "An Urban Convalescence," "Childlessness," "Swimming by Night," "The Broken Home," "The Kimono," from *Selected Poems: 1946–1985*, by James Merrill. Copyright © 1992 by James Merrill.

Merwin, William S.: "Rain Travel," from *Travels*, by William S. Merwin. Copyright © 1992 by W. S. Merwin.

O'Hara, Frank: "Chez Jane," "In Memory of My Feelings," from *The Selected Poems of Frank O'Hara*. Copyright © 1971 by Maureen Granville-Smith, Administratrix of the Estate of Frank O'Hara.

Ransom, John Crowe: "Bells for John Whiteside's Daughter." Copyright © 1924 by Alfred A, Knopf and renewed 1952 by John Crowe Ransom. "Blue Girls," "Janet Waking," "Piazza Piece," from *The Selected Poems*, by John Crowe Ransom. Copyright © 1927 by Alfred A. Knopf and renewed 1955 by John Crowe Ransom.

Snodgrass, W. D.: "April Inventory," from *Heart's Needle*, by W. D. Snodgrass. Copyright © 1959 by William Snodgrass.

Stevens, Wallace: "Anecdote of the Jar," "Nomad Exquisite," "Sunday Morning," "The Snow Man," "Thirteen Ways of Looking at a Blackbird." Copyright © 1923 and renewed 1951 by Wallace Stevens. "Final Soliloquy of the Interior Paramour." Copyright © 1951 by Wallace Stevens. "Of Modern Poetry." Copyright © 1942 by Wallace Stevens and renewed 1970 by Holly Stevens. "The Idea of Order at Key West." Copyright © 1936 by Wallace Stevens and renewed 1964 by Holly Stevens. "To an Old Philosopher in Rome." Copyright © 1952 by Wallace Stevens. From "Notes toward a Supreme Fiction (It Must Be Abstract)," from *The Collected Poems*, by Wallace Stevens. Copyright © 1942 by Wallace Stevens.

Strand, Mark: "Shooting Whales," "The Garden," "The Kite," from *Selected Poems*, by Mark Strand. Copyright © 1979, 1980 by Mark Strand.

Van Duyn, Mona: "Moose in the Morning, Northern Maine," from *If It Be Not I*, by Mona Van Duyn. Copyright © 1982 by Mona Van Duyn.

Wylie, Elinor: "Castilian." Copyright © 1923 by Alfred A. Knopf. "Let No Charitable Hope." Copyright © 1932 by Alfred A. Knopf and renewed 1960 by Edwina C. Rubenstein. "Malediction upon Myself." Copyright © 1928 by Alfred A. Knopf and renewed 1956 by Edwina C. Rubenstein. "Wild Peaches," from *Collected Poems of Elinor Wylie*. Copyright © 1921 by Alfred A. Knopf and renewed 1949 by William Rose Benét. Reprinted by permission of Alfred A. Knopf.

BEACON PRESS

Oliver, Mary: "Some Questions You Might Ask," "When Death Comes," from *New and Selected Poems*, by Mary Oliver. Copyright © 1992 by Mary Oliver. Reprinted by Permission of Beacon Press.

GWENDOLYN B. BENNETT

"Hatred." Published in *Opportunity* 4 (June 1926). "Heritage." Published in *Opportunity* 1 (December 1923). "To a Dark Girl." Published in *Opportunity* 5 (1927).

BLACK SPARROW PRESS

Reznikoff, Charles: from "Testimony," from *Poems 1918–1975: The Complete Poems of Charles Reznikoff*. Copyright © 1977 by Marie Syrkin Reznikoff. Reprinted by permission of Black Sparrow Press.

GWENDOLYN BROOKS

"Jessie Mitchell's Mother," "Langston Hughes," "Negro Hero," "Notes from the Childhood and the Girlhood," "Of Robert Frost," from *Selected Poems*, by Gwendolyn Brooks. Reprinted by permission of Gwendolyn Brooks.

CARCANET

H.D. (Hilda Doolittle): "At Baia," "At Ithaca," "Helen," "Oread," "Pear Tree," "The Shrine," from *H.D. Collected Poems: 1912–1944*, edited by Louis L. Martz. Copyright © 1982 by the Estate of Hilda Doolittle.

Ransom, John Crowe: "Bells for John Whiteside's Daughter." Copyright © 1924 by Alfred A. Knopf and renewed 1952 by John Crowe Ransom. "Blue Girls," "Janet Waking," "Piazza Piece," from *The Selected Poems*, by John Crowe Ransom. Copyright 1927 by Alfred A. Knopf and renewed 1955 by John Crowe Ransom.

Williams, William Carlos: "It Is a Small Plant," "Spring and All," "The Red Wheelbarrow," "The Sadness of the Sea," "The Young Housewife," "To a Poor Old Woman," "Woman Walking," from *The Collected Poems of William Carlos Williams: Volume I, 1909–1933*, edited by A. Walton Litz and Christopher MacGowan. "Mists over the River," "To Ford Madox Ford in Heaven," from "Paterson" ("The Falls"), from *The Collected Poems of William Carlos Williams: Volume II, 1939–1962*, edited by Christopher MacGowan.

Winters, Yvor: "Summer Noon: 1941," "The Slow Pacific Swell," from *Summer Noon 1941*, by Yvor Winters. Reprinted by permission of Carcanet Press Ltd.

FRANCES COLLIN, LITERARY AGENT

Hacker, Marilyn: "Rondeau after a Transatlantic Telephone Call," from *Taking Notice*, by Marilyn Hacker. Copyright © 1980 by Marilyn Hacker. Reprinted by permission of Frances Collin, Literary Agent.

CARL COWL

McKay, Claude: "Harlem Shadows," "If We Must Die," "The Lynching," from *The Selected Poems of Claude McKay*. Copyright © 1957 by Harcourt Brace. Reprinted by permission of the Archives of Claude McKay, Carl Cowl, Administrator.

DIANE CLEAVER, INC.

Jackson, Laura Riding: "All Things," "Helen's Burning," "Nothing So Far," "Prisms," "The World and I," from *The Poems of Laura Riding*, by Laura Riding Jackson. Copyright © 1938, 1980 by Laura Riding Jackson. Reprinted by permission of Persea Books, Inc., and Diane Cleaver, Inc. "In conformity with the late author's wish, her Board of Literary Management asks us to record that, in 1941, Laura (Riding) Jackson renounced, on grounds of linguistic principle, the writing of poetry: she had come to hold that 'poetry obstructs general attainment to something better in our linguistic way-of-life than we have.' "

DOUBLEDAY

Roethke, Theodore: "Big Wind." Copyright © 1947 by The United Chapters of Phi Beta Kappa. "Cuttings (Later)" ("This urge, wrestle, resurrection of dry sticks"), "Cuttings" ("Sticks-in-a-drowse droop overy sugary loam"), "Orchids." Copyright © 1948 by Theodore Roethke. "Elegy for Jane." Copyright © 1950 by Theodore Roethke. "My Papa's Waltz." Copyright © 1942 by Hearst Magazines, Inc. "Root Cellar." Copyright © 1943 by Modern Poetry Association, Inc. "The Far Field," from *The Collected Poems of Theodore Roethke*. Copyright © 1962 by Beatrice Roethke, Administratrix of the Estate of Theodore Roethke. Reprinted by permission of Doubleday, a division of Bantam Doubleday Dell Publishing Group, Inc.

THE ECCO PRESS

Bogan, Louise: "M., Singing," "Winter Swan," from *The Blue Estuaries*. Copyright © 1923, 1929, 1930, 1931, 1933, 1934, 1935, 1936, 1937, 1938, 1941, 1949, 1951, 1952, 1954, 1957, 1958, 1962, 1963, 1964, 1965, 1966, 1967, 1968 by Louise Bogan. First published 1977 by The Ecco Press.

Glück, Louise: "Messengers," from *The House on Marshland*, by Louise Glück. Copyright © 1971, 1972, 1973, 1974, 1975 by Louise Glück. First published 1975 by The Ecco Press. "Mount Ararat," from *The House on Marshland*, by Louise Glück. Copyright © 1990 by Louise Glück. First published 1992 by The Ecco Press. "The Pond," from *The House on Marshland*, by Louise Glück. Copyright © 1990 by Louise Glück. First published 1992 by The Ecco Press. "The School Children," from *The House on Marshland*, by Louise Glück. Copyright © 1990 by Louise Glück. First published 1992 by The Ecco Press. "The Wild Iris," from *The House on Marshland*, by Louise Glück. Copyright © 1990 by Louise Glück. First published 1992 by The Ecco Press.

Hass, Robert: "Meditation at Lagunitas," from *Praise*, by Robert Hass. Copyright © 1974, 1975, 1976, 1977, 1978, 1979 by Robert Hass. First published 1979 by The Ecco Press.

Pinsky, Robert: "Shirt," from *The Want Bone*, by Robert Pinsky, "The Questions," from *History of My Heart*, by Robert Pinsky.

Tate, James: "The Lost Pilot," from *The Lost Pilot*, by James Tate. Copyright © 1978 by James Tate. First published 1982 by The Ecco Press. Reprinted by permission of The Ecco Press.

EDNA ST. VINCENT MILLAY SOCIETY

Millay, Edna St. Vincent: "Renascence," "The Buck in the Snow," Sonnet XXXVI from "Fatal Interview" ("Hearing your words, and not a word among them"), Sonnet I from "Sonnets from an Ungrafted Tree" ("So she came back into his house again"), "Ragged Island," from *Collected Poems*, by Edna St. Vincent Millay. Copyright © 1912, 1923, 1928, 1931, 1940, 1951, 1954, 1955, 1958, 1982 by Edna St. Vincent Millay and Norma Millay Ellis. Reprinted by permission of Elizabeth Barnett, Literary Executor.

FABER AND FABER LTD.

Berryman, John: "Henry's Fate," from *Henry's Fate and Other Poems 1962–1967*, by John Berryman; from "Homage to Mistress Bradstreet," from *Homage to Mistress Bradstreet*, by John Berryman; from "The Dream Songs" (1: "Huffy Henry hid the day"; 4: "Filling her compact & delicious body"; 5: "Henry sats in de bar & was odd"; 14: "Life, friends, is boring"), from *The Dream Songs*, by John Berryman.

Clampitt, Amy: "A Baroque Sunburst," from *What the Light Was Like*, by Amy Clampitt.

Elliot, T. S.: "Gerontion," "The Love Song of J. Alfred Prufrock," "The Waste Land," from *Collected Poems 1909–1962*, by T. S. Eliot.

Jarrell, Randall: "The Death of the Ball Turret Gunner," "The Knight, Death, and the Devil," "The Woman at the Washington Zoo," from *The Complete Poems*, by Randall Jarrell.

Lowell, Robert: "For the Union Dead," "Grandparents," "History," "Man and Wife," "Mr. Edwards and the Spider," "Skunk Hour," "The Quaker Graveyard in Nantucket," from *Selected Poems*, by Robert Lowell.

Moore, Marianne: "In Distrust of Merits," "Marriage," "Poetry," "The Fish," "The Steeple-Jack," "When I Buy Pictures," from *The Complete Poems of Marianne Moore*.

Plath, Sylvia: "Ariel," "Daddy," "Fever 103°," "Morning Song," from *Ariel*, by Sylvia Plath.

Pound, Ezra: "Canto I" ("And then went down to the ship"), "Canto XLV" ("With Usura"), from *The Cantos*, by Ezra Pound. "A Pact," "A Virginal," "In a Station of the Metro," "Sestina: Altaforte," "The Return," "The River-Merchant's Wife: A Letter"; from "Hugh Selwyn Mauberley," from *Collected Shorter Poems*, by Ezra Pound.

Roethke, Theodore: "Big Wind," "Cuttings (Later)" ("This urge, wrestle, resurrection of dry sticks"), "Cuttings" ("Sticks-in-a-drowse droop overy sugary loam"), "Elegy for Jane," "My Papa's Waltz," "Orchids," "Root Cellar," "The Far Field," from *Collected Poems of Theodore Roethke*.

Stevens, Wallace: "Anecdote of the Jar," "Final Soliloquy of the Interior Paramour," "Nomad Exquisite," "Of Modern Poetry," "Sunday Morning," "The Idea of Order at Key West," "The Snow Man," "Thirteen Ways of Looking at a Blackbird," "To an Old Philosopher in Rome"; from "Notes toward a Supreme Fiction (It Must Be Abstract)," from *The Collected Poems of Wallace Stevens*.

Tate, Allen: "Mr. Pope," "Ode to the Confederate Dead," from *Collected Poems 1916–1976*, by Allen Tate.

Wilbur, Richard: "Still, Citizen Sparrow," "A Baroque Wall-Fountain in the Villa

Sciarra," "Love Calls Us to the Things of This World," "Mind," from *Things of This World*, by Richard Wilbur. Reprinted by permission of Faber & Faber Ltd.

FARRAR, STRAUS AND GIROUX, INC.

Berryman, John: "Henry's Fate," from *Henry's Fate and Other Poems 1962–1967*, by John Berryman. Copyright © 1975, 1976, 1977 by John Berryman. From "Homage to Mistress Bradstreet," from *Homage to Mistress Bradstreet*, by John Berryman. Copyright © 1956 and renewed 1984 by Kate Berryman. From "The Dream Songs" (1: "Huffy Henry hid the day"; 4: "Filling her compact & delicious body; 5: "Henry sats in de bar & was odd"; 14: "Life, friends, is boring"), from *The Dream Songs*, by John Berryman. Copyright © 1969 by John Berryman.

Bishop, Elizabeth: "A Cold Spring," "In the Waiting Room," "Little Exercise," "Questions of Travel," "Seascape," "The Armadillo," "The Map," from *The Complete Poems: 1927–1979*, by Elizabeth Bishop. Copyright © 1979, 1983 by Alice Helen Methfessel.

Bogan, Louise: "M., Singing," "Men Loved Wholly beyond Wisdom," "Winter Swan," from *The Blue Estuaries*, by Louise Bogan. Copyright © 1968 by Louise Bogan.

Jarrell, Randall: "The Death of the Ball Turret Gunner," "The Knight, Death, and the Devil," "The Woman at the Washington Zoo," from *The Complete Poems*, by Randall Jarrell. Copyright © 1969 by Mrs. Randall Jarrell.

Lowell, Robert: "For the Union Dead," from *For the Union Dead*, by Robert Lowell. Copyright © 1964 by Robert Lowell and renewed 1992 by Harriet W. Lowell, Caroline Lowell, and Sheridan Lowell. "Grandparents," "Man and Wife," "Skunk Hour," from *Life Studies*, by Robert Lowell. Copyright © 1956, 1959 by Robert Lowell and renewed 1981, 1986, 1987 by Harriet W. Lowell, Caroline Lowell, and Sheridan Lowell. "History," from *History*, by Robert Lowell. Copyright © 1973 by Robert Lowell. Reprinted by permission of Farrar, Straus & Giroux, Inc.

Snyder, Gary: "Axe Handles" from *Axe Handles*, by Gary Snyder. Copyright © 1983 by Gary Snyder. "Mid-August at Sourdough Mountain Lookout," from *Riprap and Cold Mountain Poems*, by Gary Snyder. Copyright © 1965 by Gary Snyder. Reprinted by permission of North Point Press, a division of Farrar, Straus & Giroux, Inc.

Tate, Allen: "Mr. Pope" "Ode to the Confederate Dead," from *Collected Poems 1919–1976*, by Allen Tate. Copyright © 1977 by Allen Tate. Reprinted by permission of Farrar, Straus & Giroux, Inc.

GEORGE BRAZILLER, INC.

Simic, George: "Against Whatever It Is That's Encroaching," "Ancient Autumn," "Clouds Gathering," "Fork." Reprinted by permission of George Braziller, Inc.

GEORGES BORCHARDT, INC.

Merwin, William S.: "For the Anniversary of My Death," from *The Lice*, by W. S. Merwin. Copyright © 1967 by W. S. Merwin. Reprinted by permission of Georges Borchardt, Inc.

HARCOURT BRACE AND COMPANY

Eliot, T. S.: "Gerontion," "The Love Song of J. Alfred Prufrock," "The Waste Land," from *Collected Poems 1909–1962*, by T. S. Eliot. Copyright © 1963, 1964 by T. S. Eliot.

Lowell, Robert: "Mr. Edwards and the Spider," "The Quaker Graveyard in Nantucket," from *Lord Weary's Castle*, by Robert Lowell. Copyright © 1946 and renewed 1974 by Robert Lowell.

Sandburg, Carl: "Bas-Relief," from *Smoke and Steel*, by Carl Sandburg. Copyright © 1920 by Harcourt Brace & Company and renewed 1948 by Carl Sandburg. "Chicago," "The Harbor," from *Chicago Poems*, by Carl Sandburg. Copyright © 1916 by Holt, Rinehart and Winston, Inc., and renewed 1944 by Carl Sandburg. "Cool Tombs," "Grass," from *Cornhuskers*, by Carl Sandburg. Copyright © 1918 by Holt, Rinehart and Winston, Inc., and renewed 1946 by Carl Sandburg. "Languages," from *Chicago Poems*, by Carl Sandburg. Copyright © 1916 by Holt, Rinehart and Winston, Inc., and renewed 1944 by Carl Sandburg.

Wilbur, Richard: "A Baroque Wall-Fountain in the Villa Sciarra," "Love Calls Us to the Things of This World," "Mind," from *Things of This World*, by Richard Wilbur. Copyright © 1956 and renewed 1984 by Richard Wilbur. "Still, Citizen Sparrow," from *Ceremony and Other Poems*, by Richard Wilbur. Copyright © 1950 and renewed 1978 by Richard Wilbur.

Willard Nancy: "Angels in Winter," from *Household Tales of Moon and Water*, by Nancy Willard. Copyright © 1982 by Nancy Willard. Reprinted by permission of Harcourt, Brace & Company.

HAROLD OBER AND ASSOCIATES

Bontemps, Arna: "A Black Man Talks of Reaping," "God Give to Men," "Nocturne of the Wharves," from *Personals*, by Arna Bontemps. Copyright © 1963 by Arna Bontemps. "Blight," from *The Book of American Negro Poetry*. Copyright © 1963 by Arna Bontemps.

Hughes, Langston: "As I Grew Older," "Cross," "Esthete in Harlem," "Jazzonia," "The Negro Speaks of Rivers," "The Weary Blues." Copyright © 1926 by Alfred A. Knopf and renewed 1954 by Langston Hughes. "Po' Boy Blues," from *Selected Poems*, by Langston Hughes. Copyright © 1927 by Alfred A. Knopf and renewed 1955 by Langston Hughes. "Theme for English B," from *Montage of a Dream Deferred*, by Langston Hughes. Copyright © 1951 by Langston Hughes and renewed 1979 by George Houston Bass. Reprinted by permission of Harold Ober and Associates.

HARPERCOLLINS

Ginsberg, Allen: "To Aunt Rose," copyright © 1958, "Wales Visitation," copyright © 1967, from *Collected Poems 1947–1980*, by Allen Ginsberg. Copyright © 1984 by Allen Ginsberg.

Jong, Erica: "The Buddha in the Womb," from *At the Edge of the Body*, by Erica Jong. Copyright © 1961, 1962, 1971, 1973, 1975, 1977, 1979, 1981, 1983, 1987, 1991.

Plath, Sylvia: "Ariel," copyright © 1965 by Ted Hughes, "Daddy," copyright © 1963 by Ted Hughes, "Fever 103°," copyright © 1963 by Ted Hughes, "Morning Song," copyright © 1961 by Ted Hughes, from *Ariel*, by Sylvia Plath. Reprinted by permission of HarperCollins.

HENRY HOLT AND COMPANY, INC.

Frost, Robert: "Design." Copyright © 1936 by Robert Frost. Copyright © 1964 by Lesley Frost Ballantine. Copyright © 1969 by Henry Holt & Co., Inc. "Directive." Copyright © 1975 by Lesley Frost Ballantine. Copyright © 1947, 1969 by Henry Holt & Co., Inc. "Fire and Ice," "Stopping by Woods on a Snowy Evening," "Nothing Gold Can Stay." Copyright © 1951 by Robert Frost. Copyright © 1923, 1969 by Henry Holt & Co., Inc. "Spring Pools." Copyright © 1956 by Robert Frost. Copyright © 1928, 1969 by Henry Holt & Co., Inc. "The Gift Outright," "The Silken Tent," "Out, Out—," "The Subverted Flower," from *The Poetry of Robert Frost*, edited by Edward Connery Lathem. Copyright

HOUGHTON MIFFLIN COMPANY

JJKR ASSOCIATES

JEAN NAGGAR LITERARY AGENCY, INC.

THE JOHNS HOPKINS UNIVERSITY PRESS

JONATHAN CAPE

DONALD JUSTICE

tures, by Donald Justice. Copyright © 1973 by Donald Justice. Reprinted by permission of Donald Justice.

LAWRENCE POLLINGER LTD.

Levertov, Denise: "The Ache of Marriage," from *Poems 1960–1967*, by Denise Levertov.

Schwartz, Delmore: "The Heavy Bear Who Goes with Me," from *Selected Poems: Summer Knowledge*, by Delmore Schwartz. Copyright 1959 by Delmore Schwartz. Reprinted by permission of Laurence Pollinger Ltd.

LIVERIGHT PUBLISHING CORPORATION

Crane, Hart: "Repose of Rivers," "The Broken Tower"; from "The Bridge" ("To Brooklyn Bridge"), "To Emily Dickinson," "Voyages," from *The Complete Poems and Selected Letters and Prose of Hart Crane*, edited by Marc Simon. Copyright © 1933, 1958, 1966 by Liveright Publishing Corporation. Copyright © 1986 by Marc Simon.

Cummings, E. E.: "anyone lived in a pretty how town," "i sing of Olaf glad and big," "my father moved through dooms of love," "you shall above all things be glad and young" from *Complete Poems 1904–1962*, by E. E. Cummings, edited by George J. Firmage. Copyright © 1931, 1938, 1940, 1959, 1966, 1968, 1991 by the Trustees for the E. E. Cummings Trust. Copyright © 1979 by George James Firmage. Reprinted by permission of Liveright Publishing Corporation.

Hayden, Robert: "A Road in Kentucky," "Middle Passage," "Night, Death, Mississippi," "Those Winter Sundays," from *Angle of Ascent*, by Robert Hayden. Copyright © 1966 by Robert Hayden.

Toomer, Jean: "November Cotton Flower," "Reapers," from *Cane*, by Jean Toomer. Copyright © 1923 by Liveright Publishing Corporation, renewed 1951 by Jean Toomer.

MARVEL PRESS

Snodgrass, W. D.: "April Inventory," from *Heart's Needle*, by W. D. Snodgrass. Copyright © 1959 by William Snodgrass.

HILARY MASTERS

Masters, Edgar Lee: "The Lost Orchard," from *Invisible Landscape*, by Edgar Lee Masters, originally published by the Macmillan Co. "Petit the Poet," "The Hill," from *The Spoon River Anthology*, by Edgar Lee Masters, originally published by the Macmillan Co. Reprinted by permission of Ellen C. Masters.

MARGARET NEMEROV

Nemerov, Howard: "Blue Suburban," "The War in the Air," "The Western Approaches," from *The Collected Poems of Howard Nemerov*. Copyright © 1977 by Howard Nemerov. Reprinted by permission of Mrs. Margaret Nemerov.

NEW DIRECTIONS PUBLISHING CORPORATION

H.D. (Hilda Doolittle): "At Baia," "At Ithaca," "Helen," "Oread," "Pear Tree," "The Shrine," from *H.D. Collected Poems: 1912–1944*, edited by Louis L. Martz. Copyright © 1982 by the Estate of Hilda Doolittle.

Duncan, Robert: "Often I Am Permitted to Return to a Meadow," "Passage over Water," from *The Opening of the Field*, by Robert Duncan. Copyright © 1960 by Robert Duncan.

Levertov, Denise: "The Ache of Marriage," from *Poems*, by Denise Levertov. Copyright © 1964 by Denise Levertov Goodman.

Pound, Ezra: "Canto I" ("And then went down to the ship"), "Canto XLV" ("With Usura"), from *The Cantos*, by Ezra Pound. Copyright © 1934, 1948 by Ezra Pound. "A Pact." Copyright © 1926 by Ezra Pound. "A Virginal." Copyright © 1934, 1948 by Ezra Pound. "In a Station of the Metro," "Sestina: Altaforte," "The Return," "The River-Merchant's Wife: A Letter"; from "Hugh Selwyn Mauberley," from *Personae*, by Ezra Pound. Copyright © 1926 by Ezra Pound.

Schwartz, Delmore: "The Heavy Bear Who Goes with Me," from *Selected Poems: Summer Knowledge*, by Delmore Schwartz. Copyright © 1959 by Delmore Schwartz.

Snyder, Gary: "The Snow on Saddle Mountain," by Miyazawa Kenji, translated by Gary Snyder, from *The Back Country*. Copyright © 1967 by Gary Snyder.

Williams, William Carlos: "It Is a Small Plant," "Spring and All," "The Red Wheelbarrow," "The Sadness of the Sea," "The Young Housewife," "To a Poor Old Woman," "Woman Walking," from *The Collected Poems of William Carlos Williams: Volume I, 1909–1939*, edited by A. Walton Litz and Christopher MacGowan. Copyright © 1938 by New Directions Publishing. "Mists over the River," "To Ford Madox Ford in Heaven"; from "Paterson" ("The Falls"), copyright © 1946, 1948, 1949, 1951, 1958 by W. C. Williams, from *The Collected Poems of William Carlos Williams: Volume II, 1939–1962*, edited by Christopher MacGowan. Copyright © 1944, 1948, 1962 by William Carlos Williams.

Winters, Yvor: "Summer Noon: 1941," from *Summer Noon 1941*, by Yvor Winters. Reprinted by permission of New Directions Publishing Corporation.

OHIO UNIVERSITY PRESS / SWALLOW PRESS

Winters, Yvor: "The Slow Pacific Swell," from *The Collected Poems of Yvor Winters*. Reprinted by permission of The Ohio University Press / Swallow Press. Copyright © 1980 by Yvor Winters.

SIMON J. ORTIZ

"The Creation: According to Coyote" from *Dacotah Territory*, No. 6, Winter 1973–74, James L. White, guest ed., "The Serenity in Stones," from *Carriers of the Dream Wheel: Contemporary Native American Poetry*, edited by Duane Niatum.

OXFORD UNIVERSITY PRESS

Aiken, Conrad: "Dear Uncle Stranger," "Hatteras Calling," "Solitaire," from *Collected Poems*, Second Edition, by Conrad Aiken. Copyright © 1953, 1970 by Conrad Aiken.

Eberhart, Richard: "A Loon Call," "For a Lamb," "The Fury of Aerial Bombardment," from *Collected Poems, 1930–1986*, by Richard Eberhart. Copyright © 1988 by Richard Eberhart. Reprinted by permission of Oxford University Press, Inc.

OXFORD UNIVERSITY PRESS UK

Stevenson, Anne: "In the Orchard," "The Spirit Is Too Blunt an Instrument," from *Selected Poems 1956–1986*. Copyright © 1987 by Anne Stevenson. Reprinted by Permission of Oxford University Press.

ROBERT PACK

"Proton Decay," from *Before It Vanishes*, by Robert Pack. "The Thrasher in the Willow by the Lake," from *Waking to My Name*, by Robert Pack. Reprinted by permission of Robert Pack.

PENGUIN USA

Ashbery, John: "A Blessing in Disguise," "At North Farm," "Crazy Weather," "Darlene's Hospital," "Some Trees," "Spring Day," "Train Rising Out of the Sea," from *Selected Poems*, by John Ashbery. Copyright © 1985 by John Ashbery.

PERSEA BOOKS

Jackson, Laura Riding: "All Things," "Helen's Burning," "Nothing So Far," "Prisms," "The World and I," from *The Poems of Laura Riding*, by Laura Riding Jackson. Copyright © 1938, 1980 by Laura Riding Jackson. Reprinted by permission of Persea Books.

PRINCETON UNIVERSITY PRESS

Pinsky, Robert: "First Early Mornings Together," from *Sadness and Happiness*, by Robert Pinsky. Copyright © 1975 by Princeton University Press. Reprinted by permission of Princeton University Press. "Serpent Knowledge," from *An Explanation of America*, by Robert Pinsky. Copyright © 1979 by Princeton University Press.

RANDOM HOUSE

Jeffers, Robinson: "But I Am Growing Old and Indolent." Copyright © 1963 by Garth Jeffers and Donnan Jeffers, from *The Beginning and the End and Other Poems*, by Robinson Jeffers. "Hurt Hawks." Copyright © 1928 and renewed 1956 by Robinson Jeffers. "Night." Copyright © 1925 and renewed 1953 by Robinson Jeffers. "Rock and Hawk." Copyright © 1934 and renewed 1962 by Donnan Jeffers and Garth Jeffers. "Shine, Perishing Republic." Copyright © 1925 and renewed 1953 by Robinson Jeffers. "To the Stone-Cutters," from *The Selected Poetry of Robinson Jeffers*. Copyright © 1924 and renewed 1952 by Robinson Jeffers.

Warren, Robert Penn: "Amazing Grace in the Back Country," "Blow, West Wind," "Evening Hawk," "Vermont Ballad: Change of Season," "What Voice at Moth-Hour." Copyright © 1985 by Robert Penn Warren. "Bearded Oaks." Copyright © 1942 and renewed 1970 by Robert Penn Warren. "Heart of Autumn," from *New and Selected Poems 1923–1985*, by Robert Penn Warren. Copyright © 1977 by Robert Penn Warren. Reprinted by permission of Random House, Inc.

WILLIAM L. RUKEYSER

Rukeyser, Muriel: "I Saw What the Calling Was," "Iris," from *The Collected Poems*, by Muriel Rukeyser. Copyright © 1978 by Muriel Rukeyser. Reprinted by permission of William L. Rukeyser.

ST. MARTIN'S PRESS

Monaday, N. Scott: "Carriers of the Dream Wheel," "Winter Holding off the Coast of North America," from *Carriers of the Dream Wheel: Contemporary Native American Poetry*, edited by Duane Niatum.

SIMON AND SCHUSTER

Lindsay, Vachel: "General William Booth Enters into Heaven," from *Collected Poems of Vachel Lindsay*, published 1925 by the Macmillan Co.

Moore, Marianne: "In Distrust of Merits." Copyright © 1944 and renewed 1972 by Marianne Moore. "Marriage," "Poetry," "The Fish." Copyright © 1935 by Marianne Moore and renewed 1963 by Marianne Moore and T. S. Eliot. "The Steeple-Jack." Copyright © 1951 by Marianne Moore and renewed 1979 by Lawrence E. Brinn and Louise Crane. "When I Buy Pictures," from *Collected Poems of Marianne Moore*.

Copyright © 1935 by Marianne Moore and renewed 1963 by Marianne Moore and T. S. Eliot.

Teasdale, Sara: "Open Windows," "Over the Roofs," from *Collected Poems of Sara Teasdale*. Copyright © 1920 by Macmillan Publishing Co. and renewed by 1948 by Mamie T. Wheless. Reprinted by permission of Simon and Schuster.

DOROTHY STAFFORD

Stafford, William: "At the Bomb Testing Site," "The Rescued Year," "Travelling through the Dark," from *Stories That Could Be True*, by William Stafford. Reprinted by permission of the Estate of William Stafford.

STERLING LORD LITERISTIC, NYC

Sexton, Anne: "The Starry Night," "The Truth the Dead Know," from *All My Pretty Ones*, by Anne Sexton. Copyright © 1962 by Anne Sexton and renewed 1990 by Linda G. Sexton. "Wanting to Die," from *Live or Die*, by Anne Sexton. Copyright © 1966 by Anne Sexton. "Music Swims Back to Me," from *To Bedlam and Back*, by Anne Sexton. Copyright © 1960 by Anne Sexton and renewed 1988 by Linda G. Sexton. Reprinted by permission of Sterling Lord Literistic, NYC.

THUNDER'S MOUTH PRESS

Jones, LeRoi / Baraka, Amiri: "Legacy," "Return of the Native," from *The Leroi Jones/ Amiri Baraka Reader*, by Amiri Baraka. Copyright © 1991 by Amiri Baraka. Used by permission of the Publisher, Thunder's Mouth Press.

MELVIN B. TOLSON, JR.

Tolson, Melvin: "African China," "Dark Symphony." Reprinted by permission of Melvin B. Tolson, Jr.

LÉONIE A. TROY

"Light at Equinox," "April Mortality," from *High Falcon*, by Léonie Adams.

UNIVERSITY OF CALIFORNIA PRESS

Creeley, Robert: "The Rain," from *The Collected Poems of Robert Creeley: 1945– 1975*. Copyright © 1983 by the Regents of the University of California.

Olson, Charles: from "The Maximus Poems," Book III (Poem 143: "The Festival Aspect"), from *The Maximus Poems: Volume Three*, by Charles Olson. Copyright © 1975 by the Estate of Charles Olson and the University of Connecticut. Reprinted by permission of the Regents of the University of California and the University of California Press.

UNIVERSITY OF ILLINOIS PRESS

Miles, Josephine: "Album," "Belief," "Conception," from *Collected Poems: 1930– 1983*. Copyright © 1983 by Josephine Miles.

Smith, Dave: "August, on the Rented Farm," "The Roundhouse Voices," from *Roundhouse Voices*, by Dave Smith. Copyright © 1979 by Dave Smith. Reprinted by permission of the University of Illinois Press.

UNIVERSITY PRESS OF NEW ENGLAND

Dickey, James: "Cherrylog Road," "The Dusk of Horses," "The Heaven of Animals," from *The Whole Motion: Collected Poems 1945–1992*, by James Dickey. Copyright © 1992 by James Dickey.

Wright, James: "Autumn Begins in Martins Ferry, Ohio," "Beginning," "Lying in a Hammock at William Duffy's Farm in Pine Island, Minnesota," "Milkweed," "Sparrows in a Hillside Drift," from *Collected Poems*, by James Wright. Copyright © 1972 by James Wright. Reprinted by permission of the University Press of New England.

W. W. NORTON AND COMPANY, INC.

Ammons, A. R.: "Corsons Inlet," "So I Said I Am Ezra," "Triphammer Bridge," from *The Selected Poems*, Expanded Edition, by A. R. Ammons. Copyright © 1986 by A. R. Ammons.

Kunitz, Stanley: "The Science of the Night," from *Selected Poems 1926–1958*, by Stanley Kunitz. Copyright © 1963 by Stanley Kunitz. "The Snakes of September," from *Next to Last Things: New Poems and Essays*, by Stanley Kunitz. Copyright © 1985 by Stanley Kunitz.

Lorde, Audre: "The Night-blooming Jasmine," from *The Marvelous Arithmetics of Distance*, by Audre Lorde. Copyright © 1993 by Audre Lorde.

Rich, Adrienne: "Aunt Jennifer's Tigers," "Diving into the Wreck," "In the Evening," "Integrity," "Power," from *The Fact of a Doorframe, Poems Selected and New, 1950–1984*, by Adrienne Rich. Copyright © 1975, 1978 by W. W. Norton & Company, Inc. Copyright © 1981 by Adrienne Rich. "Tattered Kaddish," from *An Atlas of the Difficult World, Poems 1988–1991*, by Adrienne Rich. Copyright © 1991 by Adrienne Rich. Reprinted by permission of W. W. Norton & Company, Inc.

W. W. NORTON AND COMPANY, LTD.

Cummings, E. E.: "anyone lived in a pretty how town." Copyright © 1940, 1968, 1991 by the Trustees for the E. E. Cummings Trust. "i sing of Olaf glad and big." Copyright © 1931, 1959, 1979, 1991 by the Trustees for the E. E. Cummings Trust. "my father moved through dooms of love." Copyright © 1940, 1969, 1991 by the Trustees for the E. E. Cummings Trust. "you shall above all things be glad and young," from *Complete Poems 1904–1962*, by E. E. Cummings, edited by George J. Firmage. Copyright © 1938, 1966, 1991 by the Trustees for the E. E. Cummings Trust. Reprinted by permission of W. W. Norton & Co., Ltd.

WILLIAM MORRIS AGENCY

Warren, Robert Penn: "Amazing Grace in the Back Country," "Bearded Oaks," "Blow, West Wind," "Evening Hawk," "Heart of Autumn," "Vermont Ballad: Change of Season," "What Voice at Moth-Hour," from *New and Selected Poems 1923–1985*, by Robert Penn Warren.

CHARLES WRIGHT

"California Spring," "Portrait of the Artist with Li Po" from *Bloodlines*, by Charles Wright, "Sitting at Night on the Front Porch," "Snow," "Stone Canyon Nocturne," from *China Trace*, by Charles Wright, "Virgo Descending," from *Bloodlines*, by Charles Wright.

INDEX OF AUTHORS

INDEX OF TITLES AND FIRST LINES